I0831357

Record of Daily Knowledge and *Collected Poems and Essays*

Translations from the Asian Classics

Record of Daily Knowledge and Collected Poems and Essays

SELECTIONS

Gu Yanwu

Translated and edited by Ian Johnston

Columbia University Press
New York

Columbia University Press
Publishers Since 1893
New York   Chichester, West Sussex
cup.columbia.edu

Library of Congress Cataloging-in-Publication Data
Names: Gu, Yanwu, 1613–1682, author. | Johnston, Ian, 1939– |
Gu, Yanwu, 1613–1682. Ri zhi lu. English. | Gu, Yanwu, 1613–1682.
Tinglin shiwenji.
English.
Title: Record of Daily Knowledge and Collected Poems and
Essays : selections / Yanwu Gu ; translated and edited by Ian Johnston.
Description: New York : Columbia University Press, [2017] |
Series: Translations from the Asian classics | Includes bibliographical
references and index.
Identifiers: LCCN 2016003673 (print) | LCCN 2016023628 (ebook) |
ISBN 9780231170482 (cloth : alk. paper) | ISBN 9780231542678 (electronic)
Subjects: LCSH: Gu, Yanwu, 1613–1682—Political and social views. |
Gu, Yanwu, 1613–1682—Philosophy. | Learning and scholarship—
China—History—17th century—Sources. | Philosophy, Confucian—
China—History—17th century—Sources. | China—Intellectual life—
17th century—Sources. | China—Social life and customs—
17th century—Sources. | China—History—Ming dynasty,
1368-1644—Sources. | China—History—Qing dynasty,
1644–1912—Sources.
Classification: LCC PL2716.A2 2017 (print) | LCC PL2716.A2 (ebook) |
DDC 895.18/4809—dc23
LC record available at https://lccn.loc.gov/2016003673

Columbia University Press books are printed on
permanent and durable acid-free paper.
Printed in the United States of America

JACKET DESIGN: Jason Gabbert

To the memory of Agnes Stefanowska
(A. D. Syrokomla-Stefanowska, 1936–2008),
who contributed so much to Australian Sinology generally
and to my own work on Gu Yanwu specifically

Traveling the Hard Road (4)

When water falls on level ground
it flows where it will—east, west, north, south.
A man's life too has its destiny.
How can I walk in sorrow, sit in sadness?
So I fill my cup and raise it,
and cease to sing "Traveling the Hard Road."
A heart is not made of wood or stone.
How can it help but have feelings?
I remain silent and uncertain
and dare not speak.

Bao Zhao (414–446)

CONTENTS

ACKNOWLEDGMENTS

It is a considerable pleasure to be able to express my thanks to a number of people whose contributions have helped greatly in bringing this work to completion and endowing it with whatever merit it may have. First, I must mention Agnes Stefanowska, to whom this book is dedicated. She was the supervisor for my doctoral dissertation at Sydney University on Gu Yanwu's *Record of Daily Knowledge*, done part-time between 1984 and 1991. She was, however, much more than a supervisor—she was a friend. Every Thursday during the years in question I would slip away (if possible) from my very demanding "other life" for a couple of hours to discuss my translations completed during the previous week but also to enjoy a cup of tea and talk of other things, both personal and general. I missed the meetings very much when the project came to an end and was deeply saddened when I learned of Agnes's death in 2008 after a short illness. By that time I had retired and moved to Tasmania, but we had kept in touch and in fact had plans to work jointly on the translations with a view to publication by Wild Peony Press, run by Agnes and her close friend Mabel Lee. Sadly, other things got in the way, as they do, and these plans were never realized.

I am also very grateful to my friend and colleague in other projects, Wang Ping, now at the University of New South Wales, who, coming to Australia from China via America, also did her doctoral work at Sydney under Agnes's supervision. We share the same deep respect and affection for Agnes. Ping has helped greatly by responding with invariably helpful and clarifying comments and suggestions on passages that I found difficult.

I am very indebted to the two reviewers of the original manuscript for Columbia. The first, Thomas Bartlett, a noted authority on Gu Yanwu, made very detailed comments on, and criticisms of, the translations, which helped significantly, as did his more general comments and earlier writings on Gu. The other, anonymous, reviewer made several important suggestions, which were acted upon with benefit.

I would also like to thank Jennifer Crewe of Columbia University Press for taking the project on in the first place, for her advice during the preparation of the manuscript, and especially for her tolerance in dealing with my sustained impulse to increase the number of translations, thus taking the book beyond what was deemed a desirable length. In reining in the burgeoning manuscript, she invoked the help of Victor Mair, who has been of great help to me in other matters in the past and whose specific suggestions for reduction were very helpful and largely followed. Susan Collis, my partner, has been of great assistance throughout and in many ways. She has, perforce, become very familiar with the writings of Gu Yanwu and has developed something of a liking for the man as he appears from his writings—as indeed I have. Finally, my friend Barry Hill, himself a noted poet, made very helpful specific suggestions on the translated poems.

To all these people I am very grateful, as I am to others, unnamed, who have helped more indirectly. I am particularly happy to be able to acknowledge here my debt to Agnes.

BIBLIOGRAPHICAL ABBREVIATIONS

CHC	*The Cambridge History of China*
CSJC	*Congshu Jicheng* 叢書集成
DMB	*Dictionary of Ming Biography*
ECCP	*Eminent Chinese of the Ch'ing Period*
ECP	*Encyclopedia of Chinese Philosophy*
ECT	*Early Chinese Texts*
HCP	*A History of Chinese Philosophy*
ICCL	*The Indiana Companion to Traditional Chinese Literature*
LCC	*The Chinese Classics*
QSGW	*Quan Shanggu Sandai Qin Han Sanguo Liuchao Wen* 全上古三代秦漢三國六朝文
SB	*A Sung Bibliography*
SBBY	*Sibu Beiyao* 四部備要
SBCK	*Sibu Congkan* 四部叢刊
SKQS	*Siku Quanshu* 四庫全書 and *Siku Quanshu Zongmu Tiyao* 四庫全書總目提要
SSJZS	*Shisanjing Zhushu* 十三經注疏

Record of Daily Knowledge and
Collected Poems and Essays

Introduction

Gu Yanwu 顧炎武 (Ku Yen-wu, 1613–1682) is a figure of considerable importance in Chinese intellectual history. His work was substantial and his influence significant, extending across several areas of scholarship and continuing into the twentieth century. However, for such a significant scholar the course of his life was unusual. He never held an official position or played any active part in politics, and yet his political and social philosophy was highly relevant. He never undertook any formal teaching or developed any coterie of followers. He only ever had one disciple, Pan Lei 潘耒 (1646–1708), to whom we must be grateful for his role in preserving Gu's work. Nor did he follow the path of the more or less eremitic scholar, unlike his contemporary Wang Fuzhi 王夫之 (1619–1692), who, after a brief flirtation with Ming restoration (like Gu), withdrew to his native place to study and write for the remaining forty or so years of his life. Instead, Gu became an itinerant, always on the road, traveling widely and availing himself of the hospitality (and libraries) of a number of friends. Quite how he managed to achieve so much in terms of scholarship while following such a path is something of a mystery, particularly when considering some of the major vicissitudes that marked his travels. So he remained on the road and somewhat elusive for the last thirty-odd years of his life—his friend Gui Zhuang 歸莊 (1613–1673) likened him to "a wily rabbit with three burrows"—while Wang Fuzhi was working away diligently in his own home. Even Gu's death was travel related. He fell off his horse while setting off on yet another journey and died some days later as a consequence of the fall.

Such difficulties notwithstanding, Gu is recognized as a true polymath who made his mark in several fields. And in fact he became quite well known during his lifetime, renowned for his erudition. However, only two of his works were published before he died—an early version of the *Rizhi Lu* 日知錄 (*Record of Daily Knowledge*) and his work on phonetics and phonology, *Yinxue Wushu* 音學五書 (*Five Books on Phonetics*). It is the former, in its final form, together with the *Gu Tinglin Shiwenji* 顧亭林詩文集 (*Collected Poems and Essays of Gu Tinglin*), which contains his thought on the classics, politics and statecraft, ethics, philosophy, literature, and sundry other subjects, together with his roughly three hundred extant post-1644 poems. The *Record of Daily Knowledge* is the culmination of many years of assiduous and painstaking work presented as a substantial collection of a little over a thousand essays covering these subjects. It was this book above all that established his importance in the redirection of Chinese thought, away from what were seen as the sterile Ming developments of neo-Confucianism and toward what later became known as Han learning (*Hanxue* 漢學) and *kaozheng xue* 考證學 (evidential, empirical, or textual research). Moreover, what emerges from this work, together with his other collected essays and poems, is an engaging portrait of the man himself—that of a highly intelligent, thoughtful, and humble scholar of exemplary integrity whose purpose was to make study and learning directly relevant to the betterment of society.

There is a considerable secondary literature on Gu in Chinese and other Asian languages. Unfortunately, despite his importance being well recognized also in the West, there is very little of his writings available in Western languages. In sum, there is one book in French on his thought and four doctoral dissertations in English, along with some journal articles and discussions in books of a more general nature.[1] In the Chinese literature different writers have focused on different aspects of his work. And interpretations have varied, especially in the fields of political philosophy and social philosophy, depending in no small part on the political leanings of the interpreter. Gu was, however, a writer of notable clarity. Although in the *Record of Daily Knowledge*, for example, his ideas are embedded in a mass of historical and literary detail, with specific and at times lengthy quotes from various sources, his own position is expressed clearly and often forcibly. This clarity is made more apparent in the *Shiwenji* essays.

What is signally lacking for Western students of Chinese thought is any significant and readily available translation of his work. Translations exist in only two dissertations: Bartlett's, which contains translations of several of the key essays in the *Collected Poems and Essays* plus excerpts from a number of other writings, and my own, in which material from the *Record of Daily Knowledge* predominates. The present work is an attempt to redress this deficiency, at least in part. It is a deficiency that should be addressed insofar as his work has an obvious relevance that is not limited to China or his own time; his thought is both timeless and universal. The present translations are taken from two works only, the *Record of Daily Knowledge*, which Gu himself saw as his most important work, and the *Collected Poems and Essays*, which contains several substantial essays and letters, as well as various other writings, including his extant poems. In this relatively brief introduction, I consider the course of his life, particularly as it pertains to his work; his writings, focusing primarily on the two works in question; his philosophy; and his legacy.

A TURBULENT LIFE

The essential details of Gu's life are set out chronologically in appendix 1.[2] Here I consider in greater detail certain aspects of particular importance.

Family Background

Gu was born into a family that could trace its ancestry back to Song times in the person of Gu Qing. His forebears over the centuries included scholars, officials, and writers of varying degrees of importance, and, notably, a number of bibliophiles. The family's move to Gu Yanwu's birthplace was made in 1524 by Gu Jian, a man who reached the position of superintending secretary in the Office of Scrutiny for Justice. A brief excerpt from a memorial he wrote early in the reign of Shi Zong (1522–1566) presages some of Gu Yanwu's own firmly expressed thoughts: "Establishing laws is not difficult; abiding by laws is difficult. Listening to remonstrances is not difficult; being pleased with remonstrances is difficult."[3] Gu Yanwu's father, Gu Tongying, born in 1585, enjoyed very limited success in the official examinations, although he did achieve some renown as a poet. He died in 1626 at the young age of forty-two, when Gu Yanwu was a thirteen-year-old boy. By this time, Gu Yanwu had, in fact, been adopted as the heir of Tongying's paternal uncle, Gu Shaofei 顧紹芾 (1563–1641), and Shaofei's deceased (and only) son, Gu Tongji, who had died at the age of eighteen. At the time of his death, Tongji was betrothed to a woman of the surname Wang, who, according to custom, remained unmarried, attaching herself to the household of her intended husband's parents and becoming Gu Yanwu's adoptive mother.

The Early Years

Two people of particular importance to Gu during these formative years were his adoptive mother, Wang, and his adoptive grandfather, Gu Shaofei. Their influences on the boy's developing character and his approach to learning were profound. On the former, Peterson writes, "In the same year [i.e., 1618] she instructed her six-year-old son in the *Highest Learning* [*Daxue*]. She also taught him manners, and from the stories she told him about historical figures, he learned to recognize characters and distinguish names."[4] Perhaps more important was her nature as a person. Gu expressed his feelings toward her in the substantial tribute he later wrote, "Xianbi Wang Shouren Xingzhuang," which is included in his *Shiwenji*. Shaofei became increasingly important in Yanwu's education as it progressed. Gu's reading, under his adoptive grandfather's direction, was notable for its breadth and focus on historical writings. Works studied included the Four Books, as arranged by Zhu Xi; the *Changes* (*Zhou Yi*); the *Huainanzi*; *Zuo Zhuan*; *Guoyu*; and *Shiji*. Shaofei is said to have given the eleven-year-old Gu a copy of the *Zizhi Tongjian* (*Comprehensive Mirror Aiding Government*), a work that was to feature significantly in Gu's *Record of Daily Knowledge*. Importantly, Shaofei's own profound regard for the original classics, his disdain for later commentaries and examination-centered writings, and his focus on the value of historical writings seem to have been transmitted to his adopted grandson.

The Examination Years

Gu's engagement in the obligatory struggle with the official examination system began in 1626 when he passed a qualifying examination to become a so-called "government student" (*shengyuan*—a category of student he later came to criticize vigorously) and ended in 1640, when, despondent at his series of failures, he finally abandoned the struggle. In the preface to his *Tianxia Junguo Libing Shu* (*Advantages and Disadvantages of the Empire's Prefectures and States*), he wrote, "Rejected in the autumnal triennial examination in 1639, I retired and read books. Being aware of the many grievous problems facing the state, I was ashamed of the meager resources that students of the classics possessed to deal with these problems. Therefore, I read through the twenty-one dynastic histories as well as gazetteers for the whole empire. I read the collected literary works of the famous men of each period as well as memorials and documents. I noted down what I gained from my reading."

Other significant events during these years included his marriage in 1631 to a woman also named Wang; the formation of a number of enduring friendships, including that with Gui Zhuang (apparently the two were known as strange Gu and odd Gui); and his joining the Fushe (Restoration Society), founded by Zhang Pu 張溥 (1602–1641) in 1628. Peterson quotes from Wm. Theodore de Bary's translation of Zhang's statement on the purposes of the society as follows: "Since traditional teachings have been neglected, scholars do not understand classical thought and can do no more than pick their ears and paint their eyes. If one of them is fortunate enough to obtain office, at court he is incapable of serving the Emperor and in the districts he does not know how, as a magistrate, to help the people. The capabilities of men daily decline, and the administration of government daily deteriorates—all due to this [neglect of the classics]."[5]

The Years Immediately Prior to the Fall of Beijing

These years signaled the beginning of the turbulence that was to follow Gu for the rest of his life. First, there were two deaths in the family, both of which had a major impact on him. In 1641, Gu Shaofei died, and then, in the following year, his brother, Gu Xiang, also died. So, at the age of twenty-nine, Gu not only lost one of the two people most influential in directing his life but also was elevated to head of the household, which meant he was faced with the funeral expenses and other consequences of the two deaths. This was against the background of his own relative lack of examination success and the rapidly accelerating breakdown of Ming society. Second, he began to collect information toward the compilation of his two major treatises on historical geography. Third, beset by financial pressures, he was compelled to mortgage part of the family estate to one Ye Fangheng, a move that proved to have most unfortunate repercussions.

The Decade Following the Fall of Beijing

This was, of course, a time of considerable turbulence generally. The two things that particularly occupied Gu were the need to provide for his family and keep them safe and to work toward a Ming restoration. On the first matter, Gu moved his adoptive mother and the rest of his household to Tangshi in Changshu (in the fourth month) and then to the family residence at Qiandun (in the tenth month). Following further reverses—a robbery personally and the advance of the alien dynasty generally—he moved the household again, this time to the village of Yulianjing, between Kunshan and Changshu, in the twelfth month. However, as the Manchu advance continued south, family members became embroiled in the conflict. Two of his younger brothers were killed in the fighting and his biological mother injured. It seems probable that Gu himself was not involved in the fighting. He had gone to Nanjing, but in the fifth month the Manchu forces entered the southern capital. Shortly after this Gu returned to Yulianjing, where, in all likelihood, he remained during the fighting in Kunshan. At the end of 1645, Gu's adoptive mother starved herself to death rather than submit to the alien regime. She is said to have elicited a vow from her adopted son on her deathbed that he would never serve the Manchu regime, and he never did.

On the second matter, there are two aspects, one of which is the extent of his direct involvement with an alternative Ming government. There is little evidence to suggest this was significant, although it is recorded that, when the alternative government was being established in Nanjing late in 1644, the magistrate of Kunshan, Yang Yongyan, recommended Gu for office. He was appointed to a post with the Ministry of War, which he apparently never took up. The second aspect concerns his literary activities, which were directed in part at examining the political and social issues that had led to the downfall of the Ming—the four early essays on military, geographical, agricultural, and financial policies are examples. In addition, there was his focus on geographical and historical matters, especially to the extent they might bear on a possible Ming restoration. His two major works on the subjects—*Tianxia Junguo Libing Shu* and *Zhaoyu Zhi* (*Record of the Origins of Regions*)—are examples of this.

We know relatively little about Gu's movements and activities during the several years following 1645. Not only was it a time of general upheaval but also Gu's own activities may have been somewhat clandestine in support of Ming loyalists. Moreover, information about such activities may have been retrospectively suppressed by his relatives anxious not to offend the ruling Manchus. Thus, the actual extent of Gu's involvement in the abortive attempts at Ming restoration remains unknown. What we do know is that after the burial of his adoptive mother in 1647, he traveled in the south, assuming an appearance in accord with Manchu requirements, presumably to facilitate free movement. We also have several poems from this period that reflect his feelings about the Manchu conquest and the ensuing sufferings of the people. In 1651, at the age of thirty-eight, he made the first of a series of visits to the tomb of Ming Tai Zu, the founding emperor of the dynasty, at Nanjing. In fact, in the early 1650s, he basically resided at Nanjing, although his wife continued to live at Kunshan.

Legal Troubles

During his lifetime Gu was caught up in two major legal disputes. The first stemmed from his sale of land to Ye Fangheng. In essence, a former servant of the Gu household, Lu En, transferred his allegiance to Ye Fangheng. No doubt under instruction from Ye, Lu En sought to discredit Gu by informing local officials that he had been connected with the southern Ming court at Fuzhou. On his return to Kunshan in 1655, Gu and some associates seized Lu and drowned him. As a result, Gu was arrested, tried, and sentenced to forced labor in a trial influenced by Ye.

Ultimately, through the intercession of friends, in particular Gui Zhuang and Lu Zepu, he was retried in a different court and his sentence commuted to a beating. He was released in the spring of 1656. This was not, however, the end of the matter. During a journey to Nanjing later in the same year, after the death of his natural mother, he was attacked by an assassin in the employ of Ye Fangheng. Gu was lucky: although he was knocked from his mule and suffered a head wound, he was able to escape thanks to the intervention of a passerby. Also in the same year, his house in Kunshan was robbed by a gang of Ye's ruffians.

The second dispute occurred much later, in 1668. Along with several other scholars, he was accused of sedition by a certain Jiang Yuanheng. The basis of the charge was that the men concerned were sympathetic to the deposed Ming regime and, through their writings, slanderous toward the Manchu rulers. Gu was held for about six months and then released in the tenth month of 1668. According to Peterson, the reason why "Gu was exonerated after being accused of defaming the Qing government" was to be "found in his extensive contacts with influential members of the bureaucracy who were able to exert pressure on his behalf."[6]

The Northern Travels Begin

The effect of the disturbing events involving Ye Fangheng signaled the beginning of Gu's northern travels. This period also saw a redirection of his intellectual endeavors away from his studies of historical geography and its implications for a possible Ming restoration and toward a concentration on his studies of the classics and statecraft in particular. During the decade 1657 to 1667, his travels took in visits to the tombs of Confucius, Mencius, and the Duke of Zhou, to the northern Ming tombs near Beijing, climbing Tai Shan, and meetings with noted scholars—men such as Li Yong, Sun Qifeng, Zhang Erqi, Fu Shan, and Yan Ruoqu. Throughout this period, he continued to work on the *Rizhi Lu* and to gather material for his geographical and epigraphical writings. The end of the decade saw the first publication of his influential work on phonetics, the *Yinxue Wushu*, printed at Shanyang in Jiangsu with the help of Zhang Chao.

In 1668, after resolution of the second legal matter, Gu's northern travels continued. In 1669 he acquired a student, Pan Lei (also Pan Cigeng 潘次耕), who traveled from Shanyang to Jinan to join Gu. Pan Lei was of particular importance in the preservation and publication of his teacher's works. The following year saw the first publication of the *Rizhi Lu* in eight *juan*. Gu never really settled down, although in 1675 he did establish a study in Jixia in Shanxi in a house built for him there by Dai Tingshi, a man who had supported a number of Ming loyalists. Another friend, Wang Hongzhuan, apparently also discussed with Gu the possibility of setting up a residence for him in Shanxi. This, however, never eventuated. Gu declined at least two offers to become involved in official matters: the first, in 1671, was to assist in the compilation of the Ming history and the second, in 1678, was to take up a magistrate's position at Fuping in Shanxi. Other overtures, notably by Chang Yinyi, were also rejected. In 1679, on another visit to Wang Hongzhuan at Huayin, the two men were involved in planning a shrine to commemorate a journey there by Zhu Xi in 1185. Also in 1679, Gu petitioned the History Board to have his adoptive mother's name included in the biographies of women in the Ming. Also during his travels in the 1670s, Gu spent time with his three nephews, sons of his sister, who had risen to positions of some prominence in Beijing. Since they had never served the Ming regime, it was acceptable for them to serve the Qing, and acceptable also for Gu to associate with them. In 1676 he adopted Gu Yansheng, the child of a distant cousin.

The Final Years

In 1680, while with his adopted son at Fenzhou, he received news of his wife's death. She had remained in Kunshan during the many years of her husband's travels. Apparently, Gu met his mourning obligations while staying at a friend's house, sending a poem to mark the occasion of her death. Still he continued to travel. In the first part of 1681 he visited several places, including Huayin to meet again with Wang Hongzhuan regarding the matter of Zhu Xi's shrine. On the second day of the eighth month, he began what was to be his last journey, setting out from Huayin to travel to Quwo. On the eleventh day of the eighth month, three days after his arrival at Quwo, he became ill and had difficulty walking. In the tenth month, he moved to the home of a friend, Han Xuan, and, while there, arranged the marriage of his adopted son to the daughter of an eminent local family. The start of 1682, his final year, found him, now aged sixty-nine, still staying with Han Xuan in Shanxi. Although his health had improved somewhat, on the eighth day of the first month, his foot slipped as he was mounting his horse and he fell to the ground. There followed a rapid decline in his condition, and he died early on the morning of the ninth day of the first month of 1682. Han Xuan attended to the funeral arrangements and, in the third month, his adopted son, Gu Yansheng, accompanied his coffin back to Kunshan, where he was buried.

A SUBSTANTIAL OEUVRE

Gu Yanwu was a prolific writer despite his peregrinations. Considering he was constantly on the road for the last thirty years of his life, living in inns and friends' houses, reliant on the books he could carry on pack animals and those he could borrow or copy, and subject to the various vicissitudes I have outlined, his literary output was truly remarkable. Moreover, his works, which include significant representatives in each of the four traditional divisions—classics, history, philosophy, and belles lettres—give some measure of the breadth of his interests. A detailed list of his works is given in appendix 2. More detailed lists are provided in the works by Jan Hagman and Jean-François Vergnaud listed in the bibliography; there are eighty titles in the latter's list. However, as mentioned, only two of Gu Yanwu's works were formally published during his lifetime: his treatise on phonology and related matters (*Yinxue Wushu*), in 1667, and the first version of his *Record of Daily Knowledge*, in 1670.

It is interesting to compare Gu with two of his close contemporaries, Huang Zongxi 黄宗羲 (1610–1695) and Wang Fuzhi, both of whom shared Gu's Ming loyalist sentiments. Both men were comparably prolific writers. One notable aspect that distinguished Gu from them was his unusual life. The other two men, following early and active attempts at supporting or restoring the crumbling Ming dynasty, retired to the traditional scholarly life of relative seclusion, devoting themselves largely to thinking and writing. The *Siku Quanshu Zongmu Tiyao* lists twenty-two works (and a possible additional one) for Gu Yanwu, fifteen for Huang Zongxi, and six for Wang Fuzhi, none of whose works were published during his lifetime.

What follows is an outline of the two works that provide the material for the translations—the *Rizhi Lu*, classified in the *SKQS* under philosophy, and the *Gu Tinglin Shiwenji* (*SWJ*), classified under miscellaneous. Brief comments have been added on several other of his major works.

1. The *Rizhi Lu*

Gu Yanwu's most influential work, the *Rizhi Lu*, was first published in 1670 in eight *juan*. Apparently there are two versions of the original work extant; one is held in the Shanghai Library, while another copy was recently discovered by Chen Zuwu in the rare books section of the Beijing Library.[7] The original preface is to be found in *Tinglin Shiwenji*, 2.2. The first full edition in thirty-two *juan*, edited by Gu's student, Pan Lei, was printed in Fujian in 1695. To quote Fang Chao-ying, the *Rizhi Lu* is a "collection of carefully written notes on a great variety of topics," these notes being "the results of thirty years of wide and thoughtful reading and on the observations he made in the course of his long journeys on horseback. Not one of these notes, he [i.e., Gu] says, was written without long meditation and many of them were revised again and again."[8] A further edition appeared in 1795; this included four additional *juan* of what have been described as supplementary notes grouped under the title of *Rizhi Luzhi Yu*. What has become the definitive version, that edited by Huang Rucheng 黃汝成 (1799–1837), was published in 1834. This includes annotations by various scholars and is titled *Rizhi Lu Jiaoshi* 日知錄集釋. It has been republished a number of times.

In the early 1930s, Zhang Ji 張繼 (1887–1947), then a prominent member of the Guomindang, discovered a hand-copied manuscript of the *Rizhi Lu* in an antiquarian bookstore in Beijing. He showed this to his friend Zhang Taiyan 章太炎 (Binglin—1868–1936), who was a noted Confucian scholar and radical nationalist. He in turn set his student, Huang Kan 黃侃 (1886–1935), to work on it. As a result of close comparison with the standard edition, these scholars judged it to be an original version prior to deletions and changes made, presumably by Pan Lei, to avoid problems with the Manchu rulers—Pan had already had a brother executed for a "literary crime" (preparing an alternative Ming history). Zhang Binglin's short preface, given in appendix 3, provides a brief account of these events. The actual manuscript was taken to

Taiwan by Zhang Binglin and was subsequently published after his death through the agency of his wife in Taiwan in 1958, under the title *Yuanchao-ben Rizhi Lu* 元朝本日知錄. The legitimacy of this claim by Zhang Binlin and his associates has been both supported and questioned by recent scholars.

Thus, Ku Wei-ying writes,

> I accept the authenticity of the *Yuanchaoben* [*Rizhi Lu*]. My first reason for doing this is that I believe Gu was conscious of the possibility of a literary inquisition, and had already prepared himself for it. He made his consciousness evident in such remarks as these: [there follow quotes from two letters in the *SWJ*]. Thus it is possible that Gu wrote extra manuscript copies of the original *Rizhi Lu*. After Gu died, all of his collections of books and writings fell into the hands of his nephews—the influential Xu brothers. It was then that Gu's *Rizhi Lu* was published. The text which was presented to the public was heavily edited to avoid trouble. The *Yuanchaoben*, if we take this view, survived the literary inquisition under the protection of the Xu brothers, possibly even without their knowledge of such manuscripts.[9]

Ku Wei-ying continues by giving three further reasons for his view. John Delury however, writes, "There are reasons to treat the reliability of the manuscript version discovered in 1933 with some skepticism. First, the text appeared on the heels of Japan's occupation of Manchuria, with Japanese 'barbarians' at the gate. Second, the manuscript is closely linked to Zhang Yaiyan, a brilliant scholar, but one who, at least in his other writings on Gu Yanwu, let his political agenda get the better of scholarly rigor."[10]

Although this is an issue of some scholarly interest and also has a bearing on Gu's status as a Ming loyalist, it is essentially immaterial as far as an understanding of the substance of Gu Yanwu's ideas is concerned. It is noteworthy that, of the two recent editions that include both original annotations and footnotes citing, among other things, sources, one follows the Huang Rucheng (HRC) version and the other the *Yuanchao-ben* (*YCB*) version.[11] It should also be mentioned that the many scholars influenced by Gu during the eighteenth and nineteenth centuries presumably had access only to the HRC version.

The work, in its final form, contains over a thousand essays,[12] ranging from less than a complete vertical column in length to the longest essay, "Su Song Erfu Tianfuzhi Zhong," which is 161 vertical columns (including interlinear annotations) in the Chen Yuan edition of 2007. Gu initially made a notional division of the material in the original eight-*juan* edition into three sections: *jingshu* 經術 (classics), *zhidao* 治道 (way of government), and *bowen* 博聞 (wide-ranging learning). While this division is still broadly applicable, a number of more detailed subdivisions have been proposed by later commentators. The table gives the *Siku Quanshu Zongmu Tiyao* division of the HRC version and Xu Wenshan's division of the *YCB* version. While such divisions are helpful to an extent, the overall organization of the work is less than tight, so there is a degree of crossover between the sections in terms of subject matter.

There are, in fact, three very recent versions the *Rizhi Lu*: the three-volume version edited by Chen Yuan, *Rizhi Lu Jiaozhu*, published in 2007; the two-volume version edited by Zhang Jinghua, *Rizhi Lu Jiaoshi*, published in 2011; and the version in the twenty-two-volume *Gu Yanwu Quanji*, also published in 2011. The *Rizhi Luzhi Yu*, in four *juan*,

Table 1 Comparison of subdivisions of two editions of the RZL

Section	*HRC version*	*YCB version*
1	1–7: Jingyi 經義 (classics)	1–8: Wujing 五經 (Five Classics)
2	8–12: Zhengshi 政事 (government affairs)	9–10: Sishu 四書 (Four Books)
3	13: Shifeng 世風 (customs and mores)	11–16: Zhongyang Difang Zhengzhi Jianji Shehui Zhidu 中央地方政治兼及社會制度 (central and local government relations and social institutions)
4	14–15: Lizhi 禮制 (ritual and ceremonial practices)	17: Fengsu 風俗 (customs and mores)
5	16–17: Keju 科舉 (official examinations)	18: Lizhi 禮制 (ritual and ceremonial practices)
6	18–21: Yiwen 藝文 (literature and the arts)	19: Keju 科舉 (official examinations)
7	22–24: Zalun Mingyi 雜論名義 (miscellaneous names and terms)	20: Xinxue Deng 心學等 (learning of mind and heart, etc.)

(continued)

(*continued*)

Section	HRC version	YCB version
8	25: Gushi Zhenwang 古事真妄 (old stories, true and false)	21: Shangban Yanwen Xiaban Jiangshi 上半言文下半講史 (part writing and literature, part explanations of the histories)
9	26: Shifa 史法 (historical methods)	22: Shifu 詩賦 (*shi* and *fu* poetry)
10	27: Zhushu 注書 (annotation of books)	23–26: Za Kaogushi 雜考古事 (mis cellaneous archaeological matters)
11	28: Zashi 雜事 (miscellaneous matters)	24–25: Xingshi, Chengwei, Guanzhi 姓氏、稱謂、官制 (family and clan names)
12	29: Bing Ji Waiguo Shi 兵及外國事 (matters concerning warfare and foreign countries)	27: Ping Shishu 評史書 (criticizing history books)
13	30: Tianxiang Shushu 天象術數 (astronomy and mathematics)	28: Lun Zhushu 論注疏 (miscella neous notes and commentaries)
14	31: Dili 地理 (geography)	29: Zhongwai Fuzhi 中外服制 (Chi nese and foreign dress regulations)
15	32: Za Kaozheng 雜考證 (miscellaneous evidential research)	30: Tianwen Ji Shenguai 天文及神怪 (astronomy and ghosts and spirits)
16		31: Dili 地理 (geography)
17		32: Bowen Ji Zakao 博聞及雜考 (wide-ranging learning and miscel-laneous studies)

is appended to both the Huang Rucheng and Zhang Jinghua editions, while the former also has the *Guzhong Suibi* (*Notes from amid the Wild Rice*). This has also been published separately in both one- and three-*juan* versions.

The groupings adopted in the present work are as follows:

1. The Classics—*juan* 1–7
2. Administration and Economics—*juan* 8–12
3. Customs and Mores—*juan* 13–15
4. The Examination System—*juan* 16–17
5. Literature and Philosophy—*juan* 18–21

6. Miscellaneous (including history, geography, military matters, astronomy, terminology, philology, and other topics)—*juan* 22–32

2. The *Gu Tinglin Shiwenji*

The *Gu Tinglin Shiwenji* was first published in its present form by Zhonghua Shuju in Beijing in 1959 and is described quite aptly by Vergnaud as "très utile." It includes the following six previously published works:

1. *Tinglin Wenji*: In six *juan*, this work was prepared using an edition dating from the Kangxi reign period (1662–1723). It was completed in respect of doubtful passages using the manuscript of the *Jiang Shangyong Cangao* and the Guangxu edition of Zhang Xiufu and Dong Jiujian. It is a collection of 105 pieces—essays, prefaces, letters, records, inscriptions, and other writings. The essays include Gu's four early political essays on military, geographical, agricultural, and fiscal matters and his important later multipart essays on commanderies and districts (the *junxian* system), taxation, and government students.
2. *Tinglin Yuji*: This is a collection of twelve pieces originally prepared during the early part of the Qianlong reign period and subsequently published in 1876 by Peng Guangdian from a manuscript belonging to Fu Cengxiang. It contains his long memorial to his adoptive mother, Wang.
3. *Jiang Shangyong Cangao*: This was based on a manuscript in the Osaka Library. It comprises three *juan* containing 37, 33, and 28 pieces, predominantly letters and replies, many of which are also in the *Wenji*.
4. *Tinglin Yiwen Zhibu*: This contains nineteen pieces of which several are multipart and are letters or other documents.
5. *Tinglin Shiji*: This was prepared from Pan Lei's annotated manuscript and contains 332 poems in five *juan*. There are two more recent editions with detailed annotations, as listed prior to the translations of the poems in part III.

6. *Ximiao Liangyin Jishi*: This brief work, in one *juan*, is about events during the Tianqi reign period of Emperor Xi Zong (1621–1627).

The division of material in the *Tinglin Wenji* is relatively clear-cut and is as follows:

1. Statecraft Essays—*juan* 1
2. Prefaces (to various works)—*juan* 2
3. Letters—*juan* 3 and 4
4. Records, Inscriptions, and Other Writings—*juan* 5
5. Miscellaneous (essays, letters, and prefaces)—*juan* 6

His three other major works are as follows.

3. The *Yinxue Wushu*

This work, in thirty-eight *juan*, was first printed in 1667 with the assistance of Zhang Chao. It comprises five sections: a catalogue of ancient sounds ("Guyin Biao"—two *juan*), a study of pronunciations in the *Changes* ("Yiyin"—three *juan*), an examination of pronunciations in the *Odes* ("Shi Benyi"—ten *juan*), a comparison of Tang rhymes with those used in ancient times ("Tangyun Zheng"—twenty *juan*), and a general discussion ("Yinlun"—three *juan*). On this work, Fang Chao-ying writes, "Ku Yen-wu adopted Chen's [i.e., Chen Di—1541–1617] method in his own extensive phonetical researches and, by adducing still more examples to show its applicability, he so popularized it that it became one of the most effective tools of Ch'ing [Qing] scholarship."[13] This work has come under fire in more recent times. A succinct and informative account is provided by Bartlett.[14] Despite the criticisms, it remains a work of considerable importance in the development of the text-critical movement.

4. The *Tianxia Junguo Libing Shu*

This work, in 120 *juan*, is a collection of material from historical records, veritable records, local records, collected works, and various other official documents, supplemented and corrected by Gu's own observations made during his extensive travels. It is said that whatever had a bearing on the nation's economy and the people's livelihood he considered worthy of examining and recording, with particular stress being placed on issues of strategic military importance, taxation, and waterways. Gu began his collection of data in 1639; the preface was written in 1662. He subsequently set it aside, and it wasn't published until after his death.

5. The *Zhaoyu Zhi*

This is an extensive work of historical geography begun in 1639 but never published in a completed form. In his preface, Gu writes, "First I took the general gazetteers of the empire, then the gazetteers of each of the *sheng*, *fu*, *zhou*, and *xian*. Next, I took the twenty-one dynastic histories and various works, reading, in all, more than a thousand writings." Fang Chao-ying, in Arthur Hummel's *Eminent Chinese of the Ch'ing Period*, originally published in 1943, speaks of two incomplete manuscripts in the Guoxue Library in Nanjing.

Thus, from his substantial body of published and unpublished writings, there are perhaps five that can be regarded as being of particular importance. The two from which selected translations are included in the present work, the *RZL* and the *SWJ*, contain the substance of Gu Yanwu's thinking on a wide range of subjects but especially the classics, philosophy generally, and statecraft. This material undoubtedly has a timeless quality, while the letters particularly give important insights into the nature of the man himself. The three more specialized works are predominantly of historical interest, although the first was certainly influential in determining the direction of scholars during the Qing period.

A PRACTICAL PHILOSOPHY

In attempting to identify key concepts in Gu Yanwu's thought, two things in particular must be taken into account. First, in none of his writings does he set out a detailed and extensive exposition of these concepts. They must be extracted piecemeal from the very large number of short, or relatively short, essays, which are themselves often heavily laced with quotations from other writers. Second, his criticisms of, and reflections on, other ideas and practices are, for the most part, inextricably interwoven with the expression of his own ideas. Typically, what he proposes is to be seen reflected in the mirror of what he opposes. In addition, as alluded to earlier, his thought is wide-ranging and encompasses the study of the classics, philosophy (social, political, and ethical), the methods and aims of learning, literature, history, geography, and sundry other matters. And above all, in each of these subjects, the pursuit of knowledge is for the purpose of its practical application to the moral cultivation of the individual and the general betterment of society. In summarizing his thoughts on these matters, I follow the divisions in the *Rizhi Lu* as used for the translations. Material from the *Shiwenji* is considered briefly and separately.

1. *Record of Daily Knowledge*

RZL 1–7: The Classics

The classics are covered in the first seven *juan* of the HRC edition and the first ten *juan* of the *YCB* edition. Works considered in detail are the *Changes* (*Yi Jing*), *Documents* (*Shu Jing*), *Odes* (*Shi Jing*), *Spring and Autumn Annals* (*Chunqiu*) and its three commentaries, the three works on *li* 禮—that is, the *Rites of Zhou* (*Zhou Li*), the *Book of Etiquette* (*Yi Li*), and the *Record of Rites* (*Li Ji*), the last including the two later extracted chapters, the *Doctrine of the Mean* (*Zhongyong* 中庸) and the *Highest Learning*—the *Analects* (*Lunyu*) and the *Mencius*. Delury makes a point of the inclusion of the *Zhongyong* and the *Daxue* in the section on the *Li Ji*, taking this as an implicit rejection of the creation of the Four Books by Zhu Xi 朱熹 (1130–1200).[15] Notably, however, in the *YCB* edition, they are treated together in sections 9 and 10, separate from the *Li Ji*.

Among these canonical works, Gu gives pride of place to the *Changes*. In fact, his approach to the *Changes* can be taken as a paradigm of his attitude to the classics in general. He is concerned with matters of fact, such as the origins and authorship of the particular work, and with the historical development of its interpretations, as shown by the commentaries and analyses of later scholars. He is concerned with the subject matter of textual research, and especially with the applicability of the work to a person's life and activities—that is, the classic as a vehicle for "the cultivation of the self and the ordering of the people." In this he is typical of the exponents of Han learning. In regard to the *Changes* specifically, he saw this as a work of major significance in the Confucian canon and not just a somewhat obscure tract on prognostication. It was, for him, a work embracing all the important components of learning. Indeed, as he asks rhetorically, is everything of value not contained in the *Changes*?[16]

The importance he accorded to the *Changes* is made particularly clear in the following excerpt from a letter to a friend on the subject:

> Thus is it said that the *Changes* contains the fourfold Way [*dao*] of the revered sages. In speaking, we should be guided by its judgments. In acting, we should be guided by its changes. In making objects, we should be guided by its images. In seeking an oracle, we should be guided by its pronouncements. Previously, when I encouraged men to study the *Changes*, I suggested this should be preceded by study of the *Odes* and the *Documents*, and by attention to the *Record of Rites*, with the *Changes* being used to preserve what is central. If this is done, there may subsequently be examination of its diagrams and contemplation of its judgments. Then the Way [*dao*] will not be empty action, and the Way [*dao*] of the sages can be understood. I wonder if you consider this to be true or not?[17]

He goes on to give similar detailed treatment to each of the other classics in turn, with the identification of the general issues running through all these works and with attention also to specific issues pertaining to the individual works. Moreover, in his considerations on the origin, authorship, and authenticity of a particular text, he is unafraid to enter areas of uncertainty and controversy. A central tenet of his thinking is that only through detailed clarification of all matters pertaining to the text can the meaning be made clear. For Gu, too ready an acceptance of a text, given in uncritical fashion, is not to be countenanced. His attitude is well encapsulated in the words of Mencius, apropos the *Documents*: "It would be better to be without the *Documents* than to give undue credence to it."[18] Specifically, for the *Changes* he writes on the no longer extant precursors of the work and on the final formulation of the definitive text. For the *Documents*, he gives attention to the old text–new text controversy, and for the *Odes* he examines Confucius's role in ordering and arranging the verses. In relation to the *Spring and Autumn Annals*, he also examines Confucius's role and offers a critical appraisal of the three ancient commentaries.

In his focus on the lessons to be learned from each of these works, whether they be ethical, philosophical, or political, he is clearly sympathetic to all the basic concepts of Confucianism and reaffirms the purpose of learning, which must necessarily be firmly founded on the ancient classics—that is, to cultivate the self in order to govern others. Two issues that are fundamental to Gu's thought, and are derived directly from Confucius, also emerge in this section: the importance of the "broad study of literature [*wen*]" and "in one's actions to have a sense of shame." Also permeating his writings on the classics is his implacable opposition to the development of abstruse and esoteric flights of metaphysical fancy supposedly based on the classics—developments exemplified by the writings of Zhou Dunyi 周敦頤 (1017–1073) and Shao Yong 邵雍 (1011–1077). Indeed, Gu's essays on the classics are a vehicle for him to express his antagonism to the ramifications of Song and Ming neo-Confucianism in particular and metaphysical speculation on mind and nature in general.

Also of central importance to Gu are the issues of textual analysis alluded to previously. It is critical for Gu to bring clarification to the text as a route of access to the underlying concepts. For all the classics a substantial part of his writings is devoted to these issues—the meanings of characters, the interpretation of areas of controversy, and matters of historical or biographical importance. Finally, he gives thought to the use of the texts for didactic and examination purposes.

RZL 8–12: Administration and Economics

The essential themes running through these essays (HRC 8–12, *YCB* 11–16) are those of decentralization, devolution, and local autonomy. The cornerstone of an effective system of government was, for Gu, a well-structured local administrative apparatus staffed by men of exemplary character. Indeed, he would see moral cultivation as the foundation of an effective local officialdom, hence the importance he attaches to the education and selection of officials. In terms of particular offices, it is the prefects and district magistrates who assume central importance. In

Gu's view, history had seen a progressive decline in the prefectural system (*junxian*), which therefore needed to be restructured and revivified by major changes. He saw the process as depending on the injection of elements of the *fengjian* system (feudalism, decentralization). The restoration of a satisfactory situation, he thought, required the appointment of prefects and district magistrates, men of quality, with sufficient autonomy to allow them to function effectively. These men must, moreover, be motivated purely by the desire to further the well-being of the people and the land under their control.

In this section Gu also identifies several of the factors inimical to his concept of the ideal administrative structure. First, there is the proliferation of a complex bureaucracy that will shackle even the most able and upright of local administrators. Second, growing within, there is the canker of conniving and self-seeking petty functionaries motivated by base considerations of personal gain. Third, there are the defects in the way local officials are selected and deployed, including, particularly, the method of drawing lots, the dispatch of the men selected to far-flung regions with which they are unfamiliar, and the deleterious effects of short terms of office. Fourth, there are the harmful effects of an overelaborate and enmeshing network of legal restraints by which local officials can be entirely hamstrung. Finally, there are the evils associated with the participation of eunuchs in administrative matters, an issue to which Gu devotes two important essays. Thus, for Gu, the local magistrates must be men of worth, appointed to areas with which they are already familiar and which they can come to know better by long acquaintance. In their work, they must remain untrammeled by an oppressive overseeing superstructure and a debilitating gain-seeking infrastructure.

On a number of other administrative issues, Gu also makes clear and specific recommendations. Thus, in taxation the central pillar of his argument is that tax levies must be made in whatever commodity is most convenient to those being taxed, predominantly what is being produced by the taxed population (e.g., grain), and that tax imposts must be realistically linked to the capacity of the region concerned. In addition, there must be strict avoidance of corrupt misappropriation of tax revenue. Gu was also clearly opposed to schemes of "taxation in advance," such as those proposed by Wang Anshi 王安石 (1021–1086). On land distribution, Gu harks back to the ancient well-field system, while, on the apportionment of wealth, he identifies two aspects as fundamental. First, there must not be excessive concentration of wealth in the hands of the ruling house. Second, the individual pursuit of profit must be discouraged. Other matters to which he gives specific attention include the payment of officials, the reporting and control of malfeasance, the restriction of private ownership of military equipment, the utilization and maintenance of natural and man-made amenities, the rationalization and unification of the currency system, and the control of commodity and market prices.

Gu's social prescription can be summarized by the somewhat idyllic picture of a contented peasantry laboring in equitably distributed land untroubled by needlessly meddlesome officials. A satisfactory distribution of the populace would see the majority occupying this position under the unobtrusive control of a wise and effective, paternalistic local administration thoroughly conversant with, and sympathetic to, the particular needs and capacities of the area under its jurisdiction. There would be, as a corollary, the avoidance of a concentration of people in the cities with the attendant evils of excessive corvée and litigation.

RZL 13–15: Customs and Mores

Much of the substance of Gu's position on ethical matters is contained in sections 13–15 of the HRC edition and 17 and 18 of the *YCB* edition. The first of these sections in each case begins with a series of essays on different historical periods. In these, Gu links the flourishing and decline of society to the prevailing moral climate and in so doing establishes himself as both a proponent of the cyclical view of history and an adherent of the basic Confucian concept of virtue. Here, too, he articulates his opposition to the neo-Daoist developments of the Zhengshi reign period (240–248), with particular opprobrium being visited upon the practice of "pure talk" (*qingtan* 清談). The next three essays deal with specific factors important in regulating conduct, the first two (disinterested criticism and the role of trying to preserve a good reputation) are somewhat outside the standard Confucian teaching, while the third, on the importance of being honest and having an appropriate sense of shame, is well within it. There is also trenchant criticism of Wang Anshi for his administrative and educational policies. In subsequent essays, he further develops his basic ethical views, stressing the fundamental nature of *li* 禮 (proper conduct in interpersonal relationships, rites, ceremonies) and *yi* 義 (right action, righteousness, justice). He also stresses, in separate essays, frugality and the avoidance of extravagance. Having outlined the fundamentals of morality, he goes on to say that the manifestation of these should be the basis for the selection of officials. In his treatment of the laws, he embraces a rather Legalistic position, somewhat at odds with his earlier Confucian leanings in this area. Strict laws strictly enforced with clear delineation and unswerving application, he sees as desirable. In sections 14 and 15 (HRC) and 17 (*YCB*) he gives specific consideration to various aspects of *li* 禮, dealing with practices in terms of their moral worth and historical development.

RZL 16–17: The Examination System

The essays on this topic are in two sections in the HRC edition (16, 17) and in one section in the *YCB* edition (19). In the initial essays, Gu deals with terminology, endeavoring to bring clarity to derivation and usage. These several essays preface a discussion of the two paramount evils he thought had developed in the examination system during the course of history. First, he identifies the progressive diversion of attention away from the original classics and their commentaries and toward writing directed purely at examination topics. Second, he speaks of the progressive intrusion of corrupt practices into the conduct of the examinations. The main consequence of these two evils is, inevitably, a profound overall decline in scholarship. He also states here what he sees as the importance of historical studies and the desirability of incorporating them into the examination framework. Having outlined what might be termed the broad issues, he then directs his attention to more specific matters and offers some historical deliberations.

RZL 18–21: Literature and Philosophy

The essays in this category are grouped in four sections (18–21) in the HRC edition and in three sections (20–22) in the *YCB* edition. As with his writings on other matters, Gu's essays on these topics are wide-ranging. On literature, he covers various issues, including storage of literary works and their accessibility, the means of documentation of official business, and questions arising in a number of individual works. He does, however, focus especially on two aspects: literature as a social instrument and the technicalities of composition. For Gu, writing should be original and not derivative nor imitative and certainly not tainted by the least drop of plagiarism. It should manifest simplicity—prolixity must be eschewed. Writing should be well wrought, with attention being given to technique, but at the same time it should be easy to understand. With regard to poetry, he embraces the view that verse, like prose, should be didactic and utilitarian, although not at the expense of style. It should, moreover, reflect the spirit of the era. Although Gu was much concerned with rhyme and other technicalities of verse, these are, for him, clearly secondary in importance to content, and he warns against the danger of too great a degree of attention being given to technicalities. Finally, and most importantly, writing should be an effective social instrument.

This section also contains two essays of fundamental importance for an understanding of Gu Yanwu's philosophical position. In the first (18.12), he outlines the development of Daoism and Buddhism, linking the latter historically to the doctrines of Mo Di in the pre-Qin period. He subscribes to the conventional view of parallel streams in the development of Chinese philosophy, a variable combination of Daoism and Buddhism coursing alongside Confucianism. Not surprisingly, he voices his opposition to the former. In the second (18.13), he focuses on the development of neo-Confucianism, tracing this back to its origins in the classical writings and displaying how, in his view, later interpretations had become increasingly divorced from original meanings and how fundamental Confucianism had been rendered impure by admixture with the alien strains of Daoism and Buddhism.

RZL 22–32: Miscellaneous

The final major division of the *Rizhi Lu* (HRC 22–32, *YCB* 23–32) covers a variety of topics. Many of these essays are devoted to clarifying the meanings and usage of terms. On the issue of quotations, he stresses the importance of accuracy and appropriate attribution. In his writings on history and geography, there is a focus on the names of places and people. These are broadly related to questions of textual analysis and aimed at bringing clarity to predominantly ancient texts. He also gives consideration to matters of interest relating to historical events and personages and deals with various controversial or contentious passages, particularly in early writings. A section is devoted to ritual and ceremonial practices, with the underlying theme of the superiority of the ancient over the modern. In a further section, some general consideration is given to astronomy—that is, the development of the science and how, in ancient times, it formed part of the general body of knowledge rather than being an area of special expertise, as it later became. Consideration is also given to the relationship between celestial and terrestrial affairs. The final two sections are devoted to place-names and the usage and origin of certain common characters.

2. *Collected Poems and Essays*

The divisions in this work are based on the form of the writing rather than the subject matter. The style in this work is different in that there are far fewer quotes from other writings, while those that are used tend to be shorter. Overall, there is a much more personal tone in this material, especially in the letters, which is hardly surprising. As with the *RZL*, I consider the work under the six sections of the recent *Tinglin Wenji*.[19] I treat the poems separately.

SWJ 1: Statecraft Essays

There are six essays in this section. The first three are relatively short and are about matters similar to those dealt with in the miscellaneous sections of the *RZL*. The other three essays, all multipart, correspond to material in the government and statecraft sections of the *RZL* (13–15 in the HRC edition) in two instances and to the sections on official examinations (16–17 in the HRC edition) in the third. All three are included in the translations and are considered in some detail here as they are important and direct statements of Gu's developed position on these topics.

In the nine-part essay on the prefectural system, the fundamental tenet is that some of the principles of the earlier feudal system should be grafted onto the existing prefectural system as a means of effecting a significant degree of devolution. While Gu makes explicit his recognition of the inevitability of progression from a feudal to a prefectural system, he sees no insurmountable obstacle to a reintroduction of some aspects of the earlier system. For him, the major evil in the later system was an excess of centralized, bureaucratic control with the attendant paralysis of effective local administration and the probability of an increasing role for minor officials motivated by less-than-altruistic impulses. The key to bringing about decentralization, as proposed in this essay and elsewhere, is to appoint district magistrates who are men of proven integrity and scholastic worth as revealed by an appropriate selection system. Give these men a permanent position, and they will develop a substantial commitment to the area and community they serve. An effective local administration, based on the central role of district magistrates, obviates the need for an oppressive structure of overseeing officials and reduces the likelihood of minor officials' stepping outside their prescribed functions.

In considering possible objections to this administrative framework, Gu recognizes three major areas of difficulty. First, without a suitable body of overseeing officials, the power of the district magistrates may become too great. Second, the hereditary succession of titles, which he proposes to achieve continuity of office and therefore commitment, may result in too great a concentration of power in the hands of one family. Third, the appointment of men to their own district, which Gu also advocates, may lead to preferential treatment for family and friends. Gu's counterargument is, essentially, that none of these objections is relevant if the men selected are of a sufficiently high quality. This brings him back to the methods of selection, in which he favors the ancient over the modern, as one might expect. Thus, Gu envisages a series of semiautonomous local regions under the control of a district magistrate, appointed from the area and remaining within the area so his interests will coincide with those of the community he serves. As far as possible, each region should be responsible for its own destiny in matters such as provision of food and taxation.

In the two-part essay on taxation, Gu's central thesis is that the tax levy should be paid in a commodity readily available to those paying; in other words, the people should be taxed on what they produce. On this score, he is particularly opposed to the use of silver as the medium of taxation. He recommends that the tax levied from various regions be in the commodity or substance appropriate to that region, and if this is not feasible, then in cash. In addition, he was opposed to excessive taxation, especially where this involved manipulation of tax levies for personal gain by officials. Nevertheless, in such instances he did not hold the officials themselves to be intrinsically at fault; he saw them, rather, as victims of the system. At different periods of history, officials were no more or less venal but merely likely to succumb to the human tendency to avail themselves of whatever advantage a particular system might offer.

The three-part essay on government students offers a trenchant criticism of this category of student, in terms of both concept and means of selection. As a consequence of the establishment of such a category, there was, in Gu's opinion, an extraordinary proliferation of officials lacking a secure educational foundation. These were men who were concerned primarily with furthering their own interests and those of their families, without due consideration being given to the state—men, moreover, who were not averse to adopting illicit means to achieve their objectives. Much of the first part of this essay is devoted to possible alternatives, while the second part provides an extended consideration of the evils attendant upon the use of this system—in particular, faction or clique formation. Gu strongly advocates the scrapping of the category of government student and stresses how vital it is for all examinations to be devoted to the true concepts of the original classics and dynastic histories rather than to analyses prepared purely for examination purposes. The final part of the essay provides a detailed discussion of possible alternative methods of selection followed by some concluding remarks on the benefits that might accrue from the application of appropriate methods.

SWJ 2: Prefaces

Two of the prefaces in this section are included in the translations. The first is that to the *Yinxue Wushu*, a work of great importance in the development of the evidential learning (*kaozheng xue*) movement. Gu's aim in this work was to bring clarity to the understanding of ancient rhymes—a clarity that could be gained only by a detailed study of the classics themselves and would, in turn, aid that very study. Once the foundation was established, the rhymes and pronunciations of later times could be properly understood and the accumulated errors of the centuries rectified. This most detailed and comprehensive work is, as clearly outlined in the preface, a component of Gu's program to persuade scholars to return to their ancient, and Confucian, roots. The second preface is Gu's own brief introductory statement to the first, eight-*juan* edition of the *RZL* published in 1670. In his preface to the *Yi Li Zheng Zhangju Zhu* (not included in the translations), written by Gu's contemporary Zhang Erqi 張爾岐 (1612–1678), Gu makes two important points: (1) he stresses the purpose of the *Yi Li* 儀禮 (*Book of Etiquette*) itself and the desirability of its inclusion in the official curriculum and (2) he reiterates his criticism of the more abstruse developments of neo-Confucianism. He also takes the opportunity to comment on the value of the stone carvings of the classics as a means of correcting textual errors.

SWJ 3, 4: Letters

These sections include two long letters to unnamed recipients on issues of particular importance to Gu (the *Changes* and learning or study generally), three letters to named recipients (his nephew, Xu Bingyi, Shi Yushan, and his student, Pan Lei), and twenty-five short letters to unnamed friends. The first of the long letters (included in the translations), "Letter to a Friend Discussing Learning," allows Gu to expand on some of the central pillars of Confucianism, taken from the foundational writings, which might be expected to sustain the whole edifice of ancient learning in the face of possible degradation and destruction at the hands of later and misguided interpreters. The second long letter is about the *Changes*. In this, Gu stresses again the fundamental importance of this work. In the letter to his nephew, Gu offers a further strong criticism of the examination system, in particular the use of the eight-legged essay and its utterly derivative nature. Turn once more, Gu exhorts, to a broad study of the original classics. The letter to Shi Yushan contains a clear statement of Gu's equation of the study of principle (*lixue* 理學) with the study of the classics (*jingxue* 經學), an important component of his philosophical position, and is a further statement of his opposition to Song neo-Confucianism. The twenty-five short letters to unnamed friends offer, in many instances, personal, and somewhat pithy, statements of a number of Gu's major theses: the importance of diligent application to learning; the need to make one's studies broad based; the importance of certain classical texts (here the *Changes*, *Odes*, and the *Spring and Autumn Annals*); the need for literature to be created with a view to practical application—that is, some ethical, social, or didactic purpose; the need to be cognizant of the old in planning the new; and, finally, the importance of rectifying the mind and benefiting from self-criticism.

SWJ 5, 6: Records, Inscriptions, and Other Writings

There are forty-three essays in these two sections. One essay from *juan* 5 is included in the translations, titled "The Pei Village Record," which Gu uses to present his ideas on the importance of the clan system in local administration. From *juan* 6 only the four early essays on matters of administrative importance are included. On these, Peterson has written, "It is apparent [from their content] that they were written before the fall of Nanjing and may have been intended originally as bases for memorials to be presented to the Ming court."[20] In the essay on military matters, Gu contrasts favorably the system introduced by the first Han emperor with that introduced by his Ming counterpart—the *weisuo* 衛所 system—and further contrasts the early and later developments of this system. He is opposed to the separation of agricultural and military components and also to the subdivision of functions within the military itself. The essay on historical geography focuses on identifying places of strategic importance in military terms and examining the reasons for their importance. The recognition of each place is generally prefaced by a consideration of its role in earlier conflicts. The essay on agriculture is a broad statement of the fundamental importance of the activity itself and the need to devise a suitable scheme for its effective pursuit. As in the preceding essay, the connection between agricultural and military matters is recognized, especially in the border regions, where an appropriate arrangement establishing a resident military force and the means to provide for it is seen as essential. The essay on money begins with a historical survey of the different monetary systems as a basis for a vigorous criticism of the then current system. In Gu's opinion, there should be a more equitable and rational collection of taxes and a more appropriate redistribution of the wealth acquired by taxation. In general, Gu is very critical of the current dynasty's use of money.

In summarizing Gu Yanwu's ideas, it is clear that the opinions acquired by a detailed, critical, and analytical study of the classics formed the bedrock of his philosophical position. Thus he might reasonably be characterized as a "fundamentalist Confucian," espousing the ethical and other philosophical views of the foundational texts and rejecting the increasingly elaborate metaphysical superstructure fashioned particularly by the Song dynasty neo-Confucians and further elaborated by their Ming successors. He was also strongly opposed to non-Confucian doctrines, most notably Daoism and Buddhism. On matters of statecraft, he makes many specific recommendations, but his basic position is one favoring a simplified, decentralized social organization, looking back to an idealized ancient model with a minimization of centralized control and avoidance of a complex and meddlesome apparatus of overseers. He was deeply concerned with the means of selection of officials and the examination system on which this depended. The key element of his thinking on these issues was that in order to create and identify officials of sufficient moral worth to serve society properly, teaching and examinations must be based on the original classics—and on all of them, not just one or two or later interpretative texts. On literary and textual issues he was wedded to the idea of writings that were carefully crafted, nonderivative, and easy to understand, and he emphasized the need for detailed textual study along the lines practiced by Chen Di 陳第 (1541–1617).

On the matter of intellectual influences, there is no question as to what Gu looked to as authoritative texts. The writings that formed the entire foundation of his intellectual life were the classics—that is, all the classics in their original forms and accompanied by their early commentaries. In addition, the accumulated dynastic histories and other factual records of the vicissitudes of society were taken as reliable sources useful for forming or supporting his own views. Many postclassical writers are quoted by Gu—indeed, his essays are laced with quotations—but no one individual can be singled out as being especially influential. Certainly, Gu was not a member of any particular school that could be traced to postclassical sources, nor did he come under the influence of a particular philosopher. Nonetheless, some precursors can be identified: Song opponents of neo-Confucianism such as Chen Liang 陳亮 (1143–1194) and Ye Shi 葉適 (1150–1223),[21] the scholars of the Donglin Academy with their focus on practical issues, and to some extent Liu Zongzhou 劉宗周 (1578–1645) in his opposition to Wang Shouren 王守仁 (Wang Yangming—1472–1528). Much clearer are those whom he oppugns—Xun Shuang 荀爽 (128–190) in Han times, those responsible for the development of the "pure talk" movement in the Three Kingdoms period, men such as Wang Yan 王衍 (256–311), and the Song neo-Confucians (although his attitude to Zhu Xi [1130–1200] was somewhat ambivalent). He was also fiercely critical of Wang Anshi. Finally, among his Ming predecessors, Gu was clear in his opposition to Wang Yangming and Li Zhi 李贄 (1527–1602).

A LASTING LEGACY

Unquestionably Gu Yanwu had a substantial and sustained influence on Chinese thought, extending from his own time into at least the early part of the twentieth century. He was a major force in the redirection of Confucianism away from the metaphysical abstractions that characterized the Song and Ming periods and back to what Gu saw as the fundamental components of Confucian teaching as fully articulated in the classical writings of the pre-Qin period, clarified and elaborated on where necessary by the textual studies of Han scholars. He was, then, a pioneer in the movements that became dominant during the Qing period—*kaozheng xue* and Han learning. There were many outstanding scholars over the last centuries of the second millennium who followed Gu along this road. Several important formative factors that were clearly instrumental in establishing the direction of Gu's own thought have been outlined in the earlier sections—his unusual family situation and early education; the social, political, and philosophical climate; his contacts with friends and peers; and his experiences with the examination system. These and other factors, acting on the substrate of Gu's "decreed nature," led him to recognize the fundamental objective of learning and scholarship as being the ethical development of the individual, who then directed his attention to the ethical and social betterment of society as a whole. The central pillars of his endeavor, obvious particularly in the works considered in the present book, were as follows:

- the importance of a detailed and painstaking study of the original classic texts and their early commentaries as a means of returning to the roots of Confucianism
- the study of language as a means of gaining a deeper understanding of classical texts
- the importance of studying a wide range of sources, particularly historical and geographical, to identify and understand which forces are favorable and which harmful to the proper functioning of society

Thus the key teachings and information were already there. It was discovering them and understanding them that Gu was concerned with. Added to this was the way he lived his life, with patent integrity and a manifest desire to improve society. This explains in part why Gu could appeal to a wide range of scholars and persuade them to follow him along the road he had set out on with the intent of leading society out of the chaos arising from the fall of the Ming house. What follows is a brief consideration of his influence in chronological sequence.

During the last part of the seventeenth century, both before and immediately after his death, it seems that Gu had relatively little actual influence given the limited availability of his writings and his political isolation due to his intransigent anti-Manchu stance. Moreover, he lacked any body of students absorbing and propagating his teachings. However, it does seem he had already established a reputation as an erudite and thoughtful scholar of some consequence while still alive. The eighteenth century was essentially a period of social stability in China. This may have developed under the alien Manchu regime, but it was stability nonetheless. During this period Gu's influence was felt mainly in the flourishing of evidential research—here Gu's methodology was much admired. It was characterized by Jiang Fan 江藩 (1761–1831) as "taking past and present situations as references and using various materials to reinforce his arguments." Scholars such as Zhao Yi 趙翼 (1727–1814) and Qian Daxin 錢大昕 (1728–1804) produced works like the *Rizhi Lu*. The following three comments are of interest in this respect.

The first is a statement on the *Rizhi Lu* from the chief editor of the *SKQS*, Ji Yun 紀昀 (1724–1805):

> Yanwu's studies had a solid foundation. He read broadly but could also make something out of everything he studied. When he wrote on something, he must have studied meticulously its beginning and its end, and he adduced very strong evidence. His writing quoted facts extensively to support his arguments, and very few of them were shaky. . . . However, Yanwu lived in the late Ming and loved to talk about statecraft. He was prompted by what was happening then, and determinedly took the restoration of antiquity as his duty. Some of his ideas were awkward and difficult to implement; some of his other ideas were wishful thinking and too demanding.[22]

The second is a statement by Dai Zhen 戴震 (1723–1777), which encapsulates comprehensively, but succinctly, what might be considered the underlying motive driving Gu in his textual studies: "The classics provide the route to the Dao. What illustrates the Dao is their words. How words are formed can be grasped only through [a knowledge of] philology and paleography. From the study of primary and derived characters we can master the language. Through the language we can penetrate the mind and will of the ancient sages and worthies."[23]

The third is a brief comment from a modern scholar, Yu Ying-shi, who wrote, with reference to the early Qing period, "Philological explication of classical texts . . . replaced moral metaphysical speculation as the chief method for the attainment of Confucian truth."[24] In this endeavor, Gu Yanwu was at the forefront, his influence extending into the twentieth century, for example, in the person of Sun Yirang 孫詒讓 (1848–1908).

The nineteenth century saw rapidly changing circumstances in China with the beginning of a relentless downward spiral that was to see the end of the imperial period. In particular, there were major internal uprisings such as the Taiping Rebellion and increasingly aggressive incursions from Western nations, driven by unworthy aims and employing unworthy means. The situation was somewhat similar to that in which Gu's thought developed—decay of the social structure and domination by an alien race. These developments saw attention turn more toward the political and social components of Gu's thought. A notable example of his continuing influence was the building of a temple to Gu in Beijing in 1843, organized by He Shaoji and group of scholars who met there annually between 1843 and 1873 to discuss current affairs. Notable among the members of this group were Zeng Guofan 曾國藩 (1811–1872) and Feng Guifen 馮桂芬 (1809–1874), two of the most politically significant men in nineteenth-century China. Brief quotes from both follow.

Zeng brackets Gu with Qin Huitian 秦蕙田 (1702–1764) in considering the importance of *li* 禮, an increasingly important concept in Gu's work. On Gu himself, he says, "The scholars of our dynasty regard Gu Tinglin as their master. Gu was put in first place in the *Biographies of Qing Scholars*. When I was reading his books, especially his writings which dealt with rituals, social customs and education, his determination to preserve what has been handed down and which waits for newcomers, and his determination to take responsibility into his own hands, really struck me. . . . I portrayed Gu and Qin as the first and second sages of our dynasty. Is there not a profound meaning in them!"[25]

Paul Cohen, in his work on Wang Tao (b. 1828), quotes Mary Wright as saying of Feng Guifen that he was "in many respects the very embodiment of restoration Confucians" and that in advocating as he did radical institutional reform at the local level, he was "following the ideas of his philosophical mentor Gu Yanwu."[26]

Gu's influence certainly remained strong in the early part of the twentieth century. In fact, the names Gu Yanwu, Huang Zongxi, and Wang Fuzhi were added to the Imperial Temple of Confucius in 1909. Two of his strongest advocates during this time were Liang Qichao and Zhang Binglin. The former was especially complimentary about Gu's methodology, as the following quote from Benjamin Elman reveals. Having drawn attention to Liang Qichao's account of Gu Yanwu's *Rizhi Lu* as "the exemplary work that influenced scholars to record their findings with precision and detail," Elman himself articulates what might be termed a definitive judgment on the work: "The dignity of the step-by-step empirical approach to knowledge based on wide reading and meticulous observation was an important element that model works such as the *Rizhi Lu* conveyed to scholars during the eighteenth century."[27]

Zhang Binglin, who changed his name to honor Gu, saw part of Gu's social prescription aimed at strengthening local power as relevant to defense against the Japanese threat from Manchuria.

In a relatively modern article quoted by Ku Wei-ying, probably from the Communist era (the actual source is not given), Gu is praised on the following four counts:

1. his patriotism and admirable spirit of integrity and setting an example by his own actions;
2. his adherence to existing reality and his spirit of studying in the service of existing politics;
3. his uncompromising attitude toward, and criticism of, wrong ideas; and
4. his methodologies of study[28]

These are, indeed, features that are not limited to any particular time or place!

NOTES ON THE TRANSLATIONS

In the present work there are translations of fifty-one essays from the *RZL*, thirty-one essays, letters, and prefaces from the *SWJ*, plus a small selection of poems from this work. In the majority of instances the initial translations were made using the two-volume, 1985 edition of Huang Rucheng's *Rizhi Lu Jishi* and the 1980 edition of the *Yuanchaoben Rizhi Lu*. In the case of the *RZL*, revisions of previous translations and new translations were made using a combination of the 2007 *Rizhi Lu Jiaozhu* edited by Chen Yuan, which follows the HRC text and arrangement, and the 2011 *Rizhi Lu Jiaoshi* edited by Zhang Jinghua, which follows the *YCB* text and arrangement. In the case of the *SWJ*, the translations of the essays, letters, and prefaces were made using the 1959 edition of the *Tinglin Shiwenji* supplemented by the *Xinyi Gutinglin Wenji* edited by Liu Jiuzhou and published in Taiwan in 2000. For the poems the two editions listed in the introduction to that section were used.

The aim with the prose writings was to include at least one piece from each of the sections of both the *RZL* and *SWJ*. Each section is prefaced by a summarizing analysis of the contents of the section. In the case of the poems, a small selection was made from each of five periods of Gu's life into which editors have divided them. Brief comments are appended to each poem to cite and clarify references where this was deemed necessary. Also translated and included in appendixes 3 and 4, respectively, are Zhang Binglin's short preface to the then newly discovered manuscript that became the *Yuanchaoben Rizhi Lu* and Liu Zongyuan's 柳宗元 (773–819) well-known essay on the *fengjian* system, which should, as Bartlett has suggested, be read in conjunction with Gu Yanwu's writings on the decentralization-centralization issue.

I

ESSAYS FROM THE *RECORD OF DAILY KNOWLEDGE* (*RIZHI LU*—*RZL*)

1

RZL 1–7

THE CLASSICS

Seven of the thirty-two sections of the *RZL* in the Huang Rucheng edition are devoted to the classics: one each to the *Changes*, *Documents*, *Odes*, *Spring and Autumn Annals* and its three early commentaries, two to the *San Li* (*Yi Li*, *Zhou Li*, and *Li Ji*), and one to the *Lunyu* (*Analects*) and *Mencius*. In the *Yuanchaoben* edition these same essays plus two additional ones are divided into nine sections. There are in all 370 (372) essays. What follows is a summary of each of the seven sections accompanied by one or more essays from that section.

Section 1, the *Changes*: There are fifty-three essays on the *Zhou Yi* 周易 (or *Yi Jing* 易經, *Changes*). The first five are of a general nature: 1.1 considers the origin of the work; 1.2 is a brief comment on King Wen's role in its creation; 1.3 is about Zhu Xi's interpretation in his work *Zhou Yi Benyi*; 1.4 compares the interpretations of Confucius and the later scholars Xun Shuang and Yu Fan; and 1.5 is about changes in the diagrams. Essays 1.6–37 are essentially comments on specific diagrams. Essays 1.38–44 pertain to the "Great Commentary" (*Da Zhuan* 大傳 or *Xi Ci* 繫辭). Essays 1.45–46 are about, respectively, the contrast of opposites in the work and its arrangement and function with specific reference to the term *ni shu* 逆數. Essays 1.47–49 concern the three "Discussions on the Trigrams"—*shuo gua* 說卦, *xu gua* 序卦, and *za gua* 雜卦. The final four essays are of a more general nature: 1.50 is about Su Shi's comments on phrases for diagrams 35 and 36; 1.51 is a brief consideration of Confucius's comments on the work; 1.52 discusses aspects of the arrangement of lines and diagrams; and 1.53 is a long historical discussion of divination using stalks and plants.

1.1 THE THREE *CHANGES*

Comment: The issue here is the origin and naming of the *Book of Changes* (for a discussion in English, see the translation of the work by I. K. Shchutskii, *Researches on the I Ching* [London: Routledge, 1980], particularly 56–128). In essence, the *Lian Shan* and *Gui Zang*, neither of which is extant, are traditionally linked with, respectively, Fu Xi and the Xia dynasty and Huang Di and the Shang dynasty.

Now, the Master [Confucius] did say Bao Xi Shi [Fu Xi][1] was the first to draw the eight diagrams, but he did not say he wrote the *Changes*. And he said, "Did the *Changes* not have its origin in Middle Antiquity?"[2] He also said, "Did it not arise during the declining years of the Yin and the burgeoning virtue of the Zhou, at the time of the matter between Kings Wen and Zhou?"[3] This indicates the words written by King Wen were first given the name *Changes*. Moreover, the Grand Diviner of the *Zhou Guan* had charge of the rules for the three *Changes*: the first was called *Lian Shan*, the second, *Gui Zang*, and the third, *Zhou Yi*. That the *Lian Shan* and the *Gui Zang* were not the *Changes* and yet three *Changes* were spoken of was because men of later times used the term *Changes* to name them. It is like the *Mozi*, which speaks of the *Spring and Autumn Annals* of Zhou, Yan, Song, and Qi.[4] That the histories of Zhou, Yan, Song, and Qi were certainly not all *Spring and Autumn Annals* and yet were called *Spring and Autumn Annals* was because the name of the Lu history was used to name them.

In the *Zuo Zhuan*, for the fifteenth year of Duke Xi [644 B.C.E.], it is said that a battle was fought in Han, at which the diviner Tu Fu, using the milfoil, predicted good fortune.[5] The diagram found was *gu* 蠱, which said, "The thousand chariots are thrice put to flight; from what remains of the three flights, seize the brave fox."[6] For the sixteenth year of Duke Cheng [574 B.C.E.], it is said that a battle was fought at Yanling, at which the duke consulted the milfoil and the diviner predicted good fortune.

The diagram found was *fu* 復, which said, "The southern kingdom is in distress; its king has been struck in the eye by an arrow."[7] These are both instances where the *Zhou Yi* [the Zhou *Changes*] was not used and words were quoted from other sources. This is what is referred to as the method of the three *Changes*. But the *Zuo Zhuan* does not speak of the *Yi* [*Changes*].

1.3 ZHU XI'S *THE ORIGINAL MEANING OF THE ZHOU "CHANGES"* (*ZHOU YI BENYI*)

Comment: This is a detailed essay on the arrangement of the *Changes*, focusing particularly on several important commentaries—those of Zheng Xuan (127–200), Wang Bi (226–249), Cheng Yi (1033–1107), and Zhu Xi (1130–1200). Gu's main aim is to stress the need for a thorough understanding of the classic, which includes a knowledge of the commentaries and how they are arranged in relation to the basic text. He also draws attention to the trivialization that developed as a result of the examination system.

The Zhou *Changes* [*Zhou Yi*], from Fu Xi's drawing of the diagrams, the *tuanci* 彖辭 [explanations of the diagrams] written by King Wen, and the *yaoci* 爻辭 [explanations of the lines] written by the Duke of Zhou, was referred to as a classic [*jing* 經]. The classic was divided into two chapters [*pian* 篇]. Confucius wrote the ten "wings," and these were referred to as a commentary. The commentary was [in turn] divided into ten chapters as follows: the *tuanzhuan* A and B, the *xiangzhuan* A and B, the *xici* A and B, all in two chapters, and the *wenyan*, the *shuoguazhuan*, the *xuguazhuan*, and the *zaguazhuan*, each in one chapter. From Han times on, the situation was confused by Fei Zhi, Zheng Xuan, and Wang Bi,[8] who took the words of Confucius and appended them piecemeal to the trigrams and lines. Cheng Zhengshu's [Cheng Yi's] commentary followed this.[9] It was not until Zhu Xi's *Zhou Yi Benyi* that reliance on the ancient writings began. Thus, in his heading of the "Zhou Yi Shangjing" section, he said, "In the *Changes* there is what was confused to some extent by many scholars. In the present age, Chao Shi[10] was the first to correct these errors, but he was not able to completely bring the text into line with the ancient text. Lü Shi[11] also changed and rearranged it, editing the classic to create two sections [*juan* 卷] of the classic itself and ten sections of commentary, returning to the original discussion of Confucius."[12]

At the beginning of the Hongwu reign period [1368–1399], there was promulgation of the study of the Five Classics among the Confucian scholars of the empire, and in the case of the *Changes*, the combined writings of Cheng Yi and Zhu Xi were used. Also, each of these men himself wrote a work [on the *Changes*]. During the Yongle reign period [1403–1425], the *Daquan* was compiled, and the various sections of Zhu Xi's work were divided up and appended to [the appropriate sections] of Cheng's commentary.[13] In this way the ancient text that Zhu Xi had established was returned to disorder and confusion. "The *tuan* 彖 were the words [of explanation] added by King Wen." "The *zhuan* 傳 were the words Confucius used to explicate the classic. Subsequently, whoever spoke of the *zhuan* was referring to this."[14] This, then, properly followed the "Tuan Shangzhuan." Nowadays, the three characters *tuan shang zhuan* have been deleted [from here] and added to follow the statement, "Great indeed is the originating power of *qian* 乾."[15] "In regard to the images, the two [upper and lower] as well as the six lines of the two images were explanations appended by the Duke of Zhou."[16] This was an explanation following the section "Xiang Shangzhuan." Now the three characters *xiang shang zhuan* 象上傳 have been deleted [from here] and added to follow "Heaven in its motion is full of power."[17] "This section extends the meaning of the *Treatise on the Tuan* and the *Treatise on the Symbols* by bringing together the profundity of the two diagrams, *qian* 乾 and *kun* 坤, and the rest of the explanation, because of this, can be inferred from what was said." This was the interpretation following the *wenyan* section, but now the two characters *wen yan* 文言 have been deleted [from here] and the statement added to follow "Originating is the chief quality of goodness."[18] These "*tuan* says," "*xiang* says," and "*wenyan* says" were all absent from Zhu Xi's original work. They were included on the basis of Cheng Yi's commentary. Later scholars who disliked Cheng's commentary were numerous, and they cast it aside without reading it, using only the *Benyi*. And the *Daquan* was what the court promulgated, so no one dared to make frequent alterations. Subsequently, with respect to the National University edition of the commentaries and explanations, there was the excision and discarding of Cheng's commentary, although his sequence was used as Zhu Xi's sequence. This arrangement was handed down for almost two hundred years. It is indeed unfortunate that the book with Zhu Xi's established corrections could not be seen in the world. How can this be construed as other than a misfortune with respect to this classic!

Zhu Xi, in his *Ji Songshan Chao Shi Guayao Tuanxiang Shuo*, says, "The ancient classic was first changed by Fei Shi and finally brought to a state of great confusion by Wang Bi."[19] This relies on Kong Shi [Kong Yingda], who, in his "Zhengyi" [orthodox interpretations], said, "What the Sage wrote explaining the images originally followed the classical explanations of the six lines. Because of his modest and retiring nature, he did not dare disturb the explanations of the first Sage correcting the classic. Wang Fusi's [Wang Bi's] idea was that in considering the images, it was appropriate to bring the original images of the classical text into close proximity so the meaning could be easily understood. Therefore, he separated the explanations of the images of the lines and added each subdivision to follow the appropriate line. This was like Du Yuankai, in his notes on the *Zuo Zhuan*, dividing the classic into years and appending the commentary to each year." Therefore, to say that combining a classic with its commentary began with [Wang] Fusi is not to recognize that its true origin was in Kangcheng [Zheng Xuan].

[In the] "Wei Annals" [of the *Sanguo Zhi* there is],

> Gaogui Xianggong made an imperial progress to the National Academy, where he questioned the erudite Chunyu Qi, saying,[20] "Confucius prepared the *tuan* and *xiang* while Zheng Xuan wrote the annotations. [Although the latter was not the equal of the Sage in worthiness],[21] nevertheless their explanations of the classic have one and the same purpose. Nowadays the *tuan* and *xiang* are not connected with the text of the classic and yet the notes are. Why is this?" Qi replied, "Zheng Xuan's combining the *tuan* and *xiang* with the classic was motivated by the wish to give scholars ease of understanding in their investigation and examination of the work." The emperor said, "If he joined them to make it truly convenient, why didn't Confucius join them so scholars could understand?" Qi replied, saying, "Confucius feared he might be confused with King

> Wen; this is why he didn't join them. His not doing so is a measure of his humility." The emperor said, "If the Sage, by not joining [his commentary to the text] is showing his humility, why is Zheng Xuan not humble too?" Qi replied, saying, "The ancient meaning was vast and deep and the Sage's questions mysterious and far-reaching. It is not something I am able to comprehend completely."[22]

So Kangcheng's writings were already the first combining [of text and commentary]; this did not begin with Fusi [Wang Bi].

In the "Rulin Zhuan" of the *History of the Former Han* [*Han Shu*] [there is], "Fei Zhi brought order to the *Changes* without paragraphs and sentences [analytical notes], using only the *tuan*, *xiang*, *xizi*, and *wenyan* to explain the two parts of the classic."[23] From this it can be concluded that the addition of the commentary [ten wings] to the classic also did not begin with Kangcheng. Zhu Xi, in his *Ji Songshan Chao Shi Guayao Tuanxiang Shuo*, says, "When disorder first came to the ancient regulations, this was like the *qian* diagram pertaining to the present."[24] Now, from *kun* onward, all depend on this, and those of later times also dispersed it to follow each *yao* writing, preserving only the one diagram, *qian*, by which we can see the old, original pattern of the interrelationship between text and commentary. I previously inferred from this that, in the present *qian* diagram, *tuan yue* is one section and *xiang yue* is one section. I don't think this was something Fei Zhi added to the original text. In the *kun* diagram the *xiaoxiang* is split up and added to follow each line, with *xiang yue* occurring eight times and with the remaining diagrams, seven times. Zheng Xuan was responsible for this, and it was this edition Gaogui Xianggong saw.

Although Cheng, in his commentary, used Fusi's edition, "also" indicates that this was not the ancient *Changes*. [For the diagram] *xian*, nine in the third place, the *xiang* says, "He moves his thighs—he 'also' does not want to rest in his place."[25] The commentary says, "Saying 'also' indicates that the *xiangci* was originally not juxtaposed with the text of the *Changes* but came from another place, therefore all the explanations of the images of the lines were connected." This says that "also" [*yi* 亦] refers to the explanation of the *yao* [line] above.

Qin, through the burning of the books, lost the Five Classics, while our own dynasty, through the selection of scholars, also lost the Five Classics.

Nowadays, those scholars who are studying for the official examinations are all thoroughly conversant with the words of the examination essays but are unable to understand and know the great principles. With respect to the *Changes* and the *Spring and Autumn Annals*, this reaches a particular level of absurdity. Through the *tuanzhuan* being joined with the *daxiang*, the *daxiang* with the *yao*, and the *yao* with the *xiaoxiang*, the second line is certainly the minister and the fifth line certainly the prince; the *yin* diagrams certainly speak of the lesser man and the *yang* diagrams certainly speak of the noble man. As a consequence, this one classic became like spilled water that could not be gathered up, and so the *Changes* was lost.

With respect to the *Spring and Autumn Annals*, one or two sentences were selected from Hu Shi's [Hu Anguo's][26] commentary as being important, and these were related to similar events recounted in the classic to make a topic. So the commentary became the "host" [major part] and the classic the "guest" [minor part]. There was the use of "that classic" to verify the topic of "this classic" and the use of "that classic" to conceal the topic of "this classic." As a result, this one classic became a work for use in *shefu* 射覆,[27] and so the *Spring and Autumn Annals* was lost. Recovering the writings of Cheng and Zhu was how the *Changes* was preserved. Likewise, the completion of the three commentaries and the writings of Dan, Zhao, and others was how the *Spring and Autumn Annals* was preserved.[28] However, these developments certainly had to await the later rise of men of cultivation.

Section 2, the *Documents*: There are forty-one essays in this section on the *Documents* (*Shu* 書). The great majority of these (2.3–37) are about specific chapters, passages, or terms in the work. Essay 2.1 is a general discussion of the naming of emperors (*ming* 名 and *hao* 號) in ancient times, although with particular reference to the *Documents*, while 2.2 is about the term *jiu zu* 九族 (nine generations). This appears in the "Canon of Yao," but Gu's discussion also covers other works. The final four essays are somewhat different: one considers the historical aspects of the state of Qin (2.38); one is a general discussion of the preservation and transmission of the *Documents* and touches on the old text–new text issue (2.39); one considers the preface to the *Documents* (2.40); and one is a discussion of the "false" *Shang Shu*, attributed to the Ming scholar Feng Xi.

2.39 THE OLD TEXT *DOCUMENTS* (*GUWEN SHANG SHU*)

Comment: This long essay is a significant contribution to the old text–new text debate. It is a good example of Gu's detailed study of ancient texts. A recent account of the issues involved is provided by Edward L. Shaughnessy in *Early Chinese Texts: A Bibliographical Guide*, ed. Michael Loewe, 376–89 (Berkeley: Society for the Study of Early China and Institute of Asian Studies, University of California, 1993).

In Han times there were two versions of the *Documents* [*Shang Shu*]—the new text and old text versions, with the latter also having two versions itself. The bibliographical chapter of the *History of the Former Han* [*Han Shu*, "Yiwen Zhi"], states, "The old text *Documents* [*Shang Shu, guwen jing*] had forty-six *juan* 卷 [rolls, sections] and fifty-seven *pian* 篇 [chapters]." Yan Shigu said, "Kong Anguo's preface to the *Documents* ["Shuxu"] stated, 'Altogether there are fifty-nine *pian* making up forty-six *juan*. I received an order to prepare a commentary with a preface at the head of each section, defining fifty-eight *pian*.' Zheng Xuan, in his *Xuzan*, says, 'Subsequently one of these sections was lost,' therefore there were fifty-seven." It is also said in the *Han Shu*, "The classic, as recognized by the greater and lesser Xia Hou, had twenty-nine *juan*, and by Ouyang, thirty-two *juan*." Shigu says, "This work in twenty-nine *juan* was what Fu Sheng handed down."[29]

Thus the new text and old text versions were two [distinct] works. [In the *Han Shu*] it is also said,

> The old text *Documents* came from the walls of Confucius's house. At the end of Emperor Wu's reign, King Gong of Lu was about to destroy Confucius's house, wishing to enlarge his own palace. He came across the old text *Documents* [*guwen Shang Shu*], as well as the *Record of Rites* [*Li Ji*], *Analects* [*Lunyu*], and the *Classic of Filial Piety* [*Xiao Jing*], totaling several tens of *pian*, all in the ancient script. When King Gong entered this house, he heard the sounds of the drum, lute, bell, and musical stone, whereupon he was afraid, so he stopped and did not destroy the house. Kong

Anguo was a descendant of Confucius's, and he acquired all his books. He verified the twenty-nine *pian* and obtained a further sixteen *pian*. Anguo presented them, but because of the court's involvement with [magic and sorcery], they were not classified by the education officials.[30] Liu Xiang compared the old text [version] in the Imperial Library with the texts of the three scholars, the greater and lesser Xia Hou and Ouyang [Sheng]. He found the "Announcement About Drunkenness" to be lacking one tablet and the "Announcement of Shao" to be lacking two tablets. If the tablet had twenty-five characters, there were twenty-five characters lacking, and if it had twenty-two characters, there were twenty-two characters lacking. In more than seven hundred places there were different characters, and in several tens of places [individual] characters were lacking.[31]

In the "Biographies of Confucian Scholars" ["Rulin Zhuan," in the *Han Shu*] it is stated,

The Kong family had the *guwen Shang Shu*, and Kong Anguo studied it using the new text version. As a result of the lost books that came from the walls of his house, he obtained ten or so chapters, thus increasing the *Shang Shu* still further. Because of his involvement with witchcraft and sorcery, they were never classified by the education officials. Anguo held the position of grand master of remonstrance. He passed the work on to Duwei Chao, who in turn passed it on to Yong Sheng of Jiaodong. Yong passed it on to Hu Chang of Qinghe, also known as Shao Zi. He also transmitted the *Zuo Zhuan*. Chang passed it on to Xu Ao of Guo and also transmitted the Mao *Odes*. It was then transmitted to Wang Huang and Tu Yun of Pingling, who was styled Zichen. The latter then handed it on to Sang Qin of Henan, styled Junchang. At the time of Wang Mang, these scholars were all established. Liu Xin was preceptor of state while Huang, Yun, and the others were all held in high esteem.[32]

It is also stated [in the *Han Shu*], "What was transmitted as the 'Bailian' chapter came from Zhang Ba of Donglai, who, by dividing and combining the twenty-nine chapters [*pian*], created several tens of sections. He also gathered the *Zuo Shi Zhuan* and the "Shuxu" and made a beginning and end, giving in all 102 chapters. Some of these chapters were on several strips of bamboo and in content were meager and superficial. At the time of Emperor Cheng [32–6 B.C.E.), among those who sought the old text works, Ba considered he was able to verify his 102 chapters, but when these were collated with the writings in the imperial storehouse, this was not so."[33] This indicates that Kong Anguo's old text version and the *Documents* of Zhang Ba were two distinct entities.

In the "Biographies of Confucian Scholars" [in the *History of the Later Han*], it is stated, "Kong Xi was from the kingdom of Lu. From [Kong] Anguo onward, the *guwen Shang Shu* was transmitted for several generations."[34] It also says, "Du Lin of Fufeng transmitted the *guwen Shang Shu*. Jia Kui, from the same commandery, wrote his 'Instructions' for it, Ma Rong his commentary, and Zheng Xuan his 'Notes and Explanations.' For this reason the *guwen Shang Shu* became distinguished in the world."[35] Further, it says, "In the Jianchu reign period [76–83], there was a proclamation that scholars of high talent should receive the *guwen Shang Shu*, the Mao *Odes*, Guliang and Zuo Shi *Spring and Autumn Annals* and that, although such men were not established among the educational officials, they would, nevertheless, all be promoted as able scholars to be 'court gentlemen for lecturing' in close association with the emperor."[36] This being so, what Kong Xi received from [Kong] Anguo was finally not this transmission, so Du Lin, Jia Kui, Ma Rong, and Zheng Xuan did not see Anguo's commentary but themselves wrote their "Instructions," "Commentary," and "Notes and Explanations," respectively. This means that the scholarship of Kong and Zheng also cannot reliably be verified as being two.

In Liu Tao's biography [in the *Hou Han Shu*], it is stated, "Tao understood the *Shang Shu* [*Documents*] and the *Chunqiu* [*Spring and Autumn Annals*] and prepared exegeses on them. He held in high esteem the *Shang Shu* of the three scholars [the greater and lesser Xia Hou and Ouyang Heba] and the old text [version]. He made over three hundred corrections to the text and called his work the *Zhongwen Shang Shu*."[37] In the confusion at the end of the Han era it was not handed down. [Works] like Ma Rong's notes on the *guwen Shang Shu* in ten *juan* and Zheng Xuan's notes on the same work in ten sections can be seen [listed] in the bibliographical chapter ["Yiwen Zhi"] in the *Old Tang History*.[38] In the Kaiyuan reign period [713–741], these works were still extant and had not yet been lost. In Lu Deming's *Jingdian Shiwen*, it is said, "The twenty-nine chapters on which Ma and Zheng made notes were merely the twenty-eight chapters of Fu Sheng and the 'Great Declaration' separately found among the people and joined with the other twenty-eight. This latter was not, however, the present-day 'Great Declaration.' What were referred to earlier as the further sixteen chapters obtained were not included in this total."[39]

In the "Jingji Zhi" of the *Sui History*, there is the statement, "What Ma Rong and Zheng Xuan handed down consisted of twenty-nine chapters [*pian*], and there was some admixture with the new text; it was not Confucius's old *Shu* [*Documents*]. Apart from this there was absolutely no discussion. In the Jin period, among what was preserved in the secret repository [palace storehouse], there was the classic text of the *guwen Shang Shu*, which today has not been handed down. During the confusion of the Yongjia reign period [307–312], the *Shang Shu* of Ouyang and the greater and lesser Xia Hou were all lost. By the time of the Eastern Jin, the Yuzhang administrator Mei Ze first obtained Anguo's commentary and presented it."[40] He added a further twenty-five chapters, combining these with the twenty-eight chapters of Fu Sheng, and did away with the false "Great Declaration." He also divided off the "Canon of Shun" ["Shun Dian"], "Yi and Ji," "Pan Geng"*zhong* and *xia*, and "The Announcement of King Kang" ["Kang Wangzhi Kao"], making each a separate chapter. It is this that constitutes the present-day arrangement of the fifty-eight chapters. As for the lost "Canon of Shun" ["Shun Dian"], he chose Wang Su's original commentary following [the words] *shen hui* and connected it. In the fourth year of the Jianwu reign period [497] of Emperor Ming of Qi, there was a certain Yao Fangxing who is said to have found, in a large boat,[41] a volume that had the twenty-eight characters following the words "examining into antiquity Emperor Shun. . . ." He presented this. The court discussed the matter, and everyone took it to be false. By the time of the Jiangling lawlessness, the writings had entered the central plain and scholars were surprised at them. Liu Xuan subsequently arranged the various original sections in order.[42] So then, the present-day *Shang Shu* has both old text and new text components in its thirty-three chapters, which are surely a mixture of the texts of

Fu Sheng and [Kong] Anguo. And twenty-five chapters came from Mei Ze, while the twenty-eight characters of the "Canon of Shun" that came from Yao Fangxing were also joined to make one book. Mencius said, "It would be better to be without the *Documents* than to give undue credence to it."[43] In the present times, this is even more apposite.

I doubt that in ancient times there was a "Canon of Yao" ["Yao Dian"] without a "Canon of Shun" ["Shun Dian"], and that there was a *Documents* of Xia and not a *Documents* of Yu, or indeed that the "Canon of Yao" was [one of the chapters] of the *Documents* of Xia. Mencius quotes these words, "After twenty-eight years the highly meritorious one [the emperor] died,"[44] and speaks of them as being from the "Canon of Yao," so the preface's separating [the text] to make the "Canon of Shun" is wrong. There are the following statements in the *Zuo Zhuan*: For the eighth year of Duke Zhuang, "Gao Tao vigorously sowed his virtue abroad"; for the twenty-fourth year of Duke Xi, "The earth is reduced to order and the influences of Heaven operate with effect"; for the twenty-seventh year [of Duke Xi], "They were appointed by their speech"; for the seventh year of Duke Wen, "Caution them with gentle words"; for the fifth year of Duke Xiang, "When one's good faith is established, one can accomplish one's undertakings"; for the twenty-first and twenty-third years [of Duke Xiang], "Think whether this thing can be laid on this man"; for the twenty-sixth year [of Duke Xiang], "Rather than put an innocent person to death, you run the risk of irregularity"; for the sixth year of Duke Ai, "Where sincerity proceeds from, therein is the result"; and for the eighteenth year [of Duke Ai], "The officer of divination, when the mind is made up on a subject . . ."[45] In the *Guoyu*, the Zhou royal secretary, Guo, has this quote: "If the multitude were without their sovereign, whom should they serve? If the sovereign were without the multitude, there would be none with whom to guard the country."[46] All these quotes are from the "Xia Documents" [in the *Documents*], but those of later times who thought there was a Yu *Documents* were very numerous. Why was this then? Those who recorded these writings certainly came from the historians and officials of Xia, although they transmitted this as being from Tang, and their adornment and composition certainly awaited men of later times. Thus, at the head of the chapter, there are the words "on examining into antiquity."[47] The use of the word "antiquity" makes it clear that this was not a contemporary record.

The world still had three sages, but they served the same house. If, through the officials of Xia, there was a retrospective recording of the affairs of the two emperors, how can we not speak of a Xia *Documents*? Now if it was only by Xia officials that there was retrospective recording of the affairs of the two emperors, then saying Yao can reveal Shun is not as good as the historians of later times establishing an original record for each emperor and afterward making this a complete book.

"The emperor said, 'Come Yu, you must also have admirable words to bring before me.'" These words are a continuation of the statement of Gao Yao made at that time.[48] "The king came forth and stood in the space within the fourth gate of the palace" is a continuation from the "princes all went out from the temple gate and waited," and these are matters occurring at one time.[49] It is absurd that the preface should divide them into two chapters.

Section 3, the *Odes*: There are forty-two essays devoted to the *Odes* (*Shi Jing* 詩經). The first three are general—3.1 on the distinction between verses with musical accompaniment and those without; 3.2 on the four verse forms *nan* 南, *bin* 豳, *ya* 雅, and *song* 頌, to which *feng* 風 (airs) is added; and 3.3 on Confucius's editing of (or excisions from) the *Odes*. The next thirty-seven essays are specific and concern particular terms and their meanings and the social implications of individual lines or verses. The final two essays return to general matters: 3.41 is on why the verses of Lu were called *song*, with a comment on the sequence of Zhou, Lu, and Shang *song*; 3.42 is a general discussion of the ordering of the work.

3.3 CONFUCIUS'S EDITING OF THE *ODES*

Comment: This short essay addresses the issue of Confucius's role in bringing the *Odes* to its definitive form. Tradition has it that Confucius, in correcting and editing the *Odes*, made substantial changes in the material to bring the work to its present form. Thus James Legge quotes Zhu Xi as follows: "Poems had ceased to be made and collected and those which were extant were full of errors and wanting in arrangement. When Confucius returned from Wei to Loo he brought with him the *Odes* which he had gotten in other states and digested them along with those which were found in Loo, into a collection of 300 pieces." Legge himself concludes, however, that "before the birth of Confucius the *Book of Poetry* existed substantially the same as it was at his death and that while he may have somewhat altered the arrangement of its Books and Odes, the principal service which he rendered to it was not that of compilation, but the impulse to the study of it which he communicated to his disciples" (*Odes*, LCC, 4[prolegomena].2).

Confucius's editing of the *Odes* is how the *feng* [airs] of the various states were preserved. Whether they were good or not, he collected and preserved them, just as the grand music master of old arranged the *Odes* in order to observe the people's customs, and as Ji Zha listened to them to know about the rise and decline of states. They were corrected by these two men, who arranged them so they could be read and listened to. If the age had not been that of the two emperors and the time had not been remote antiquity, it would surely not have been the case that the *feng* were pure and without licentiousness, and orderly without elements of chaos.

The transformation wrought by King Wen was effective in the southern states,[50] but he was unable to change the sounds of slaughter in Northern Pi.[51] If these odes are still preserved and are included in the Master's compilation, there will certainly be preservation of the southern sounds to secure the *feng* of King Wen and preservation of the northern sounds to secure the *feng* of Zhou and not allow them to merge into one. This is why both the "Sang Zhong" and the "Qin Wei" were not omitted by the Master, although he considered them to be lewd verses. The "Shu Yu Tian" is in praise of the words of Duan, while the "Yang Zhi Shui" and the "Jiao Liao" follow the talk of Wo.[52] The Master did not omit them and so displayed the basis of disorder. As for poems on elopement, he included them all without exception, hence the importance of his recording of these *feng*. If the verses of one state were all lewd and yet among them there were things that could not be changed, then he hastily recorded them. In the "Jiang Zhong Zi" [there is] "fearing the people's words."[53] In the "Nü Yue Ji Ming" there is an admonition to live a life of diligence.[54] In the "Chu Qi Dong Men" there is no admiration of beauty,[55] while in the "Heng Men" there is no wish to leave home.[56] In choosing these words and comparing their sounds, he set aside what was vexatious and excessive. This is what the Master meant by editing [deleting]. Men of later times who adhered to Confucianism did not attain this excellence. Nevertheless, they said that poems on elopement were not appropriate for inclusion in the Sage's classic. How is this different from the Tang heir apparent Hong saying that the murder of the sovereign by Shang Chen is not appropriate for inclusion in the *Spring and Autumn Annals*?[57]

Zhen Xiyuan, in the selection of poems for his *Wenzhang Zhengzong*,[58] swept away at a stroke the vulgarity of the ancients and returned to true goodness. Nevertheless, his fault lay in taking *li* 理 [principle, pattern, coherence] as a teaching and so failing to attract the interest of poets. Moreover, like the *Nineteen Old Poems*,[59] although they are not the work of one man, the customs of the Han period are included in this collection. Nowadays, if one takes what Xiyuan deleted and reads it, there is the line, "Is it not better to drink good wine and wear fine white silk?"[60] How does this differ from the "Shan You Shu" in the Tang odes?[61] Further, the line, "My husband thought of our former joys, he kindly came in his carriage and gave me the forestrap"[62] has the same meaning as, "The male pheasant flies away" from the "Xiong Ji" in the Bei odes.[63] The idea of the herd boy and the weaving girl appears in the "Da Dong,"[64] while with the dodder and the ivy, the meaning is the same as in the "Che Xia."[65] In the *Nineteen Old Poems* there is not much variation in quality. Certainly, with the purpose of guarding against licentiousness, rectifying vulgarity, and being strict in restraining deletions, even if there was correction of Zhaoming's[66] mistake, I fear we would lose the meaning of the *feng* of the states. The empty vanities of the Six Dynasties should be discarded, but if Xu and Yu[67] are not regarded as men [i.e., are forgotten] and the Chen and Sui are not recognized as dynasties, would it not be too much? Would this not be the fault of holding too firmly to *li* 理 [pattern, principle, coherence]?

3.16 THE ONE-YEAR-OLD BOARS ARE FOR THEMSELVES

Comment: Gu uses these lines from the *Odes* to stress the general point of the importance of privileging the public interest over private interests and how the inevitable conflict between them must be taken into account in any prescription for social improvement.

Let it rain first on our public fields,
and then come to our private fields![68]

This is to put the public first and make the private subsidiary.

The one-year-old boars are for themselves.
The three-year-old boars are for the duke.[69]

This is to put the private first and make the public subsidiary.

From the time the world had families, each one treated its family members as family members and its sons as sons. People having what is private was certainly something human feelings could not be free of. Therefore, the former kings did not make it a prohibition. Indeed, not only did they not prohibit it; they accepted and understood it. In establishing the kingdom, they were close to the nobles, conferring lands and granting clan names.[70] In drawing up the well-field system and demarcating the fields, they joined what was private in the world to perfect what was public. This is why it is considered to have been a kingly administration. When it came to instructing officials, they said to use the public to eliminate the private. Despite the fact that salaries were enough to substitute for farming, and the land was enough to provide for sacrifices, letting them be free of anxiety as to the lamentations of mothers and the reproaches of their families,[71] they were also sympathetic toward the private. But for a long time now this principle has not been clear. The noble men of the age certainly say there is the public and not the private. These are the favored words of later generations but not the perfect teaching of former kings.

Section 4, the *Spring and Autumn Annals* and its commentaries: There are seventy-seven essays devoted to the *Spring and Autumn Annals* itself and its three early commentaries (*Zuo Zhuan*, *Guliang Zhuan*, and *Gongyang Zhuan*). The first two essays are general: one is a brief comment on Confucius's role in the creation of the work (4.1), and the other is a survey of omissions and doubts in the *Spring and Autumn Annals* (4.2). Essays 4.3–37 are for the most part about specific terms and passages in the *Spring and Autumn Annals*. One exception is 4.6, which is about writing both the season and the month in dating an event. Here the examples are predominantly from the *Documents*. Also, 4.23, which focuses on the use of *ren* 人 in the entry for the eighteenth year of Duke Xi, refers to the *Guliang Zhuan*. Essays 4.38–62 are concerned particularly with passages in the *Zuo Zhuan*. Essay 4.63 is about discrepancies in the use of certain characters in the Five Classics generally. Essays 4.64 and 4.65 are about the *Spring and Autumn Annals* itself. Essays 4.66–72 consider issues in the *Gongyang Zhuan*, while 4.73–77 consider issues in the *Guliang Zhuan*.

4.2 OMISSIONS AND DOUBTS IN THE *SPRING AND AUTUMN ANNALS*

Confucius said, "I am old enough to have seen scribes [historians] leave a blank in their texts."[72] What the historian omitted, the Sage did not dare to add. Thus, in the *Spring and Autumn Annals* for the seventeenth year of Duke Huan, there is, "In winter, in the tenth month, on the first day of the moon, the sun was eclipsed."[73] In the *Zuo Zhuan* [Zuo commentary], there is, "The day of the cycle is not written because the officials had lost it."[74] In the fifteenth year of Duke Xi, there is, "In summer, during the fifth month, there was an eclipse of the sun."[75] In the *Zuo Zhuan*, there is, "The first day of the month and the day were not written because the officials had lost the day."[76] Given the Sage's intelligence and the fact that "one can calculate the solstices for a thousand years without leaving one's seat,"[77] if the calendar is examined, how difficult can it be to remedy these omissions? And yet the Master did not dare to do so. How much more, then, would he not choose to correct errors in historical writings? How much more, in arranging the affairs of the states, would those things learned of by hearsay not be recorded in historical writings?

The completion of the writing of the *Zuo Zhuan* was not the work of one man, nor was the record itself of one time. It can be said to be rich in content, and yet the Master did not necessarily see it at that time. If there is something not recorded by the official historian's chronicles, then even a sage might not know of it. Moreover, the *Spring and Autumn Annals* is the history of the state of Lu, so if there were many official visits, he would necessarily hear about their government and subsequently could add to the Veritable Records of the 120 states, incorporating them into the records and notes of his own state. If matters such as the death and burial of Duke Hui are not recorded,[78] then the old histories have deficiencies. That Cao Dafu, Song Dafu, Sima, and Sicheng are not named represents a deficiency.[79] That the Earl of Zheng, Kun Wan, the Viscount of Chu, Qun, and the Marquis of Qi, Yang Sheng, were actually murdered,[80] although the writings state that they died, is an example of hearsay not being superior to the memorandum tablets that, in these cases, follow the old historical writings.

Zuo Shi, continuing on from the capture of the *lin*, collected an extensive array of material that, in reality, the Master never saw.[81] Nevertheless, later Confucian scholars [Ruists] seemed to say there was already this writing that the Master relied upon and revised. Accordingly, in Zuo Shi's explanation of the classic, in what doesn't tally, there are many erroneous explanations. Further, in the discussions of the classic's origins, scholars subsequently were of the view that what the Sage did not know should be avoided. Hence new theories became increasingly numerous, and the rights and wrongs of a matter were not established. Therefore, the words of present-day scholars who study the *Spring and Autumn Annals* are all writings of Ying and explanations of Yan and are not things on which the Master can adjudicate. Did the Sage not say, "Hear much and put aside what is dubious; speak cautiously about what remains"?[82] Why he particularly told Zizhang[83] this is because the methods of rectifying the *Spring and Autumn Annals* don't go beyond it.

The *Spring and Autumn Annals* is rectified in accord with the Lu history. The *Zuo Zhuan* is written as a collection of the histories of all the states. Therefore, what is written of the affairs of Jin, from the time of Duke Wen's being president of covenants[84] and the administrative changes within the Middle Kingdom, is recorded in the histories of the various states, and all followed the first month of the Zhou calendar. From Duke Hui and before,[85] the historical chronicles did not use the first month of the Xia calendar. This did not emerge from the understanding of one man. The statements [in the *Spring and Autumn Annals*] that the funeral presents of Zhong Zi arrived prior to her death;[86] that the death of King Ping was announced on *gengxu*,[87] and that the death of Bao, the Marquis of Chen, was announced twice[88] are all matters that must be examined thoroughly so there can be an explanation.

Section 5, the *Zhou Li* and *Yi Li*: In this section there are forty-nine essays on two of the three works included in the *San Li*—the *Zhou Li* and the *Yi Li*. As with the other texts, these essays are essentially about specific phrases or passages. Essays 5.1–20 relate to the *Zhou Li*, which Gu describes as the standard for the administration of the kingdom, and are predominantly on what might broadly be termed administrative matters. Two essays of particular interest in this group are the one on the control of functionaries in the inner palace (5.1) and the one on the detrimental effects of clique formation among scholars (5.19). Essays 5.21–29 relate to the *Yi Li*, which Gu describes as the model for gravity and reverence; they are mostly about aspects of etiquette. Seventeen of them are on one chapter of the *Yi Li* ("Sangfu") to do with mourning practices.

5.7 DOCTORS

Comment: In this essay, Gu uses several famous doctors as examples to reflect on the quotation from the *Rites of Zhou* and also to make an adverse comparison between doctors of his own time and those of ancient times. The treatment of bodily ailments is used as an extended metaphor for the treatment of social and political ills.

In ancient times, quack doctors killed people. In the present times, such charlatans don't kill people, but they also don't save their lives. Rather, they cause them to exist in some intermediate state between life and death, their sickness becoming worse each day until they do finally die. Now, among medicines, there are "princes" and "attendants" and, among people, there are the strong and the weak.[89] So, because there are "princes" and "attendants" among medicines, much or little can be used; and because there are strong and weak people, the dose can be halved or doubled. If much is used, then it is used alone; and if it is used alone, it is rapidly effective. If a double dose is used, then it is substantial, and if it is substantial, its potency is profound. Nowadays, those who use medicines are, for the most part, confused and careless and don't prescribe an accurate dose. Since they are not able to see things clearly and also lack courage in their treatments, they cannot cure the illness. Nevertheless, the world still takes not killing people to be a measure of a doctor's worth. Don't they know that superior doctors of ancient times could not avoid failure?

In the chapter on doctors in the *Rites of Zhou* [*Zhou Li*] [it is written], "At the year's end, there was examination into the medical affairs of a doctor in order to regulate his livelihood. Those doctors who, out of ten patients, lost none were ranked highest; those who lost one out of ten were next; those who lost two out of ten were next; those who lost three out of ten were next; and those who lost four out of ten were lowest."[90] Even those who lost three or four out of ten were still employed by the ancients. Chunyu Yi, in replying to Xiao Wen [Emperor Wen of Han—r. 179–157 B.C.E.], even said, "From time to time I fail. I cannot claim complete success."[91] In the *Changes* it is written, "To view a father's wrongdoing indulgently will bring regret as one goes forward."[92] Why only choose this "viewing wrongdoing indulgently"? It is to deny personal responsibility for someone's death. Ah, alas! This is why Zhang Yu lost the Han[93] and Li Linfu lost the Tang.[94]

In the *History of the Tang Dynasty*, Xu Yunzong[95] said,

> The leading doctors of ancient times only distinguished the pulse. Once the pulse was accurately analyzed, it was possible to recognize the disease. Then the medicine prescribed for the illness could be correct and appropriate, and it was necessary only to use one agent to overcome the disease. Since the strength of the medicine lay in its purity, the disease was completely cured. In the present times, men are not able to distinguish the pulse and so cannot identify the origin of the disease. They must rely on guesswork, often being content to try one medicine after another. It is like hunting without knowing the hare's whereabouts. Many men and horses set out, and the empty land is surrounded in the hope that one man will catch the animal. This is a far cry from being an exercise of skill. If one medicine is prescribed that happens to be right for the disease but other concoctions oppose it, then its vital strength is not effective. What is difficult or wrong can be thought to arise from this.[96]

In the *History of the Later Han Dynasty* [it is said that] Hua Tuo was skilled in prescribing medicines and that his healing potions were few in number.[97] [For the diagram] *shi*, six in the fifth place and nine in the second place mean good fortune. This can be compared to the third and fourth places, which mean misfortune.[98] This is why, if officials are numerous, there is disorder, and why, if generals are numerous, there is defeat. The affairs of the empire are like this too!

Section 6, the *Li Ji*: There are fifty-two essays, devoted predominantly to the *Li Ji* (*Record of Rites*). In general terms, the essays are about specific passages from the *Li Ji*, although other works are mentioned in a number of instances. Essays 6.1–35 relate to chapters other than the "Zhongyong" and "Daxue," while essays 6.36–37 focus mainly on the *Xiao Jing* 孝經 (*Classic of Filial Piety*), although the *Li Ji* is mentioned. The two chapters of the *Li Ji* that were later extracted from the work by Zhu Xi in his creation of the Four Books (i.e., the "Daxue" 大學 and "Zhongyong" 中庸) have a number of essays devoted specifically to them. Thus, 6.38–42 relate to the former and 6.43–51 to the latter.

6.24 LOVE FOR ORDINARY PEOPLE IS THE REASON FOR PENALTIES AND PUNISHMENTS

Comment: This statement from the *Li Ji* (*Li Ji* 34, "Da Chuan," *SSJZS*, 5.622) is taken as the basis for some brief reflections on bringing about order and delegating responsibility.

A ruler cannot govern the world by himself. If there is government by one person alone, punishments become complicated. If there is government by many, punishments are properly managed. The kings in ancient times did not permit punishments to impoverish the people of the world. For this reason, within each household, government was by the father and elder brother; within each clan, government was by descendants of the ancestor. If there were any seeds of badness, they were, without exception, transformed in the inner chambers, and if there were still those who would not be directed and taught, they were subsequently handed over to the chief judge. This being so, what the ruler governed was kept under control. Then there was the loving relationship between father and son and the establishment of *yi* 義 [right action, righteousness, duty] between ruler and minister, each having the appropriate authority. Thinking about and discussing the order of trivial and important, and the measure of the careful evaluation of the shallow and deep, were achieved by distinguishing these. All this understanding and awareness extends to making loyalty and love complete. Now, if this obtains, can there be penalties and punishments that are not correct? This is why the lineage method was established and punishments became clear. In each case, the clan head governs his clan and thus supports the governance of the ruler. "The ruler himself does not appear in the government orders,"[99] and the people do not oppose those in charge. The purity of customs and the simplicity of orders and laws come from this. The *Odes* says, "Acknowledge them as rulers and as ancestors."[100] This is how I know the position of the clan head [son of the ancestor] is part of the *dao* of ruling.

6.38 PERFECTING KNOWLEDGE

Comment: To perfect (or extend) knowledge (致知 *zhi zhi*) is a key phrase in the opening section of the *Daxue* (*Highest Learning*), as is "knowing where to come to rest." One of the most contentious statements in this opening section is, "The perfection of knowledge lies in the investigation of things." What are "things"? This brief essay expresses Gu Yanwu's thoughts on this question.

"To perfect knowledge is to know where to come to rest."[101] What is "knowing where to come to rest?" "As a ruler, he came to rest in *ren* [loving-kindness, benevolence]; as a minister, he came to rest in reverence; as a son, he came to rest in filial piety; as a father, he came to rest in compassion; in his dealings with people of the state, he came to rest in trust."[102] This can be called "to come to rest." Know where to come to rest, and then one can speak of knowledge being perfected. From the intercourse between ruler and minister, father and son, and state and subjects, right up to the "three hundred rules of ceremony and the three thousand rules of demeanour,"[103] all can be termed "things."

The *Odes* says, "Heaven gave birth to the multitude of people; there were things and there were rules."[104] Mencius said, "Shun clearly understood the myriad things and closely observed the relationships among people."[105] In former times, King Wu's enquiring[106] and Ji Zi's statement,[107] as well as Zengzi's and Ziyou's questioning,[108] and Confucius's replying, were all such things. Therefore, it was said, "The ten thousand things are all complete in oneself."[109]

Only the noble man can be in sympathy with the things of the world. Thus, the *Changes* says, "The noble man, in his words, encompasses things; in his actions, he displays constancy."[110] In the *Li Ji* [*Record of Rites*], it is said, "The man of *ren* does not go beyond things; the filial son does not go beyond things."[111] The investigation of things is more than just becoming well versed in the names of birds and beasts, plants and trees.[112] "Those who know truly know; they direct their attention to what is most important."[113] The hearing of litigation is one aspect of the conduct of relationships with people of the state.[114]

6.45 GHOSTS AND SPIRITS

Comment: There are two statements in the *Zhongyong* that are relevant to this essay. For these, together with the commentaries of Zheng Xuan, Kong Yingda, and Zhu Xi, see the following references in Ian Johnston and Wang Ping, trans., *Daxue and Zhongyong* (Hong Kong: Chinese University Press, 2012): *ZY* 10, 265–68 and *ZY* 31, 358–69 (*Li Ji* text, Zheng Xuan and Kong Yingda commentaries), and *ZY* 16, 436–37 and *ZY* 29, 478–81 (*Sishu Jizhu* text and Zhu Xi commentary).

The greatness of the kingly *dao* 道 [Way] begins at the doors of the inner apartments. Happy union with one's wife, harmony with one's older and younger brothers, and obedience toward one's parents constitute a *dao* that is near at hand and simple.[115] There are sacrifices and the heavenly spirits are provided for. There are temples and the spirits and ghosts of people are provided for.[116] This is a *dao* that is distant and lofty. "The former kings served their fathers with filial piety, therefore their serving Heaven was manifest. They served their mothers with filial piety, therefore their serving Earth was conscientious."[117] Cultivate this by being constant; manifest it in the conduct of government; base it on Heaven but bring it to fulfillment on Earth. It is given order by ghosts and spirits and extends to funerals, sacrifices, archery, charioteering, the capping ceremony, marriage, formal visits, and invitations. Thus the kingdoms of the world can acquire it and be correct. It resembles what

Shun, Kings Wen and Wu, and the Duke of Zhou called "the practice of ordinary virtue"[118] and "the apogee of human relationships."[119] Therefore it is said, "The *dao* of the noble man takes its origin from ordinary men and women; in reaching its perfection it is manifest throughout Heaven and Earth."[120]

As a man has a father and mother, at cockcrow he must enquire how they spent the night, and being at their side, he must nurture them constantly. How near at hand this is. When it comes to their death and they are neither seen nor heard and cannot be found or met with, some seek them in the yin and some in the yang. Subsequently, "their likenesses may certainly be seen in the sacred tablet."[121] Afterward, this depends on the able priest to transmit it and on the filial descendants to convey it. Alive, they are father and mother; dead, they are ghosts and spirits. The Master said, "An ancestral temple is built for making sacrifices to ghosts."[122] What he said is this: "How widespread they are. They circulate and fill the world. It is as if they are above us and all around us."[123] This brings about obedience to parents and extends it.

The *Record of Rites* [*Li Ji*] states,

> When King Wen was the heir apparent, he would visit Wang Ji thrice daily. At the first crowing of the cock, he would dress and present himself outside the door of the sleeping chamber. There, through the medium of a young servant, he would ask if the king was at peace today. If the young servant said he was, King Wen was pleased. In the middle of the day, he again presented himself and made a similar enquiry, as he also did in the evening. If things were not satisfactory, the young servant would inform King Wen, who would then assume a melancholy appearance and be unable to follow a straight path when walking. When Wang Ji took his food again, King Wen would regain his composure. Before the meal, he was invariably present to check whether it was of a suitable temperature. After the meal, he enquired as to what was eaten and directed the food steward saying that none [of the dishes] should be served again. On receiving the steward's assurance, he withdrew.[124]

It also states, "King Wen, when sacrificing, served the dead as if he were serving the living. He thought of the dead as if he did not wish to live [any longer himself]. On days to be avoided, his heart was heavy. In calling his father by the name elsewhere forbidden, he looked as if he saw him, so sincere was he in sacrificing. If he saw the things his father loved, his face took on a pleased expression. Such was King Wen. In the *Odes* it says, 'Dawn breaks and I still do not sleep. There are two people in my heart.' This is King Wen's poem."[125]

It is only King Wen who, when his parents were alive, served them with this degree of filiality. When they died, he sacrificed to them so loyally it was as if he were actually seeing his parents. If, when one's parents are alive, there is not a sincere attempt to carry out their desires, then when they are dead, one will certainly not be influenced by, and comprehend, the principles of right conduct. Therefore, it is said, "Only a filial son is able to care for his parents."[126] So the Master informed Zilu, saying, "While you are not able to serve people, how can you serve ghosts?"[127] Thus, in "the practice of ordinary virtue" is not obedience toward parents of paramount importance? It is, moreover, the ritual practices [*li* 禮] of the sacrificial altars and the principles of the ancestral sacrifices that are the sources from which this arises. If there is clarity on this point, then the empire and the states can be secure and well governed. Among men in high positions, those who are able to show obedience toward their parents can subsequently serve Heaven and sacrifice to the emperor, while among men in lower positions, those who are able to show obedience toward their parents can subsequently attain higher positions and bring good order to the people.

Master Cheng said, "Ghosts and spirits are the meritorious agents of heaven; they are the traces of creation and change." Master Zhang said, "Ghosts and spirits are natural manifestations of the two material forces."[128] This is used to explain the statement in the *Changes*, "The spirits are mysterious in the ten thousand things and yet find expression [in the trigrams]."[129] This single statement is entirely fitting. Like the two Masters said, we look for them but do not see them; we listen for them but do not hear them—these are ghosts and spirits. What can be seen and heard are also spiritual beings. Now, the Master simply said "not seen" and "not heard," knowing they were what sacrifices were directed to and presenting these to ghosts and spirits without any doubts. This is similar to what is said in the commentary [*wen yan*] on *qian* in the *Changes*: "[The great man is in accord with] ghosts and spirits in his good and bad fortune."[130]

Section 7, the *Lunyu* and the *Mencius*: The fifty-six essays in this section are predominantly about passages from the *Lunyu* or the *Mencius*. Of the fifty-six, essays 7.1–24 pertain to the *Lunyu*, 7.25 is a general consideration of references to King Hui of Liang, and 7.26–45 pertain to the *Mencius*. The last eleven essays (7.46–56) are something of a mixture. Thus, essays 7.46–48 are general in nature: the first is titled "To Examine Oneself and Not Be Complacent"; the second has the title "How Should a Scholar Serve?"; and the third is about the need to experience want and show humility to successfully serve in a high position. Essays 7.49–52 are about general aspects of the *Mencius*—7.49 on the so-called outer chapters; 7.50 on quotes from the *Lunyu* in the *Mencius*; 7.51 on the form of characters in the *Mencius*; and 7.52 on Mencius's disciples, related particularly to Zhao Qi's notes. There are then two essays on specific characters, *cha* (7.53) and *ge* (7.54). Essay 7.55, "The Nine Classics," is a historical discussion of the classics and the use of the various classics at different times, while 7.56, "Sequence in Classical Writings," considers some changes in the ordering of texts by later scholars such as Zhu Xi and Su Shi.

7.8 THE MASTER'S WORDS ON NATURE AND THE *DAO* (WAY) OF HEAVEN

Comment: These were subjects that Confucius notoriously did not discuss, although they were of great importance in later Confucian thinking.

What the Master taught men were literature, conduct, loyalty, and trustworthiness;[131] nature and the *dao* [Way] of Heaven fell within this. Therefore, he said, "We cannot get to hear."[132] The Master said, "Do you think, my friends, that I am concealing anything from you? I conceal nothing from you. There is nothing I do which I do not share with you, my friends. This is my way."[133] This refers to the Master's words on nature and the *dao* of Heaven not being possible to get to hear, thus raising doubt about his claim not to be concealing anything. This is a failure to realize that the Master's "outward manifestations of conduct" [*wen zhang* 文章][134] are nothing other than his statements on nature and the *dao* of Heaven. This is why he was able to say, "There is nothing I do which I do not share with you, my friends. This is my way."

Zigong's idea was that "outward manifestations of conduct" and "nature and the *dao* of Heaven" were two different matters. Therefore, he said, "If you, Master, do not speak, what shall we, your disciples, record?" The Master replied, "Does heaven speak? The four seasons follow their courses, the hundred things come into being, and yet does heaven speak?"[135] For this reason it is possible to take up office or to retire; it is possible to continue for a long time or to withdraw quickly.[136] There is not a single thing that is not Heaven['s *dao*]. "Simple and unassuming," "cautious and precise," "direct and to the point," "reserved and formal"[137]—not one of these is not Heaven's *dao*.

When all movements of the countenance and actions of the body are in accord with *li* 禮 [propriety, ceremonial practices], this is the highest point of resplendent virtue.[138] Mencius took these to be matters pertaining to Yao and Shun.[139] In the Master's "outward manifestations of conduct," nothing is greater than the *Spring and Autumn Annals*. The meaning of the *Spring and Autumn Annals* is that "to venerate the Heavenly King," "to punish the barbarians,"[140] and "to put to death rebellious ministers and villainous sons"[141] are all aspects of nature and the *dao* of Heaven. Therefore, Hu Shi took the *Spring and Autumn Annals* to be literature stemming from the Sage's decreed nature[142] [and accepted Zigong's statement]: "If you, Master, do not speak, what shall we, your disciples, record?"[143]

At the present time men still consider the "Xici"[144] to be the Master's words on nature and the *dao* of Heaven. I, myself, have read this work three times. [There are] words such as "the crane calling in the shade" for seven lines; "[therefore] he is blessed by Heaven" for one line; "wavering and irresolute" for eleven lines; and "the basis of walking in the path of virtue" for nine diagrams.[145] How he teaches men to study the *Changes* lies in nothing other than what is in words and actions. Therefore, it is said, "First, if you follow its words and consider its method, then there are constant principles. But if you are not this right man, the *dao* cannot be followed in actions."[146]

Fan Chi asked about *ren* 仁 [loving-kindness, humanity, benevolence]. The Master said, "Be reverent in your dwelling, respectful in the conduct of affairs, and loyal in your relationships with others." Sima Niu asked about *ren* 仁. The Master said, "The man who is *ren* 仁 is deliberate." Following this and carrying it out is "for one day subduing oneself and returning to *li* 禮 [propriety, ceremonial practices]."[147] Is there a difference from the *dao* 道? Noble men of the present time, in their studies, do not reach the level of Fan Chi and Sima Niu, and yet they wish their theories to be more exalted than the two disciples Yan and Zeng.[148] This is why they spend the whole day talking about human nature and the *dao* 道 of Heaven without realizing that they, themselves, have fallen to the level of *chanxue* 禪學 [Chan Buddhism].

Zhu Xi said,[149] "What the Sage teaches men does not go beyond filial piety and fraternal submission, loyalty and trustworthiness, and the careful preservation and scrupulous practice of these. This is the basis of studying things at the lower level. Scholars of the present day regard this as the business of dull spirits incapable of understanding something that is not worthy of their consideration. [Yet] these, and the matters that such latter-day scholars ordinarily discourse on, are nothing other than what Zigong spoke of as 'cannot get to hear.'" Zhu Xi also said, "The malaise of present-day scholars lies in their love of the high-flown. Thus, with regard to the *Lunyu*, they never ask about 'studying and constantly practicing' but only the theory of 'the one thread.'[150] With regard to the *Mencius*, they never speak about 'King Hui of Liang asked about profit' but only about 'exerting the mind to the utmost.'[151] With regard to the *Changes*, they never look at the sixty-four diagrams but only read the 'Xici.'" This is the defect of skipping over the basic steps. He also said, "Sages and worthies set up their words and base themselves on the simple and plain. Nowadays [scholars] promote what is exalted and attempt to penetrate what is abstruse."

The *Huangshi Richao* states, "The Master compiled the Six Classics; those who followed him devoted themselves to exegetical analysis of the texts. Nor was this harmful. Lian and Luo[152] spoke of *daoxue* 道學, while their successors borrowed from discussions of Buddhism, and this was profoundly harmful."[153] The disciples of Confucius did not go beyond the four branches of study, whereas, from the Song onward, there were five divisions of study for scholars, the fifth being called the branch of "recorded utterances."[154]

The confusion brought to China by the five barbarian tribes [or Liu Yuan and Shi Le] originally arose out of the prevailing calamity of pure talk;[155] everyone knows this. But who knows whether the pure talk of the present day is not worse than that of former times? The pure talk of former times concerned Lao and Zhuang, while that of the present day concerns Confucius and Mencius. [Scholars] who have never attained the essential points go ahead and transmit a rough outline; those who have never looked into the basic principles go ahead and speak of the secondary aspects [nonessentials]. They have never studied the writings of the Six Classics, nor have they examined the documents of the "hundred kings." They do not give due attention to the affairs of their own times but raise the great principles of the Master's discussions of scholarship and government, and without questioning them at all speak of "the one thread" and of "no words,"[156] using the empty words of pure mind and original nature as a substitute for the true learning of cultivating the self and governing people. This means that the arms and legs grow weak, and yet the ten thousand things are neglected; it means that the talons and teeth are lost and the four kingdoms fall into confusion. The nation itself is unsettled and agitated, and the ancestral temples fall into ruin. Formerly, Wang Yan, who was well versed in profound and abstruse doctrines, compared himself to Zigong.[157] When he was on the point of death at the hands of Shi Le, he turned and said these words: "Ah, alas! Although we are not like the men of old, still if we had not given undue attention to what is insubstantial and empty but had labored together to restore the empire, then it remains possible that affairs would not have reached their present pass."[158] Among the noble men of today, who could help but feel shame on hearing these words?

7.39 THE ARRANGEMENT OF RANKS IN THE ZHOU HOUSE

Comment: This is a concept examined by Mencius in VB.2(1); LCC 2.373.

It is for the people that the ruler is established. Therefore, the idea of groups and ranks is that the Son of Heaven, along with duke, marquis, earl, viscount, and baron are each one rank, and yet these do not mark off the honors of the world. In place of farming, they get a salary from taxes, therefore the idea of ranks and salaries is that the ruler, chief minister, great officer, scholar-official, and ordinary people each are one official group or rank and must work for their sustenance.[159] It is for this reason we know that the *yi* 義 [right action, righteousness, duty] of the position of the Son of Heaven would not allow him to act without restraint or use the people for his own self-aggrandizement. And we know, too, that the *yi* 義 of salaries from farming would not allow him to take from the people in a substantial way to enrich himself. Rulers who did not understand this and who insulted and snatched from the people were many in the time after the Three Dynasties.

7.44 TO SEEK THE LOST MIND

"The *dao* 道 [Way] of learning is nothing other than seeking the lost mind—that is all."[160] If this is so, in only seeking the lost mind, can this be done without the necessity of recourse to learning? In the words of Confucius, "I have passed a whole day without eating and a whole night without sleeping just to think but it was of no use. It is better to study."[161] Is this not the same concept? On another occasion, Mencius said, "The noble man preserves his mind through *ren* 仁 [loving-kindness, humanity, benevolence]; he preserves his mind through *li* 禮 [proper conduct and ceremonial practices]."[162] What he preserves is not an empty mind. In *ren* 仁 and *li* 禮 there is nothing that can be made clear without learning. This is Mencius's purpose in saying that if you are able to seek the lost mind, then subsequently you can learn. Thus, "Suppose Chess Qiu is instructing two men in the art of chess. One of the two gives the matter the sole attention of his mind and will and listens only to Chess Qiu. The other, although he listens, has part of his mind on an approaching flock of geese, thinking to bend his bow, adjust the string, and shoot it. Although the second is learning along with the first, he will not be like him."[163] He is a man with a lost mind who does not know how to seek it. Nevertheless, only to know how to seek the lost mind and never to investigate the arrangement of chess pieces on the board or know the pattern of wild geese in flight is also necessary not to be able to follow affairs!

7.55 THE NINE CLASSICS

In the selection of scholar-officials, both Tang and Song used the Nine Classics, whereas the present dynasty established the Five Classics, and the *Zhou Li*, *Yi Li*, the two commentaries, the *Gongyang Zhuan*, and the

Guliang Zhuan are no longer included in the official curriculum. Du You, in his *Tong Dian*,[164] wrote,

> At the time of Emperor Yuan [r. 317–322] of the Eastern Jin [317–419], the chamberlain of ceremonials, He Xun, memorialized, saying, "By imperial edict, one erudite has been established for each classic. Further, because it was a period of great unrest, the Confucian Way was neglected and abandoned, and there were few scholars who could clearly understand the meaning of the classics. Moreover, the three commentaries on the *Spring and Autumn Annals* all came from the sages, and yet their meanings and purposes were not the same. So, from former times, there were no Confucian scholars who could understand their merits and failings and study them all. Nowadays, it is appropriate that two erudites be established for the two classics the *Rites of Zhou* [*Zhou Li*] and the *Book of Etiquette* [*Yi Li*], three erudites for the three commentaries on the *Spring and Autumn Annals*, and one erudite for each of the remaining classics [i.e., the *Documents*, *Odes*, and *Changes*], giving a total of eight men."[165]
>
> [Du You's *Tong Dian* continues:]
>
> The chamberlain for ceremonials, Xun Song,[166] memorialized, saying, "Formerly the number of erudites was nineteen in all. Now, for the Five Classics, there are nine men in all. So, comparing the old with the new, there is not half the number. For the *Changes* there are Zheng [Xuan's] notes. His writings probe the depths and can truly be regarded as being of great worth. On the *Book of Etiquette* [*Yi Li*], which concerns what might be termed the minutiae of etiquette, Zheng Xuan was particularly clear, with documentary proof in all instances. Formerly, during the decline of Zhou, Confucius wrote the *Spring and Autumn Annals*; Zuo Qiuming and Zixia received personal transmission from him. When Confucius died, Qiuming collected what he had heard and created a commentary that was comprehensive, subtle, and profound in its purport. This must be carefully studied. Gongyang Gao received personal transmission from Zixia. His work was established in the Han period

> and contained much that could be used. Guliang Chi was an example of master to pupil transmission; his work contained many new insights. In some instances, there were matters that Zuo Shi and Gongyang did not record, and also there was what required editing and correcting. I consider that, although these three commentaries are the same in being on the *Spring and Autumn Annals*, they are quite different in their purport and objectives, so it is entirely appropriate that each should have an erudite responsible for the transmission of its learning."

But when Wang Dun rebelled, this was not implemented.[167]

In Tang times, in the fifth month of the ninth year of the Zhenguan reign period [635], there was an imperial proclamation to the effect that from now on, all candidates for the *mingjing* [examination], considering the *Zhou Li* to be like the *Yi Li*, should reduce their prescription of study by choosing one [of these works only]. In the seventh month of the eighth year of the Kaiyuan reign period [720], the director of studies at the National University, Li Yuancui,[168] memorialized, saying,

> The three *Li*, the three commentaries [on the *Spring and Autumn Annals*], as well as the Mao *Odes*, *Documents*, and *Changes*, etc., bring together the profound intentions of sages and worthies and are works of instruction for all mortals. Nowadays, what is studied for the *mingjing* degree[169] is about the pursuit of office, and, as all consider the *Li Ji* to be short, all contend to read it. The *Rites of Zhou* is the standard for the administration of the kingdom. The *Book of Etiquette* is the model for gravity and reverence. The *Gongyang* and the *Guliang* commentaries on the *Spring and Autumn Annals* have been subjects of study through successive generations. Nowadays, in the two educational directorates and in prefectural and district schools, because men study alone, without companions, the transmission of these four classics is in danger of being cut off. So the application of teaching and instruction in serving [the ruler] and assisting [in administration] cannot be continued. May I request that students stop working on one particular classic, and also, that when men presented [as candidates] are preparing for the examinations, they study the *Rites of Zhou*, the *Book of Etiquette*, and the

> *Gongyang* and *Guliang* commentaries? Moreover, I would ask that an understanding of five out of ten topics set would allow men to pass the examination, so affording them encouragement. Accordingly, one may hope that men throughout the world would study them all equally and that an understanding of the Nine Classics would be fully realized.

[The emperor] followed this [recommendation].

In the *Tang History* for the twelfth month of the sixteenth year of the Kaiyuan reign period [728], [there is], "Yang Yang, who was chancellor of the directorate of education, memorialized, writing, 'Nowadays, those candidates for the *mingjing* degree who study the *Zuo Zhuan* number less than two or three in ten. Also, the *Rites of Zhou*, the *Book of Etiquette*, and the *Gongyang* and *Guliang* commentaries have been almost completely done away with. I request that consideration be given to adding encouragement and reward [for studying these works].' Thereupon, a decree was handed down that those candidates successful in the *mingjing* degree who studied the *Zuo Zhuan* as well as the *Rites of Zhou* and the rest of the four classics referred to above and who entered government service should avoid appointment to a sinecure."[170] Subsequently, this was written into the statutes. The ancients who were of a mind to preserve the neglected classics and who supported the mind of recondite learning considered it a pressing matter in this way. And yet now, on the contrary, this has all been done away with. It must have been that scholars of the time had difficulty with the study of the four classics, and those officials responsible for educational policy complied with their private wishes, so subsequently the classic works handed down through successive generations were cast aside and not studied.

From Han times on, could anyone not know that there were the Five Classics, that they together preserved a common meaning, and that this did not allow of one classic being studied alone. Therefore, the study of the "Sanjia" [*Zuo Zhuan*, *Gongyang Zhuan*, and *Guliang Zhuan*—i.e., three commentaries] was included with the *Spring and Autumn Annals*. As for the *San Li* [the Three *Li*—i.e., *Zhou Li*, *Yi Li*, and *Li Ji*], each was considered a separate work. Nowadays, however, the classic itself is put aside and the commentary is studied. This is particularly inappropriate. There is nothing worse than this improper use of study for private ends becoming generalized throughout the empire, deceiving the ruler and betraying the kingdom. That the study of the classics daily declines and men of talent daily diminish in number has this as its basis, has it not?

In the *History of the Song Dynasty* [it is written] that Shen Zong [r. 1068–1086] utilized [Wang] Anshi's theory that each student should specialize in one classic—the *Changes*, the *Odes*, the *Documents*, the *Rites of Zhou*, and the *Record of Rites*—while at the same time studying the *Lunyu* and the *Mencius*.[171] Zhu Wengong [Zhu Xi], in his *Qixiu Sanli Zhazi*, wrote,

> At the time of the Qin destruction of books, those on *Li* [*Rites*] and the *Yue* [*Music*] were first destroyed. What were preserved to a slight degree were the three *Li* [*San Li*], and that was all. The one work, the *Zhou Guan* [*Zhou Li*], was certainly the guiding principle of *li*, whereas, when it came to the minutiae of ceremonial methods, the *Yi Li* was the basic classic. The "Jiaotesheng," the "Guanyi," and other chapters of the *Li Ji* provided the explanations of these principles. Before this, there were still the several courses [for examination]—the *San Li*, the *Tong Li*, and the *Xuejiu*—so that although *li* 禮 [ritual practices, propriety] was not put into practice, scholars, through reading and study, were still able to comprehend its theory. From the Xining reign period [1068–1077] on, Wang Anshi brought change and disorder to the old system, doing away with the *Book of Etiquette* and preserving only the *Record of Rites* as a subject, discarding the classic and relying on the commentary. This was tantamount to neglecting what was fundamental and conferring primary authority on what was incidental; this was especially misguided.[172]

Thus, doing away with the *Book of Etiquette* started with Wang Anshi and, when it came to Ming times, its study remained in abeyance.

Zhu Xi also wrote a preface for Xie Jianyue's *Wenji* [*Collected Writings*] in which he said, "Xie Chuozhong was from Zhenghe in Fujian. During the time, my late father was military governor of Zhenghe. As he was walking between the fields, he heard the sound of somebody reading aloud. When he went to investigate, he found the book was the *Book of Etiquette*. Because at that time there was only specialization in Wang

[Anshi's] program of learning, my father took this man to be uniquely capable and was very surprised. He walked home with the man and encouraged him to continue to study those parts of the work he had not yet mastered. Subsequently, in the third year of the Shaoxing reign period [1133], Xie was ranked as a *jinshi*."[173] In Song times, such a person was already like "the sound of footsteps in an empty valley." At the present time there are no footsteps to be heard at all!

2

RZL 8–12

ADMINISTRATION AND ECONOMICS

Section 8: There are fifteen essays in this section. The first three (8.1–3) deal predominantly with the question of how the kingdom should be subdivided, especially in relation to modes of administration and taxation. The fourth essay (8.4) offers a detailed treatment of the usage of the term *fu* 府 (prefecture—Ming and Qing). The fifth essay (8.5) is an extended argument for devolution in which Gu advocates the appointment of relatively autonomous local officials—men able to provide not only effective administration but also inspiring moral leadership. Essay 8.6 gives brief consideration to one particular form of local administrative organization (*lijia* 里甲—community self-monitoring systems). Essays 8.7–9 are devoted to types of minor officials, the methods of their selection, and the dangers of undue delegation of official matters to them. Essay 8.10 considers the nature of an appropriate legal system, based on Confucian rather than Legalist principles. Essay 8.11 deals with the issue of finding a balance between too many and too few officials. The final four essays (8.11–15) are concerned primarily with the means of selection of officials.

8.5 THE GOVERNING OF TOWNSHIPS (*XIANG* 鄉) AND NEIGHBORHOODS (*TING* 亭)

Comment: In this long essay, Gu gives detailed and specific information about administrative positions in small communities. A number of dynasties are covered, and there are difficulties associated with terminological change over time—in particular with the term *ting*, which is not listed in standard dictionaries with the meaning used here. Translations of the terms follow Charles O. Hucker, *A Dictionary of Official Titles in Imperial China* (Stanford, Calif.: Stanford University Press, 1985).

In the "Hundred Officials" chapter of the *History of the Former Han* [*Han Shu*][1] [there is]: *Xian ling* 縣令 and *chang* 長 were both Qin officials responsible for the administration of their districts. For [a district of] 10,000 or more families, there was a *ling* 令, ranked from 1,000 down to 600 piculs, and for [districts of] less than 10,000 families, there was a *chang* 長 ranked from 500 down to 300 piculs. Both had aides and military officials ranked from 400 down to 200 piculs. These were senior officials. Ranked at 100 piculs and below, there were *doushi* 斗食 and *zuoshi* 佐史, and these were minor officials. In general, every 10 *li* there was a *ting* 亭, with each *ting* having a *chang*. Ten *ting* constituted a *xiang* 鄉, with each *xiang* having a *san lao* 三老 [elder] who was ranked, a *se fu* 嗇夫 [bailiff], and a *you jiao* 游徼 [patroller]. The elder was responsible for the control of education, the bailiff for the hearing of law suits and the collection of taxes, and the patroller for the patrolling of boundaries to prevent crime or theft. A *xian* 縣 was, in general, 100 *li* square. If its population was dense, then it was less; if it was sparse, then it was more extensive. The *xiang* and *ting* were also like this. Both were part of the Qin [administrative] system.

In the "Record of Emperor Gao" [in the *History of the Former Han*] for the second month of the second year, there was an order that, "Those over fifty years of age who are able to cultivate morality and lead the people to goodness should be appointed as *san lao*, there being one [such elder] for each *xiang*. One of the *san lao* from the *xiang* should be selected as *san lao* for the *xian*. He, the district magistrate, his aides, and military officials should consult one another about affairs and not again be sent for labor or frontier duty."[2] This system did not originate in the Qin and Han periods but began at the time of the annexations of the feudal lords. The principles whereby Guan Zhong, Wei Ao, and Zi Chan ruled their kingdoms were in no wise different from this.[3] According to the "Di Guan" chapter of the *Rites of Zhou* [*Zhou Li*], from the rank of *zhou chang* 州長 down, there were *dang zheng* 黨正, *zu shi* 族師, *lü xu* 閭胥, and *bi chang* 比長. From the rank of the *xian zheng* 縣正 down, there were *bi shi* 鄙師, *zan chang* 贊長, *li zai* 里宰,and *lin chang* 鄰長.[4] Thus, under the rule of the wise kings of the Three Dynasties [Xia, Shang, and Zhou], there was also nothing that exceeded this.

Now if, within a single *xiang*, the officials were to put things in order and to apply the laws with meticulous care, then subsequently, in the governing of the empire, this would be like the main rope in a net, and there would be order, not chaos. Yet when it comes to the present day, all this has been completely lost and there is nothing preserved. Moreover, if prefects and magistrates are not sufficiently responsible in the conduct of their duties, numerous overseers need to be appointed. Likewise, if the overseers are also deficient in responsibility, it is important to establish regional inspectors. If there is an accumulation of honor and a piling up of importance through the occupancy of higher positions and there are none beneath them who can share their duties, then even if just, incorrupt, diligent, and skilful officials are found, it is still impossible to conduct good government with them. And on top of this, it is not possible to find good people. In the Taihe reign period of the later Wei [477–499], the supervising secretary, Li Zhong, sent up a memorial, saying, "It is appropriate to follow the ancient practices as follows: For five families establish one neighborhood chief [*lin chang* 鄰長]; for five neighborhoods establish one village chief [*li chang* 里長], and for five villages establish one ward chief [*dang chang* 黨長]. These chiefs should be selected from among the strong and diligent men of the township. The neighborhood chief should in turn select one man, the village chief two, and the ward chief three, and those selected should go on frontier duty while those remaining should be normal citizens. If there were a three-year period without transgressions, then there should be a promotion in employment, and this promotion would be of one rank."[5] Xiao Wen [r. 471–500] agreed to these measures and issued a proclamation, saying, "The system of neighborhood, village, ward, and township had its origins in antiquity. I wish to put into effect the customs and practices of Zhou, so families of the present time can see that the great should oversee the small and the near the distant, just as the body controls the hands and makes their functioning orderly. Then tax levies will be equitable, *yi* 義 [right action, righteousness, duty] will flourish, and litigation will cease."[6]

The histories say[7] that with the start of these laws, many complained they were unsatisfactory, and yet when it came to putting them into practice, the expenses saved were greater than tenfold, and as a result all within the Four Seas was peaceful.

In the Later Zhou period, when Su Chuo wrote the Six Articles,[8] there was an imperial proclamation that said, "Not only must the regional and prefectural officials all be good men but also, when it comes to the overseeing of the headmen of townships and villages, all should be examined with great care and one selected for each township, so bringing about effective local government."[9] Emperor Wen of Sui [r. 589–604], based on his own opinion, changed the ancient [practices] and in the fifteenth year of the Kaihuang reign period [596] for the first time did away with officials completely in the prefectures and townships. Moreover, in the words of Liu Zongyuan of the Tang period, "There were village assistants and then there were district leaders. There were district leaders and then there were feudal lords. There were feudal lords and then there were regional earls and provincial surveillance commissioners. There were regional earls and provincial surveillance commissioners and then there was the Son of Heaven."[10] According to this argument, the ordering of the empire starts with the village assistants and ends with the Son of Heaven—this much is obvious. For this reason, from ancient times to the present day, when small officials are numerous, the age flourishes, and when great officials are numerous, the age falls into decay. The paths of prosperity and decline are nothing other than this.

In Han times, lowly officials such as *se fu* 嗇夫 [functionaries] could still, by their own efforts, fulfill their duties. Thus, when Yuan Yan was a functionary in the Waihuang district [*xiang*], goodness [*ren* 仁] and reform were widely practiced, and the people knew only of the functionary but did not know about prefectures or districts.[11] And when Zhu Yi, himself a functionary [*se fu*] in Tongxiang in Shu who reached the rank of *dasinong* 大司農 [chamberlain for the national treasury], was ill and approaching death, he instructed his sons, saying, "In the past I was a Tongxiang official and the people loved me, therefore you must bury me in Tongxiang. Descendants of later generations who offer the autumnal sacrifices for me will not be like the Tongxiang people." Then he died and his sons buried him in the western outskirts of Tongxiang. The people erected a great sacrificial temple, and through the yearly festival period right up to the present, the sacrifices have continued without interruption.[12] These two gentlemen were both people of the district. Certainly they changed the region so there was good administration and they changed the people so there was good order. How is this so!

In the present dynasty, before the district gates, there are mostly tablets saying that for false accusation, three degrees should be added to the punishment, and for improper appeals to higher courts, fifty lashes of the bamboo should be given. This was an old regulation of former dynasties and was traditionally conducted at the official entrance to the county court. Nowadays, the people do not go through the district court officials but appeal to higher authorities [such as] those controlling the prefecture, this being "appealing to a higher authority in an irregular manner"—this is wrong. In the *Veritable Records of Tai Zu* for the twenty-seventh year of Hongwu [1394], on *renwu* in the fourth month, it is written, "The civil authorities received an order to select from among the people an old man of advanced years who would be able, in a just and equitable fashion, to fulfill his duties in managing legal matters of his township. If there were disputes regarding matrimonial matters or fields and dwellings, then the local officials should resolve them. If the issue was complex and weighty, it was first presented to the district officials."[13] If the matter was not presented for resolution to the local elder but directly to the district officials, this was termed appealing to a higher court in an irregular fashion. Only if great and small support one another and the finer points are all attended to can those above not be unduly troubled and those below not be unnecessarily disturbed.

In Tang times, after the Dali reign period [766–779], military problems arose and taxes became troublesome. And Liu Changqing, in his *Tizha Xili Mingfu*, wrote,

> The sun sets and there are no affairs of state.
> The green hills are at the district gate![14]

If the duties of the district magistrate still do not encroach on those below, then lesser men may be able to find peace in their occupations. In this way, it was possible to extend the kingdom's decree for more than a hundred years right up to the great calamities of Xi and Zhao [the last two Tang emperors]. After this, there was the great defeat. So then, whether by the singing lute [i.e., government by nonaction] or by carrying the stars [i.e., government by hard work], the emperor and his ministers should have a way to manage things.

In the first year of the Hongxi reign period [1425], in the seventh month on *pingshen*, [there is]:

> The regional inspector of the censorate for Sichuan, He Wenyuan, said, 'Tai Zu, Emperor Gao Huang, ordered that in the *zhou* 州 [subprefectures] and *xian* 縣 [districts] of the empire, old men should be established—men necessarily selected on the basis of high virtue—in whom the people had trust and who would be able to direct them toward goodness. Also, in townships and villages, they would be responsible for the regulation and resolution of litigation. Thus, below, they would be of benefit in the people's affairs, and above, they would be of assistance to legal officials. Every year many who were used [in this role] were not such men, some even coming from the ranks of orderlies who took the position to avoid service. Moreover, the district officials did not examine the age and virtue [of the appointees] but ordered the immediate filling of positions, causing [an undue] reliance on the administrative body, which led to the reckless wielding of power and oppression of villages and hamlets. When high officials came to make an inspection, they just indulged in slanderous remarks, stirring up disorder foolishly and intimidating lesser officials. Those who have recently transgressed should be carefully examined according to the law. I am concerned for the subprefectures and districts of the empire on this kind of matter and ask that situations such as outlined above be made the subject of prohibitory regulations.' The emperor ordered that the old system of Hongwu be reinforced, so if there were excessive appointments of evil people, even the officials of the subprefectures and districts would all be punished according to the law.[15]

And so, out of this, it came about that the selection of village elders was made on trivial grounds, and their authority was devalued.

In the Han era, elders [*san lao*] were appointed and given a rank and official salary. And Emperor Wen's [r. 179–157 B.C.E.] proclamation caused each according to his intention to provide leadership for the people. At that time there were many among the *san lao* who were loyal, trustworthy, venerable, and accomplished scholars. Superiors treated these men particularly well, and this was why the people knew a natural goodness. Thus, men of worthiness and ability frequently came from among them. The Xincheng elder Dong Gong[16] intercepted and advised the Han king that he must escort the funeral of Emperor Yi to the grave and he would subsequently receive the empire. The Huguan elder Mao[17] presented a memorial on an injustice to Li Taizi,[18] which the historical records made apparent. This is something the ten thousand ages will praise. The elders of our time comply with the terms of their office but will not go beyond these terms. As a result, those who are to any degree knowledgeable and modest are not willing to serve, while those who do serve are for the most part all followers of villainous and treacherous practices—men who wish to rely on their administrative authority to oppress ordinary people. This is, of course, quite contrary to Ming Tai Zu's purpose in establishing the role of the elders.

At the start of the Ming dynasty, tax captains were appointed from influential families who were responsible for the collection of taxes from their districts; many of them reached the rank of one hundred thousand piculs or more, and in transporting grain to the capital, they might obtain an audience with the emperor. In the Hongwu reign period [1368–1398], official status was conferred on some by virtue of their ability. When it came to the fifth year of the Xuande reign period [1431], in the intercalated twelfth month, the investigating censor of Nanjing, Li An[19] (an elder of the two districts Luling and Jishui in Jiangxi), and also, in the fourth month of the sixth year [1432], the investigating censor Zhang Zheng,[20] both spoke of the evils of tax captains—their doubling of the number of lawsuits, and their undue influence over government officials. This was repeatedly prohibited, and consequently the evil decreased slightly, although the position was not done away with because of this. In the position of elder, the name only was preserved but the reality was lost.

The position of police chief was like the ancient position of patroller. In the Hongwu reign period, this was [a position] of particular importance and specially bestowed by imperial order. Also established was the method of periodically examining the service of officials. In this regard, the Marquis of Jiangxia, Zhou Dexing, made a tour of inspection in Fujian and increased the establishment of the police office by forty-five.[21] From the Hongzhi reign period [1488–1505] on, there was considerable impetus to reduce and do away with these positions until what remained did not amount to half of what was in existence in former times. As the number of police chiefs was reduced so [the burden] of the governor-general was increased. Why was this? The police office could stop evil before it started, whereas control by the governor-general was exercised only when there was already disorder.

8.10 LAWS AND REGULATIONS

Laws and prohibitory regulations are what a king cannot set aside, and yet they are not what make for good order. The foundation of good order lies in rectifying men's minds and making their customs and mores substantial—that is all. Therefore, it is said, "To dwell in reverence and act with simplicity is the way to come near to the people."[22] The Duke of Zhou, in writing "The Establishment of Government" in the *Documents*, said, "King Wen did not involve himself in the various government orders and notifications, legal processes, and precautionary measures." He also said, "With regard to the legal processes and precautionary measures, King Wen would not presume to know of these."[23] His intention to give repeated injunctions to men of later times may be said to be excellent. In the rule of Qinshi Huang Di, "the matters of the empire, whether great or small, were all decided by the emperor, the stage being reached where the emperor weighed out 120 catties of writings, which was the measure for a day and a night, and unless he fulfilled the measure, he did not rest."[24] Through this, Qin subsequently perished.

Taishi Gong [Sima Qian] said, "In former times, the emperor's laws were especially complex. Consequently, deceit and falsity arose. In the end, there was mutual deceit between those above and those below, so the situation could not be relieved."[25] This being so, a multiplicity of laws and prohibitions can be considered an instrument for hastening collapse, and yet a foolish and befuddled ruler would still consider he had not reached perfection.

Du Zimei [Du Fu], in one of his poems, said,

Shun made use of the sixteen assistants,
yet he himself was honored and the Way exalted.
In Qin times responsibility was given to Shang Yang,
laws and regulations were like the hairs of an ox.[26]

And also,

You watch the lamp and candlelight spread,
which makes the flying moths grow dense.[27]

How appropriate these words are to the affairs of the present dynasty!

Emperor Wen of Han issued this proclamation: "Set up elders [*san lao*], filial and fraternal and strong in their agricultural work, as permanent officials, and order each of them to teach the people according to their own concepts."[28] Thus, to have the elders as humble officials and to have them follow their own intentions was the method of rule of Wen and Jing and the reason why they were able to change the customs of the people and modify their mores. The honesty and purity of the people can then be compared to the glory of Cheng and Kang [the second and third emperors of the Zhou dynasty, ruling from 1115 to 1079 B.C.E. and from 1078 to 1053 B.C.E., respectively]. Zhuge Kongming [Zhuge Liang] had a sincere heart and established a just way, so in the exchanges between superiors and inferiors, no one complained.[29] Even a small and insignificant state such as Shu could become comparatively prosperous. Cao in Wei and Quan in Wu relied on Legalist methods to control their officials, yet disorder and rebellion continued to arise with almost never a year of peace.[30] In the affairs of the empire it is certainly not laws that can act as protection.

Shu Xiang, in his letter to Zi Chan, said, "When a kingdom is about to collapse, there are inevitably many regulations."[31] If laws and regulations are complex, then artful and cunning people all take the law to be like the marketplace, and even if there are worthy men, they are not able to find employment for themselves. This is why the affairs of such a state decline day by day. How apt are the words of Du Yuankai [Du Yu], who in his explanations of the *Zuo Zhuan*, said, "If the laws are effective, then people follow the laws. If the laws fail, then the laws follow the people."[32] When men of former times first established laws, they were not able to examine the trends of affairs carefully, so they made provisions for change. Men of later times inherited what was already corrupt and were restrained by old regulations, which they were unable to change or do away with, and so they sought to remedy the situation by further legislation. As a result, laws became increasingly numerous and corrupt practices increased pari passu. Indeed, the affairs of the empire grew more vexatious by the day. In the end, there was "bewilderment and inaction."[33] In the intercourse between superior and inferior officials there was deception, consideration being given only to not losing the regulations of the ancestors. At no time was this more so than in the Ming period, as exemplified in the two matters of the management of military affairs and the practice of using paper currency, where laws were established to save laws that were already in place and yet ultimately were ineffectual.

The words of Ye Shi of the Song period were,

> As a consequence of the extreme malpractices of the Tang and Five Dynasties periods, the powers of the military commissioners were completely reappropriated by the emperor, so even the registration of one soldier, the origin of one aspect of wealth, or the guarding of one piece of land were all matters undertaken by the ruler himself. In the desire to derive only the greatest benefits and not suffer the greatest harms, subsequently laws were used and the people disregarded, subofficial functionaries were used and officials disregarded, and prohibitions and bans were trivial and vexatious. This was notably different from ancient times, when the authority and its implementation were especially not divided. Nonetheless, how could this be right? As a result, men of ability diminished in number, the outer provinces were reduced, and the central government was weak. And despite the greatness of the empire, men were fearful. All this was brought about by the legal system of one generation.

He also said,

> In recent times, in the court and in the provinces, both among those above and those below, no matter how small the issue nor how trifling the crime, all first had some law to deal with them.

> Ultimately, all the people of one generation had their thoughts entirely circumscribed, so if a wise person were to be found, they thought it very unusual, and a law would be established to make provision for this. Thus the laws became complex and all-encompassing such that men of ability could not reach the highest level of expression and men of purpose could not have full scope. In their confusion, the people bowed their heads and complied with the laws, so the conduct of affairs became more disrupted while customs decayed further with every passing day. The poor people became increasingly destitute and helpless, while artful villains increasingly achieved their purposes. This is what caused concern to the empire and why officials dared not make a false accusation.

He also said,

> For a distance of ten thousand *li*, if a brow is wrinkled, a groan emitted, or a breath indrawn, all is known to the emperor. Even so, when nothing is entrusted to officials, the empire will float aimlessly, and that is all. The sorrows of a hundred years or the misfortunes of a moment were all the emperor's sole responsibility—the multitude of officials played no part. If, for a distance of ten thousand *li*, all is under the control of the emperor, then the emperor himself certainly benefits. If the sorrows of a hundred years or the misfortunes of a moment are all the sole responsibility of the emperor, then are the harmful effects like this? This is the reason why barbarians were able to usurp power and could not be resisted, and why shame at the hands of enemies became extreme and could not be requited.[34]

Chen Liang, in a memorial sent up to Xiao Zong, said, "In the Five Dynasties period the authority over military and financial matters had reverted to those in lower positions. Yizu Huang Di [Tai Zu of Song] gathered control into the hands of the emperor and in this way brought stability when there had been calamity and disorder. Later generations did not, however, understand his original intention and so continued the process without end. As a consequence, prefectures and districts were empty names, root and branch were both weak."[35]

In the sixth year of the Hongwu reign period [1373], in the ninth month, on *dingwei*, there was an order to officials responsible for general business that the monthly announcements be changed to quarterly, and if this was thought to be too frequent, then in general they could become annual announcements. In all the prefectures, subprefectures, and districts, the legal cases and prisoners, whether in relation to trivial matters or weighty, relied upon legal processes for resolution with no need to transfer them to a higher authority. If there was some perversion of the course of justice, then such misdeeds were exposed and rectified by the censors of the surveillance commission. The promulgation of this edict brought general benefit to the empire.[36]

Section 9: There are twenty essays in this section. The first two continue the treatment of the selection of officials: finding men of ability (9.1) and the matter of recommending such men (9.2). There are two short essays on official seals (9.3 and 9.4). Essays 9.5 and 9.6 deal with "regional inspectors" (*duci shi* 都刺史). The next four essays (9.7–10) are concerned with several official titles considered in a historical context. The essay titled "Prefects and District Magistrates" (9.11) provides an extended treatment of the pivotal role of these officials in an effective, equitable administrative structure. Essays 9.12–14 continue with this theme. Essay 9.15 is about the roles appropriate for members of the ruler's clan. There are then three essays on military matters: frontier defense commands (9.16), bulwark departments (9.17), and border districts (9.18). The last two essays are about eunuchs: the first is an extended general treatment of the subject (9.19) and the second a consideration of the practice of self-castration to gain advancement (9.20).

9.1 MEN OF ABILITY

Ye Shi of the Song period said, "Laws and regulations daily became more troublesome, the essential instruments for ruling the nation daily more arcane, and prohibitions and restrictions daily more binding, until it came to the point where it was impossible to move. Men of wisdom and foresight were unable to escape the enmeshing network of bonds and constraints, so their own abilities could not find an effective outlet."[37] Nowadays, in discussions among men, topics outside the regulations are barely considered; men abruptly wave their hands and don't dare [to dwell on such matters]. By virtue of Han's being able to utilize completely men of ability, Chen Tang was able to indulge his passion for literary pursuits [i.e., able to express his ability].[38] But what of the present times? It is little wonder that brave and outstanding scholars no longer see themselves as determined and impetuous but fall back on being commonplace and weak. If Mei Cheng or [Sima] Xiangru[39] had studied the modern interpretations of the classics, it is certain they would not have been able to produce their literary works. If Guan Zhong or Sun Wu[40] had studied modern laws, it is certain they would not have been able to employ their strategies. Therefore, the laws and decrees bring harm to the expression of men's abilities. Those who are effective in their guarding against lewdness number perhaps three out of ten, while those who are effective in their hindrance of brave and eminent scholars number, as a rule, seven out of ten.

From the time of the Wanli reign period [1573–1619] and before, the laws were complicated, and yet they were supported by education. Their administrative efficacy created a peaceful era [as under the rule of the ancient kings]. After the Wanli period, the laws were still preserved, but the effects of education were lost, so opportunism daily increased while talent and ability daily diminished. The noble men of these times worked at the "cutting of cap strings"[41] but were unable to obtain the heads of their enemies. These lesser men were skilled in the theft of horses but were not willing to save the ruler from misfortune.

Truly, it is as the *Mozi* says: "Those who are put in charge of the official treasury will plunder and steal from it. Those who are charged with defending the city will betray and forsake it. . . . Those employed to decide cases at law will not be just. Those responsible for the distribution of wealth will not do it equitably."[42] The *Lü Shi Chunqiu* says, "When officials take office, they are wild and disorderly; when they are in the presence of wealth, they become avaricious; when they advance in rank, they become flatterers; and when they lead the multitudes, they are hesitant and cowardly."[43] It is also as Liu Fen said: "Planning is not enough to eradicate villainy and violence, but deception is enough to disturb the emperor's serenity. Bravery is not enough to guard and protect the nation, but violence is enough to disrupt and bring harm to the rural areas."[44] Ah, alas! I have realized that the law alone [i.e., without any civilizing influence] is of no use.

The *Shilu* says,

> In the fifth year of the Xuande reign period [1430], on *bingxu* in the eighth month, the emperor brought the morning audience to a close and traveled to the Wenhua palace. Of the scholars such as Yang Pu[45] and others who waited on him, he asked, "In the selection of the various officials, which method should be used in order to be completely sure of obtaining the right men?" Yang Pu replied, "If there is strictness in [the matter of] recommendations and purity [in the conduct of] the periodical examinations of the service of officials, how will you suffer the misfortune of not getting the right men?" The emperor said, "In recent times there have been faults in the method of recommendation; with one word of recommendation there is the desire to make a whole lifetime secure. Is this not a problem?" I consider that, if the Way is followed in education and upbringing, then men of ability will spontaneously emerge. Dong Zhongshu of the Han period said, "[As a rule] not nurturing scholars and yet desiring to seek worthy men is like not polishing gems and yet seeking the beauty of adornment." This is the theory of knowing the essentials.[46]

If there is merely compliance with the form of the triennial examination of the service of officials, but the code of teaching of the Three Matters is not practiced, then even if the emperor were to be Yao or Shun, he would still not be able to complete the regulation of government.[47]

Section 10: There are thirteen essays in this section, which is something of a miscellany. With one exception, the first six essays are about aspects of land management. The exception (10.2) is about the standardization of weights and measures. Essays 10.7 and 10.8 are about financial matters, including land taxes (10.7) and the practice of drawing money in advance (10.8). Essay 10.9 is about spinning and weaving and the profits therefrom. As for the final four essays, 10.10 and 10.11 are about horses and dispatch stations, 10.12 is about travel by water, and 10.13 is about the smuggling of salt.

10.8 DRAWING MONEY IN ADVANCE

In the third year of the Tianbao reign period of Emperor Xuan Zong of the Tang [744], there was a decree that said, "Every year personal service to the state and household taxes are to be levied in the eighth month. But if the agricultural work has not been completed, there is the fear that it might be difficult to fulfill these requirements, so from the present time on, [collection] will be deferred, with the twelfth day of the ninth month being set as the limit."[48] By the time of the *gengzi* day in the seventh month of the second year of the Guangde reign period of Dai Zong [764], the cultivated land throughout the empire was taxed "green sprouts money" as a means of providing salaries for the hundred officials.[49] What was called "green sprouts money" arose when the nation's needs were pressing and the government was unable to wait until autumn, levying taxes as soon as the fields showed green sprouts. This was the reason for the term "green sprouts money." Those responsible [for collection] were called "green sprouts officials." This was the origin of the term "drawing money in advance" used by later generations.

Lu Xuangong [Lu Zhi][50] said, "When sericulture flourished, a silk tax was introduced; when agricultural work was not yet complete, a grain tax was hurriedly demanded. If the demands of high officials are heavy, the harshness and cruelty of lesser officials becomes increasingly manifest. Those who have possessions sell hastily, reducing their prices by half; those who do not are compelled to borrow and repay at double the rate."[51] In the second month of the sixth year of the Yuanhe reign period of Xian Zong [811], there was a regulation to the effect that, because the new arrangements were not well received and the management of military encampments was particularly difficult, wherever these were in use, a surveillance commissioner was to be put in charge of the contributions to military expenses. All around there was borrowing for this purpose, and if the [necessary] sum was not obtained, a levy was applied to the ordinary people.[52] Therefore, Han Wengong [Han Yu], in his poem "Wandering South of the City," wrote,

Long robes of white calico and a purple neck scarf,
before taxes fall due, this is a time of leisure.
Young growing wheat, full mulberry trees,
ripe grain and new-borne fruit.
Together we go to the head of the field.
Happy is the god of soil.[53]

This refers to the time during the third and fourth months before the *chaike* [a demand for either service or money] has been levied.

When it came to Zhuang Zong of the Later Tang, in the fourth year of the Tongguang reign period [926], on the *wuchen* day in the third month, because army provisions were insufficient, there was an imperial order to the overseers in Henan to obtain money in advance for the summer and autumn taxes. At this time, there was rebellion within and without, and in less than a month the country was lost and the ruler killed. When Ming Zong was established on the throne [926], it was clear that he loved the people, and this can be seen by what is recorded in the *Wenxian Tongkao*[54] for the fourth year of the Changxing reign period [933]: the earliest time for collection of tax levies was the fifteenth day of the fifth month, and by the first day of the eighth month, enough was received. It was then altered and made later, the latest being on the twentieth day of the sixth month, so that by the ninth month enough was received. In the third year of the Xiande reign period of Shi Zong of Zhou [956], on the *bingzi* day in the tenth month, the emperor spoke to his attendant officials, saying that in recent times, in the collection of taxes, either of grain or silk, many did not await the completion of the harvest or the reeling of the silk. Further, he proclaimed to the Three Offices[55] that from now on the collection of summer taxes should be in the sixth month and that of the autumn taxes in the tenth month.[56] Thus, although Zhuang Zong issued an edict for the drawing of taxation monies three months in advance, this was never actually put into practice. In later generations, there were times when the kingdom's strength was in danger, although never so extreme as in the Tongguang period. And yet, when in spring there were the first placards [announcing] the commencement of the tax levies, the suffering among the people was very great.

The *Odes* says, "Large rats, large rats. Do not eat our springing grain."[57] Xie Junzhi [Xie Fangde] said, "If the springing grain is eaten when still in flower, this is avarice in the extreme."[58] Nowadays, the government that draws money in advance is one that eats the springing grain. Does this not drive the people away and cause them "to go to the happy borders"?[59] Yu Qian, who in the later years of the Hongwu reign period [1368–1399] was the prefect of Hangzhou prefecture, offered this advice: "Buddhists and Daoists are the plunderers of the people. Now, in Jiangnan the fields associated with temples are extensive, perhaps several hundred *qing*, and yet forced labor on government service is never imposed on them. It is the poor people without fields who are frequently pressed into such service, and this creates hardship. I request that there be a regulation to the effect that, among the Buddhists and Daoists, the fields of every person should not exceed ten *mou* and that the remaining land be distributed equitably among the people."[60] At first this was approved, but later it was said not to be an old regulation and was subsequently done away with.

Section 11: There are sixteen essays in this section. Essays 11.1 and 11.2 are about weights and measures, looking at terminology in a historical context. The remaining fourteen essays are all to do with fiscal matters, and again the main focus is on terminology. Three of these essays discuss the historical aspects of the use of particular materials for currency—gold (11.6), silver (11.7), and copper (11.8). Two of the essays focus on specific forms of a single currency—*wuzhu qian* 五銖錢 (11.9) and *kaiyuan qian* 開元錢 (11.10). The next five essays are something of a mixture: 11.11 is on the changes in coinage throughout history; 11.12 is about the uses of copper; 11.13 concerns what is written on the surfaces of coins; 11.14 is on the practice of taking one hundred to represent less than a hundred (*duan mo* 短陌); and 11.15 is about paper money. The final essay, 11.16, is a short historical consideration of the debasing of silver and gold coinage.

11.16 DEBASING SILVER

Nowadays superiors and inferiors all use silver. This has led to a great upsurge of clever swindling among the people. Not only do they cheat merchants but also some even cheat senior officials. The people of Jinan particularly indulged in this form of deception, until it reached a point where many tens or even hundreds used it. What is said is that those who are robbers are not only those who grasp spears and bows. According to the law, whoever makes false gold or silver is given a hundred lashes or is banished for three years. Those who aid and abet them, if they are cognizant of the circumstances surrounding the transaction, are in each case reduced in rank by one grade. This law is relatively lenient and also is not invariably applied, therefore people don't think twice about transgressing. This variability in the imposition of penalties highlights the deficiencies of the legal process.

In Han times, gold was used. In the twelfth month of the sixth year of Xiao Jing's [Emperor Jing's] reign [144 B.C.E.], a law was promulgated to the effect that the casting of coins using debased gold would result in public execution. The law was that those who manufactured debased gold and privately cast coinage would, in like manner, be publicly executed.[61] In the fifth year of the Yuanding reign period of Emperor Wu of Han [112 B.C.E.], there was a shortage of gold in the privy purse from the *yinzhou* levy, and the number of nobles on trial for their failure to provide for this levy exceeded a hundred. Ru Chun said, "According to the *Hanyi Zhu*, if the gold is deficient in weight, or poor in color [i.e., debased], the king will lose his lands and the feudal lords will flee their states."[62]

In the seventh month of the fourth year of the Kaibao reign period of Tai Zu of Song [971], on the *jisi* day, there was a proclamation to the effect that those making false gold should be publicly executed.[63] And in the sixth month of the third year of the Taihe reign period of Wen Zong of Tang [829], according to a memorial from the secretariat-chancellery, those who debased money with lead or tin, if it exceeded ten *guan*, were to be immediately executed in the place where they were gathered.[64] Nowadays, the crime of debasing silver is not as serious as that of debasing gold but is a more serious matter than the exchange of lead for silver in currency, so it is appropriate that a severe penalty, comparable to that of former times, should be established. Perhaps, then, villainy can be done away with and there can be a return to what is straightforward.

When, in Han times, money was taken as a commodity, the copper was not of uniform quality, therefore the commandant of the Imperial Gardens included within his office an assistant for distinguishing copper. This was a continuation of the traditional Zhou office of Overseer of Treasures.[65]

Section 12: In this final section on government and economics there are fifteen essays. The first two are about wealth—its distribution (12.1) and the adverse effects of its pursuit by individuals, especially if they are officials (12.2). The remaining essays in the section can be divided into two broad groups, with one additional essay. The first group concerns official matters and contains five essays, as follows: 12.3 on the payment of officials; 12.4 on methods of raising revenue; 12.10 and 12.11 on the reporting and control of malfeasance; and 12.12 on the need to control the private ownership of military equipment. The second group deals with natural and man-made amenities: 12.13 on conservation of water; 12.14 on rain and rainfall; 12.15 on rivers and creeks; 12.6 and 12.7 on roads; 12.5 on inns; and 12.8 on bridges. The odd one out is 12.9, "Gathering of People," which is a statement of Gu's social prescription.

12.2 OFFICIALS WHO SPEAK OF PROFIT

Mencius said, "Without government control, the utilization of wealth will be unsatisfactory."[66] Rulers in ancient times never avoided talking about wealth. What they abhorred was the glorification of profit because this would inevitably bring harm to the people. Formerly, Tai Zu of Ming [r. 1368–1398] dismissed those censors who spoke of profit, saying to his officials in attendance that the noble man, in attaining his position, wishes to act in accordance with the Way, while the lesser man, in attaining his position, is bent on pursuing his own private ends. Those who wish to follow the Way have hearts that are concerned for the empire and the kingdom, while those who are motivated by self-interest have hearts that are concerned with harmful things that injure the people.[67] This, then, was Tang Tai Zong's tradition of responsibility and authority handed down for almost a millennium.[68] Further, the minor official [subofficial functionary] of Guangping prefecture, Wang Yundao, said, "Regarding the production of iron in the Linshui commandery of Cizhou, I request permission to establish a smelting furnace." The emperor said, "I have heard that to bring good order to the age, the empire should not neglect worthy men. I have not heard that the empire should not neglect profit. Moreover, profit lies not with the officials but with the people, and if the people obtain profit, then the source of wealth is universal and there is also benefit to the officials. If the officials alone secure profit, then the source of profit dries up, and this is inevitably harmful to the people. Nowadays, the various smelting furnaces are numerous, military resources are not lacking, and the livelihood of the people is already established. If this is again set up, there will certainly be a significant disturbance."[69] [Wang] was punished by beating and exile. The sage ancestors did not disregard the significance of fondness for money, which can be said to be very deep-rooted. From the middle of the Wanli reign period [1573–1619], mining taxes arose and the objective of seeking profit brought disorder for a further several decades, so the people became increasingly impoverished and political life increasingly troubled. This being so, the distinction between good order and disorder, gain and loss, can be known. Can those who are in high position simply seek profit and not consider [the welfare of] the people to be important?

The *New Tang History*, in the biographies of Yuwen [Rong], Wei [Jian], Yang [Shenjin], and Wang [Hong], says in acclaim,

> In the Kaiyuan reign period [713–741], Yuwen Rong, by first speaking of profit, secured the imperial favor at that time, and the emperor, seeing that all within the seas was settled, ceased to have a mind to drive out the four barbarians. Rong, in devising for the emperor a means of arranging military provisioning, discussed the seizure of the remaining fields of unregistered households in conformity with the wishes of the landlords. Once this theory of profit was founded, the emperor regretted that he had come upon it so late. Not ten years passed before Rong was chosen as prime minister, although he was subsequently found guilty of crimes, punished, and reviled. Still, the emperor regretted that his talent had not been fully utilized. From the Tianbao reign period [742–755] on, armed uprisings occurred without, while within there was the poisonous effect of beautiful concubines to the degree that the waste and excess could not, in material terms, be determined. As a result, Wei Jian, Yang Shenqin, Wang Hong, and Yang Guozhong were each responsible for the introduction of oppressive taxes. This harmed those below while benefiting those above. For the yearly offering, there was an excessive demand for cash to fill the private coffers of the emperor so that he might make numerous unreasonable bestowals, the expenditure of the empire being as it was before [Rong]. This being so, those who deserted the empire daily became more numerous than before and there were officials who, in filling their posts, did not attend to affairs. Thus, what Jian and the others desired was fulfilled and there was a return to the abuse of power, flattery, and internecine strife. The four tribes all rebelled, and the empire regarded it as a joke. Therefore, can what Mencius said, to wit, 'Superiors and inferiors will try to snatch their profits the one from the other, and the state will be lost,' not readily be believed?[70]

Ah, alas! Rui Liangfu, in his criticism of Li Wang, said, "What is resented is very considerable, and yet there is no provision for great difficulties."[71] The rulers of the Three Dynasties [Xia, Shang, and Zhou] were all like this. When the cart in front overturns and the cart behind doesn't recognize this as a warning, people and officials destroy themselves and rulers lose their states. How sad is this!

To study the writings of Confucius and Mencius and become conversant with the methods of Guan [Zhong] and Shang [Yang] is something that, for these past forty years, officials have not been willing to do. As a consequence, there is now ferment everywhere. If there were one man here who could speak but did not speak, he would be esteemed by the multitude and considered to be a scholar-official who had a sense of shame. If those above act in a particular way, then those below will follow them. Thus the responsibility for the collection of taxes and the levying of bridge and ferry tolls, which is something men formerly avoided and did not put into practice, is something that they are now prepared to bare their arms and fight over. *Li* 禮 [ritual practices, propriety] and *yi* 義 [right action, righteousness, duty] are in tatters while thieves and robbers contend. "If *yi* 義 is put second and *li* 利 [profit, benefit] is given primacy, the people will not be satisfied until they have snatched everything."[72] If kings who will arise in the future consider what is important to be the establishment of good order and the transformation of those within the empire who are avaricious and heterodox, they must not give precedence to profit *li* 利.

3

RZL 13–15

CUSTOMS AND MORES

Section 13: There are thirty-seven essays in this section, which constitutes the main statement of Gu's opinions on ethics and related matters. Considerable attention is given to the variation of customs through different eras and how this reflects a changing moral climate. The first five essays are about customs during specific periods: Late Zhou (13.1), Qin (13.2), Western and Eastern Han (13.3), Three Kingdoms (13.4), and Song (13.5). The next part of the section—essays 13.6–16—contains important statements on what might be termed pure and applied ethics. Of particular note are 13.6, on what he calls pure (disinterested) criticism, 13.7 on *ming jiao* 名教 (the teaching of names), and 13.8 on honesty and a sense of shame. In the last two essays of this subsection (13.15 and 13.16), he turns to the question of laws and their application and seems here to embrace a somewhat Legalist position. Essays 13.17–23 consist of a series of comments on relatively specific aspects of national and domestic administration, the former being exemplified by some observations on the practice of incarcerating the relatives of treacherous ministers and the latter by a consideration of the acquisition of male slaves. Essays 13.24 and 13.25 are brief statements of what Gu sees as the different failings in the northern and southern regions. The following two essays (13.26 and 13.27) are about individuals from the Song era. Essay 13.28 is an interesting deliberation on what scholars study in their later years, particularly their tendency to turn to Buddhism in the south and the Immortals in the north as they come to recognize the limits of possible achievement in self-cultivation and other studies and the difficulty of applying their acquired moral precepts in the face of the vicissitudes of the practical world. The final nine essays (13.29–37) cover a miscellany of unrelated topics.

13.1 THE CUSTOMS AND MORES OF THE LATE ZHOU

Comment: This is the first of several essays on what Gu refers to as the customs and mores (*feng su* 風俗) of a particular era. His concerns are primarily ethical and social. In this case he focuses mainly on the period between the end of the time recorded in the *Spring and Autumn Annals* and the *Zuo Zhuan* and the establishment of the vertical alliance of states—that is, 468 to 334 B.C.E.—lamenting the inadequacy of the recording of history during those years. More generally, he is lamenting the overall decline of ethical standards and ceremonial practices through the later centuries of the Zhou dynasty. He sees this decline as not starting to be reversed until the initial emperors of the Eastern Han (beginning 25 C.E.). One of his chief points is the need to examine the customs of a particular time to make an evaluation of the leaders.

The *Spring and Autumn Annals* end with the thirty-ninth year of the reign of King Jing, which was the year *gengshen* [481 B.C.E.]. [The final words are:] "The hunter in the west captured a *lin*."[1] Fourteen years later, in the first year of the reign of King Zhen Ding, which was the year *guiyou* [468 B.C.E.], Duke Ai of Lu fled. Two years after this he died at the hands of Youshan Shi. The *Zuo Zhuan* ends with this.[2] Then, sixty-five years later, in the twenty-third year of the reign of King Weilie, which was the year *wuyin* [403 B.C.E.], the Jin high officials, Wei Si, Zhao Ji, and Han Qian, were first proclaimed feudal lords.[3] Seventeen years after that, in the sixteenth year of the reign of King An, which was the year *yiwei* [386 B.C.E.], the Qi high official, Tian He, was first proclaimed a feudal lord.[4] Fifty-two years further on, in the thirty-fifth year of the reign of King Xian, which was the year *dinghai* [334 B.C.E.], the six states were in succession designated kingdoms and Su Qin became the leader of the vertical alliance.[5] From this time onward affairs can be ascertained and were recorded.

From the end of the *Zuo Zhuan* up to this time [i.e., 334 B.C.E.] spanned a total of 123 years. The historical writings for this period were deficient, so those studying the ancients were confused. In the Spring and Autumn period [722–484 B.C.E.], *li* 禮 [proper conduct, ceremonial practices] was still revered and *xin* 信 [trust, good faith] was still regarded as important, and yet in the Seven States period [403–221 B.C.E.] nothing was said about *li* 禮 and *xin* 信. In the Spring and Autumn period, the Zhou king was still revered, and yet in the Seven States period, nothing was said of the Zhou king.[6] In the Spring and Autumn period, there was still strict observance of the sacrifices and due weight given to presentations and offerings, and yet in the Seven States period, there is nothing about these matters. In the Spring and Autumn period, there was still discussion of family and clan, and yet in the Seven States period, there is not one word about them. In the Spring and Autumn period, banquets were still given and poems recited, and yet in the Seven States period, nothing is heard of this. In the Spring and Autumn period, there were still announcements of celebration and mourning, and yet in the Seven States period, these ceased. Countries were without established relationships and scholars were without established masters. These were all changes that occurred in this period of 123 years. And yet, despite the lacunae in historical writings, there were those in later times who thought they could infer what had happened. The exhaustion of the *dao* [Way] of Wen and Wu did not have to wait for Qinshi Huang Di's unification of the empire.[7] When peaceful times returned in the Western Han, these customs didn't change. Thus Liu Xiang could say, "The sequel to a thousand years of Zhou decline was the excessive evil of the tyrannical Qin, and there was rapacious greed, deceit, and wrongdoing without the restraints of *yi* 義 [right action, righteousness, justice] and *li* 理 [pattern, coherence, principle]."[8]

It can be seen, then, that what history records is nothing but the doings of men who achieve fame, power, and profit, given expression by the various classes of writers and mouthpieces. Only very few see the words of Dong Sheng[9] on true goodness and the enlightened *dao*. Now, from after the Spring and Autumn period, it was not until the time of the Eastern Capital [Eastern Han] that there was some return to ancient customs and mores. I know this because Guang Wu, Ming, and Zhang[10] brought about a change to the merits of the time from Qi to Lu, but it is a pity they never purified the *dao*. In later times, the Song period between

Qingli and Yuanyou [1041–1086] was one of excellence. But alas, if you discuss the age without examining its customs, you will not make clear the merits of rulers. What I reprove the Late Zhou and commend the Eastern Han for is also the purport of the *Spring and Autumn Annals.*

13.2 THE KUAIJI MOUNTAIN STONE CARVINGS OF THE QIN ANNALS

Comment: The locations of the three inscriptions considered were Mount Tai in Qi (modern Shandong)—paragraph 1; Mount Jieshi in Yan (modern Hebei)—paragraph 2; and Kuaiji Mountain in Yue (modern Zhejiang)—paragraph 3.

The stone carvings of the first Qin emperor [Qinshi Huang Di] numbered six in all. In each case much was made of his conquest of the six kings and his unification of the empire. Their words at Mount Tai, in regard to the customs of the common people, said, "Men and women should act in accordance with propriety; they should be cautious and honorable in the conduct of affairs; they should clearly differentiate without [i.e., men] from within [i.e., women] and do nothing that isn't conducive to peace and tranquility."

At Jieshi Gate it is said, "Men find pleasure in the land; women devote themselves to their tasks." The writings are like this and that is all. But at Kuaiji there is one carving, the words of which read, "To gloss over faults and proclaim oneself righteous, to have a son and yet remarry, is to behave with particular impropriety and to be impure. He [Qinshi Huang] took the precaution of separating men and women and prohibiting lewdness and licentiousness to keep the relationships between them pure. If a husband pays court to someone else's wife, he may be killed without it being a crime, so men are made to follow the path of righteousness. If a wife deserts her husband to remarry, leaving her children without a mother, this is, in every respect, a transformation of goodness and purity."[11]

How is it that there are so many [statements] and they are not reduced? Examine the matter in the *Guoyu*. From the time the King of Yue, Gou Jian,[12] settled at Kuaiji, he feared only that the population of the kingdom would not be sufficient. Therefore, he ordered that able-bodied men should not take an old wife, nor should an old man marry a vigorous young woman. If a daughter reached the age of seventeen unmarried, this was considered a crime on the part of the parents; so, too, was the case of a young man reaching the age of twenty unmarried. If a male child was born, [the parents were given] two flasks of wine and a dog. If a female child was born, the gift was two flasks of wine and a sucking pig. If three children were born, a wet nurse was provided. If two children were born, there was a gift of grain.[13] In the *Inner Chronicles* [*Neizhuan*], Zixu [Wu Yuan] says, "In the tenth year of the King of Yue, many were born."[14]

In the *Spring and Autumn Annals of Wu and Yue* it is said that Gou Jian dispatched those widows who had transgressed in the matter of licentious behavior to a mountaintop. Scholars who were beset by melancholy thoughts were ordered to wander on the mountain in order to alleviate their melancholy. Gou Jian's wish at that time was for the population to increase, so there was no return to the prohibition of licentious behavior. This was handed down until the end of the six states [i.e., the Qin unification], and as the custom was still in existence, so the first Qin emperor [Qinshi Huang] strictly prohibited it and made a particular point of incorporating it into the text of the stone carvings. Considering this was raised and mentioned [in the Kuaiji inscription] together with the destruction of the six states and the unification of the empire, and that they were, moreover, matters that were not evident in Yan's and Qi's inscriptions but only in Yue's, then although the punishments put into practice by the Qin were excessive, they were, nevertheless, framed with the intent of protecting the people and correcting their customs and certainly never differed from [those of] the Three Kings. When the Han arose, the Qin laws were inherited and utilized. Indeed, many have been preserved to the present day. Confucians of every generation, in speaking of the Qin, clearly consider their laws to be the cause of the fall of a kingdom. This is because they don't examine them in depth.

13.3 THE CUSTOMS AND MORES OF THE TWO HANS

In Han times, subsequent to Xiao Wu's [r. 140–87 B.C.E.] proclamation commending the Six Classics, although the study of Confucianism flourished, its central meaning remained obscure. Therefore, when Xin

Mang [Wang Mang][15] assumed the regency, those who wished to praise his virtue and offer auspicious omens in relation to his appointment were to be found everywhere throughout the empire. Guang Wu [r. 25–57 C.E.] had these as his examples. Therefore, he honored and revered *jie* 節 [purity, moderation, frugality] and *yi* 義 [right action, righteousness, duty] and regarded name [*ming* 名] and entity [*shi* 實] as important, so those whom he employed in official positions were invariably men who understood the classics and were cultivated in conduct. As a result, customs underwent a change. When it came to the last years of the Eastern Han, the court and administration were disordered and corrupt, the nation's affairs declined by the day, and yet those of the proscribed party[16] and those given to independent action, who followed the path of *ren* 仁 [loving-kindness, benevolence, humanity] and *yi* 義, continued to risk their lives. [In the *Odes* it is written,]

Wind and rain, all looks dark,
Yet the cock crows without ceasing.[17]

After the Three Dynasties period, the excellence of the customs still did not reach that of the Eastern Han. Therefore, Fan Ye, in discussing this matter, wrote that he "considered the period of Huan [r. 142–167] and Ling [r. 168–188] to be one during which the Way [*dao* 道] of the noble man declined and the principles of government grew worse by the day. Disputes between kingdoms were constantly arising, so that even those of moderate wisdom or less could not fail to recognize this deterioration. And yet powerful officials ceased their plans to seize the ultimate power; indeed, those in power yielded to the criticisms of scholars from remote parts."[18] [He also said,] "The reason why [the empire] would lean but not topple, burst its confines but not catastrophically, was in all instances through the strength of men who were *ren* 仁 and noble."[19] It can be said that his words embodied wisdom. If rulers of later dynasties were to abide by these precepts and not change them, how is it not possible for these customs to continue to the present time? And yet Mengde [Cao Cao],[20] when he held control of Jizhou, rewarded and encouraged unconventional and unrestrained scholar-officials, as is seen repeatedly in his edicts, even to the point of seeking those with a reputation for debauchery and profanity whose actions might be sneered at—men without *ren* 仁 or *xiao* 孝 [filiality], who nonetheless had mastered the art of administering the kingdom and organizing the army. Thus, those who practiced trickery or deception were repeatedly promoted and evil actions flourished. Therefore, Dong Zhao, in his memorial during the Taihe reign period [227–232], had already said, "Young men of the time did not turn to scholarship as the foundation but looked rather at the forging of friendships as the matter of importance. The foremost scholars of the nation did not give filial and fraternal behavior, purity, and self-cultivation primacy but took hastening to curry favor with those in power and seeking profit to be primary."[21]

When it came to the Zhengshi reign period [240–248], there were some men, unruly in speech and behavior, who were given to displays of their wisdom and ability. These men disdained the writings of Zhou and Confucius while studying the teachings of Lao [Zi] and Zhuang [Zhou]. So customs and mores again underwent a change. Now, it can be seen that the policy of using an administration based on an understanding of the classics and the guarding of *jie* 節 and *yi* 義, as pursued by Guang Wu, Ming, and Zhang[22] for several generations, was not enough, since one man, in the shape of Mengde, was able to effect a change with the destruction and breakdown of customs. Rulers of later times, if they are going to establish a suitable moral climate and lay down laws and ethical standards utilizing good customs to influence men, cannot do otherwise than examine this.

Guang Wu, using his personal diligence and frugal living as a way of transforming officials and subordinates, expounded and discussed the meanings of the classics, often late into the night. On one occasion, a meritorious official, Deng Yu,[23] had thirteen sons and made each master one of the arts. If there is order within the inner apartments, this can be a model for the age. Further, relatives of the emperor, like Fan Zhong,[24] maintained the integrity of the family through three generations, with sons and grandsons devoting themselves unremittingly to *li* 禮 [ritual practices, propriety] and *jing* 敬 [reverence]. They were always like a noble family. For this reason, although in the Eastern Han the talents of men were unrestrained, they were inferior to those of the western capital [i.e., Western Han]. Nevertheless, the style of scholars and the domestic regulations did seem to exceed those of the former time.

In the last period of the Eastern Han, there was a decline in *jie* 節 and *yi* 義, with a rise of elegance and sophistication, and this began with Cai Yong.[25] His appointment by Dong Zhuo[26] was without integrity, and his expression of surprise and regret on learning of [Dong] Zhuo's death was ill-advised. If one examines his collected works, there is an excess of funeral inscriptions and eulogies. From this it can be inferred how he conducted himself in his daily affairs. Because his literary talents were rich and his friends numerous, men of later times gave him a most complimentary biography. Ah, alas! Scholars and noble men who live in the final stages of a dynasty must bear the reputation of the times. Those who would effect a change in the moral climate of the empire should examine Bojie's[27] conduct and be warned by it.

13.4 THE ZHENGSHI REIGN PERIOD (240–248)

At the death of Emperor Ming of Wei, Emperor Shao ascended the throne, and the title of the reign period was changed to Zhengshi, which lasted for nine years in all. In the tenth year the grand tutor, Sima Yi, killed the general in chief, Cao Shuang, and the great power of Wei was transferred.[28] The tripartite balance of power between the Three Kingdoms had, up to this point, been in existence for thirty years. At one time, unconventional scholars of high repute filled Luoyang. They set aside the classics and esteemed the works of Lao and Zhuang. They despised *li* 禮 [ritual practices, propriety] and *fa* 法 [laws, standards] and revered unrestrained freedom. If they saw their ruler in distress or danger, they acted like bystanders, and all worthy men took their lead from them. From this time on, there was dispute about following what was handed down by the ancestors.

The *Jin History* [*Jin Shu*] says Wang Dun, on seeing Wei Jie, addressed the aide Xie Kun, saying, "I never thought to hear again, at the end of Yongjia [307–312], the sounds of Zhengshi!"[29] The monk Zhi Dun became famous at that time through his 'pure talk' [*qing tan* 清談].[30] Everyone respected and honored him, taking him to have achieved great subtlety—enough to be compared to those of the Zhengshi period. In the *Song History* [*Song Shu*], it says that Yang Xuanbao had two sons on whom Tai Zu conferred names, calling one Xian and the other Can. To Xuanbao he said, "I wish to order your two sons to have styles left over from the bamboo grove of the Zhengshi [reign period]."[31] Wang Wei, in a letter to He Yan, said, "When you were young you were fond of *xuanfeng* 玄風. You are a man of deep refinement and clarity and in this you are like someone from the Zhengshi period."[32]

In the *History of the Southern Qi* it says that Yuan Can spoke to the emperor, saying, "I see that Zhang Xu has the customs handed down from the Zhengshi period."[33] The *Southern History* records that He Shangzhi said to Wang Qiu, "The customs of the Zhengshi period are still preserved."[34] This shows that men of later times desired to be like this. However, in the "Records of the Writings of Confucian Scholars" in the *Jin History* [*Jin Shu*], the preface states, "To set aside the established classics of Queli and practice the unorthodox theories of the Zhengshi period indicates the prevalent customs in relation to *li* 禮 and *fa* 法 and enables one to see that unrestrained indulgence and boastful talk were taken to be pure and lofty."[35] Although at that time scholars often had empty reputations, nevertheless there were those who did not lose sight of true scholarship. Thus, through the clear explanations of the Six Classics, Zheng [Xuan] and Wang [Su] epitomized the late Han period,[36] while in their discourses on Lao [Zi] and Zhuang [Zhou], Wang [Bi] and He [Yan] were identified with the start of the Jin period.[37] When it comes to the collapse of the nation above, the ruination of teaching below, the inroads made by barbarians, and the constant changing of rulers and officials, if this is not the fault of those worthies who sit beneath the trees [the Seven Worthies of the Bamboo Grove], then whose fault is it?

There is loss of the kingdom and there is loss of [the moral basis] of the world. How may these two things be distinguished? It is said that a change in the family name of the emperor and in the reign period constitutes loss of the kingdom. But when *ren* 仁 [loving-kindness, benevolence, humanity] and *yi* 義 [right action, righteousness, duty] are entirely obstructed, it comes to a point where beasts are led on to devour men and men to devour one another.[38] It is this that is referred to as loss of the moral basis of the world. How can the "pure talk" of the men of the Wei and Jin [periods] be taken as responsible for the loss of the moral basis of the world? This is what Mencius was referring to when he said that the words of Yang [Zhu] and Mo [Di] reached a point where they caused the empire "not to acknowledge ruler or father" and to enter the state of "birds and beasts."[39]

In former times, Ji Shao's father, [Ji] Kang, was put to death by King Wen of Jin.[40] When it came to the time of Emperor Wu's change of the mandate, Shan Tao recommended him for an official position. Shao was at that time living privately and in isolation and wished to refuse and not go. Tao spoke to him, saying, "On your behalf I have been contemplating the matter for some time. Through heaven and earth and the four seasons, there is still the ebb and flow of fortune. How much more is this so in the affairs of men."[41] At one time these were taken to be famous words and were on everyone's lips. But this was a failure to recognize the harm they did to *yi* 義 and their damage to *jiao* 教 [teaching, education], until the stage was reached of leading the world not to acknowledge fathers. Now, in the case of Shao of Jin, this was not his proper ruler, so that he not only forgot his father but also served an improper ruler. Thus for thirty or so years before his death, he had already been a man without a father for a considerable period. How can his death at Dangyin atone for his crime?[42] Moreover, when he first took up his official position, how could he have been aware of the inevitability of the affair of the imperial carriage? And yet it was possible through this to establish his reputation for loyalty, which lasted beyond his own time.

From the Zhengshi period on, great *yi* 義 [right action, righteousness, duty] became obscured everywhere in the empire. With people like Shan Tao, heterodox theories were predominant and subsequently caused the worthiness of Ji Shao to oppose what was not right in the world without thinking of the consequences. Heterodox and orthodox doctrines cannot be allowed to coexist. If you say that Shao was loyal, then you must say that Wang Pou[43] was not loyal—this would subsequently be permissible. Is it any wonder that people of this sort led one another to serve as officials under Liu Cong and Shi Le,[44] and when they saw their former ruler reduced to blue garments and serving wine, their hearts were unmoved by this? For this reason, it is necessary to know how to protect all under heaven before it is possible to know how to protect the state. Protecting the state is something that is planned by the ruler, ministers, and high officials. Protecting all under heaven is the responsibility of every man, even the meanest.

13.6 DISINTERESTED ("PURE") CRITICISM (*QING YI* 清議)

How the wise kings of ancient times rectified the "hundred princes" was to have already in place a system of official punishments and admonish those holding official positions while also establishing supervisors in the neighborhoods and setting up township schools, preserving the practice of disinterested [pure] criticism in subprefectures and villages in order to add to the limited effect of penalties and punishments. "They were moved to the outskirts of the city" is recorded in the *Li Ji*: "Mark off the boundaries of their hamlets" is what is designated in the "Bi Ming."[45] Since the two Hans, this system has been followed. In recommendations from the townships and selection from the villages, there must first be scrutiny of the person's life. If there is one flaw coming out in "pure [disinterested] criticism," "throughout their lives they will be excluded from distinction."[46] The noble man has an inherent fear of the law; the lesser man is accustomed to avoiding shame. If the teaching is successful among those below and those above are not strict, discussion is resolved in the townships and the people do not rebel.

When it came down to the Wei and Jin periods, the setting up of the Nine Ranks was of central importance; even though there were many failings, the traditional concept was never lost. "In general, people were reprimanded if they were subject to 'pure [disinterested] criticism' and were cast aside for the rest of their lives."[47] It was the same with prohibitions and restraints. When it came to Song Wu Di's usurpation of the throne [420], there was a proclamation as follows: "If there are the transgressions revealed by township discussions and disinterested criticism, taking bribes, vile conduct, debauchery, and theft will be washed away and cleansed, and there will be a new beginning."[48] From this time on, everything encountered was very kind and gracious writing, and there was this kind of language as well.[49] When the "Xiao Ya" were done away with, the central states declined, customs and mores decayed, and rebellion arose. Nevertheless, if the impurities of public [township] discussion reached the point of causing trouble, there was an imperial edict to clear the insult to someone's name. Did the true *dao* [Way] of the Three Dynasties not still exist among the people and, fearing people's criticism, occur only in the days when customs were changing? I have heard from what has come down that because there was such a man [as Shun], he was advanced instead of the three evil sons, who were cast aside for want of ability. Even with decisions of the two emperors [Yao and Shun], the opinions of grass and reed cutters were invariably sought. This being so, honoring the first day of the lunar month is a way of assisting the Autumn Office, and promoting public [township] criticism can facilitate state affairs. Therefore, above all, local government should listen to comments from all quarters—this is something the kingly way of government cannot do without.

When Chen Shou was grieving for his father, he became ill and sent a young maidservant for some medicines. The medicine seller went to see him. The district community censored and disparaged him, and he spent many years without progressing to an official position.[50] Ruan Jian, when he was grieving for his father, went out walking and encountered a heavy snowfall. It was bitterly cold. Subsequently, he reached the home of the district magistrate of Lingyi. The magistrate had laid out some millet and meat broth for other guests. Jian ate this. As a result, he incurred public [pure] criticism and was rejected, remaining without a position for almost thirty years.[51] Wen Qiao was persuaded by Liu Sikong [Liu Kun] to take office. His mother, Lady Cui, tried strongly to prevent him from going. Qiao tore his robe in breaking free of her grasp and left. When finally he was venerated and honored, the people of his native district still did not accept him. Every time he was being ennobled, a proclamation had to be issued.[52] Xie Huilian gave primary importance to his friendship with the Kuaiji subofficial functionary Du Deling. While Xie was grieving for his father, he sent Du ten or so poems of the five-characters-per-line type, and this writing was distributed to the world. Xie was then sent away and did not receive an honorable position.[53] Zhang Shuai left his official position because of grief over his father. His father had engaged several tens of singing girls; one of them was not only a good singer but was beautiful as well. Gu Wanzhi, a court gentleman with the Ministry of Rites, sought to acquire her as a wife with gifts, but the singing girl was unwilling. Subsequently, she left the house and became a nun. On one occasion, when she joined a religious gathering at Shuai's house, Wanzhi wrote an anonymous letter accusing the nun and Shuai of debauchery. The Censorate included the matter in a report to the emperor. Gao Zu, who valued Shuai's ability, set the report aside. Nevertheless, it still became part of the discussion of the time. After the period of mourning was over, it was a long time before he got an official position.[54] In the promotion and demotion of officials, rank is basically given or taken away according to public opinion. Does this not still come close to the ancient custom?

In places where the world's customs and mores are very degenerate but public criticism is still preserved, it may be enough for it to continue for a little while. But when public criticism is lost, warfare follows. In the fifteenth year of the Hongwu reign period [1382], in the eighth month on *yiyou*, there was the following discussion at the Ministry of Rites: "In general, the ten evils, debauchery, robbery, fraud and deception, and offending against the well-known principles of what is right, there is damage to customs and mores, and when opposition to bribes reaches a point where it is fruitless, offenders' names are written in the Shenming pavilion[55] to display a warning and admonition. If anyone damaged the pavilion and erased the surname and name, a surveillance commissioner from the Department of Investigating Censors would examine the matter according to the time, and the offender would be charged with a crime according to the law. This system was acceptable."[56] In the eighteenth year of the Hongwu reign period [1385], in the fourth month on *xinchou*, [this is recorded], "There was a decree that the Bureau of Punishments should record all inner and outer administrative associates who transgressed the law or committed a crime, and this should be written in the Mingbai pavilion."[57] What was handed down from a previous age was the idea of local criticism. However, people of a later time saw this as an empty name in respect of customs and regulations and took it to be a matter of the name of the punishment. They didn't see the point of enlightening people by public opinion, as if it were irrelevant. No wonder things have gone from bad to worse in the country!

13.7 THE TEACHING OF MING (*MING JIAO* 名教)

Comment: The term *ming jiao* can be taken as referring to the fundamental elements of Confucian teaching, one of which is the correct correspondence between name and actuality, as in the *Lunyu* XIII.3. Brook Ziporyn, in contrasting Daoist *xuanxue* 玄學 (abstruse learning) with *ming jiao* 名教, writes, "Spontaneity was commonly associated with the teachings of the *Laozi* and *Zhuangzi*, while morality, 'the teaching of names' (i.e., specifically defined hierarchical social roles and the obligations that go with them) concerned with the ordering of society, was associated with Ruism, which had been the dominant ideology throughout most of the Han" (*The Penumbra Unbound* [New York: SUNY Press, 2003], 23).

Sima Qian, writing in the "Biographies of the Traders" [Huozhi Zhuan] in the *Historical Records* [*Shiji*], said, "Scholar-officials, whether in palace chambers and audience halls or in mountains and caves, all come back to wealth and substance. When we come to those below, scribes and officers use clever phrases to tamper with the laws, carve fake seals and create false documents, regardless of what maiming punishments might await them, because they are inundated by bribes and gifts."[58]

And Zhong Changao, in his *Close Examination of Nature*, wrote, "Of the three hundred naked animals [i.e., those without fur, feathers, or scales], men are the most vile. Claws, teeth, skin, and fur are not enough to protect them. They rely only on falsehood and deception, repeatedly snapping at and biting one another. At a lower level, when we come to lesser officers and young servants, all they do is rob and plunder."[59] If we look at this from the present-day viewpoint, there is no official who doesn't accept bribes, and everybody wants to be an official. There is no prefect who doesn't rob and plunder, and everybody wants to be a young servant. From the time a bound-haired scholar begins his studies, what encourages him are only what may be called "a thousand measures of grain" and "a house full of gold." As soon as a man gains an official position, he immediately seeks out what he most desires. Rulers and ministers, superiors and inferiors, from top to bottom cherish profit in their exchanges, so this lack of restraint can no longer be controlled. In later times, what methods are appropriate for those who govern to adhere to?

I say that only *ming* 名 can overcome this. Whenever *ming* exists and those above use it, then loyalty, trust, honesty, and purity are manifest throughout the world. Whenever *ming* is done away with and those above reject it, then presumption, extravagance, avarice, and acquisitiveness will cast off restraint in households. Even if there are one or two false and dissembling men, this is still better than the widespread and wanton pursuit of profit. The *Southern History* has this to say: "In Han times scholar-officials regarded cultivation of the self as fundamental, therefore loyalty and filial conduct were established customs. As for those who boarded carriages and wore ceremonial caps [i.e., officials], nothing that deviated from this occurred. However, from Jin and Song times on, customs decayed and *yi* 義 [right action, righteousness, a sense of duty] was lacking."[60] Therefore, the terms the ancients used—*ming jiao* 名教 [the teaching of names], *ming jie* 名節 [the regulation of names], and *gong ming* 功名 [living up to the name]—even if they can't make the people of the world regard *yi* 義 as "profitable" can still make them regard *ming* 名 as "profitable and beneficial." Although there may not be the customs of a pure king, these concepts can still save the world's customs from defilement.

In the *Old Tang History*, Xue Qianguang, who was rectifier of omissions on the left, sent up a memorial, saying,

> I humbly venture to observe that the ancients, in selecting scholar-officials, were truly different from those of the present time. First, they looked at the origins of a candidate's correspondence of word and deed [name and actuality], examined his standing in township and district, whether he used his respect for *li* 禮 [propriety, proper conduct] and *rang* 讓 [complaisance] to restrain himself, whether he used his displays of *jie* 節 [purity, moderation] and *yi* 義 to show sincerity, and whether he regarded *dun* 敦 [honesty] and *pu* 樸 [simplicity] as being of first importance, while ability in minor matters was regarded as being of secondary importance. Therefore, there was respect for a spirit of encouragement and yielding, while scholars eschewed actions that were unimportant and trivial. Those who aspired to official positions had to cultivate virtue and constantly maintain their personal integrity, practicing the rule of "difficult to advance, easy to retire." When public evaluation had already established their merits or demerits, it was then difficult for the head of a prefecture to falsify the rights and wrongs. Therefore, in assessing the worthiness or foolishness of a candidate, honor or shame might reflect on the head of the prefecture, while the disclosure of improper behavior would reflect a lack of shame in the men of a township. This was the reason for Li Ling's submission to allegiance and the disgrace to Longxi, and for Ganmu's retiring and the glory to Xihe.[61] Thus, if *ming* 名 triumphs over *li* 利 [profit, benefit], the way of the lesser man disappears. But if *li* 利 triumphs over *ming* 名, then an atmosphere of avarice and cruelty prevails.

From the period of the Seven Kingdoms, although there were various political theories and the Han dynasty sought men of talent, there was still examination of a wide range of conduct. This is why scholar-officials who, through their proper conduct and integrity were diligent in their virtue and cultivated in themselves, were advanced to high positions in their local areas and subsequently assumed government positions. Nowadays, in recommending men, there is a perversion of what is right. In the townships, decisions are based on the writings of lesser men and the cultivation of conduct is not discussed at any length. On the posting of examination ranks, there is noisy contention in subprefecture and prefecture, while requesting favor doesn't go beyond bowing and prostrating oneself. As soon as some clear regulation is issued, candidates seek to praise it, gathering hastily at the gates of the prefectural office and scurrying to and from the mansions of nobles. In sending up statements and presenting poetry, they hope only to gain the benefits of fine phrases. "Rubbing smooth the whole body from crown to heel,"[62] they hope to receive the kindness of guidance and support. Therefore, those commonly called *juren* [recommendees] could all be called "those seeking recommendation" and those who do the seeking themselves seek such an appellation. When the pursuit of self-interest is paramount, then the public interest will be obstructed. When the coveting of government office manifests itself, then the spirit of honesty and purity is diminished. This is how we know that the prefectural decrees, although lofty, were different from Shudu's [Huang Xian's] diligence and earnest complaisance, and that the palace office, although honorable, did not match the resignation of Qin Jia when he was distressed.[63] Although they were not able to suppress the self and promote further worthiness, they were also not willing to await the "three decrees." Therefore, in the selection of officials to fill vacancies, there was a clamor at the doors of the Board of Rites. The tribute from the subprefectures [i.e., the candidates], when paying their respects, struggled and contended on the steps of the palace. Slanderous talk and disordered alliances gradually became established practice.

Those who contend for glory must have a heart that is opposed to profit. Those who are humble and compliant are not concerned with the accumulation of wealth. If the person himself is not lofty

> and wise, how can he avoid being influenced? If he dwells among ordinary people, he is influenced by their practices and customs. If weight is given to diligent and substantial scholars, then those who seek public office must venerate virtue in cultivating their reputations. If the door is open to mutual contention, then those seeking office will do so through flattery and party affiliations, and in the forming of such affiliations, the common people will suffer. However, if there is a cultivation of *ming* 名, the ordinary people will be grateful for the blessing. Can the gradual change of customs come about in any other way?[64]

Ah indeed! Should these words not be considered particularly apposite in the light of the malpractices of the present day?

The Han people established good order through *ming* 名 [being of good repute], therefore men of talent waxed. At the present time, good order is imposed through laws, therefore men of talent wane. During Song times, Fan Wenzheng, in a letter to Yan Yuanxian, said, "If the teaching of *ming* [*ming jiao* 名教] is not held in high esteem, then those who are rulers could say that Yao and Shun are not adequate as exemplars, while Jie and Zhou are not enough to fear. Those who are officials could say the Eight Good Ones are not sufficient to venerate, while the Four Wicked Ones are not sufficient to regards as shameful. Within the empire, will excellent men again be found? If men no longer hold *ming* 名 precious, the authority of the sages will be dissipated."[65]

At the present time, among the means of changing and transforming men's minds and of reforming and purifying evil customs, nothing is more pressing than these two matters—encouragement of learning and exhorting people to be pure. If there are, among the scholars of the empire, those who are able to respect trustworthiness and love learning and can continue to do so into old age without growing weary, they will be eminently able to advance correctness and the possession of the *dao* [Way]. And if officials ranked by the Hanlin Academy go out and take office complying with their rank, the people will all recognize the inclination toward learning, and there will be no contention about the topics of study. All the officials will be able and honest, will cherish the people, and will resign from office only through old age, according to propriety [*li* 禮]. Families that do not have savings will have five or ten *qing* of land bestowed on them so sons and grandsons can have an occupation and be exempt from the burdens of taxation and compulsory service. Then people will all know self-control and not covet goods and gifts [bribes]. Can we await Zichuan's [Gongsun Hong's] twice being sent away and then accept a scholar who tends pigs or Youmeng's [Sunshu Ao's] statement that first recorded the sincerity of one who carried firewood?[66] And Fufeng's son had specially bestowed on him yellow gold, while Zhuojun's worthiness [was such that] he often bestowed a gift of sheep or wine.[67] As a result, those scholars of high repute living in retirement made manifest their virtue to all officials. At that time, those who revered the glory of seeking out the ancient ways looked up to the richness of this purity of abnegation throughout their lives. Is this not better than exhorting others to aim for examination success, rank. and emolument, causing them to pursue advancement and become greedy for profit? If order is to be achieved by *ming* 名, then a start must be made along this path.

In the Yuanshi reign period of Emperor Ping of Han [1–5], there was an imperial proclamation that said,

> Since the rise of the Han and the establishment of ministers and assistants, in the frugality of personal conduct, the disregarding of wealth, and the importance placed on *yi* 義 [right action, righteousness, duty], there has never been anyone to equal Gongsun Hong. When he occupied the position of prime minister and feudal lord, he used coarse cloth for his clothing and ate unpolished rice for his food. He donated his official salary to his friends and guests, leaving nothing remaining. This can be said to have effected a lessening of regulations and have led his inferiors toward sincere customs. There was a distinction between those who were rich and substantial within and those who were falsely adorned and sought empty praise without. . . . The title of Marquis of Guannei [*guannei hou*] and a fiefdom of three hundred households were bestowed on Hong's later descendants, sons and grandsons, who were legitimate heirs.[68]

In the *Wei Annals* [*Wei Zhi*] for the sixth year of the Jiaping reign period [254], it is recorded that the court, reflecting on scholars who were pure and restrained, proclaimed the bestowal on the families of the former minister of works, Xu Mao, the general for subjugating the east, Hu Zhi, and the military governor, Tian Yu, two thousand *hu* of grain and thirty bolts of silk. This was made known throughout the empire.[69] In the fourth year of the Yanchang reign period of Emperor Xuan Wu of the Northern Wei [516], there was a proclamation that said, "The former retired scholar Li Mi, who constantly refused to be summoned to court and steadfastly guarded his compliance and simplicity, as well as the principle of scholarship and retirement, can especially be considered a man of excellence. He can be compared to Hui and Kang of past times, and to Xuanyan in more recent times, and was posthumously titled Zhenjing Chushi. Further, an insignia was attached to his dwelling proclaiming his great purity."[70] In the *Tang Liudian* [there is], "For his nurturing of morality among hills and gardens, his substantial reputation and manifest intelligence, despite not being a member of the official class, he was posthumously granted the title of teacher."[71] From what I have seen, during the Chongzhen reign period [1628–1644], the words of the provincial censor, Qi Biaojia, were used to confer on the recommendees Gui Zimu and Zhu Jiexuan the position of Hanlin Academy editorial assistant.[72]

In the [*New*] *Tang History* [there is], "Niu Sengru was a descendant of the Sui vice-director, Qizhang Gonghong. When he was a young orphan living in Xiadu, Fanxiang had fields to the extent of several *qing* bestowed upon him, which he relied on for a living."[73] Then it is known that the bequest of land extended from Sui times into the Tang period for two hundred years and was still preserved by descendants. By comparison, gifts of gold and silk or the conferring of official salaries would rapidly have changed into dust. During the present dynasty, in the Zhengtong reign period [1436–1449], lands in Wujin that were bestowed on the secretary of the Board of Rites, Hu Ying, have been preserved by his sons and grandsons to the present time.[74] In my humble view there is nothing as good as the bestowing of lands as a reward for honesty.

13.8 HONESTY AND A SENSE OF SHAME

In Feng Dao's[75] biography in the [*Xin*] *Wu Dai Shi*, the discussion says,

> *Li* 禮 [propriety, ritual practices], *yi* 義 [right action, righteousness, duty], *lian* 廉 [honesty], and *chi* 恥 [a sense of shame] are the four bonds of the state. If the four bonds are not made manifest, the

> state is then doomed to destruction.[76] How excellent were Guan Sheng's abilities in speaking. Propriety [*li*] and righteousness [*yi*] are the great rules for bringing good order to people; honesty [*lian*] and a sense of shame [*chi*] are the great regulators for establishing people. Now, if there is not honesty, there is nothing that will not be taken; if there is no sense of shame, there is nothing that will not be done. If people are like this, then misfortune, failure, disorder, and loss know no bounds. How much more will this apply if those who are great officials have nothing they will not take and nothing they will not do, for then how can the world be without disorder and the state not be lost?[77]

This being so, within these four bonds a sense of shame has particular importance. Thus the Master, in discussing scholars, said, "In conducting themselves they have a sense of shame."[78] Mencius said, "A man cannot be without a sense of shame. If a man feels shame at being without a sense of shame, he will not have any occasion to be ashamed."[79] And again, "A sense of shame in a man is a good thing. Those who display clever opportunism do not do so through a sense of shame."[80] The reason why this is so is that, if a man is not honest and goes so far as to rebel against propriety [*li*] and oppose righteousness [*yi*], the origins of such behavior can, in all cases, be traced to the absence of a sense of shame. If the official classes are without a sense of shame, this can be spoken of as the state's shame. If I look at things from the Three Dynasties on, the decline of society and the trivialization of the Way, the abandonment of propriety [*li*] and righteousness [*yi*] and the rejection of honesty [*lian*] and a sense of shame [*chi*] are not the work of one night and one day. Still "the leaves of pine and cypress are the last to fall in the winter of the year" and "the crowing of the cock is not stilled by wind and rain." Moreover, in these days of darkness, there was certainly never "a man who was sober."[81]

Recently I was studying the *Yanshi Jiaxun*, which has this to say: "There was a scholar at the Qi court who once said to me, 'I have a son, seventeen years old, who knows something about writing letters and memorials. I taught him the language of the Xianbei and to play the lute. This was with the hope that he might gain proficiency in both and, with these accomplishments, that he might serve dukes and nobles and all would favor and love him.' At the time, I bowed but did not reply. Strange, is it not, this man's teaching of his son! Even if, through these accomplishments, you yourself were to reach the level of minister, I, too, would not wish you to do so."[82] Ah, alas! Zhitui had no alternative but to serve in a disordered world. And like what has been said, there is still the meaning of the poet who wrote the "Xiao Yuan."[83] Are there those who, "eunuch-like, flatter their generation"?[84] How can they not be ashamed!

Luo Zhongsu said, "Transformation by education is the court's primary responsibility. Honesty and a sense of shame are the finest virtues of the scholar-official. Customs and mores are the great matters of the empire. If the court has transformation by education, then scholar-officials will have honesty and a sense of shame. If scholar-officials have honesty and a sense of shame, then the empire will have satisfactory customs and mores."[85]

In the way the ancients managed military matters, there was nothing that was not based on honesty and a sense of shame. The *Wuzi* says, "Whoever regulates the state and manages the army must teach through propriety [*li*] and encourage through righteousness [*yi*] to ensure there is a sense of shame. If men have a sense of shame, at the most this will be sufficient for offensive war, and at the least it will be sufficient for defense."[86] The *Weiliaozi* says, "A state must have the mores of compassion, filial piety, honesty, and a sense of shame—then there can be a transformation from death to life."[87] And yet Duke Tai, responding to King Wu, said that for leaders there are three kinds of overcoming. The first is through proper conduct [*li* 禮], the second is through strength, and the third is through a suppression of desires. Thus, *li* 禮 is how to manage the court and regulate the army.[88] The martial men in the "Rabbit Net" are all based on the civilizing influence of King Wen and his empress and consort.[89] How can there then be the leading astray of fuel gatherers, the stealing of oxen and horses, and the oppression of the ordinary people!

In the *History of the Later Han* [there is],

> Zhang Huan was the defender for pacifying the dependent states. The Qiang general was moved by Huan's kindness and virtue and made him a gift of twenty horses. The Xianling chieftain also made him a gift, of eight golden drumsticks. Huan received them all together and ordered a scribe to anoint the ground with

> wine before the assembled Qiang, saying, "I shall treat the horses like sheep and not put them in a stable. I shall treat the gold like corn and not let it enter my pocket," whereupon he returned all the gold and horses. The Qiang were, by nature, covetous, and yet they prized purity in officials. Previously there were eight defenders, who, in the main, loved wealth and goods, and this was what brought calamity and suffering. When it came to Huan, by his self-rectification and purity, he effected a great change in conduct.[90]

Ah, alas! From ancient times to now, in the failures of border affairs, is there anything that doesn't take its origin from covetousness and greed? In the affairs of Liaodong,[91] there is that which moves me.

In one of Du Zimei's [Du Fu's] poems there are the lines,

> How can it be that the Lianpo general,
> got the three armies to lie peacefully together?[92]

In one edition there is "Lianchi general." The poet's meaning does not necessarily extend to this. Nevertheless, I note that the *Old Tang History* says,

> Wang Bi was military commissioner for Wuling. Prior to this, the Tufan [Tibetans] decided to complete the Wulan bridge. Every time they came to the riverbank, they first stored up materials and timber, but everything was carried away and thrown into the flowing current by people the military commissioner sent, so in the end they were not able to complete the work. The Fan people knew that Bi was avaricious and without a plan, so they first gave him a substantial gift. Afterward, they doubled the number of workmen to complete the bridge and also built a wall to protect it. From this time on, there was no respite from the northern-based rebels, and right up to the present this has been a problem.[93]

It all stems from Bi's defilement by material possessions. Therefore, if someone who is avaricious is the leader, then the area beyond the Great Wall is vulnerable. Those who understand the meaning of this, as in the case of Ying's writing to Yan,[94] may perhaps act as guides in bringing good order to the kingdom!

13.28 WHAT OFFICIALS STUDY IN THEIR LATER YEARS

In their later years, many officials from the southern regions like to study Buddhism, whereas of those from among the northern regions, many like to study Daoism. When a man who has been an official throughout his life grows old and finds leisure, what he really should do is to develop virtue and cultivate scholarship to make up for the shortcomings of his earlier existence. And yet, if he knows he cannot achieve this, he may turn to heterodox doctrines. Although men who are interested primarily in bettering their own material circumstances may differ in their activities, nevertheless they are the same in having a mind that strives to gain benefit.

In Lü Dalin's biography in the *Song History* [it is written],[95]

> Fu Bi resigned from office and retired to his home to study Buddhism. Dalin wrote him a letter, saying, "In ancient times, the Three Dukes [*san gong*][96] did not have specific duties; only the virtuous could hold this office. Within, they discussed the *dao* [Way] at court; without, they supervised teaching in the countryside. Great men of ancient times who conducted themselves properly in office invariably intended to 'use this Way to teach the people'[97] and 'complete themselves by completing things.'[98] How can one, whether in office or retiring from office, whether in the prime of his life or in his declining years, change on account of circumstances? Nowadays, the great *dao* [Way] is no longer clear, and men hasten toward heterodox learning. Those who don't turn to Zhuang [Zhou] turn to Buddhism. They suspect that the sages did not achieve perfect goodness; they make light of *li* [propriety] and *yi* [right action] as being matters not worthy of their study. Personal relations are not clearly defined, and all creation is distressed and grieving. This is the time when mature and virtuous men of high standing, and with the feeling of compassion preserved in their hearts, should take manifesting the *dao* [Way] as their personal responsibility and vigorously restore degraded customs. As for moving semen and transforming the vital essence and devoting their attention to seeking a long life, these are matters that officials who have retired to seclusion and think only of what is good for themselves, especially love. How, then, can the world hope for anything from you?" Bi apologized to him.

That a man of high office and great virtue should receive such a rebuke from a young man is truly something rarely seen.

In the sixth year of the Kaiyuan reign period of the Tang emperor Xuan Zong [718], the Henan administrator, Zheng Xian, and the aide from Zhuyang district in Guozhou, Guo Xianzhou, placed their proffered verse in a box. The emperor responded thus: "I see that the unity of the principles expressed in your writings pays homage to the methods of Daoism. But when it comes to the matter of being useful for these times, there is no correspondence with the nation's circumstances. Each of you may follow what you love." Both were relieved of their positions and became Daoists.[99]

Section 14: There are twenty-three essays in this section devoted to what might broadly come under the heading of *li* 禮 (ritual practices, propriety, proper conduct in personal relationships). The first three essays (14.1–3) concern aspects of regal succession. There are then six essays (14.4–9) that deal with what might be termed retrospective veneration; two of these are directed primarily at the clarification of terminology (14.4 and 14.5). The next three essays focus on court practices: abdication (14.10), imperial conduct (14.11), and enfeoffment (14.12). Essay 14.13, "Wet Nurses," is largely about terminology, and 14.14 concerns the celebration of the emperor's birthday. The next eight essays pertain to matters of mourning, funerals, and sacrifices. Although much of the discussion is historical, in some instances there are recommendations regarding current practices. The final essay (14.23) examines the role of *nü wu* 女巫 ("sorceresses" or "witches").

14.20 THE TEN WISE ONES

Comment: The ten wise ones are Confucius's disciples. For the list of those concerned, see *Lunyu* XI.2(2); LCC 1.237 and Legge's note, 237–38.

Mencius said, "On another day, Zixia, Zizhang, and Ziyou, thinking that You Ruo was like the Sage, wished to serve him as they had served Confucius. They tried to force Zengzi to do so, too. Zengzi said, 'I cannot! Like something that has been washed in the waters of the Jiang and Han Rivers and bleached in the autumn sun, how immaculate he was. There is nothing to equal him.' "[100]

Master Huang [Huang Zhen] of Cixi[101] said,

> The disciples considered You Ruo's words, actions, and demeanor to be like those of Confucius and wished to serve him by means of the ceremonial practices they used to serve the Sage. But what was You Ruo's learning like? Zengzi thought that because there had never been anyone like Confucius since the beginning of human existence, they could not continue the same practices for You Ruo, and he stopped them. And yet he did not undervalue You Ruo. Although You Ruo was in no way comparable to Confucius, it can still be recognized in what the Master's disciples considered worthy of esteem at that time that no one reached the level of You Ruo. In the third year of the Xianchun reign period [1267], there was promotion of those to whom accessory sacrifices were made, giving them the same position as the "ten wise ones." The general opinion was certainly favorable toward You Ruo. However, the libationer wrote strongly disparaging You Ruo, claiming it was not appropriate to advance him, and that Zizhang should be advanced.[102] He did not know that in the *Lunyu* [*Analects*] Confucius never deeply approved of Zizhang.[103] According to the *Mencius*, Zizhang was someone who wished to serve You Ruo. Lu Xiangshan, whose natural abilities were high and bright, directly pointed to mind and sudden enlightenment and did not want men to follow events as topics for study.[104] Therefore, he criticized You Ruo's words on filial and fraternal piety as trivial and jumbled. What is to be done about someone who doesn't look into how You put his words into practice and yet attacks him a thousand years later?[105]

The discussions of the time in question were like this. In my humble opinion the first chapter of the *Lunyu* records the words of You Zi on three occasions, and he along with Zengzi is given the title "philosopher" [*zi*].[106] The disciples truly wished to continue the transmission of Confucius's teachings through these two philosophers. The records handed down state that on Confucius's death, Duke Ai presented the eulogy,[107] and at You Ruo's funeral, Duke Dao offered condolences.[108] From this it can be realized that he was someone the people of Lu regarded as important. The sacrifices to the "ten wise ones" may, then, be appropriately reformed.[109]

Section 15: There are twenty essays in this section, all but one of which continue the consideration of matters pertaining to funerals and burial. In many instances, Gu does no more than look at a particular practice historically; here, as in other matters, there is a clear preference for ancient practices as opposed to modern modifications. Broadly, the first eight essays (15.1–8) are to do with terms and practices; for example, the terminology relating to *ling* 陵, "burial mounds" (15.1). and the practice of cremation (15.8), whereas the next eleven (15.9–19) consider mainly personal conduct during and after a funeral. The final essay (15.20) examines what Gu terms "domestic regulations" at the Song court, stressing the need to clearly establish such regulations—something that was not done during the Song period.

15.3 EXTRAVAGANT BURIALS

Suo Lin's biography in the *Jin History* [states],

> In the Jianxing reign period [313–316], robbers opened the two Han tombs at Ba and Du, seizing much of the precious material within. The emperor questioned Lin, asking, "Why were there so many things in the Han tombs?" Lin replied, "When the Han emperors had been on the throne for one year, they built a tomb. The tax revenue of the empire was divided into three parts, one of which went to the ancestral temples, one to foreign embassies, and one to the emperor's tomb. Emperor Wu of Han enjoyed a long reign [140–87 B.C.E.]. When he died, the Mao tomb could not accommodate any more things, and all the trees at the tomb were already of a thickness to be encircled with the hands. The Red Eyebrows, who seized things from within the tomb, were not able to reduce the amount by half, and even now rotting silk is piled up and the pearl and jade is not exhausted. And these two tombs were frugal, so this might serve as a warning to a hundred generations."[110]

The "Xiao Wen Record" in the *Historical Records* [*Shiji*] says, "The building of the tomb at Ba was entirely with earthenware material and it was not decorated with gold, silver, copper, or tin."[111] And Liu Xiang, in a memorial on the Chang tomb, exhorted the emperor to consider Xiao

Wen's simple funeral and that this was enough to act as a model for later generations.[112] Nevertheless, if one examines Zhang Tang's biography, then [it can be seen that] at Emperor Wu's time there had already been robbers who had taken away the buried wealth of Xiao Wen's tomb at Yuan.[113] Indeed, from the various kingdoms of the Spring and Autumn period onward, with regard to the matter of extravagant burials, even if Xiao Wen provided a clear example in favor of frugality, elaborate burials were a custom that could not be entirely done away with. Thus, what is written in the historical chronicles is not necessarily a true record in all cases.

In the *Zuo Zhuan*, for the eighth month of the second year of Duke Cheng, [there is],

> Duke Wen of Song died and was the first [duke of Song] to have an elaborate burial, using mortar made of [burned] frogs for the walls of the grave and more than the usual number of [earthen] carriages and [straw] horses. For the first time men were interred with the corpse. The number of articles prepared for such an occasion was increased. The outer coffin was made with four pillars, and the inner coffin was decorated with colored patterns on all sides and above. The noble man will say, "Hua Yuan and Yue Ju did not act in this matter as ministers should. It is for ministers to control the anxieties and get rid of the errors of their ruler, striving to do this even at the risk of contention and death. Now, these two officers allowed their ruler to follow the path of error while he was alive, and when he died, they increased his extravagance. They abandoned their ruler to wickedness. How were these the proper actions of ministers!"[114]

In the "Moderation in Burials" [Jie Sang] chapter in the *Spring and Autumn Annals of Mr. Lü*, it is said,

> To examine and understand life is the essential duty of the sage; to examine and understand death is the apogee of being a sage. Those who understand life don't, in doing this, harm life but can be said to nourish it. Those who understand death don't, in doing this, harm death but can be said to make it tranquil. These are two matters only a sage can determine. In general, whatever is born between heaven

and earth must die; this is something that cannot be avoided. A filial son's reverence for his parents and compassionate parents' love for their son are both feelings of the greatest depth—this is human nature. That someone who is venerated and loved should die and be left in a ditch is something human feelings cannot endure. Therefore, there is a purpose in burying the dead. To bury is to conceal; this is what compassionate parents and filial sons are very careful about. Being careful is to use the mind and forethought of the living and, with the mind of the living, give forethought to the dead. In doing this there is nothing as good as not moving them and not exposing them. To achieve this aim of not moving and not exposing, there is nothing as good as not having anything from which benefit can be obtained. This is what is called giving importance to keeping enclosed ["doubly enclosing"].[115]

The ancients who were concealed in the vast wilderness and remote mountains found tranquility there, not because there was talk of pearls and jade or the nation's treasures but because there was no possibility of the burial not being concealed. If burial is too shallow, foxes will dig up the corpse; if burial is too deep, springwater will reach it. Thus, in all burials it is necessary to have a high mound above to avoid harm from foxes and dampness from the waters of springs. This, then, is good. And yet would it not be foolish to forget about the problems caused by evil people such as robbers and bandits? This could be compared to a blind musician's avoiding a pillar only to run into a stake. Foxes, springs, and the calamity of evil people such as robbers and bandits are the greatest of stakes. Compassionate parents and filial sons avoid them because they grasp the true objectives of burial. Having good inner and outer coffins is how to avoid ants and moles. In the great disorder that characterizes rulers of the present age, they have become increasingly extravagant in their burial preparations, but this is not because they are thinking about the situation when they are dead. It is because they are trying to outdo one another while living—extravagance is equated with glory and moderation with parsimony. Their intention is not to bring benefit to the dead; their concerns are about the censure or praise of the living. This is not the heart of the compassionate parent or the filial son.

The people, in their pursuit of profit, will risk the flight of arrows, will pass through naked blades, and will face death and destruction and yet still seek it. There were men, rustic and unheard of, who were able to endure the sufferings of their parents and their older and younger brothers in their pursuit of profit. Nowadays, these dangers and causes of shame no longer exist. If a person's profit is very substantial, then rich carriages, fine food, and beneficence extend to his sons and grandsons. If even a sage could not prevent this state of affairs, how much less could a nation in great disorder! The greater the state and the richer the family, the more extravagant the burial. The mouth of the corpse is filled with pearls, the body is covered with jadelike fish scales, there is an excess of items collected, money, valuables, musical instruments, tripods, and vases. There are carriages, horses, clothes, quilts, daggers, and swords too numerous to count. No implement that is of use in life does not accompany them. The walls of the outer coffin come together at the apex, and there are several layers in the inner and outer coffins.[116] Moreover, there is a piling up of stones and charcoal to encircle the outside. When evil people hear of this, they pass the information on to one another. Although those above may be stern and imposing and prohibit this as a felony, it still cannot be stopped. Further, the dead are dead for a long time and become increasingly distant from the living. As the living become increasingly distant, so their guarding becomes increasingly lax. As this happens, the buried materials remain there as they were, so the dead inevitably become less and less secure.[117]

In the "Peaceful Repose for the Dead" [An Si] chapter of the *Lü Shi Chunqiu* it is said,

The custom of the age in creating burial mounds is to make them as tall as a mountain and surround them with trees like a forest. Towers and courtyards are built to create a kind of mansion with a stairway for guests, as if it were a city or town. If you look at the structures at the time, it is possible to see the display of wealth, but after death this is no longer possible. Now, for those who are dead, ten thousand years is like an instant. The life of man at its longest doesn't exceed a hundred years, while the average life doesn't go beyond sixty years. To take "a hundred" or "sixty" in planning for what is without limit is to have feelings that certainly don't mesh with one another. To plan by considering death as being without limit is the proper approach. Suppose, then, there was a man who made a stone tablet with an inscription and placed it above the mound, and the inscription read that the things within included pearls, jade, things specially collected, valuable things, and precious instruments to a great number, it would be impossible for them not to be dug up. This digging up would certainly provide great wealth, so that, for generations, there would be rich chariots and fine food. Others would certainly laugh at this and consider it to be foolish in the extreme. This is exactly what the world's having extravagant burials is like.

From ancient times to the present, there has never been a state that did not perish. And in states that invariably perish, there have never been graves that were not dug up. From what the ears have heard and the eyes have seen, Qi, Jing, and Yan previously perished. Song and Zhongshan have already perished. Zhao, Wei, and Han have all perished. These were all old states. Going back before this, the number of lost states cannot be counted. For this reason, there are no great graves that have not been dug up. How is it not lamentable that the whole world still strives to make such graves? A ruler's recalcitrant people, a father's nonfilial sons, and an older brother's nonfratemal younger brothers are all to be driven out by those in districts and villages who cook in pots and pans. They dread the labor of plowing fields and gathering firewood, they are unwilling to attend to the affairs of men, and yet they strive for the pleasures of beautiful garments and fine food. Although their wisdom and skill are entirely expended in this, they don't have the means to achieve it. As a result, great bands of fellows take to remote mountains, wide marshes, forests, and overgrown lakes and rush at people, striking them down and seizing their goods. Also, when they see famous mounds and great graves and tombs, they seek to establish a suitable shelter nearby, from which they secretly plunder them. Day and night they don't rest but must obtain what is profitable and distribute it among themselves. So there are those who are loved and revered, and yet crafty and evil men, robbers, and bandits ultimately and inevitably bring shame and disgrace to them. This is something that is a great calamity for filial sons, loyal ministers, loving parents, and dear friends.

Yao was buried at Gulin and all around there were trees. Shun was buried at Ji marketplace, and there was no change in the functioning of the market. Yu was buried at Kuaiji, and there was no disturbance to the people. This was why former kings were frugal and moderate in their burial of the dead. It was not that they grudged the expense, nor that they were averse to the labor involved—they were showing consideration to the dead. What was anathema to former kings was only that those who died should be disgraced. If the graves were opened, this certainly meant disgrace, whereas if the graves were simple and frugal, without ostentation, they were not opened. Therefore the graves of the ancient sage-kings were necessarily simple, were necessarily in accord, were necessarily the same. What is the meaning of being in accord, and of being the same? It is that, if there is burial in the mountains and forests, [the grave] should be in accord with the mountains and forests. If there is burial in mounds or low-lying places, [the grave] should be in harmony with the mounds or low-lying place. These things are what are called "loving others." Now, there are many who love others but few who know how to love others. Thus, even before Song perished, the eastern burial mound [of Duke Wen—original note] was dug up. Even before Qi perished, Duke Zhuang's burial mound was dug up. If a state is peaceful and secure and yet such things still happen, how much more likely are they to happen after a hundred generations and the state has already perished! Therefore, filial sons, loyal ministers, compassionate parents, and dear friends cannot do otherwise than examine this. To love something and yet, perversely, to endanger it—what can be said of this?

When Jisun of Lu had a funeral, Confucius went to offer his condolences. Confucius entered the door and went to the left, taking up the position appropriate to guests. As the master of the funeral was receiving the precious jade, Confucius, who was some way away, hastened forward and, step-by-step, came up to him, saying, "Don't receive this precious jade; this is tantamount to leaving him exposed on the open plain." Being some way away and step-by-step are not in accord with *li* 禮 [ritual practice, propriety]. Nevertheless, they were a means of remedying the fault.[118]

4

RZL 16–17

THE EXAMINATION SYSTEM

Section 16: There are seventeen essays in this section on examinations, focusing particularly on specific forms of examination but also dealing with some other issues. The first four essays are on major categories: *mingjing*, "senior graduates" (16.1); *xiucai*, "cultivated talent" (16.2); *juren*, "recommendees" (Tang) or "provincial graduates" (Yuan-Qing) (16.3); and *jinshi*, "presented scholars" or "metropolitan graduates" (16.4). There are four essays on more particular forms of examination: *zhike* (16.6), *san chang* (16.10), *niti* (16.11), and *pan* (16.15). There are two essays about the classics: one on questions and themes in interpretation (16.9) and one on the style of writing on them (16.16). There are two essays on the style of writing in examinations (16.13 and 16.14). Of the five remaining essays, 16.5 and 16.7 are on issues of classification and ranking, 16.8 is on the term *fang* 方, 16.12 concerns the use of current affairs as an examination topic from the Song period on, and 16.17 is a general discussion on the decline in the study of history (an important issue for Gu) related to its lack of relevance to the examinations.

16.5 EXAMINATION CATEGORIES (THE CLASSIFICATION OF SCHOLARS)

Comment: In this short essay Gu gives brief consideration to the term *ke mu* 科目, which probably originates from the "Xuanju Zhi" of the *Xin Tang Shu* (44, 4.1159), from which the first paragraph of the present essay is taken. In the entry for the term in the *Zhongwen Da Zidian*, the present essay is quoted in extenso.

[Under] Tang regulations, the examination categories by which scholars were selected [for official positions] were *xiucai* [cultivated talent], *mingjing* [senior graduate], *jinshi* [presented scholar], *junshi* [refined scholar], *mingfa* [adept at laws], *mingzi* [adept at characters], *mingsuan* [adept at calculations], *yishi* [single history], *sanshi* [three histories], *kaiyuan li* [rites of the Kaiyuan era], *daoju* [recommended Daoist], and *tongzi* [juvenile].[1] The *mingjing* were differentiated into [the following subcategories]: *wujing* [five classics], *sanjing* [three classics], *erjing* [two classics], *xuejiu yijing* [single classic specialist], *sanli* [the three *Rites*], *sanzhuan* [three commentaries], *shike* [histories].[2] This was the ordinary selection of the annual recommendation. That which the emperor himself proclaimed was called *zhiju* [special recruitment].[3]

Categories like Yao Chong's "fluent and quick writing"[4] and Zhang Jiuling's "way like Yi and Lü"[5] that are seen in the *Histories* number in all more than fifty classifications.[6] Therefore, there was reference to a classification list. At the present time, there is only one class—*jinshi*—so there is a class but no list. To still speak of a classification list is wrong. Wang Weizhen[7] wished to go beyond the regular recruitment[8] and follow the systems of Han and Tang, establishing several classes as a means of gathering the empire's extraordinary scholars. What he did not realize was that the fault of placing undue emphasis on the *jinshi* had increasingly developed over two or three hundred years, so that, if the established system were not completely destroyed, even though there might be others with talents, there would be no way of advancing and employing them.

16.6 *ZHIKE* 制科 (SPECIAL EXAMINATIONS)

Comment: The term *zhike* refers to special examinations held irregularly by imperial decree and designed primarily to lure into the ranks of officialdom extraordinary scholars who, for one reason or another, did not follow the regular examination system. See Charles O. Hucker, *A Dictionary of Official Titles in Imperial China* (Stanford, Calif.: Stanford University Press, 1985), p. 159, no. 1011, and, in particular, Ichisada Miyazaki, *China's*

Examination Hell: The Civil Service Examinations of Imperial China, trans. Conrad Shirokauer (Tokyo: Weatherhill, 1976), 107–10, where he refers to Gu Yanwu in relation to the "[special] examination for great scholars" held in 1678 by decree of the Kangxi emperor.

Under Tang regulations what the emperor himself announced was called the *zhiju*.[9] This was how exceptional talent was treated. The *Tang Zhi* states,

> What is spoken of as *zhiju* came from long ago. From Han times on, the emperor frequently made a proclamation, personally framing those questions that he wished to ask. When the Tang arose, the world venerated Confucian scholars. Although in this period there may have been differences among rulers in terms of worthiness and foolishness, goodness and badness, nevertheless, in the intention to take pleasure in goodness and to seek worthiness, from the very beginning they had never been even slightly remiss. Therefore, from the capital outward to the prefectures and districts, the officials always recommended scholars according to the needs of the times. Moreover, the emperor himself made a proclamation to the four corners of the empire [calling for] virtuous, talented, and literate scholars. Those men living far off in seclusion who were unable to make themselves successful, down to those conversant with military matters, those with exceptional strength, and those with particular skill in the arts were all equally acceptable. The list of titles followed that which the ruler particularly desired at the time. These were arranged in established categories, such as those who were worthy and good, those who were upright in character, those who were "plain speaking and ready to admonish,"[10] those who could thoroughly penetrate the most ancient records, those who were fully conversant with culture, those whose military strategies were far-reaching and who were suitable for military leadership, and those who had a clear and detailed understanding of administrative methods and were able to manage men. It is these titles whose reputation stood highest. The emperor, in conducting the imperial progress and circuit, would make his sacrifices on

> Tai Shan and Liang Fu and then generally meet with them in his place of temporary residence. The propriety wherewith he received them was particularly noteworthy. Men of great talent, men who were fine speakers or otherwise extraordinary would also at times appear and would not fail to be accepted.[11]

At the beginning of the Song the system continued in existence during the Xiande reign period [960] of the [Later] Zhou, establishing three categories that were not limited to previous lists of talents [i.e., those qualified as examination candidates]. If they were seen to undertake the responsibilities of officials, whether they wore yellow clothing or dwelled in the country, they were also permitted to write verse at the emperor's behest. In the Jingde reign period [1004–1007], there was an increase to six categories, but after the Xining reign period [1068–1077], this was repeatedly discontinued and restored.[12] The Song people called it the *dake* [great classification].[13] Nowadays, the palace examination *jinshi* is also erroneously called the *zhike* [special examination].

Xu Du of the Song period,[14] in his *Notes Compiled in Seclusion*, wrote,

> This dynasty's special examinations [*zhike*] followed the Tang system at the beginning in that there were three categories in all: those who were wise and upright and were able to speak frankly and issue reprimands; those whose classical learning was deep and profound and could be used as models; and those who had a full and clear understanding of official and administrative matters and were well versed in educational matters. If it was appropriate, metropolitan and provincial officials could be employed on the basis of previously demonstrated capacities. It was also permissible for the various *zhou* [regions] and local officials to send those who wore yellow garments or dwelled in the countryside to the Board of Civil Office [to attempt] the emperor's examination, which was restricted to essays of at least three thousand words. In the Xianping reign period [998–1003], there was also a proclamation to the effect that the civil officials, both metropolitan and provincial, and those officials responsible for management of the regions and districts should go to the country districts and from there each promote one man who was worthy, good, and upright.

In the Jingde reign period [1004–1007], there was also a proclamation to the effect that the following six categories should be established: those who were worthy, good, and upright and were able to speak frankly and issue admonitions; those who had a broad understanding of the works of the Three Emperors and Five Rulers and were well versed in education; those who were talented, discerning, and altogether excellent and clear in respect of theory and practice; those whose valor was sufficient to pacify the border regions, who had a clear concept of military strategy, and could prepare schemes for decisive victory; those with far-reaching plans who could be sent to the border regions; and finally those who brought scrupulousness and perspicacity to the conduct of government and were successful in the administration of affairs.

In the seventh year of the Tiansheng reign period [1029], there was again an imperial command to the effect that officials of the court at the capital who did not involve themselves in the official business of the Department of State Affairs and in the academies and institutions, who were unable to oppose bribery and crime or personal gain, and who treated Heaven's principles with scant respect certainly ought to be investigated by the censor and made the subject of memorials to the throne. There were also some who proffered their biographies and begged to be presented before the six categories. Those who were first presented were examined on questions and themes to the extent of ten essays, [each] essay comprising five *dao*. They then waited until they were sent down to the two departments to be examined. Thus, if expression and reasoning were of a high standard, and if they were able to respond in this special examination, their names would be raised and heard of in memorials.

Further, for irregular officials, there were examinations under the six headings, and if they passed, they took the emperor's examination. The following three categories were also established: those who dwelled in seclusion in hills and gardens; those who dwelled lost in the country; and those with fine and varied talents of above-average ability. The recruitment was of men dwelling in the country and of recommended men who were not in the miscellaneous group of artisans and merchants and should be permitted to be recommended by functionaries, such as those of the fiscal commission and the district and township heads, or who put forward an application to ask for registration in their native places. The regions and districts would investigate those whose behavior was unorthodox but were without blemish or transgression. Such men were to be given questions and themes in which they were to practice to the extent of ten *juan*, each *juan* consisting of five *dao*. If there was some excellence of words and principles, then a senior official of the fiscal commission [was deputed] to investigate their reputations in townships and villages. In the ministry, there was selection of instructing officials, and this also had to be examined carefully. If there were literate and moral men who could be praised, their writings [or dispatches] were sent to the Board of Rites and a student administrative assistant deputed to examine them carefully. Those of excellence in expression and principle were all named and heard of in memorials. The remainder, like those who were worthy and excellent, straightforward and upright [*xian liang fang zhen*][15] and others of the six classes, were, during the Xining reign period [1068–1077], entirely brought to an end. Further, there was an order that the *jinshi* in the formal palace examination would cease [to be examined in] the three topics but would have examination questions in one *dao*. In the Jianyan reign period [1127–1130], there was a proclamation that the one category, *xian liang fang zhen*, be restored, although it should not include writing a verse at the emperor's behest.[16]

Gao Zong established the class of *boxue hongju*[17] with twelve topics in all: *zhi* [regulations], *gao* [granting of titles], *zhao* [imperial proclamations], *biao* [addresses to the emperor], *lubu* [manifestos], *xi* [summonses to war], *zhen* [remonstrances], *ming* [inscriptions], *ji* [recordings], *zan* [admonitions], *song* [commendations], and *xu* [prefaces]. Six topics were chosen from among these and divided into three examinations. Every examination embodied a system that was one part ancient and one part new. After the southern crossing, the right sort of men rose to prominence, and many even reached the level of cabinet minister or Hanlin graduate. Nowadays, in the second examination, three subjects [imperial proclamations, granting of titles, and addressing the emperor] in one *dao* roughly follow this example, but it is so simple and awkward that even people who know nothing about allusions or tones [poetry] can pass. This is the fault of putting too much emphasis on the first examination.

Section 17: This section, comprising twenty-one essays, begins with two essays on the restriction of numbers for two categories of students—*shengyuan* and *jinshi*. The third essay considers the special situation when none of the examinees reaches the standard necessary for ranking. Essays 17.4–17.16 deal with a miscellany of topics all broadly related to examinations, considered predominantly in a historical context. One of these essays ("Examination Masters and Disciples," 17.11) has a more general relevance than the others. In it, Gu focuses on the practice of having those students who pass a recruitment examination regard themselves as being disciples of the examiner and under an obligation to support him in what Hucker describes as "any partisan struggles and controversies" (p. 330, no. 3950). The consequent tendency toward clique formation is then discussed. The remaining five essays (17.17–17.21) move away somewhat from the immediate topic of examinations: 17.17 is on the time of a man's life when he is most fitted to serve in an official capacity; 17.18 concerns the importance of an understanding of the classics in the functioning of an official; 17.19 is about the establishment of a military school (*wuxue*) during the Song period; and 17.20 and 17.21 are about particular official positions.

17.13 THE SAME YEAR

Nowadays, people take the same recommendation [*tong ju*] to be the same year [*tong nian*]. "Xian Zong of the Tang [r. 806–820] questioned Li Jiang, asking, 'Do men of the same year necessarily have an emotional connection?' Li replied, 'Men of the same year are still men from the Nine Regions and the Four Seas. Perhaps they may have the same graduation rank, or, after passing the examination, may know each other, but how does this create an emotional bond?' "[18] Nevertheless, when Emperor Mu Zong [r. 821–824] wished to punish Huangfu Bo, the grand councilors Linghu Chu and Xiao Mian, who were *jinshi* of the same year, protected him.[19]

It would seem the Han already had this sort of thing. Thus, the biography of Li Gu in the *History of the Later Han*, states, "There were graduates of the same year who committed an offense in Ji."[20] The *Fengsu Tong* states, "In Nanyang a fifth-generation gentleman became governor of Guanghan. He was a graduate of the same year as the aide to the Ministry of Education, Duan Liaoshu." It also states, "He was of the same year as the governor of Donglai, Cai Boqi." It also states, "The Xiao director, Wu Bin, and the aide Han Yan were of the same year."[21] In the Wei Wu Di record of the *History of the Three Kingdoms*, it is stated, "The Duke and Han Sui were *xiaolian* ["filial and incorrupt"—a recommendation category] of the same year."[22] In Han times, on the tablet of the Dunhuang aide, Wu Ban, it was stated, "The scribe Hui, from Gaoyang, between Jinxiang and the Yangzi, recalled the 'filial and incorrupt' officials from former times."[23] On Liu Min's tablet it is stated, "The district magistrate of the same year made Qian a tributary state of the Zhaobai Duke."[24] In Tao Kan's biography in the *History of the Jin* [*Jin Shu*], there is the statement, "Kan and Chen Min were from the same prefecture and were also recommended officials of the same year."[25] This saying of "same year" [*tong sui*] is the same as the present-day "same year" [*tong nian*]. The rise of the bond of private favors between individuals and the decline of public right action [*yi*] are not the result of a single generation.

5

RZL 18–21

LITERATURE AND PHILOSOPHY

Section 18: There are twenty-three essays in this section dealing with a range of literary, philosophical, and examination matters. Six reasonably distinct subgroups can be recognized, as follows:

1. Five essays on the thirteen classics and the dynastic histories—writing that Gu sees as the foundation of a scholar's education: one is about government-organized repositories of books (18.1), two are about the compilation of and commentaries on the classics (18.2 and 18.10), one is about a particular edition of the dynastic histories (18.3), and one is about Zhao Can's work on the Five Classics (18.4).
2. Four essays on textual matters: one on errors in characters (18.5), one on plagiarism (18.20), and two on comparison and revision of ancient texts (18.21 and 18.22).
3. Six essays on specific works or authors: 18.6, 18.11, 18.17–19, and 18.23, which include essays on two Ming scholars, Wang Shouren and his work *Zhu Xi Wannian Dinglun* (18.17) and Li Zhi (18.18). The final essay (18.23) is on the *Yi Lin*.
4. Three essays on particular (and unrelated) official practices: one on "secret memorials" and their contribution to Veritable Records (18.7); one on *tie huang* 貼黃, or summarizing statements to memorials (18.8); and one on the recording of notes on business conducted with the emperor (18.9).

5. Three essays pertaining to examination matters: one on the literary basis of examinations considered in a historical context (18.14), one on the use of Daoist writings in the examinations (18.15), and one on prohibitory regulations directed against material not considered suitable for examination candidates (18.16).
6. Two essays on philosophical matters: one on the historical development of the study of Daoism and Buddhism as parallel streams of philosophical thought coursing alongside Confucianism (18.12) and one on the "learning of mind and heart," or neo-Confucianism (18.13). This includes an important statement of his own philosophical position.

18.12 THE INNER CANON (*NEI DIAN* 內典)

The statements that the sages of ancient times used in teaching people were as follows: their conduct should be filial and fraternal, loyal and trustworthy; their duties should be sprinkling and sweeping, answering and responding, and advancing and withdrawing; their reading should be of the *Odes*, the *Documents*, the *Rites* [*San Li*], the *Changes*, and the *Spring and Autumn Annals*; their use of themselves should lie in taking up office, retiring from office, and social intercourse; their service to the world should lie in carrying out official orders, influencing others by teaching, and administering penalties and punishments. Although "a harmonious conformity [to virtue] is realized within and the blossoming display of it is conspicuous without,"[1] there is also the division between theory and practice [substance and function] that intersects with the theory of "not using the heart within." This began from the study of Lao and Zhuang as practiced in the Warring States period, and there was the "beyond *yi* [right action, righteousness, justice]" of Gao Zi, as well as the "beyond the world, beyond things, and beyond life" of Zhuang Zi. From this, lofty and intelligent scholars rejected and slighted the *Odes* and *Documents*, taking them to be the dregs of what former kings used to bring good order to the world. Buddhism later entered China, and the theories they spoke of about peace, tranquility, and compassion were of the sort to move the affections and inclinations of the men of the times, and the various noble men of the Six Dynasties followed and embraced it. Taking the theory of quiet, tranquil, and free of delusion and extending this to the limit, they come to the perfection of no life and no death, and then entering Nirvana. This, then, is Yang Zhu's egotism. Taking the theory of being kind, merciful, and benefiting things and extending this to the limit, they come to the perfection of saving all sentient beings and releasing them from the sea of suffering. This, then, is Mo Di's universal love. What the world says is that if there is not a return to Yang, then there is a return to Mo, and Buddhism combines the two. The transmission was gradual, and later students of this subsequently referred to their books as the "Inner Canon" (Nei Dian).[2] Going on from the purport of their established words, will they not come to, "I am a Buddhist within but outwardly a Confucian"? Internally a Buddhist and externally a Confucian—did this not come from the statements of the followers of Sengzhao,[3] so how could men who were accomplished scholars also speak about it?[4]

The *Huangshi Richao*[5] states,

> The collected notes on the *Lunyu Zengzi Sansheng Zhang* record Yin Shi as saying, "Zengzi maintained moderation, therefore in acting one must seek it in the self." The meaning of the phrase is already sufficient. They also record Xie Shi as saying, "The studies of the various schools all came forth from the Sage, and as they became increasingly distant from him, they also increasingly lost their truth. Only Zengzi's studies emphasize using the mind on what is within and are therefore transmitted without being corrupted." Now, the mind is what collects together the many principles and responds to the ten thousand matters. One who corrects his mind, corrects desires and acts to bring good order to the state and peace to the world. Confucius's disciples never had the theory of exclusively using the mind that is within. Using the mind that is within is the theory of the Chan Buddhists of the present age. Lu Shi of Xiangshan responded by saying that Zengzi's studies affirm what is within coming forth. The various schools affirm what is without entering and going out. Now, what is transmitted to the world are all the studies of the external entering and are not Master Kong's truth. Subsequently, outside the *Lunyu*, he himself said he attained the teaching of nontransmission, and in general everything had its source in the theories of Xie Shi.[6]

Subsequently there was Zhu Xi, and he appropriately did away with this section in his "Collected Notes."

Chu Shaosun revised the "Huaji Zhuan" [of the *Shiji*] using biographical records and various opinions as "*wai jia*" [outer schools]; in this he took the Six Classics to be "inner."[7] Confucians of the Eastern Han then took the Seven Appendixes to be "inner studies" and the Six Classics to be "outer studies."[8] Raising the writings of the books of prophecy and omens was the nature of one return and the heavenly *dao* 道 [Way] and could not be attained and heard.[9] And now, after a hundred generations, all are obviously aware that this is not so. What are nowadays referred to as "inner studies" are no longer works of prophecy but have changed to be Buddhist books.

18.13 THE LEARNING OF MIND AND HEART (*XIN XUE* 心學)

Comment: This is, perhaps, Gu Yanwu's most detailed statement of his opposition to Song neo-Confucianism. Although in the title I have followed de Bary's rendering of the term *xin xue* (i.e., as "mind-and-heart"), in the essay itself I have abbreviated this to "mind" only. De Bary offers a detailed analysis of the term and discusses Gu Yanwu's essay (Wm. Theodore de Bary, *Neo-Confucian Orthodoxy and the Learning of the Mind-and-Heart* [New York: Columbia University Press, 1981], sp. pp. 168–75). The final paragraph is taken from the *Yuanshaoben Rizhi Lu* and does not appear in the Huang Rucheng edition.

The *Huangshi Richao*[10] offers an explanation of the statement in the *Documents* that reads, "The mind of man [*ren xin*] is wavering; the mind of the Way [*dao xin*] is subtle. Be discriminating, be undivided, and firmly hold fast to the center." One section says,

> This section originally recorded the words of Yao in his decree to Shun, who extended this through his decree to Yu with the addition of further detail. Yao, in his decree to Shun, said, "Firmly hold fast to the center." Now, Shun added the words "wavering, subtle, discriminating, and undivided" to come before "firmly hold fast

to the center" as words that would cause him to examine carefully and be able to grasp the center. They were his words of instruction. They all gave primary importance to Yao's statement, "Hold fast to the center" and developed it. Yao, in his decree to Shun, said, "If there is distress and want within the Four Seas, the position of emperor will come to a permanent end." Now, Shun added [the passage from] "do not listen to unsubstantiated words" up to "respectfully cultivate any virtues that are desired in you," this to come before "the heavenly revenue will come to a permanent end." These were also a means of urging caution, so causing him to avoid "distress and want" and "coming to a permanent end." These were words of warning. They all gave primary importance to Yao's expression "permanent end" and developed it.[11]

The counsel to "hold fast to the center" was one of positive words; the warning of a "permanent end" was one of negative words. That is to say, Shun took all instructions and warnings that he formerly received from Yao, joined them together with his daily endeavors, and included them in his decree to Yu so the latter would know how to "hold fast to the center" and not come to a "permanent end," and that is all. How could it have been for the sake of discussing mind [that Shun] set out his instructions and warnings! The present generation delights in talking of the study of mind, but this is to set aside the basic meaning of the whole passage and discuss only the mind of man [*ren xin* 人心] and the mind of the Way [*dao xin* 道心]. The extreme position is to focus only on the two characters *dao* 道 and *xin* 心 and equate the mind directly with the Way. That is, those who immerse themselves in the study of Chan Buddhism do not realize they are departing a very long way from the original purposes of Yao, Shun, and Yu in their giving and receiving of all under heaven.

Cai Jiufeng, in the commentary he wrote on the *Documents*,[12] quotes Master Zhu's [Zhu Xi's] words, saying, "In ancient times, when the sages were going to hand on all under heaven to their successors, they never failed to hand on the method of government with it." This may be said to show a profound understanding of the basic intent of the passage quoted. Not only did Jiufeng make clear by this the mind of emperors and kings, and that it was the foundation of government of the kingdom and pacification of the empire; his interpretation is certainly a correct [reading] of the principles [involved]. Those who subsequently presented his commentary on the *Documents* to the court took it to embody the theory of the three sages' transmission of mind. The scholars of the age subsequently pointed to these sixteen characters from the *Documents* as being the essence of the transmission of mind.

And yet students of Chan [Buddhism] availed themselves [of these words] as proof [of their own theories]. I cannot help but think that the mind does not depend upon any such transmission. What prevails between Heaven and earth, what is the thread linking ancient and modern and is everywhere the same is *li* 理 [principle, pattern, coherence]. *Li* 理 is altogether encompassed in our minds and is verified in affairs and things. The mind is what creates a synthesis of this principle and distinguishes clearly between right and wrong. Whether a man is worthy or not, whether affairs are successful or not, and whether order or disorder prevails in the world are all determined by this. This is why the sages looked to and examined the matters of "insecurity," "subtlety," "refinement," and "singleness [of mind]" and transmitted the way of "holding fast to the center," so there was nothing that did not accord with *li* 理 and no tendency toward either "going beyond" or "not reaching."

Chan studies had their origins in the works of Zhuang [Zhou] and Lie [Yukou][13]—comical and playful words that were unrestrained and without scruple. They feared the manifestations of principle as being abnormal and erroneous, so any writings of the sages and worthies in the classics and commentaries that spoke of principle were all seen as bringing harm to the self. Therefore, [students of Chan] take principle to be a veil and point only to the mind. They say it cannot be set out in writings but can only be transmitted by its mental imprint. And so they do not wish to speak of principle, considering it to be a misleading word that has been passed down without sufficient analysis. The studies of sages and worthies extend from one mind to the practical application of mind throughout the empire and kingdoms, which is nothing other than the prevalence of principle. This is perfectly clear and comprehensible and is shared by all. It is something that has continued for a thousand years without interruption. How can one speak of its "transmission"! Common statements are insidious; even sages and worthies cannot help appropriating and using their words sometimes. Therefore, unworthy as I am, I offer my opinion on this.[14]

[Zhu Xi, in his] *Zhongyong Zhangju*, quotes Cheng Yi's words, which say, "This tract is, then, the model of the mind as handed down by Confucius's disciples."[15] That this also borrows the words of Buddhists cannot but be considered. In the entire *Lunyu* there are three references to mind. [The first] says, "At seventy I could follow what my mind desired without transgressing what was right." [The second] says, "In the case of [Yan] Hui, for three months his mind would never be in opposition to *ren* 仁 [loving-kindness, benevolence]. [The third] says, "He stuffed himself with food the whole day and did nothing that used the mind."[16] These are similar to the admonition, "Hold it fast and it stays with you; let it go and you lose it."[17] The disciples never recorded this, so it is seen only in the *Mencius*. Now, not to study the Sage's "grasping of the mind" and yet to recklessly speak of "following the mind" is what may be called "stuffing oneself with food all day and doing nothing that uses the mind" and "what he does in the course of the day once again dissipates what he had gained."[18]

Tang Renqing,[19] in replying to a friend's letter, said,

Since the rise of the new learning and the celebrated scholars who wrote about it, those who pretended to put it into practice were by no means few in number. Nevertheless, when they spoke of learning, it was mind and nothing else. I have heard [he said] that in ancient times there was study of the Way; I have not heard of the study of mind. The two words *xin* 心 and *xue* 學 [mind and learning] are not mentioned in the Six Classics, nor are they in Confucius or Mencius. Nowadays, those who speak of learning say that mind is equivalent to the Way. And yet I do not understand this. How is it so? The purport of "insecure" and "subtle" lies in this, even if the great sages didn't dare speak of it. Today many people castigate me for speaking of learning and neglecting mind; how is that easier to understand than your upbraiding me for not studying? I have no answer for you on this point. The Master said, "Is there a man who, for one day, can use his strength for *ren* 仁?" He also said, "If a man can for one day subdue himself and return to *li* 禮 . . ." And he said, "Respectfully attentive for a whole day" in the conduct of affairs.[20] I have not been able to do this.

Even if the disciples of the Master were to sustain it for a day or a month, he would still not acknowledge their love of learning. Even more so does this apply to those who are not able to sustain it even for a day.[21] It is possible to say it is not learning, but I don't know if what you refer to as learning is really *ren*. Or is it *li*? Or is it affairs? Or are you referring to mind? To set aside *ren*, *li*, and affairs [*shi*] in order to speak of mind is something even you know is impossible. Your purpose is surely to say that *ren* 仁, *li* 禮, and *shi* 事 [affairs] are all subsumed under mind, so that to use one's strength for *ren* is to use one's strength for mind; to recover *li* is to recover mind;[22] and to conduct affairs is to make mind manifest. This I don't understand, as I said before, and so may be said to be without learning.

He also says,

Addressing oneself earnestly to the practice of goodness is mind. Surely, then, "addressing oneself earnestly to the pursuit of gain" is also mind?[23] An insecure mind distinguishes between good fortune and bad fortune and discriminates between man and beast. Even though a great sage must always maintain his guard, can he do so and dare to speak of the study of mind? The study of mind takes mind to be [the object of] learning. To take mind to be learning is to take mind to be nature. The mind may be able to make nature complete, but it cannot be nature. Therefore, to seek "lost mind" is right, but to seek "mind" is wrong.[24] To seek "the mind," then, is wrong, but to seek "in the mind" is right. What I consider to be the defect in this study of mind is precisely this seeking of mind. If the mind really depends on being sought, then mind is not of the same order as the self. The mind undoubtedly can be studied, so that to speak of controlling the mind through *li* 禮 or preserving the mind through *ren* 仁 is still a protection for the mind, is it not?

In the *Lunyu* [there is], "Those who are *ren* 仁 [loving, kind, benevolent, humane] come to rest in *ren* 仁."[25] Xie Shi [Xie Liangzuo], in his

Collected Annotations [*Jizhu*], says, "The mind of *ren* does not differentiate between internal and external, near and far, coarse and fine. It is not the case that what is preserved is naturally not lost; it is not the case that what is ordered is naturally not disordered."[26] These are all words of Zhuang [Zhou] and Lie [Yukou] and are not what I take to be Confucian studies. In the *Tai Jia*, it is said, "He contemplated and studied the lucid decrees of Heaven."[27] The Master said, "Hui was a man who chose the use of the center. When he attained one good, he held it fast within his breast and did not lose it."[28] Therefore, hold it fast and it will be preserved; let it go and it will be lost. Not to rely on preserving it and yet naturally not to lose it—what kind of man is that?

Section 19: There are twenty essays in this section on various aspects of writing and literature. Essays 19.1–6 are on general matters: writing must be of benefit to the empire (19.1), not much writing is prized (19.2), the difficulties of writing (19.3), direct language (19.4), established words that are not of one time (19.5), and the large number of writers (19.6). There are then four essays on some negative aspects of literature—deceptive words, overelaboration, and imitation 19.7–10). Essay 19.11 examines the issue of simplicity versus complexity in writing. The next three essays are again on negative aspects: the affectation of imitating the ancients (19.12), repetition (19.13), and the unnecessary proliferation of prefaces and postfaces (19.14). There is an essay on the origins of biographical writing (19.15). The final five essays are on specific and essentially unrelated topics: tomb inscriptions and obituaries (19.16), rewards for writing (19.17), the relation of the writing to the writer (19.18), empty words (those that don't contribute to meaning) (19.19), and obscure passages in ancient writings that can't be corrected (19.20).

19.6 THE PROLIFERATION OF THE LITERATI

Since Tang and Song times, how numerous the literati have become! Certainly there are those who are not conversant with classical accomplishments and do not understand ancient and modern and yet style themselves literary men. Han Wengong [Han Yu], in his poem "Fu Dushu Chengnan," wrote,

Why do you think literature is valued?
It is a field sown with the learning of the classics.
There is no source for muddy trickles in the streets;
at dawn they are full, by evening they are gone.
If a man cannot understand ancient and modern,
he is just like a horse or ox wearing clothes.
When such men act, they sink into wrongdoing,
much less can they hope for fame and praise.[29]

And yet when Liu Zhi of the Song gave instruction to his sons and grandsons, he always said, "Scholars ought to consider ability and judgment to be paramount. Once they acclaim themselves as literary men, they are no longer worthy to be so regarded."[30] This being so, is being renowned in the world as a literary man of sufficient importance? This is what Yang Ziyun meant when he spoke of "someone who collects my fine writings but does not accept what I really am."[31] Huang Luzhi said, "For the past several decades, teachers and noble men have used essays only to raise up and exhort later generations. There is, therefore, splendor without real substance."[32]

In our own times, from the Jiajing reign period [1522–1566] on, there has only been this custom, and yet Lu Wenyu [Lu Shen] recorded the words of Liu Wenjing's announcement to auspicious scholars, which Kongtong [Li Mengyang] strongly considered to be unjust.[33] In the *Song History* it says, "Ouyang Yongshu, in speaking to his students, never touched on the subject of literature but only discussed politics, saying that literature stopped at being beneficial to the self, whereas a consideration of affairs can extend to things and others."[34]

19.11 COMPLEXITY AND SIMPLICITY IN WRITING

Han Wengong [Han Yu], in writing Fan Zongshi's epitaph, said, "In antiquity all words certainly came from the men themselves, but in coming down to us the unskilled then plundered them. Subsequently, all pointed to former worthies, plagiarizing one another, and from Han times down to the present time, one style has been used."[35] This gets to the heart of the failings of the men of the present time. Thus, Zongshi's writings can serve as a warning against the failings of the present day, and yet he, too, fails. In writing [literature] it is essential to have notes. For the time before Qin and Han it is possible not to have notes, but writings of the present day cannot be understood without them. This is to seek simplicity and yet to achieve complexity—it is a double failure. Confucius said, "In writing, all that is required is to convey the meaning."[36]

The most important thing in writing is that it be comprehensible, regardless of whether it is complex or simple. When discussion of complexity and simplicity arises, the literature itself is forgotten. The complex passages in the *Historical Records* [*Shiji*] are certainly superior to the simple passages in the *History of the Former Han*. The simplicity in the *New Tang History* is not simplicity in the matters but simplicity in the writings; this is how it is defective.

"Shi Zi used Chen Zi to convey his message to Mencius, and Chen Zi used Shi Zi's words to inform Mencius."[37] In this case there was no need for repetition; the meaning was already clear. [Elsewhere Mencius writes,] "A man of Qi lived with his wife and concubine. When his wife asked him with whom he had wined and dined, [he replied] that they were all worthy men. The wife informed the concubine, saying, 'When our husband goes out, he sates himself with wine and food and then returns. When I asked him with whom he wined and dined, he told me they were all wealthy and honorable men, and yet no men of distinction ever come here. I shall watch closely and see where he goes.' "[38] And again, "Formerly, someone gave Zichan of Zheng a live fish. Zichan directed his pond keeper to keep it in the pond. The pond keeper, however, cooked the fish, went back to Zichan, and said, 'When I first let the fish go, it seemed restrained, but after a little while it seemed more at ease and then swam away joyfully.' Zichan said, 'It is in its element! It is in its element!' "[39] In this case the repetition is important in describing the situation fully.

This is the subtlety of Mencius's writings. If this were in the *New Tang History*, for the man of Qi it would certainly say, "His wife doubted him and watched him closely." And in the case of Zichan, it would certainly say, "The pond keeper went out and laughed at him." There would be these two sentences and nothing more. This is why the most important thing in writing is to be understood; it is not important for writing to be simple. Liu Qizhi said, "The *New Tang History*, in recounting events, prized simplicity and brevity in its words, therefore its descriptions of events were very condensed and not at all clear. In writing history this is a defect. Moreover, how is there complexity and simplicity in writing? Men of former times, in discussing this, said that when the wind blows, the water naturally rises, completing the pattern. If it does not come out naturally but has its meaning in complexity and simplicity, then this is a failing."[40] At that time the *Jin Xin Tang Shu Biao* said, "Its subject matter is greater than previously, but the writing is less good than that of the old [*Tang History*]."[41] That in which the *New Tang History* falls short of the ancients—indeed, its defects—can truly be identified in these two statements.

In the *Huangshi Richao* it is written,

> Su Ziyou, in his *Gu Shi*, changed the *Historical Records* [*Shiji*] in many instances where it was not right. For example, in the biography of Chu Lizi, the *Shiji* says, "His mother was Han's daughter. Chu Lizi was humorous and very wise." The *Gu Shi* says, "His mother was Han's daughter. She was humorous and very wise." This indicates that the mother was humorous. This being so, how can the three characters "Chu Lizi" be omitted? In the biography of Gan Mao, the *Shiji* has, "Gan Mao was from Xiacai. He served the Xiacai historian in raising the study of the theories of the hundred schools." The *Gu Shi* says, "The Xiacai historian raised the study of the theories of the hundred schools." This is as if the historian himself studied the theories of the hundred schools. If this is the case, how can the one character *shi* [historian] be omitted?[42]

From these examples we know that it is impossible to achieve merit in writing by reducing the number of characters. If it were possible to reduce the number of characters, the Grand Historian [Sima Qian] would have reduced them long ago.

Section 20: There are thirty essays in this section covering a range of topics of a literary nature. The first (20.1) concerns the word *gong* 公, particularly in the term *san gong* 三公 (Three Dukes). Essays 20.2–8 are about the recording of times and the dating of events, especially in early works such as the *Spring and Autumn Annals*. There are six essays on various aspects of reign titles (20.9–12, 20.15, 20.16). Essay 20.13 is on a specific work—*The Western Study Record* by the Tang scholar Sun Qiao 孫樵. There are three essays on the *Comprehensive Mirror* (*Tong Jian*), dealing with, respectively, the recording of reign titles (20.14); the use of the word *zang* 葬 ("to bury"—20.17); and the use of the term *run yue* 閏月 (intercalary month, 20.18). Of the remaining twelve essays, five are about the recording of the names of persons or places in historical writings (20.19–23), and four concern aspects of the approach to, and quoting from, ancient writings (20.24–27). The final three essays are of a somewhat general nature: 20.28 is on the use of *yue* 曰 to introduce quotations, 20.29 is about the introductory sentences in historical writings, and 20.30 is on the division of topics in historical writings.

20.23 TRANSMITTING THE WORDS OF THE ANCIENTS

Whenever there is transmission of the words of the ancients, it is certainly appropriate to quote the one who established the words.[43] Also, if one of the ancients transmitted the words of another, then both should be quoted. It is not acceptable to plagiarize and consider the words to be one's own. In the *Odes* it is written,

> From of old, before our time,
> former men set the example.[44]

Cheng Zhengshu [Cheng Yi], in his commentary on the *weiqi* diagram in the *Changes*, says that the three yang lines have all lost their position; and he says this meaning was what he heard from a hermit of Chengdu.[45] This, then, is a case of someone's not daring to fail in giving due recognition to the words of a contemporary. The humility of the noble man is a prerequisite for being able to make progress in scholarship.

Section 21: There are thirty-six essays in this section, and they are predominantly about poetry. The first three are somewhat general: on the purpose of poetry (21.1); on the point that it is not necessary for all men to write poetry (21.2); and on the titles of poems, referring to the ancient practice of taking the title from within the poem and the later practice of deciding on a title first (21.3). There are seven essays on aspects of rhyme (21.4–9, 21.15). Essays 21.10–14 are about technical aspects of verse. There are then four essays on other and diverse aspects: 21.16 on the Bailing Terrace, built by Han Wu Di to house poets; 21.17 on the evolution of styles in poetry; 21.18 on calligraphy in poetry; and 21.19 on variations in old stories in poems by later writers. There are then five essays on errors in the verses of specific poets (21.20–24). Two essays are about certain characters in writing more generally (21.25 and 21.26). There are six essays on specific works: the *Shuowen* (21.27); the *Shuowen Changjian* (21.28); the Five Classics in the old text (21.29); the *Jijiu Pian* (21.30); the *Qianzi Wen* (21.31); and the *Jinshi Lu* (21.33). The remaining four essays are on draft writings (21.32), the use of simplified characters in printing (21.34), drawings (21.35), and literary references to ancient implements (21.36).

21.1 THE PURPOSE OF POETRY

Shun said, "*Shi* 詩 poetry is an expression of [the poet's] aspirations toward virtue."[46] This is the fundamental aspect of *shi* poetry. In the "Royal Regulations" chapter of the *Book of Rites*, there is the statement, "An order was given to the grand preceptor to arrange the *Odes* as a means of examining the ways of the people."[47] This is the use of poetry. Xun Zi, in discussing the "Xiao Ya" section of the *Odes*, said, "There was criticism of the government of the day in order to recall that of the past. The words have an elegance in them; the sounds have a melancholy in them."[48] This is the emotion of poetry. Thus, the *Odes* was the "traces of kings."[49] From the Jian'an period [196–219] on down to the Qi [479–501] and Liang [502–556] periods, the *fu* 賦 [rhymed prose] of *ci* 辭 [elegiac] poets found beauty by going to excess,[50] so failing by a long way to fulfill the purpose of poetry.

The Tang poet Bai Juyi, in a letter to Yuan Weizhi, wrote, "As the years pass and experience grows, each time I speak with people, I deliberate a lot on current matters. Each time I read the *Documents* and *Histories*, I seek mainly *li* 理 [principle, pattern, coherence] and the *dao* 道 [the Way]. This was when I first realized that literature should be written to accord with the times and that poems and songs should be in accord with affairs." So in arranging his own poems, he designated as satirical poems those that praised the good and ridiculed the bad, comparing himself to Liang Hong and his composition of the "Wuyi Song." He said, "Of those who appreciate this poetry, both Deng Fang and Tang Qu are dead, while you and I are both in distress. How could it be borne if Heaven wished to destroy the six forms of verse in the first songs in the four sections of the *Odes*! Further, can we assume that Heaven does not intend to make the troubles and sufferings of ordinary people known to the emperor?"[51] Ah, alas! Bai Juyi can be said to be someone who knew "the purpose of establishing his words."[52]

Ge Hong of the Jin period, styled Baopu Zi, said, "In ancient times, poetry criticized errors and failings. Therefore, it was of benefit and was valued. Nowadays, poetry is nothing more than empty words and so is flawed and worthless."[53]

21.17 THE SUCCESSIVE FALLING AWAY OF POETIC STYLE

The three hundred verses of the *Odes* could not do otherwise than fall away to the *Chu Ci* [*The Songs of the South*]. The *Chu Ci* could not do otherwise than fall away to the verse of the Han and Wei periods. [The verse] of the Han and Wei periods could not do otherwise than fall away to the verse of the Six Dynasties. The verse of the Six Dynasties could not do otherwise than fall away to the verse of the Tang period. These changes were determined by circumstances. If one uses the style of a particular period, one will certainly conform to the literature of that period, so establishing a standard. The styles of prose and poetry fall away with time because they cannot do otherwise than change. If the literary style of one period were to continue over a long period, people would be writing the same things all the time. Now, however, after the passage of many years, there is still the use of old-fashioned words that are imitated time and again. And this is considered poetry! But is it acceptable? If there is not conformity, there is loss of what is considered poetry, and if there is conformity, there is loss of individuality. The reason why Li Bai and Du Fu are alone among Tang poets in scaling the heights is that they never failed to conform and yet never conformed. Only those who understand this can properly discuss poetry.

6

RZL 22–32

MISCELLANEOUS

Section 22: There are twenty-two essays in this section, predominantly on terminology as applied to places, designations of officials, and their modes of appointment. The first two essays deal with two general terms commonly used in ancient times—the Four Seas (22.1) and the Nine Divisions (*zhou* 州) (22.2), the first referring to the empire as a whole and the second to the early division of the empire by Emperor Yu. Of the next fourteen essays (22.3–16), all but two deal with terms applied to men (king, viscount, minister, etc.) or to places (commandery, district, village, etc.). The two exceptions are 22.3 and 22.5; the former considers the lack of family continuity in the state of Yan during the Spring and Autumn period and the latter the issue of whether Qinshi Huang Di destroyed the states of Wei and Yue. There are four essays on matters pertaining to burial: the whereabouts of the tombs of early emperors (22.17), the burial mound of Yao (22.18), and the establishment of tablets and shrines for those still living (22.19 and 22.20). Finally, there are two essays on the names of individuals, Zhang Gongsu 張公素 (22.21) and Wang Gen 王亘 (22.22), which have given rise to confusion.

22.1 THE FOUR SEAS

Comment: For a discussion of the range of application of this term, see Legge, *Documents*, LCC, 3.41n, in which he states in part that "anciently the territories occupied by the nine E ([Yi] 夷), the eight Teih ([Di] 狄), the seven Jung ([Rong] 戎), and the six Man ([Man] 蠻) were called 'the four seas.' All within the four seas was divided into the 'nine provinces.' Within the nine provinces there were arranged the 'five domains,' divided into three . . ." In this sense the phrase obviously has nothing to do with an actual sea, although later in the same note, Legge says, "The phrase must have had its origin in some idea of the habitable territories bounded on every side by water." Gu's purpose here is to clarify the use of the term "Four Seas."

The *Zhengyi* [commentary—"orthodox interpretation"] on the *Documents* states that the situation of the world is that there is water on four sides.[1] Zou Yan,[2] in his writings, said that beyond the Nine Divisions there are great oceans and seas encircling, so the Nine Divisions are surrounded by water and hence were named *zhou* 州.[3] Nevertheless, in the Five Classics, there is no mention of a northern or western sea, and the term "four seas" is also used as a general term referring to the ten thousand states.[4] In the *Erya* [dictionary] the nine Yi [Eastern Barbarians], the eight Man [Southern Barbarians], the six Rong [Western Barbarians], and the five Di [Northern Barbarians] are spoken of as the four seas.[5] In the "Jiaoren" chapter of the *Rites of Zhou*, [there is], "Whenever trouble was about to occur in the Four Seas, the hills and streams . . ."[6] According to the note, the four seas were like the four directions. Thus the word "sea" is not the name of real water. In the *Changes* the diagram *dui* 兌 is taken to indicate marsh, there being no mention of a sea.[7] The "Xiangyin Jiuyi" chapter of the *Record of Rites* states, "In reverential acknowledgment that on the left [east] of heaven and earth there is the sea."[8] From this it can be seen that on the right [west] there is no sea. In the *Yu Documents*, Yu says, "I opened up the nine streams and conducted them to the four seas."[9] According to the *Tribute to Yu*, there was only one sea, and the name Southern Sea [Nan 南海] was like the Western River [Xihe 西河], which was, in fact, the [Yellow] River.[10] So in the words of the *Tribute to Yu*, there were two seas: "On the east, reaching to the sea" truly speaks of a sea; "his fame and influence filled all within the four seas"[11] uses the term "sea" more generally.

Hong Mai of the Song period[12] says there is one sea and that is all. In physical features [topography], the north and west were high, the south and east low. What were called the three seas—eastern, northern, and southern—were in reality one. The north, where the land stretches to the azure depths of heaven, was called the northern sea. The south, reaching to Jiao and Guang, was then called the southern sea. The east, reaching to Wu and Yue, was called the eastern sea. There was no reason to have what is called the western sea. In the *Odes*, the *Documents*, and the *Record of Rites*, the term "four seas" is used in the same way. When it comes to Zhuang Zi saying, "In the barren north there is a dark sea"[13] and Qu Yuan saying, "The western sea was our meeting place,"[14] these are in both cases metaphorical.

Cheng Dachang[15] said that in the west of Tiaozhi there was a sea that the Former Han envoys had certainly seen and recorded in their chronicles. In the Later Han period, Ban Chao also dispatched Gan Ying and his family to this land.[16] And to the west of the western sea there were also the barbarians of the Roman Empire, and all frequent comings and goings by sea for commercial purposes were by sea. Huo Qubing blockaded Lang Juxu Mountain, which was, in reality, near Han Hai [the Gobi Desert].[17] Su Wu and Guo Ji were both imprisoned by the Xiongnu, having been dispatched to the shore of the northern sea.[18] Also, the *Tang Shi* states that of the Turkish tribes north of the northern sea, there was the Guligan kingdom on the sea's northern bank.[19] This being so, what the *Odes* and *History* refer to as the four seas were in reality what encircled the barbarians and the Chinese[20] in all four directions and were not metaphorical. So nowadays, Ganzhou has Juyan Hai, Xining has Qing Hai, and Yunnan has Dian Hai.[21] How do we know that what the men of Han and Tang regarded as seas were not of this kind?

Section 23: This section comprises forty-one relatively short essays on names and naming. The first three essays are broad in scope. Essay 23.1 is a general discussion on the origin of surnames (*xing* 姓), 23.2 is a discussion of clan names (*shi zu* 氏族), and 23.3 is a list of errors in the transmission of the two kinds of names. There are then two essays (23.4 and 23.5) on specific clan names, one (23.6) on the creation of clan names in relation to the state or kingdom of the particular clan, one (23.7) on the origin of surnames, and one (23.8) on the naming of those of the same clan. Essays 23.9–16 cover a range of topics, from the decline of the great northern clans to the variable use of style and rank in naming people.

The issue of taboos in naming is considered in a number of essays (23.17–22, 23.26, 23.29), one in particular (23.20) providing a long discussion of taboo names from various historical periods. The remaining essays in the section are brief considerations of various aspects of naming, with attention being directed to three main issues: the origin of the practice described, comparison of ancient and modern practices, and clarification of textual matters in relation to names.

23.10 CLANS (FAMILIES) OF THE NORTHERN REGION

Du Shi [Du You], in his *Tong Dian*, said, "At the time of the Northern Qi, the Lius of Ying and Ji, the Zhangs and Songs of Qinghe, the Wang family of Bingzhou, the Hou clan of Puyang, and all the people of this sort amounted to almost ten thousand families."[22] In Xie Yin's biography in the *Northern History* [*Bei Shi*], it says that when he was prefect of Hebei, the two surnames Han and Ma each had over two thousand families.[23] Nowadays, in the central plain, although designated the great families of the northern region, they don't reach even a thousand individuals. The population is scanty, and the clans and families have declined. This is very different from the situation in Jiangnan. If a family had one second-class graduate, this gave a preeminent position in the one region to all those on the same genealogical register, right down to those who were servants. This custom also declined from the Jin and Yuan periods on, so that deterioration up to the present is not the work of a single day.

Section 24: The forty-nine essays in this section deal mainly with terms and titles applied to family members and various official positions. Of the first fourteen essays (24.1–14), twelve examine individual terms applied to family members and their interrelationships, with the major focus on usage and the minor focus on origin, while the other two consider, respectively, interchangeable words (24.12) and repeated words (24.14). Then follows a long series of essays (24.15–42), predominantly brief, on titles used for rulers, officials, and others, with the main focus again being on origin and usage with reference to the classics and other early writings. There is one apparent interloper in this group—a historical review of the function of the Hanlin Academy and how this changed over time. The final seven essays (24.43–49) consider terms used in the intercourse between officials themselves and their exchanges with the ruler.

24.26 HANLIN (IMPERIAL ACADEMY)

Comment: On the title Hanlin 翰林, Charles Hucker writes, ". . . from the 700s on, occurs as a prefix to numerous titles of literary and editorial workers and even other specialists such as physicians, most commonly but not solely members of the Hanlin Academy" (*A Dictionary of Official Titles in Imperial China* [Stanford, Calif.: Stanford University Press, 1985], p. 222, no. 2141). See also Frédéric A. Bischoff, *La forêt des pinceaux* (Paris: Presses universitaires de France, 1963).

The "Zhiguan Zhi" chapter of the *Old Tang History* says,

> The duty of the Hanlin academician was originally, through writing and speech, to prepare responses for the emperor and to be in personal attendance during his coming out and going in, so that he might be able to participate in policy discussions and give admonitions and warnings. Moreover, the Hanlin [Academy] was the place where imperial edicts were awaited.[24] Under the Tang system, wherever the emperor was, there were invariably scholars of phraseology and diction. Those of lower rank, down to people such as diviners, doctors, and technical personnel, were all on duty in another building and undertook the preparation of banquets and audiences. Official dispatches and imperial edicts fell within the province of the secretariat drafter. At the time of Tai Zong [627–649], well-known Confucian scholars were frequently appointed to draft imperial edicts, but they still did not have an official designation. After the Qianfeng reign period [666–667], they were for the first time called "Scholars of the Northern Gate." During the time of Xuan Zong [713–755], Zhang Yue, Lu Jian, Zhang Jiuling, Xu Anzhen, Zhang Ji, and others were summoned to the inner palace,[25] called Hanlin academicians awaiting orders, and made responsible for reports to the emperor both within the palace and without,

> written instructions, verses in reply, and essays. Subsequently, in the preparation of edicts and proclamations, all of which were the responsibility of the secretariat, there was a considerable backlog. The delay led to the first selection of court officials with skills in literature and learning to enter the Hanlin [Academy] and serve the throne [i.e., to be academicians in attendance]. Nevertheless, such men also did not have established titles or duties. In the twenty-sixth year of the Kaiyuan reign period [738], there was for the first time the change of Hanlin academicians to Hanlin academicians in attendance, and they were situated in an academy. These men were responsible only for edicts relating to the inner court. After the Zhide reign period [756–757], when the empire was embroiled in warfare [the An Lushan Rebellion], there were many matters of national and military importance [necessitating] arcane plans and secret edicts, all of which emanated from the emperor. Six scholars were established, and each year one man of profound virtue and gravity was chosen from within this group to be a recipient of edicts. This man alone took responsibility for the secret edicts. De Zong [r. 780–804] loved literature and had particular difficulty with his selections. After the Zhenyuan reign period [785–804], many of those scholars who were recipients of edicts went on to become prime ministers.[26]

That such an office was not seen in the *Tang Liudian* was because this work was completed by Zhang Jiuling, and at that time this office was not yet in existence.[27]

The *Old Tang History* speaks of the Hanlin Academy as being a place in which Buddhist and Daoist [monks], those involved in divination and invocation, and those practicing methods and arts, calligraphy and chess were gathered and trained, each [group] being funded from a separate academy.[28] Lu Zhi was in disagreement with Wu Tongxuan. He said that in a time of peace, students of the technical arts, calligraphy, and painting are expectant officials of the Hanlin and are not academicians. He asked that their official positions be terminated.[29] Further, it can be learned from the histories that the following men were all expectant officials of the Hanlin Academy: the Daoist scholar Wu Yun from Songshan at the beginning of the Tianbao reign period [742–755], the star diviners Han

Ying and Liu Xuan from the middle of the Qianyuan reign period [758–759], the chess master Wang Shuwen and the court calligrapher Wang Pi from the end of the Zhenyuan reign period [785–804], the necromancer Liu Mi and the Buddhist monk Datong from the end of the Yuanhe reign period [806–820], the chess expert Wang Yi and the Daoist priest Sun Zhun from Xingtang Monastery at the beginning of the Baoli reign period [825–826].[30] Another example is Li Gan, who, although reaching the level of metropolitan governor, started out as an expectant official in star divining at the Hanlin Academy.[31] Moreover, in the second month of the twenty-first year of the Zhenyuan reign period [805], on the day *bingwu*, forty-two redundant officials were dismissed from the academy;[32] these included medical apprentices, fortune-tellers, star diviners, and those well versed in literary games [*shefu*]. In the second year of the Baoli reign period [826], in the twelfth month, on the day *gengshen*, there was a reduction in the number of redundant officials, music officials from the office of music, expectant officials in the various skills from the Hanlin Academy, as well as various kinds of supervising officials in charge of internal [inner court] matters, to the number of 1,270 men in all.[33] From this it can be known that not all the scholars of the Hanlin Academy were concerned with literary matters. Zhao Lin, in his *Yinhua Lu*, states, "Wen Zong [r. 827–840] bestowed on the Hanlin scholars ceremonial dress. [When] later there was an expectant official who wished to be honored first and a responsible official put his name forward, the emperor, in response, said. 'There cannot be a bestowal on a noble man and a lesser man on the same day. It must await another day.' "[34]

In the third year of the Chenghua reign period [1467], in preparation for the lantern festival on the fifteenth day of the first month of the following year, there was an imperial command to the phraseology officials of the Hanlin Academy to write *shi* 詩 and *ci* 詞 verses. The compilers, Zhang Mao and Huang Zhongshao, as well as the examining editor, Zhuang Chang, sent up a memorial, stating,

> Members of the Hanlin Academy consider that discussing, deliberating, and writing documents for the emperor are their duties. Even if they might be said to assist in literary matters, nevertheless how would vulgar and irregular phrases be appropriate to present to the emperor? Surely it would not be possible to indirectly quote

the words of felicitation Song Qi and Su Shi sent from the music school and to take upon themselves the fault of being rude and disrespectful. We have also respectfully read the fine piece of writing by Xuan Zong in his imperial exhortation to the Hanlin academicians, which has this to say: "May the words that inform and enrich us concern only *ren* 仁 [loving-kindness, humanitarianism, and benevolence] and *yi* 義 [right action, righteousness, and justice], the way of Yao and Shun—words that were explained by Mencius of Zou." At present, we are afraid the conduct of the lantern festival is not the way of Yao and Shun, and the writing of verse at the royal behest does not involve words of *ren* and *yi*. We know the mind of Your Majesty and we know the minds of your ancestors. Therefore, we are loath to bring these foolish statements before the emperor. We humbly desire you to adopt these, the words of grass and reed cutters, and that these matters be altogether prohibited.[35]

The emperor was angry and ordered that they be beaten. Mao was demoted to the position of magistrate of Linwu, Zhongshao to the position of magistrate of Xiangtan, and Chang to the position of administrative assistant to Guiyang Zhou, each being transferred to a distant post. Subsequently, the imperial censors interceded on behalf of the three memorialists, and their positions were changed. Mao and Zhongshao became judges at the court of judicial review, and Chang became the vice-director of the messenger office at Nanjing. From this, then, one can see the importance of the Hanlin officials.[36]

Section 25: The seventeen essays in this section are, in broad terms, devoted to clarification of a variety of specific literary and historical matters and terms. Five of the first six essays concern mythical or semimythical personages: Chong Li 重黎 (25.1), Wu Xian 巫咸 (25.2), He Bo 河伯 (25.3), Xiang Jun 湘君 (25.4), and Jie Zitui 介子推 (25.6). Essay 25.5, "Harmonious Joint Rule" (Gong He 共和), presents a historical discussion of events surrounding King Li's 厲王 flight to Zhi 彘 and the subsequent joint administration of the Dukes of Zhou and Shao. There are four essays on aspects of the lives of particular individuals thought to be of literary or historical interest: Qi Liang's 杞梁 wife (25.7), Zhuang An 莊安 (25.9), Li Guang 李廣 (25.10), and Mao Yanshou 毛延壽 (25.13).

There are three essays dealing with certain terms: *chi yu* 池魚 (25.8), *da* and *xiao shan* 大小山 (25.12), and *wai ren* 外人 as part of a name (25.13). The final four essays deal with more general literary matters that Gu sees as requiring criticism or clarification. These are as follows: where two people are involved in a single event but only one gains renown (25.14), where both gain renown but one undeservedly so (25.15), where there is mistaken identification of the people involved in a particular event (25.16), and a series of instances in which the date or time ascribed to a particular event is thought to be wrong (25.17).

25.5 HARMONIOUS JOINT RULE

The "Original Record of Zhou" in the *Historical Records* [*Shiji*] [states], "King Li fled to Zhi. His heir apparent, Jing, concealed himself in the Duke of Shao's house. The Dukes of Zhou and Shao conducted the administration jointly; this was called 'harmonious joint rule' [*gong he*]. In the fourteenth year of this period [828 B.C.E.], King Li died in Zhi, at which time the two ministers then jointly established the heir apparent, Jing, as king."[37] To take this joint ministry to be "harmonious joint rule" is wrong.

In the *Jizhong Jinian* [there is this], "King Li, in the twelfth year, fled to Zhi. In the thirteenth year, He, Earl of Gong, carried out the imperial duties. This is termed 'harmonious joint rule.'[38] In the twenty-sixth year, the king [Li] died in Zhi, whereupon Duke Ding of Zhou and Duke Mu of Shao established the heir apparent, Jing, as king, and He, Earl of Gong, returned to his [own] kingdom."[39] This is what Zuo Shi [records] the king's son, Chao, as saying: "Two of the feudal lords gave up their own positions to attend to the king's government."[40] But his words that the Earl of Gong returned to his kingdom are not in accord with this. In ancient times, during periods when there was no emperor, for visits to the court or in the conduct of litigation, there was necessarily a place to return to. The *Lü Shi Chunqiu* says, "Earl He of Gong cultivated his conduct and loved *xian* 賢 [worthiness] and *ren* 仁 [loving-kindness, benevolence, humanity]. When Li of Zhou was in difficulties, there was no one to occupy the position of emperor, so the people of the empire all came to request [that he, Earl He, assume responsibility]."[41] According to this, then, it was the people of the empire who paid a visit to the Earl of Gong, and not the Earl of Gong who came to Zhou to conduct the business of the empire [in the king's stead]. The Earl of Gong never had any intention of possessing the empire, nor did the Dukes of Zhou and Shao ever serve the Zhou altars of soil and grain [i.e., the kingdom] and entrusted this to others. Therefore, the people of Zhou did not have the shame of a change of the [ruling] family's name, and the Earl of Gong did not have any plan to assume the name of king. In the *Zhuangzi* it says, "Therefore Xu You enjoyed himself on the sunny side of the Ying River and the Earl of Gong found what he wanted on top of a hill."[42] Thus, he grasped the Way to the end of his life and mastered the art of keeping his spirit intact and nourishing his original nature.

The *Zuo Zhuan* states that Tai Shu of Zheng fled to Gong.[43] According to the note, the state of Song was near what is now Gong district in Ji prefecture. In the biography of Prince Chun Shen in the *Historical Records* [*Shiji*], there is, "Shangdang in Han was in communication with Gong and Ning, making a road through Ancheng, on which taxes were imposed when leaving or entering."[44] The "Tianjing Zhongwan Shijia" [chapter in the *Historical Records*] states that King Jian submitted to Qin. Qin sent him to Gong, where he died of hunger. The people of Qi had a song about this that went, "Ah pine, ah cypress! The one who established Jian in Gong was a guest."[45] In the "List of Meritorious Officials" in the *History of the Former Han* [*Han Shu*], there is reference to Gong Zhuang Hou, Lu Ba Shi.[46] In the "Dili Zhi" in the *Tang Shu* [it is written that] Gongcheng district in Weizhou was established as Gongzhou in the first year of the Wude reign period [618]. This is now Hui district in Weihui prefecture.[47] At the present time, Hui district has in it Gongjiang terrace, from which men of later times have drawn a wrong conclusion.

Section 26: There are thirty essays in this section, which is devoted to historical writings, predominantly the dynastic histories. Thus, essays 26.1–3 are on the *Shiji*: a comparison of the recording of military matters in it and the *Tong Jian* 通鑑 (*Comprehensive Mirror*) (26.1), on the sequence of topics (26.2), and on textual matters needing clarification or correction (26.3). There are four essays on the *Han Shu*: on textual matters (26.4), on intercalated comments in small characters in some of the chapters (26.5), on a comparison of the recording of the same event in the *Han Shu* and the *Shiji* (26.6), and a brief comparison of the *Han*

Shu and Xun Yue's 荀悅 *Han Record* (26.7). There is a single essay each on the *Hou Han Shu* (26.8) and the *Sanguo Zhi* (26.9), both dealing with textual issues. The next four essays are of a more general nature: methods of recording biographical information (26.10), place-names given differently in different places (26.11), superfluous characters (26.12), and confusion about names due to later writers perpetuating earlier errors (26.13). There are then single essays on each of the following histories dealing mainly with textual issues: *Jin Shu* (26.14), *Song Shu* (26.15), *Wei Shu* (26.16), *Liang Shu* (26.17), *Hou Zhou Shu* (26.18), *Sui Shu* (26.19), and the *Bei Shi* (26.20).There is then an essay comparing the recording of a single event in four different histories: *Song Shu*, *Qi Shu*, *Liang Shu*, and the *Nan Shi* (26.21). There are then a further six single essays on the following histories: *Jiu Tang Shu* (26.22), *Xin Tang Shu* (26.23), *Song Shi* (26.24), *Liao Shi* (26.26), *Jin Shi* (26.27), and *Yuan Shi* (26.28). Interposed in this group is a single essay commenting briefly on a person from the Yuan being chronicled in the Song history (Alutu 阿魯圖) (26.25). The final two essays are on the *Comprehensive Mirror* (26.29 and 26.30).

26.12 SUPERFLUOUS CHARACTERS IN HISTORICAL WRITINGS

In the biography of Wang Bi of Wu in the *History of the Former Han*, [there is], "In Wu there was a copper mountain in Zhang prefecture." Here there is the erroneous addition of the character *yu* 豫][48] In the "Record of Guang Wu" in the *History of the Later Han*, [there is], "Before the magistrate of Mi, Zhuo Mao, became Grand Tutor." Here there is the erroneous addition of the character *gao* 高.[49] In the "Biography of Dang Gu," [there is], "The magistrate of Huang, Mao Qin, was drilling his troops and reached the gate." One of the many mistakes is the addition of the character *wai* 外.[50] In the "Record of Huang Hou" in the *History of the Later Han*, [there is], "The Empress Dou's father, Huan Si, had the taboo name of Wu." It is not appropriate in the case of the father of an empress to speak of avoiding a name, so the character *hui* 諱 is superfluous.[51] In the "Chronicle of Writings of the Confucian Scholars" in the *History of the Later Han*, [there is], "Scholars were established for the Five Classics, each teaching by means of his own domestic regulations. For the *Changes* there were the following: Shi, Meng, Liangqiu, and Jing

Shi; for the *Documents* there were Ouyang and the greater and lesser Xia Hou; for the *Odes* there were Qi, Lu, Han, and Mao; for the *Rites* there were the greater and lesser Dai; for the *Spring and Autumn Annals* there were Yan and Yan. Altogether there were fourteen scholars, and a chamberlain was assigned to preside over them." According to this, there are fifteen, not fourteen, there being the superfluous addition of the character *mao* 毛.[52] In a subsequent section there is the statement that in the Jianchu reign period [76–83], there were "the old-text *Shang Shu*, the Mao *Odes*, and the Guliang and Zuo Shi *Spring and Autumn Annals*, although these did not have an office of scholarship set up."[53] Also, in the second part of the same *juan* [i.e., 79 *xia*], it says, "Mao Chang of Zhao collated the *Odes*, and this is the Mao *Odes* that is not yet established."[54] In the "Annals of the Hundred Officials," [in the *Hou Han Shu*] [there is], "There were fourteen scholars." The original note says, "the *Changes* had four: Shi, Meng, Liangqiu, and Jing Shi; the *Documents* had three: Ouyang and the greater and lesser Xia Hou Shi; the *Odes* had three: Lu, Qi, and Han Shi; the *Li* had two: the greater and lesser Dai; the *Spring and Autumn Annals* had two; and the Gongyang commentary had Yan and Yan Shi." It is clear, then, that this character *mao* 毛 is superfluous.[55] In the "Record of Emperor Ling," [there is], "In the sixth month of the third year of the Guanghe reign period [180], there was a proclamation that from among the dukes and nobles, one with ability should be appointed for the following works: the old-text *Shang Shu*, the Mao *Odes*, the *Zuo Zhuan*, and the Guliang *Spring and Autumn Annals*, so the court gentlemen for consultation could all be done away with." Prior to *Shang Shu* there is the omission of the two characters *gu wen* 古文 [old text].[56]

Section 27: The nineteen essays in this section concern points of contention in a number of well-known works, especially ancient writings, dynastic histories, and works of poetry. In broad terms, Gu's observations take one of two forms: his own comments on particular passages in the work in question and discussion of existing notes on difficult passages. The first three essays are, however, of a more general nature. Essay 27.1 takes up a long series of examples of notes on the various classics by Han commentators; 27.2 discusses errors in the notes to early works, mainly with reference to quotations; and 27.3 deals with errors in surnames and clan names in notes. The next seven essays consider (often briefly) the existing notes to the following works: *Zuo Zhuan* 左傳 (27.4), the "Kaogong Ji" 考工記 chapter of the *Zhou Li* 周禮 (27.5), *Erya* 爾雅 (27.6), *Guoyu* 國語 (27.7), *Chu Ci* 楚辭 (27.8), *Xunzi* 荀子 (27.9), and *Huainanzi* 淮南子 (27.10). The next three essays concern the three earliest dynastic histories. The first comprises a long series of somewhat miscellaneous observations on the *Shiji* (27.11), whereas the essays on the *Han Shu* (27.12) and the *Hou Han Shu* (27.13) are about existing notes, in the former case those of Yan Shigu 顏師古. The five essays on works of verse concern the following: the *Wen Xuan* 文選 (27.14), the works of Tao Yuanming 陶淵明 (27.15), of Li Taibo (Li Bo, 李太白) (27.16), of Du Zimei (Du Fu, 杜子美) (27.17), and of Han Wengong (Han Yu, 韓文公) (27.18). The final essay, on the *Comprehensive Mirror* (*Tong Jian* 通鑑), deals with various points of contention in relation to this work, in particular where Gu takes issue with the existing notes (27.19).

27.9 NOTES ON THE *XUNZI*

In the *Xunzi* [there is], ". . . will be gored and broken like a drooping deer, dripping and wet, and will retreat." The commentary says, "The meaning [of these words] is not clear, but they all indicate the appearance of something broken down and scattered."[57] Nowadays, if one examines Dou Gui's biography in the *Old Tang History*, [there is], "Gao Zu spoke to Gui, saying, 'On your entering Shu, those on carriages and horses were completely exterminated by your twenty followers. My broken and scattered carriages are not adequate to give to a duke.' "[58] In Li Mu's biography in the *Northern History*, [there is], "In the battle at Mang Shan, Emperor Wen of Zhou's horse was struck by a flying arrow, which startled it, causing it to bolt and throw him to the ground. Mu dismounted, struck Wen of Zhou on the back with his whip, and reviled him, saying, 'You defeated soldier! So where is your officer? Do you alone stop this?' "[59] In Zhou and Sui times men still used these words.

Section 28: The twenty-five essays in this section can be grouped under the general heading of ritual and ceremonial practices, with particular attention to relevance. The first four examine the practice of bowing. The first (28.1) provides a detailed description of the custom of bowing to the ground, dealing with its historical development and ritual significance.

The remaining three essays in this group concern, respectively, the practices of *jishou* and *dunshou* (28.2); the phrase "a hundred obeisances" from the *Record of Rites* (28.3); and the origins of the practice of "nine bows, three obeisances" (28.4). The next two essays (28.5 and 28.6) consider sitting and are followed by an essay on the northern custom of constructing a hollow earthen bed under which a fire can be lit for warmth (28.7). The next five essays (28.8–12) concern garments, mainly from a historical standpoint. There are then three essays (28.13–15) on terms: *yuefu* 樂府 (music bureau), *si* 寺, and *sheng* 省. The remaining ten essays are quite varied: 28.16 is on the beating of officials who transgress, 28.17 concerns signing documents, 28.18 is about the *Capital Gazette*, 28.19 is on the prohibition of liquor, 28.20 deals with gambling for money, 28.21 and 28.22 are on officials in the capital who incur debts, 28.23 and 28.24 concern the giving of daughters in marriage, and 28.25 is about matters pertaining to resignation.

28.1 BOWING, AND BOWING TO THE GROUND

The ancients laid a mat on the ground and sat on it.[60] If they stretched their bodies and rose, then this was *chang gui* 長跪 [prostrating oneself]. If they brought their heads to their hands, then this was *bai shou* 拜首. If they brought their hands to the ground, then this was *bai* 拜. If they brought their heads to the ground, then this was *qi shou* 稽首 [bowing to the ground]. These were grades of *li* 禮 [ritual practice, propriety]. In venerating the prince or father, there was certainly the use of *qi shou*, *bai*, and, afterward, *qi shou*, these being degrees of *li* 禮. Certainly to end by means of *qi shou* is the completion of *li* 禮 [i.e., conforms on propriety]. Nowadays, the *Daming Huidian* says, "After one bow [*bai* 拜], *kou tou* 叩頭 [kowtow] completes *li* 禮."[61] This is to abandon the intention of the ancients.

The ancients used *qi shou* 稽首 [bowing to the ground] to display the highest degree of respect. The "Taizhu" chapter of the *Rites of Zhou* [*Zhou Li*] [states], "Nine forms of bowing [obeisance] are differentiated, of which the first is called *qi shou* 稽首 [bowing to the ground]." The notes say that *qi shou* is the most important of the obeisances as it is the ritual practice [*li* 禮] between minister and ruler.[62] In the "Jiao Tesheng" chapter of the *Record of Rites* [*Li Ji*], [there is], "The minister of a great officer did not bow to the ground. This was not about not honoring the minister but about the officer's not receiving the homage that he had himself paid to the ruler."[63] In the *Zuo Zhuan* for the twenty-third year of Duke Xi, [it is said that] the Earl of Qin received the Duke of Jin, Chong'er. The earl [compared himself to] the ode 'Liu Yue.' The duke descended and bowed to the ground [*qi shou*]. The earl descended one step but declined to do the same.[64] In the third year of Duke Xiang [there is], "At the covenant in Zhangshu the Duke bowed his head to the ground. Zhi Wuzi said, 'The Son of Heaven is alive, and yet you are ashamed to bow your head to the ground. This makes my ruler afraid.' "[65] For the twenty-fourth year [of Duke Xiang] [there is], "The Earl of Zheng was going to Jin. The earl bowed his head to the ground, but Xuan Zi was about to decline. Zixi, who was in attendance, said, 'Through its reliance on the great state [of Chu], Chen erases an insolent oppression of our poor state. On this account, our ruler asks leave to call it to account for the offense—how dare he do otherwise than bow his head to the ground.' "[66] For the seventeenth year of Duke Ai [there is], "When a covenant was made at Meng, the Marquis of Qi bowed with his head to the ground, but the duke only bowed. The people of Qi were angry, but Meng Wubo said, 'Only to the Son of Heaven does our ruler bow with his head to the ground.' "[67]

In the *Guoyu* [there is], "King Xiang sent the Duke of Shao, Guo, and the Royal Secretary, Guo, to present gifts to Duke Hui of Jin. The Duke of Jin held the jade in low regard and bowed, but not to the ground. The Royal Secretary, Guo, returned and informed the king, saying, 'He [the duke] held the jade in low regard, receiving and setting aside this offering. He bowed, but not to the ground, thus insulting his superior. If the gift is set aside, this indicates no land, if the prince is insulted, this indicates no people.' "[68] From this it can be seen that bowing to the ground was a matter of great importance. Among equals, all followed the practice of *dun shou* 頓首 [bowing the head]—that is what Li Ling in his letter of reply to Su Wu termed "*dun shou*."[69]

Chen Shi [Chen Xiangdao], in his *Li Shu*,[70] says,

> Bowing to the ground [*qi shou*] was the form of propriety to be observed by a feudal lord to the emperor or by a great officer to his prince. Nevertheless, between the prince and the minister there

was also bowing to the ground. In the *Documents* there are the examples of Tai Jia bowing to the ground to Yi Yin[71] and King Cheng bowing to the ground to the Duke of Zhou.[72] A great officer could bow to the ground to one who was not his prince. In the *Book of Etiquette*, it is written that the duke made a bestowal on the guest, and the guest bowed twice with his head to the ground. With the bestowal to him, Jie's bowing to the ground twice is a case in point.[73] A noble man, in acting with propriety to someone he respects, must use the highest form of respect, so that a prince, in bowing to the ground to a minister, is manifesting his regard for the minister's virtue. A great officer who bows his head to the ground to someone who is not his prince is displaying his respect for the ruler. In the Spring and Autumn period, Muying of Jin embraced Tai Zu and bowed his head [*dun shou*] to Xuan Zi of Zhao.[74] Ji Pingzi of Lu bowed his head to Shu Sun,[75] which indicates that bowing the head is a form of *li* 禮 [propriety] that is not bestowed on one who is venerated.[76]

The *Xunzi* says, "Bowing to the level position is called *bai* 拜; bowing lower than the level position is called *qishou* 稽首; bowing to the ground is called *qi sang* 稽顙."[77] It seems that this is not so. The ancient funeral rites were the first occasion for the use of *qi sang* with the head striking the ground. This and *qi shou* are distinguished by what they are and are not permitted for.

Section 29: There are twenty-one essays in this section covering a range of more or less unrelated topics, although several subgroups can be identified. Thus, the first three essays (29.1–3) deal with beasts of burden and transport but are directed primarily at specific characters—*qi* 騎, *yi* 驛, and *lü luo* 驢贏. There are then two essays on military matters—29.4 on the rapidity of troop movements and 29.5 on a phrase from the *Shiji* describing a specific incident of an army crossing a waterway. These are followed by two essays on water transport in general (29.6 and 29.7). Military matters are again taken up in the next four essays: the term *shao huang* 燒荒 (29.8), personal troops (29.9), the soldier-monks of Shaolin (29.10), and the Maohulu 毛葫蘆 army (29.11). There are two essays devoted to language—local dialects (29.12) and the term *guoyu*

國語 (29.13). The final eight essays (29.14–21) concern non-Chinese peoples, with a range of topics being covered—in particular, customs, aptitudes, geography, and history, and, as is customary with Gu, issues of terminology.

29.12 LOCAL DIALECTS

As the dialects of the "Five Regions" [i.e., everywhere] are all different from one another, attempting to create amity between the scholar-officials of the empire while each district retains its own dialect is not a task the noble man would choose to undertake. Thus, Zhongyou's coarseness brought distress to the Master,[78] and the shrike-tongued man was upbraided by Mencius.[79] And in the *Song History*, referring to Gao Zu, [there is], "Although his family had dwelled in Jiangnan for several generations, his Chu dialect remained unchanged. However, elegant and unconventional scholars did not draw attention to it."[80] It also says, referring to the Prince of Changsha, Daolian, "In general he was without ability, and his speech had a pronounced Chu accent. Further, his deportment and behavior were for the most part rustic and clumsy."[81] In the *Shishuo Xinyu* it is said, "After Liu Zhenchang had come out from seeing the prime minister, Wang, someone asked him what Wang was like. Liu replied, 'Nothing out of the ordinary—only I did hear him use the speech of Wu.'"[82] It also says, "The general in chief, Wang, when young had the reputation of being a country bumpkin and also spoke with the dialect of Chu."[83] It also says, "When Zhi Daolin left for the east, he saw Wang Ziyu and his brothers. On his return, someone questioned him as to what these Wangs were like. He replied, 'I saw a flock of white-necked crows and heard the sound of crows cawing.'"[84]

In the *Northern History*, it is said with regard to the Prince of Danyang, Liu Chang, that when "he was berating and scolding his servants, the sound was a mixture of barbarian and Chinese. Although this was a public occasion, the various princes all ridiculed him."[85] Now, even a founding prince or a prime minister, during a period of restoration, cannot avoid the criticism of his contemporaries. How much less can an ordinary scholar do so! Yang Yin of the Northern Qi praised Pei Yanzhi, saying, "The scholarly families of Hedong provide a substantial number of metropolitan officials, but in this family only the older and younger brothers are entirely without a regional accent."[86] Thus, what was looked down upon can be known. When it comes to the writing of literature, there is particular avoidance of what is unrefined and vulgar. Gongyang, [in his commentary on the *Spring and Autumn Annals*], used many Qi words and Huainan used many words from Chu.[87] Was there never such a character in works like the *Commentary on the Changes* and *Lunyu*? As for the explications of the classics, more importance was attached to the literary form. This is why Sun Xiang and Jiang Xian formerly studied the *Zhou Guan* and yet their speech was a mixture of Chu and Xia, so their erudition was not of the highest level.[88]

Li Yexing's scholarship was profound, and yet he did not change the old sounds. Consequently, he was a laughingstock of the people of Liang.[89] The scholars of Yexiu, in their tones and diction, were rough and crude and had a demeanor that was rustic and clumsy, so Yan Zhitui did not wish to have them as tutors to his sons.[90] This being so, if a noble man has the ambition to succeed in the empire, he must certainly begin with his speech. The preface to the *Guoyu Jie* in the *Jin History* says, "In the new-text *Shang Shu* the words are in many cases strange and harsh, which is a reflection of the local dialects of the time."[91] In the *Xunzi* there is always the word *an* 案, and in the *Songs of the South* [*Chu Ci*] there is always the word *qiang* 羌—both are examples of local dialects.[92] In Liu Xie's *The Literary Mind and the Carving of Dragons* [*Wenxin Diaolong*] [there is], "Zhang Hua, in discussing rhymes, said that Shiheng [Lu Ji] used much that was from Chu, so he can be said to have continued Lingyun's [Qu Yuan's] tradition but to have lost the true sounds of the *huangzhong*."[93]

Section 30: Of the twenty-six essays in this section, the first eight concern astronomical matters. In the first (30.1), which is broad in scope, Gu examines the development of astronomy and makes the point that in ancient times the subject was much more a part of the general body of knowledge, whereas as astronomy became more specialized, more and more people grew ignorant of the subject. The next two essays consider, respectively, solar (30.2) and lunar (30.3) eclipses. The remaining essays in this subsection are concerned predominantly with prognostic aspects—the influence that celestial phenomena can have on human affairs and, conversely, the question of whether human affairs can exert a reciprocal influence on celestial events. The following subgroup of seven essays (30.9–15) continues the prognostic theme but in relation to events other than celestial. One does, however, examine the interpretation of celestial events, but by non-Chinese people (30.12), while two of the essays deal with writings on prognostication—one in general terms (30.14) and the other (30.15) specifically on the *Bifang Ji* 閉房記, a work attributed to Confucius. The next six essays are devoted to the clarification of terms: three are to do with divisions of time or periods of astronomical calculation (30.16, 17, & 19), 30.18 considers some aspects of the ancient term *wu xing* 五行 (Five Phases or Five Elements), 30.20 deals with the term used to refer to the prediction of auspicious days, and 30.21 takes up the name of a particular star. The three following essays deal with places of worship: ancestral halls (30.23), Buddhist temples (30.24), and Tai Shan (30.25). The final essay, "The Barbarian Custom of Belief in Ghosts" (30.26), gives examples of occasions when a particular act, perpetrated by non-Chinese people (barbarians), was followed by a natural calamity for which the barbarians in question attempted expiation.

30.1 THE PATTERN (*WEN*) OF THE HEAVENS (ASTRONOMY)

Before and during the Three Dynasties [Xia, Shang, Zhou], people all understood the pattern of the heavens. "In the seventh month the five stars passed the meridian" were the words of farmers.[94] "The three stars appear in the sky" were the words of women.[95] "The moon also is in the Hyades" were due to soldiers at the frontier.[96] "The tail of the dragon lies hidden in the conjunction of the sun and moon" was the song of children.[97] Among literati and scholars of later generations, there were some who, when questioned, were ignorant of these matters. Nevertheless, in the matter of calculations regarding stars and times, the ancients did not achieve the precision of the present day.

Fan Shen, in his *Hejian Fuzhi*, said, "Initially, I studied the 'Lü Shu' and saw there was prohibition of the private practice of astronomy. Subsequently, I read in the imperial orders that at an audience with Ren Miao [Ren Zong], Yang Shiqi and others said, 'This law was naturally established for the people. Should the prohibition also apply to nobles and others?' Later, by means of the *Tianyuan Yuli Xiangyi Fu*, permission was granted to many officials. If one looks at it from the viewpoint of the words of the 'Lü Shu,' one can know that what sages grieve over is deep. If one looks at it from the viewpoint of the imperial orders, one can know that what sages see is great."[98]

30.26 THE BARBARIAN CUSTOM OF BELIEF IN GHOSTS

It is the custom of foreign barbarians to believe in ghosts. The Xiongnu wished to kill Er Shi. Er Shi cursed them, saying, "If I die, there will certainly be destruction of the Xiongnu." Subsequently, they killed Er Shi as a sacrifice. Within a short time there was continuous rain and snow for several months. Domestic animals died, the people were afflicted with epidemic sickness, and the grains didn't ripen. The barbarian chieftain was afraid and established an ancestral temple for Er Shi.[99]

Murong Jun beheaded Ran Min at Longcheng and laid waste to Xingshan. For seven *li* on either side of the mountain, the grass and trees all withered, and a great plague of locusts arose. People said that Min was an evil spirit, so Jun dispatched an envoy to make a sacrifice to him and gave Min the posthumous title of Daowu Tian Wang. On that day there was a heavy fall of snow.[100]

Wei Tai Zu slew He Ba and slaughtered his family. Subsequently, Shi Zu made a tour of the west to Wuyuan and returned. On his progress, he was hunting at Chai Shan when he suddenly encountered a fierce wind with clouds and mist coming in from all quarters. Shi Zu thought it was strange and asked about it. His attendants said that Ba's ancestral home was on this land and a sacrificial mound was still preserved there, so perhaps it was Ba who was able to bring about this change. The emperor sent the Duke of Jianxing, Gu Bi, to make a sacrifice with three animals, whereupon the mist dispersed. Afterward, whenever Shi Zu spent a day hunting, he always first made a sacrifice to Ba.[101]

Boyou was taken to be an evil spirit. This could certainly be regarded as true.[102] The barbarian custom of fearing ghosts and spirits is not, then, something that can be discussed by way of a common principle.

Section 31: The fifty-three essays in this section are predominantly about places (states or kingdoms, provinces, prefectures, districts, and cities), although other places of some particular interest are also included. Points of focus are the origin of the name of the place and changes in a name over time. The former is exemplified by 31.6 on Sichuan 四川 and the latter by 31.18 and 31.19 on Wuzhong 無終 and Liucheng 柳城, respectively. Another point of interest is the situation of the place under consideration, as exemplified by 31.23 on Jiangcheng 江乘. Gu is also interested in errors in usage with regard to place-names, particularly in early writings. One work that comes in for a good deal of attention is the *Water Classic* (*Shui Jing* 水經), as in 31.11. Other works referred to include the *Spring and Autumn Annals*, the *Zuo Zhuan*, the *Shiji*, and the *Han Shu*. Apart from these topics, other points of geographic interest are given attention—for example, mountains (31.45), marshes (31.16), waterways (31.22), palaces and temples (31.12), and tombs (31.24). There is also a long historical discussion about the Great Wall (31.53). Finally, there are four nongeographical essays: one on the origin of the Stone Tablets of Tai Shan (31.43), two on official positions (their establishment and purpose—31.44 and 31.46), and one on the phenomenon of tides (31.27).

31.37 DAI 代

Comment: Dai 代 was an ancient kingdom destroyed in the Warring States period (475 B.C.E.) by Zhao Xiangzi. It was situated in what is now Yanggao district of Shanxi province.

In the Spring and Autumn period, Dai was still not in communication with the Central States. Zhao Xiangzi then said, "As the top of Changshan overlooks Dai, so Dai could be taken." The "Zhengyi" [Orthodox Interpretation] states, "The *Didao Ji* says that Hengshan is 140 *li* northwest of Shang Quyang district. If you travel north 450 *li*, you will reach the peak of Hengshan, designated Feihu Kou. To the north of this is the commandery of Dai [Dai Jun]."[103] The *Water Classic* [*Shui Jing*] commentary quotes Mei Fu on the above matter as saying that the Dai valley had Hengshan to its south and Bei Pass to its north. The land within the valley and above lay to the east and Dai commandery to the west.[104] This is what is now Weizhou but was then still the ancient state of Dai. Xiang Yu moved the King of Zhao, Xie, to be King of Dai, while Xie then established Chen Yu as King of Dai.[105] Emperor Gao of the Han established his elder brother, Liu Zhong, as King of Dai. All these matters refer to this land. In the tenth year of Han Gao Di [197 B.C.E.], Chen Xi rebelled. In the eleventh year [196 B.C.E.], Xi was overthrown, and his son Heng was established as King of Dai, with the capital at Jinyang.[106] This, then, was what is now Taiyuan district. The "Xiaowen Ji" [in the *Shiji*] states that the capital was Zhongdu[107] and that Emperor Wen passed through Taiyuan and returned to Jinyang and Zhongdu.[108] After two years he also established his son Wu as King of Dai, with the capital at Zhongdu,[109] the capital then being in what is now Pingyao district. Also, according to Wei Wan's [biography], he was a man of Daling in Dai.[110] Daling is presently in the north of Wenshui district, which is included in Dai, and this is why the Dai capital was Zhongdu. Although Dai moved three times in all, it never corresponded to what is now Daizhou. The name of the present Daizhou dates from the Sui period.

Section 32: This section comprises forty-three essays about characters, either singly or in combination, devoted essentially to clarification of meaning and usage, as well as origin in some cases. Such aspects are illustrated predominantly in relation to the canon of ancient literature, although modern texts are cited in certain instances. It is of interest that fifteen of these essays are referred to in the definition of the relevant character or character combination in the *Zhongwen Da Cidian*. The characters dealt with in the section are as follows: *er* 而, *nai he* 奈何, *yu ji* 語急, *sui* 歲, *yue ban* 月半, *si* 巳, *li* 里, *ren* 仞, *bu shu* 不淑, *bu diao* 不弔, *wang* 亡, *qian mo* 乾沒, *ru* 辱, *jian* 姦, *e* 訛, *shei* (*shui*) *he* 誰何, *xin* 信, *chu* 出, *guan gua* 鰥寡, *ding zhong* 丁中, *a* 阿, *yao* 幺, *yuan* 元, *xie* 寫, *xing li* 行李, *hao* 耗, *liang yi* 量移, *fu si* 罘罳, *chang wu* 場屋, *dou* 豆, *xing* 陘, *zhi* 豸, *guan* 關, *zhou* 宙, *shi tan* 石炭, *zhong kui* 終葵, *kui* 魁, *sang zi* 桑梓, *hu long* 胡嚨, *hu* 胡, *cao ma* 草馬, *cao lü nü mao* 草驢女貓, *ci xiong pin mu* 雌雄牝牡.

32.2 *NAI HE*

Comment: *Nai he* 奈何 is a phrase with a several meanings: "how"; "to no avail"; "what remedy or alternative is there?"; "what shall I do, then?"; "for what reason." Gu gives a number of examples of its usage. All are from early literature apart from one instance in the *Song Shi*.

The two characters *nai he* 奈何 were first used in the "Songs of the Five Sons" [as follows]: "The ruler of men—how can he not be reverent?"[111] In the *Zuo Zhuan* [there is], "When your belly is pained with fish from the river, what will you do?"[112] In the "Quli" it says, "When the prince of the kingdom was on the point of leaving his domain, those who would stop him asked, 'How can you leave the altars of soil and grain!' The great officers asked, 'How can you leave the ancestral temple!' The scholar-officials asked, 'How can you leave the graves [of your ancestors]!'"[113] In the song "Dasi" from the "Nine Songs" in the *Songs of the South* [*Chu Ci*], it says, "What is there for the melancholy man!"[114] In the "Nine Discussions" [there is], "The prince did not know; how is this possible!"[115] These were the origins of the two characters *nai he* 奈何.

In the *Zuo Zhuan*, in the "Song of Hua Yuan," [there is], "Oxen then have skins; rhinoceroses and wild bulls are still many. But what about the casting away of the buff-coats!"[116] In direct speech *na* 那 is used, whereas in the more ornate style, *nai he* 奈何 is used, and yet they are the same. Also in the *Documents* [there is], "Like the five instruments."[117] Zheng Kangcheng [Zheng Xuan] reads *ru* 如 as *nai ge fan* 乃箇反 [i.e., *ne*]. In the *Analects* [there is], "What is there I can do about it!"[118] The sound here is also the same as *nai*.[119] In the Six Dynasties period, men often wrote *nai* 奈 as *na* 那. Thus, in the notes to the *Annals of the Three Kingdoms* [there is], "Wen Qin, in a letter to Guo Huai, said, 'With respect to that which has been completely overcome, what can be done if afterward there is no continuation?'"[120] In Liu Jingxuan's biography in the *Song History* [*Song Shu*] [there is], "Lao Zhi said, 'After the pacification of Xuan, what shall I be ordered to do with the cavalry?'"[121] In the poetry of the Tang period there was much use of *wu nai* 無奈 for *wu na* 無那.

II

ESSAYS, LETTERS, AND PREFACES FROM *COLLECTED POEMS AND ESSAYS* (*TINGLIN SHIWENJI—SWJ*)

1

SWJ 1

STATECRAFT ESSAYS

There are six essays in this section. The first three are single-part essays: 1.1 is about the sacred peaks—Beiyu Bian, 1.2 deals with the term *ge chu*, and 1.3 concerns original surnames. The other three essays are multipart and are on, respectively, commanderies (prefectures) and districts (nine parts—1.4–12); money and grain (two parts—1.13 and 1.14); and government students, or *shengyuan* (three parts—1.15–17).

1.4–12 ON COMMANDERIES AND DISTRICTS (THE *JUNXIAN* SYSTEM 郡縣, CENTRALIZATION), 1–9

Comment: This is an important statement of one of the fundamental components of Gu Yanwu's political philosophy. On the question of terminology, I have, as elsewhere, followed Charles O. Hucker, *A Dictionary of Official Titles in Imperial China* (Stanford, Calif.: Stanford University Press, 1985). He has this to say on the title:

Junxian 郡縣. Commanderies and Districts: from Qin on, a generic reference to the regional and local units administered by appointees of the central government in what eventually developed, through many transformations into the territorial-administration hierarchy of Provinces (*sheng* 省), Prefectures (*fu* 府), and Districts (*xian* 縣) in the Ming-Qing era; regularly used as a shorthand reference to

> such a governmental system (centralized, bureaucratic, direct) in contrast to the ancient Zhou dynasty system of regional and local administration by hereditary nobles "established by enfeoffment" (*fengjian* 封建 . . .) and by subinfeudation (decentralized, feudal, indirect). (p. 201, no. 1758)

This essay should be read in conjunction with the material in *RZL*, section 8, and Liu Zongyuan's essay on the *fengjian* system included in appendix 4.

1. To know why the *fengjian* [feudal or decentralized] system changed to become the *junxian* [prefectural or centralized] system is to know that this system will, in turn, break down and change again. If this is so, will this change again and return to being feudalism? Impossible, I say. If a sage were to arise and lodge the ideas of feudalism in the prefectural system, the empire would be well ordered. People from Han times onward all said that Qin was lost because of isolation. What they don't know is that the Qin was not lost because it didn't practice the *fengjian* system; the *fengjian* system also died out. Undoubtedly, the decay of this system started during the decline of Zhou and not from the Qin period. It was not the work of one day. Even if a sage had arisen, it would still have changed to become the *junxian* system.

Now, the breakdown of the *junxian* system has already come to pass and yet no sage has emerged. Nevertheless, every one of the ancient practices still persists. As a result, every day the people grow poorer and the central kingdom grows weaker, moving with gathering pace toward disorder. Why is this so? The failings of the *fengjian* system lay in the concentration of power in the hands of those below; the failings of the *junxian* system lay in the concentration of power in the hands of those above. The sages of antiquity treated the people of the world with public-spiritedness, rewarding them with lands and dividing up [the administration of] the state. The rulers of today completely appropriate everything within the Four Seas as their own commanderies and districts, and still this is not enough. All men are held in suspicion, all matters are controlled. Laws, statutes, and records of cases grow more numerous every day. In addition, inspectors and overseers are appointed, as are governors, on the grounds that in this way the prefects and district magistrates will be prevented from harming the people. What is not realized is that those holding office fearfully try to save themselves from error and regard getting a transfer as good fortune. As a consequence, they are not willing to concern themselves for a single day with being of benefit. How can the people do otherwise than become poorer? How can the country do otherwise than become weaker? If this course were to be pursued without change, even if thousands of years were to pass, I know it would lead to disorder and trouble, and this would become more extreme every day.

This being so, to venerate the status of the district magistrate, conferring on him authority over financial and administrative matters, to do away with the office of overseer, to set up the rewards of hereditary office, and to permit the practice of local officials selecting their own subordinates can be termed lodging the ideas of feudalism within the framework of the prefectural system. And this may allow the deterioration of two thousand years to be reversed. If future rulers wish to improve the lives of the people and strengthen the state, they would do well to attend to my words.

2. My proposal is this: change *zhixian* 知縣 [district magistrate] to become a fifth-rank official and rectify his name to call him a *xianling* 縣令.[1] In appointing men to undertake these duties it is necessary to use those from within a thousand-*li* radius who are well versed in local customs. At first they should be called *shiling* 試令 [probationers]; after three years of competent service, they should become *zhenling* 真令 [true magistrates]; after a further three years of competent service, they should be appointed "father and mother" officials; after a further three years of competent service, they should receive an imperial letter recognizing their accomplishments; after a further three years of competent service, they should receive advancement in rank, an increase in salary, and be appointed for life. Those who resign because of old age or ill health can put forward a son or younger brother to replace them. If they can't put forward a son or younger brother, allow them to put forward someone else. When such a person has been replaced and left office, he should live in his district as a "libationer" [*jijiu*] and receive a salary for the rest of his life. The man put forward to replace him should again be a probationary magistrate. After three years of competent service, he should be confirmed in office according to the method given above.

Every three or four districts, or perhaps every five or six, should constitute a prefecture. Appoint one prefect per prefecture and replace him after three years. Appoint and send out censors to tour the regions, replacing them after one year. Let all the provincial authorities be abolished.[2] Establish one assistant under the magistrate, selected and appointed by the Ministry of Personnel. After the assistant has held his position for more than nine years, he can fill a vacant magistracy. Below the assistant there should be officers designated as follows: registrar, commandant, erudite, postmaster, granary master, patroller, and functionary. These should be established in full and not reduced. Let these men be chosen by the magistrate himself and have their names reported to the Ministry of Personnel. For the positions from registrar down, find and use men of the district to fill them.

If the magistrate is found to have committed a crime against the people, he should be banished if the crime is small and executed if it is grave. In the case of magistrates who are deemed competent and have established their home in the district, their names should be removed from the registers of their native places. See to it that those who become district magistrates of the empire are not able to transfer [out of the district] or return [to their native place] but devote the balance of their lives to the district and have their descendants for many generations live there. Banish those who do not perform their duties properly; execute those whose avarice is such as to destroy the integrity of the office. If they are living in the district, it is as district magistrate; if they are banished, they become exiles. If they are rewarded, it is as hereditary officials; if they are punished, it is by beheading or strangulation. How could there be anyone not encouraged to be a good official!

3. What is it that I call "the proper execution of duties" [i.e., being competent]? I say it is wasteland being opened up, uncultivated fields being cultivated, trees being made to grow luxuriantly, drains and ditches being kept in a good state, walls and fortifications being made secure, granaries and storehouses being kept full, schools being made to flourish, robbery and theft being eradicated, and weapons and utensils being kept in good repair. But the most important thing of all is to keep the people happy in their occupations.

Now, caring for the people is just like rearing the five domestic animals. If one man is in charge of horses and oxen, and another in charge of hay and fodder, and you also send an overseer to supervise them, and still have every minor decision referred to the master, the horses and oxen will grow much thinner day by day. To me this is not right. Better to choose a single groom who is diligent and capable, put him in charge of the horses and oxen, provide him with pastureland, and direct him to regularly produce more than is required for their feed. If you see the beasts grow fat, reward him; if not, then beat him. In this way the one who is the master will surely be a Wu Shi or a Qiao Yao.[3]

Thus, a single groom is enough to manage the afflictions of the world, and yet those who do this are numerous. And if he doesn't trust his grooms but uses overseers, and even more, if he doesn't trust the overseers, the eyes and ears of the master will be clouded with confusion. As a result, his heart that loves his horses and oxen will fail to overcome his schemes for scrimping and saving in grain, and the animals he is caring for will waste away. Thus, horses will grow fat under a single groom just as the people will be happy under a single magistrate.

4. Someone might say, "Without provincial intendants will the magistrate not become too important? If his sons and younger brothers replace him, is this not in effect a monopoly? If he comes from within a thousand-*li* radius, will he not be partial to his family and friends?"

Now, the reason why an official's concern for his family and friends disturbs him greatly is that they are all far away. If they all lived together within one city, even if they thought to disturb him, they would not be able to do so. From Han times on, there have been many who administered their own districts and prefectures. The magistrates of Qufu[4] have seldom shown the failings of greed and cruelty. And it wasn't just that the descendants of Confucius were especially worthy; it was their circumstances that made them so. If the prefect were to be succeeded by a son or younger brother and there was concern about a monopoly of power, could a small and insignificant district raise an army in rebellion? Above, there would be the prefect. Couldn't he raise forces from the neighboring districts to suppress the rebellion? If the prefect himself wished to rebel, would [the magistrates of] five or six districts be willing to set aside the possibility of handing down their official positions to their sons and younger brothers and follow the path of disorder? Would they not see that the Yang clan of Bozhou, after eight hundred years of hereditary titles, was executed because of rebellion?[5]

If you say that without overseeing officials [provincial intendants] it is impossible to bring about good order, how was it that the fourteen prefectures [*fu* 府] and four subprefectures [*zhou* 州] of the Southern Imperial Domain were directly responsible to the Six Boards? Moreover, in today's subprefectures and districts, officials don't have established responsibilities and the people don't have established obligations, which is why there is the recurring misfortune of robbers and thieves. And if the Western and Tartar barbarians reach one subprefecture, it is overthrown; if they reach one district, it is destroyed. Not to plan against this but to worry about magistrates acting on their own authority is what I call not recognizing similarities.

5. That each person in the world cherishes his own family and is partial toward his children is an invariable state of affairs. What an official feels in his heart for the Son of Heaven and the ordinary people is certainly not like what he feels for himself. Even before the Three Dynasties, this was already so. Sages relied on this and made use of it. They used the self-interest of the world to bring to perfection the public-spiritedness of one man and the world was well ordered.

Now, if a district magistrate can be brought to look on his hundred *li* of land as his personal concern, then the people of the district will all be like his descendants, the land of the district will all be like his own fields, the inner and outer city walls of the district will all be like his own boundary walls, and the granaries and storehouses of the district will all be like his own granaries and cellars. If he takes the people as his descendants, he will inevitably love them and will not harm them. If he takes the land as his own fields and arable land, he will inevitably keep it in good order and will not neglect it. If he takes the inner and outer walls and the granaries and storehouses as his own boundaries and storage places, he will inevitably keep them well maintained and will not damage them. From the magistrate's standpoint it is self-interest; from the emperor's standpoint, it is what he seeks in bringing order to the world—no more and no less.

If one day there should be an unexpected rebellion, it would surely not be like the rebellion of Liu Yuan, Shi Le, Wang Xianzhi, and Huang Chao—men who ranged without restraint across thousands of *li* as if entering uninhabited regions.[6] As a result, there would be defense to the death and the people would not flee. As a result, there would be resistance through unions and close alliances. This would not be for the emperor; it would be in their own interests. But acting on the basis of self-interest would be acting for the emperor. Thus the self-interest of the world is in effect the public interest of the emperor. "He was concerned for the general good so there was happiness; he was trustworthy so others relied on him."[7] This can come close to the good order of the Three Dynasties. Even more, the splendor of the Han and Tang may not be hard to reach.

6. Nowadays, of the misfortunes of the world, there is none greater than poverty. If, however, my theories were put to use, in five years there would be a small degree of well-being, and in ten years a great degree of wealth. For the moment, let me speak of this in terms of horses. In the empire, from the movement of couriers back and forward, the sending of records from subprefectures and districts to the capital, the sending of official reports, meeting and awaiting high officials, and the transmission of documents, right down to the use of horses by ordinary people on official business, in any one year there will be unimaginable millions of horses traveling unimaginable hundreds of millions of *li*. Now, if this were to be reduced by sixty to 70 percent, the horses and mules from the western and northern regions would be much more than sufficient.

Let me speak of this in terms of documents. A single matter must be reported to a number of district offices [yamen]; the goings and comings associated with reversals of decisions must be multiple. When it comes to the use for welcoming visitors, birthday greetings, and congratulatory messages, the overall cost of paper and materials borne by the people is not less than a great sum every year. At the present time, then, if there were to be a 70 or 80 percent reduction [in use], the bamboo stems of the southeast could not possibly be used up.

The other things to which this argument applies cannot all be enumerated. Moreover, if the one who is magistrate is able to examine plowing and harvesting, instruct on trees and domestic animals, the obtaining of the produce of the fields, the collecting of the fruits from trees and plants, the breeding of the six domestic animals, and the vigorous growth of timber, these things ought to double in amount within five years. From this, the profits from the mountains and marshes can be opened up. Now, in the matter of conscripted labor for mining, during and prior to the Yuan dynasty, there was a constant annual quota. In the Ming dynasty, the reason why the mines were closed down and did not produce was because they might call forth disorder. This is comparable to there being a vault full of gold. If this were to be brought forth at a highway crossroads, traders would come crowding to contend for it. If it were to be brought forth within the hall of a house, only the master would have access to it and those outside would not be able to contend for it. At the present time, where there are mines, if the emperor opens them up, this is like bringing forth gold at the crossroads of five highways. If the district magistrate opens them up, this is like bringing forth gold within the hall of a house. The profits from the mountains and marshes are maximized and not taken from the people. Therefore, I say this is a plan for enriching the country.

7. Among bad methods, there is none worse than taking the eastern subprefectures' grain supplies and giving them to the western border troops, or using those of the southern prefectures to sustain the relay stations of the northern region. Nowadays, if you were to take all the tax revenue and return it to that district, evaluating whether that district was an important place or remote, and estimating whether the requirements were complex or simple, this would make that one district's expenses always bearable and there would be excess. Also, let the salaries of the officials of a single district always exceed the regular amount and only afterward have the excess established as falling within the category of what is sent to the capital.

Before this, it is necessary to fix the taxes for the region, selecting upper, middle, and lower fields, arranging them in three or five grades. What comes from them should all be sent to the district magistrate who receives it. What is sent to the capital is called *gong* 貢 [tribute] or *fu* 賦 [tax]. In the case of irregular expenses, these would be treated as outlay from the fixed tax quota. If one district's income was completely used up and there was still not enough, then subsequently there would be augmentation from the taxes of another district, this being termed *xie ji* 協濟 [lending assistance]. This, then, was the emperor's wealth and could not be regarded as a regular fixed amount. Nonetheless, if this method were to be practiced for ten years, there would certainly not be a single district whose revenue was used up but was still not enough for that district.

8. Excellent, indeed, were Ye Zhengze's words when he said, "Nowadays in the empire officials don't have subinfeudation but minor functionaries do."[8] The deficiency of the subprefectures and districts is that these minor functionaries have burrowed themselves into "holes and caves," fathers handing on their positions to sons and older brothers to younger brothers. Those who are particularly cruel and cunning then advance to become clerks in agencies and bureaus, thereby interfering with the authority of subprefectures and districts. Those in high positions are clearly aware that this is very detrimental to the empire and yet they are unable to do away with it.

If officials were all men from within a thousand-*li* radius, well versed in the affairs of the people and also appointed for life, then superiors and inferiors would be clearly distinguished and the people would be stabilized in their purposes. Regulations would be done away with and official business would be simplified. The power of officials would be sufficient to control the minor functionaries with something to spare, while the latter would have no way of exerting undue influence on the former and would themselves have to comply with the laws. What men of former times called "nurturing a million tigers and wolves in the midst of the people" would be completely done away with in a single day. In the joy of bringing good order to the empire, what could surpass this!

9. In determining the selection of scholar-officials, there is a recommendation that, in summary, uses the ancients' concept of "township recommendation and village selection," and there is an examination that, in summary, uses the Tang people's methods of [assessing] personal appearance, speech, calligraphy, and judgment. For worthy and able scholar-officials recommended by districts, in alternate years one person should be examined at the Ministry [of Personnel]. Those of the highest rank should become court gentlemen [*lang* 郎]; there should be no fixed quota. Court gentlemen of the highest grade should go out and fill vacancies as district magistrates. Those of the second rank should become aides [*cheng*] and be employed near their own prefectures. Those of the third rank should return to their native districts and be appointed to the categories of registrar and military official.

In setting up schools, allow district magistrates and scholar-officials of their districts to make appointments themselves. Call the appointees teachers and not officials, and do not attach their names to the Ministry of Personnel. And at the capital, those of ducal and ministerial rank and above should imitate the Han-period method of *san fu* 三府 [Three

Dukes],[9] involving and employing them. Now, if there are scholars of the empire who have the Way and virtue and yet do not wish to serve in an official capacity, they should become teachers of others. If there are those who have learning and ability and think to involve themselves in the affairs of the age, their district magistrate should find and elevate them or the Three Dukes should find and summon them. This also makes it possible not to lose scholar- officials.

Someone might say, "One man in alternate years—is the path to merit and achievement not too narrow!" Transforming the scholar-officials of the empire so they don't contend for merit and reputation is the greatness of kingly government. Besides, Yan Yuan did not take office; Min Zi resigned his official position; Qidiao never considered himself able; and Zeng Xi had a different objective.[10] What need is there for achievement and reputation!

1.13–14 ON MONEY AND GRAIN (*QIANLIANG* 錢糧—TAXATION), 1–2

Comment: This is another important component of Gu's political philosophy. The essential message is that taxation should not produce hardship and disaffection among the ordinary people. This means two things: (1) People should be taxed in what they produce. (2) There should be no added exactions made by venal officials, such as the "meltage fee" covered in the second section.

1. From the times of Yu and Tang,[11] years of famine have been unavoidable—years when the people, driven to extremes by having no grain, sold their own children. Indeed, years of famine and the selling of wives and children were what even the times of Yu and Tang could not be free of. On the other hand, years of abundance in which there was the selling of wives and children never occurred, even in the last year of the Tang and Song dynasties.

In the past, when I was in Shandong, I noticed that the people who lived in Dengzhou and Laizhou, both coastal provinces, often said the price of grain was so low that the people living in mountainous and remote regions could not obtain the silver to pay the tax collector. Now, coming to Guanzhong from the west as far as Qixia, the year has been very abundant and grain very plentiful, and yet the people still follow one another in selling their wives and children. When it comes to the day of the grain levy, the people of the villages all come forth, and there is what is called a "human market." When I asked a senior official, he said that in one district, those sold into military camps or who request the official seal [for tax exemptions], in one year came close to a thousand people, while there is no knowing how many people run away or commit suicide. Why is this?

It is because there is grain but no silver. What they harvest is not what they have to pay; what is sought is not what they produce. Now, silver doesn't fall from the heavens. Miners have already stopped [mining]. Ocean-going vessels have already been withdrawn. The country's silver that is among the people is already being dispersed and diminished by the day, and particularly in the mountainous and remote regions where merchants never set foot. Even if the silver were to be sought under threat of flogging, how could it be obtained! Therefore, the grain becomes cheaper every day and the people become poorer every day; every day they are more weighed down by taxation. Each year more people flee to avoid debt and each year the number of registered individuals diminishes. If this situation continues unchanged, who knows where it will end!

Furthermore, from what did [the use of silver] arise? What constituted wealth for the ancients were legumes and grains, and that is all. In their carrying out of trade, there was no alternative but to use money as a measure. Nevertheless, from the Three Dynasties to the Tang, what was taken from the people was grain and cloth, and that is all. From the implementation of Yang Yan's two-tax law,[12] there was the start of change and the levying of money but never of silver. The "Han Zhi" [Han Records] [chapter of the *History of the Former Han*] states that the Qin had a currency of two grades, but that silver and tin were used for utensils and ornaments and not as currency.[13] From Liang times, starting in Jiaozhi and Guangdong, there were reports of the use of gold and silver as commodities. In the second year of the Jingyou reign period of the Song emperor Ren Zong [1035], there was, for the first time, an order to all circuits to pay the year's taxes in strings of cash. For Fujian, Guangdong, and Guangxi, this was changed to silver, and for Jiangdong, to silk. The reasons why this was chosen for Fujian and the two Guangs were that the mines and foundries were numerous and maritime trade was profitable. At the time of the Jin emperor Zhang Zong [1190–1208], the casting of silver coinage began. This was called "the precious commodity of the Chengan reign period" [1196–1200]. In public and private dealings alike, this was used as money. During the Zhengda reign period of the [Jin emperor] Ai Zong [1224–1231], the people used silver only in market transactions; they did not use the cast coinage. When we come to the present day, all levels of society use the latter universally and have forgotten what it arose from. However, if you examine the matter in the *Yuan History*, the amount of the annual tax levy that was silver was very low. This being so, then, the use of silver as a national tax doesn't exceed two or three hundred years.

Nowadays, when people speak of taxes, they invariably speak of *qian* 錢 and *liang* 糧. Now, *qian* is money [copper cash] and *liang* is grain. Why should they also speak of silver? Moreover, the amount of silver in the world has not increased, and yet taxes have doubled, so this must be an amount that is not contributed. Formerly, at the time of the Tang emperor Mu Zong [821–824], goods were cheap and money expensive, so the proposal of the minister of finance, Yang Yuling,[14] was used—that is, the order was given that the two tax grades of money were to be changed to cotton and various forms of silk for the convenience of the people.[15]

Xu Zhigao of Wu followed the words of Song Qiqiu[16] in considering that money was not what was obtained from agriculture and sericulture, so to make people pay tax in money was to teach them to neglect the root and follow the branches. As a result of this, the various taxes were received in grain and silk. This, then, was the discussion of those of former times on what was collected from the people. Moreover, since they regarded money as being difficult to obtain, for the people to seek money would mean that they did not devote attention to the root. Does this not apply much more in the case of silver?

When former kings established taxes, they certainly collected what a particular place had. Nowadays, in major metropolises and large district cities—places of great commercial activity—even if all the tax levies are in silver, the people don't report distress. But when it comes to places that are distant and remote—places that boats and carts don't reach—even if only 30 percent of the tax levy is in silver, it still cannot be obtained. Distress the people with this, which certainly cannot be obtained, and ultimately distress will come to the state. Why not, then, work out what is appropriate for the land and place, estimate the amount of the annual tax collection, give thought to the methods of transmission, and find some compromise in these things? Order all prefectures and districts that don't engage in commerce to pay entirely in what is natural for them. If this can't be done, then levy the tax in money at a rate of three parts in ten. If money passes from those below to those above, there will be the unacceptable evil of excess and the value of money will be high, so with one act there will be two effects. There will be no deficiency in the taxes remitted, and there will be a livelihood for the people. There will not be the problem of the need for restraint, and there will be the payment of all that is owed. Among the present-day schemes, there is none more suitable than this.

To plant grains and yet collect taxes in silver is like rearing sheep and yet seeking horses. To rely on silver to enrich the nation is like depending on wine to satisfy hunger. It is by this individual foolishness that the deficiencies reach a point where state and people are bound together in exhaustion. This is inferior to the scheme that came from the various officials of the last stages of the Tang and Song dynasties.

2. Sad to say, from ancient times on, those who have held states have taken from the people—this is already well known. Nevertheless, I have not heard of there being talk of a "meltage fee." Did the term "meltage fee" not arise in the era when tax was collected in silver? Is this not what is spoken of as the true tax being ten parts and the excess tax [surtax] being three parts? Is this not what is spoken of as the state misappropriating public funds and corrupt officials becoming rich? Is this not what the state rigorously guards against and yet what venal officials and knavish clerks preserve for generations, taking it to be a treasure for their descendants? Is this not the root cause of impoverishing the people, the source of exhausting wealth, the gateway to the beginning of banditry, and what ordinary timid men in official positions see with their own eyes but do not remedy?

What originally brought the meltage fee into existence was that the many taxes of the prefectures and districts, being collected as they were, household by household, and received in very small amounts, could not be sent up to the official storehouses in little fragments, which left no alternative but to melt them down. If there was melting down, then inevitably there was loss. What was termed loss amounted to only one or two parts in a hundred—that is all. There were avaricious men who thought that a levy outside the fixed quota could not escape official opposition, while selecting people and preying on them would not be enough to satisfy their greed. As a result, they made use of the term "meltage fee" as a cunning method of extortion.

Now, I don't know in what year this arose, but the method was handed down, becoming more onerous from official to official and increasing from generation to generation until we come to the present time. Thus, if officials take a 20 or 30 percent profit, the people pay 130 percent for the state's 100 percent. And if subofficial functionaries and their like take ten to 20 percent, the people end up paying 150 percent for the state's 100 percent.

In these collections a small part is in *liang* [taels] and a great part is in *zhu* [1/24 of a tael]. In all cases, when the amount collected is in taels, it will invariably be from those with large landholdings, power, and influence—people who can cope with the shortcomings, deficiencies, and excesses I have mentioned. When the collection is in *zhu*, it is invariably from poor and lowly households, and although much is taken from them, they dare not speak out. As a result of this, 20 to 30 percent is added to the collection in taels, whereas 50 to 60 percent is added to the collection in *zhu*. This is less in the regular tax levies and more in the irregular tax levies. It is the regular tax levies to which attention is primarily directed; the irregular levies receive secondary consideration. Consequently, the addition to the regular levies is 20 to 30 percent, whereas that to the irregular levies may sometimes reach 70 to 80 percent. When this is sent to the provincial treasurer, it is called a surplus; when the contribution is made to the various regional commissioners, it is called regular practice. There is no alternative to meeting these demands, which are protected as something that cannot be broken. They have given rise to the people's difficulties, which have never been greater than they are at the present time.

I have lived in Shandong for a long time. Among the people of the province there is not one who doesn't knit his brow with care and complain of the oppression of this meltage fee. Only in Dezhou is this not so. When you ask why, they say the tax for the province is 29,000 taels, of which 20 percent is silver and 80 percent copper cash. No meltage fee is added to the copper cash, so the people's resources are free from constraint compared with other districts. It is not that the officials of Dezhou are all worthy men or that the village functionaries are all good men. It is simply a matter of circumstances. I have also heard elders say that the greedy officials of recent times are much more numerous than in Tang and Song times. The reason why this is so is that copper cash is heavy and hard to transport, whereas silver is light and easy to transport. If something is hard to transport, then even if little is taken, it is considered a lot, whereas with something that is easy to transport, then even if a lot is taken, it will still be considered a little. It is not that the officials of the Tang and Song were particularly honest while those of the present time are venal. It is the circumstances that make things so. Nevertheless, the circulation of silver and the cessation of the use of copper cash mean riches for officials and robbery for the people.

At the beginning of the Ming, the people were prohibited from using gold and silver. Those who transgressed were presumed to be traitorous villains. Now, why is the use of gold and silver villainous? As for there being repeated prohibitions, the probability is that there was foreknowledge of corrupt practices inevitably coming to this [present state]. At that time, what was used in the marketplace and shops was in all cases the copper coinage of the Tang and Song along with single castings of the official coinage made to help out if there was a shortage. Nowadays, currency is weak and harmful metal has arisen; the *dao* of trading is weak and false things are made. The country's wealth is seized by those above and the people's resources are exhausted by those below. If the likes of Lu Zhi, Bai Juyi, and Li Ao were alive today, their loud sighs and lamentations would certainly be much greater than those they uttered in the mid-Tang period.[17]

Someone might say, you take the meltage fee to be a cause of distress for the people. If a change were to be made and taxes collected in grains and rice, would there be no cunning methods for taking extra grain from the people? I say I have never seen a food provisioner leaving office nor a grain measurer settling down with his family who traveled carrying a load of rice. Invariably they have bought silver before they left. And if there were two carts traveling on the road, the one in front with copper cash and the one behind with silver, then a great robber's glance would always be directed at the one behind. This being so, not only are greedy officials much more numerous than in Tang and Song times but also those called mounted highwaymen north of the Yellow River are much more numerous.

1.15–17 ON GOVERNMENT STUDENTS (*SHENGYUAN* 生員), 1–3

Comment: The proliferation of government students and the abuses of the system were a particular cause of concern for Gu Yanwu. This essay should be read in conjunction with his other writings on the subject in sections 16 and 17 of *A Record of Daily Knowledge*—and in particular *RZL* 17.1. In calling for the abolition of government students, he lists four benefits: (1) government offices will be purified; (2) the burden on ordinary people will be relieved; (3) clique and faction formation will be eliminated; and (4) talented scholars will be able to emerge more readily.

1. Why is it that the state established government students? It was to collect the outstandingly talented students of the empire and nurture them in the schools, so causing them to perfect their virtue and reveal their talents, gain a clear awareness of the Way of former kings and an understanding of the affairs of the present time. Thus they could emerge to become high officials and great officers who could join with the emperor in his plans and deliberations and, together with him, bring about good order.

This is not how things are at present. If you were to gather together the government students of the empire, reckoning on three hundred per district, there would be not less than half a million men, and yet what they are taught is only to write essays in the examination halls. However, if you want to seek those with well-developed skills, you would not find one in several tens. As for those who understand the classics and are proficient in ancient and modern learning—men who could be of use to the emperor—you would not find one in several thousand. On the other hand, those who are deceitful, litigious, indolent, and stupid to the point of distressing officials are much more numerous. Because of this, their superiors increasingly dislike them and every day treat them more disrespectfully, subjecting them to conditions and regulations that every day become more vexatious. Thus it is that government students are increasingly disliked, increasingly treated disrespectfully, and increasingly vexed. And yet lowly men still press forward urgently day and night, stopping only when all their strength is spent—why?

It is because once they have attained this [status], they escape from the labor service of the people, they are not subject to the appropriations of the village functionaries, they are registered as gentry, they get to be received with due ceremony by senior officials, and they don't suffer the disgrace of a flogging with a bamboo cane. Therefore, at the present time, those who wish to be government students are not invariably driven by the desire for achievement and rank; they wish to protect themselves and their families and nothing more. If we reckon that 70 percent of government students are those wishing to protect themselves and their families, there are almost three hundred and fifty thousand such men. This is contrary to the original intention behind establishing the category and has no benefit for the state.

But when it comes to people's feelings, who is not concerned for himself and his family? Thus, in seeking this [status] night and day, there are some whose conduct is so extreme that they suborn, transgress the laws, and have to atone for their crimes, and yet they do not stop, such are the circumstances. So among government students of the present day, 70 to 80 percent attain their positions by improper means, and there are also students of warfare and sacrifices who in all cases buy their positions with money. Now, bribery is what the court must punish, and yet feelings for oneself and one's family are something even former kings were unable to prohibit. So taking the laws of the present day, even if Yao and Shun were to be born again and could send the Four Villains away from the court, they would still be unable to put a stop to bribery within the empire.[18] This being so, what, then, can be done?

I would ask that this system be done away with entirely and a different system instituted. It is necessary to select men with a thorough understanding of the Five Classics and then fill the positions with them, and also examine them on the twenty-one dynastic histories and the affairs of the present time, and then advance them. They should still be divided into the two categories of *xiucai* [cultivated talents] and *mingjing* [classicists], but those supported by the schools should not exceed twenty in number, and if there are not [twenty who are appropriate], the places should be left vacant. As for those who are teachers, they should be selected through decorous enquiry in the prefectures and districts and not appointed centrally. If things were like this, the state would have men of genuine usefulness, the districts would have scholar-officials with an understanding of the classics, and those who are men of talent would certainly flourish in the present times.

But in one township there will inevitably be this one family of ordinary abilities that will establish itself, and in one district there will invariably be a hundred. If all of these do not attain [the status of] government student in order to protect their families and are in the same boat as the common people in suffering the mistreatment and cruelty of the village functionaries and the beatings of the senior officials, how will the ruler's intention to protect and encourage these people be realized? So then, there is the Qin and Han method of conferring noble rank. Initially there was a reward for military achievement, but later it was awarded as an imperial favor or for hard work or as a general or specific reward. Emperor Gao [206–195 B.C.E.] issued a proclamation that said, "At the present time my attitude toward noble rank is that it is not to be taken lightly. . . . I order officials to treat those of high rank well as this would be in accord with my intention."[19] However, by the time of Hui Di [194–188 B.C.E.], the people were able to purchase noble rank. Now, if the importance of noble rank attains an equivalence to an official position in terms of *li* 禮 [respect] and gives back to a family freedom from affairs, then men will be hastening to acquire it. By reinstituting that method it would be possible to put an end to the present one. Even if noble rank is confined to the giving of grain, the name would still be fair—at least it would not be as harmful as the selling of the various kinds of licentiate and the confusion this brings to the schools.

Now, in establishing merit and reputation and protecting oneself and one's family, there are two paths. For gathering together men of eminence and for treating eminent people sympathetically, there are two methods. In both cases, if the two methods are practiced separately, they will not conflict with each other, but if they are made one, there will be problems. If the ruler shares the empire with these five hundred thousand men who don't understand ancient and modern [learning], of whom three hundred and fifty thousand are trying to protect themselves and their families and avoid a beating, and he wishes to seek dukes and nobles and high officials from among them to establish the state and bring good order to the people, this is like "climbing a tree to look for fish"![20] In governing it will certainly be dangerous; in warfare it will certainly fail.

2. Do away with the government students of the world and the administration of government will become pure. Do away with the government students of the world and the difficulties of the ordinary people will be put to rest. Do away with the government students of the world and the practice of clique formation will be abolished. Do away with the government students of the world and talented men of use to the times will emerge.

Nowadays, it is government students who, by going in and out of the government offices of the world, disturb the administration of government. It is government students who rely on their authority to make arbitrary decisions in townships and villages. It is government students who are implicated with subofficial functionaries or who even become subofficial functionaries themselves. It is government students who rise up en masse and create a clamor if the government even once opposes their ideas. It is government students who take control of the government's clandestine affairs and trade in these. Those in front make a noise; those behind chime in. Those in front rush forward; those behind follow. Those above them wish to bring them to order and yet they cannot do so; they wish to get rid of them and yet they cannot do so. If some slight restraint is imposed, they say it is "slaughter of scholars" or "burial of Confucians."[21] I consider them to have been a major problem for the past hundred years. And yet the few scholar-officials who understand the principles of government and have the ability to speak about them themselves all come from the ranks of government students and don't dare to speak openly about the corruption. Therefore, it is impossible to eliminate this comprehensively at a single stroke. This is why I say do away with the government students of the empire and purify the administration of government offices.

There are three things in the world that bring distress to the people: retired officials, government students, and subofficial functionaries. These three groups all, by law, have their households exempted from taxation and labor services. Moreover, their not being called upon for miscellaneous labor services means these fall entirely on the ordinary people. Nowadays, large districts with 100,000 or more government students are commonplace. Suppose that one district has 100,000 *qing* of land and the government students hold 50,000 *qing*. Then the people with 50,000 *qing* are responsible for the miscellaneous labor services appropriate to 100,000 *qing*. If one district has 100,000 *qing* of land and the government students hold 90,000, then the people with 10,000 *qing* are responsible for the miscellaneous labor services appropriate to 100,000 *qing*. As the people's land becomes increasingly less so the practice of the false assignment of land becomes increasingly great, and as this becomes increasingly great, so the people's land becomes increasingly less and the government students increasingly important. The rich indulge in nefarious practices seeking to become government students; the poor, one after another, flee or die. Thus the government students do not bring one iota of benefit to their districts; indeed, they are a mountainous burden. Notwithstanding, all the expenses for the preliminary examinations fall entirely on the ordinary people, therefore those who especially bring distress to the people are the government students. I say this, then: do away with the government students of the empire and the difficulties of the ordinary people will be relieved.

Among the troubles of the empire, there is none greater than gathering together people from the four directions who don't know one another and teaching them, so causing there to be cliques and factions. Of the government students in the empire, those who are near to one another are several hundred or a thousand *li* apart, while those who are distant are separated by ten thousand *li*. Their speech is not the same and their surnames and personal names are unfamiliar. But as soon as they have risen in the ranks of examinees, they have what is called a "chief examination officer" whom they call "examination mentor" and an "associate examination officer" whom they call "deputy mentor." Scholars who are graduates of the same year are called *tongnian* 同年 [year mates], while sons of the year mates are called "year nephews." Sons of the examination mentor and deputy examination mentor are called "elder brothers." A student's examination mentor and deputy mentor call him "disciple," while those later chosen by the disciple are called "second-generation disciples." The second generation disciples call their master's master "grand master." These associations are firm and enduring; the bonds formed cannot be broken. They write documents and exchange them on the roads, and they seek preferential treatment from government offices.

On a small scale, this is enough to corrupt the administration and harm the people; on a large scale, it comes to the point of establishing cliques and causing subversion, taking hold of the handle of the ruler's great sword[22] and turning it upside down. Thus are all these things caused. Therefore I say: do away with the government students of the empire and the practice of clique formation will be eliminated.

The reason why the country selects government students and examines them in the interpretation of the classics and in essays, memorials, policies, and judgments is the wish for them to have a clear comprehension of the purport of the Six Classics and an understanding of contemporary affairs. Nowadays they use the interpretations printed by booksellers, calling these *shiwen* 時文 [model essays];[23] they set aside the classical writings of the sages and don't read the notes and commentaries of former Confucians or the histories of former dynasties. And yet they read these so-called *shiwen*. The *shiwen* that come out change with every examination. Young boys no taller than five *chi* [feet] can recite from memory several tens of these essays, and by making small changes in the text, can achieve an examination rank, while those who are dull witted can reach white-haired old age without attaining success. Experienced scholars may fritter away the most useful years of their lives in examination halls, whereas those who achieve rapid success at an early age also have a facile view of the affairs of empire and state, taking what constitute merit and achievement in a man's life to be just this and nothing more. Therefore, this corrupts and ruins the talented men of the empire until the point is reached where scholars are not true scholars, officials are not true officials, soldiers are not true soldiers, and generals are not true generals. Subsequently, outlaws and villains have opportunities to gain advantage while enemy states and foreign aggressors have opportunities to prevail. If the effort put into the *shiwen* were to be directed to the classics and dynastic histories, as well as current affairs, then of necessity scholars of intelligence and courage with a thorough understanding of administrative principles would arise in their midst. Therefore I say: do away with the government students of the empire and let talented men of use to the age come forth.

3. Someone might ask, if government students of the empire were to be done away with, how would scholar-officials be selected? I say, what I refer to as doing away with government students is not doing away with government students per se; it is doing away with the government students of the present day. I ask that the method of "special imperial appointment" be used, along with the preservation of the system of government students and Confucian scholars. The people of the empire would not need to be asked whether they were government students or not. All would be able to gain advancement and be presented to the court. So then, if my idea were to be accepted, the numbers would be increased and yet the number drawing a government stipend would be limited to a fixed quota, retaining and imitating the Tang system of grading prefectures and districts. A small prefecture would have a quota of ten men, and so on up to forty men for a large prefecture and then stop. A small district would have a quota of three men, and so on up to twenty men for a large district and then stop. Estimate the size of their district's population and the quality of their talented men, then rank them accordingly. If there are vacancies, fill them, and put a stop to the two methods of "tribute students" [*suigong* 歲貢] and "provincial graduates" [*juren* 舉人].

Of those who are graduates, select the ones who are accomplished and outstanding; all these should undergo an examination at the Ministry of Rites. Those who become presented scholars [*jinshi*] should merely be given the responsibilities of assistant magistrate and district defender in close relation to the people, not allowing them to advance with unseemly rapidity by restraining their feelings of greed and ambition. In arranging educational officials for them, worthy men of their district must be engaged, and they should not be added to the register of government employees. Put an end to the office of education intendant and direct these matters to the provincial administration commissioner.

Among all these students there will be some who are recommended and enter official service and some who pass the examinations and become presented scholars [*jinshi*]. There will also be some who don't comply and end up being reprimanded and dismissed. And there will be some who, through decrepitude and illness, are unable to pursue a career but who wish to retain the scholar's garb into old age. When vacancies for two or three men arise, gather together those who fall into the category of "Confucian apprentice" and select from their number those who understand the classics and are able to write well to fill the vacancies.

In this way, then, those in the empire who are government students will be few, and in being few, others will esteem them, and these men will also come to experience self-esteem. Do this, and teachers will not be troubled by teaching, while what was formerly called the gathering of scholars into factions to behave outrageously in the country will spontaneously stop without need for prohibition. If scholars "revive the old and understand the new,"[24] and in their middle years are examined and compared so that they strive to realize their abilities, then it is appropriate to examine and compare ancient and modern methods, but I have not discussed this fully.

Someone might say, in the empire men of talent arise every day—there is no limit. But if they are all obstructed at the level of Confucian apprentice, what then? I would certainly say, if men of the empire, whether they are government students or not, can all gain advancement and be recommended to the court, then the method of selecting scholar-officials will not depend only on all scholars following a single path. Now, if there is selection of scholar-officials to assist the ruler in managing the country and they all come out of a single path, there cannot but be corrupt practices.

2

SWJ 2

PREFACES

This section comprises fifteen prefaces or postfaces, either to Gu's own works or to those of other writers. The former (2.1–6) include the *Yinxue Wushu* and the *Jinshi Wenzi Ji*. The latter (2.7–15) include the *Lü Shi Qianzi Wen* and *Cheng Zhengfu Shi.*

2.1 PREFACE TO THE *YINXUE WUSHU*

The [*Li*] *Ji* [*Book of Rites*] says, "When sounds form patterns, we speak of rhymes." That is, when there are patterns, there are rhymes, and when rhymes are brought together, poetry is created. When a poem is complete, it is set to music. These things all come forth from Heaven and are not something man can create. At the time of the Three Dynasties, texts were all based on the six classes.[1] When people came forth from the family and village schools, their natures were all developed and transformed toward "central and harmonious," and the sounds that emerged from their lips were invariably in accord with what was right. Nevertheless, the *Rites of Zhou* [*Zhou Li*] says, on the responsibilities of the senior messenger, "In the ninth year, he assembles the blind musicians and historiographers, issues a proclamation on written characters, and practices listening to sounds and rhymes." This is how to bring unity to the Way and virtue and uniformity to customs—this cannot be neglected.[2]

This is why the 305 poems of the *Odes* beginning from the Shang hymns and continuing down to Duke Ling of Chen [r. 612–598 B.C.E.], over a range of fifteen states and a time of more than a thousand years, never showed any variation in their rhymes. Emperor Shun's song, Gaoyao's continuation, Ji Zi's statement, and the appendixes of King Wen and the Duke of Zhou were entirely without differences.[3] Therefore, the 305 poems are a record of the rhymes of the ancients. From the Wei and Jin periods on, antiquity became more remote every day and *ci* 詞 and *fu* 賦 [verses] more numerous every day. Subsequently, the term *yin* was changed to *yun* [finals]. When it came to Zhou Yong of the Song and Shen Yue of the Liang, tables of the four tones were created.[4] But from the writings of Qin and Han, rhymes had already turned away from the ancient [forms]. By the time of the Eastern Jin, this deviation was already very great, and when Xiuwen [Shen Yue] created his table, he was unable to base the rhymes on the earlier odes [*ya* and *nan*] or evaluate them beside the *Chu Ci* [*Songs of the South*] in order to complete a lasting classic. His work was based only on the rhymes used in the *fu* of Ban Gu and Zhang Heng, and those who came after them, and the *shi* of the Caos and Liu Zheng, and those who came after them.[5] Nevertheless, he compiled what was established as a basis, and, as a result, modern rhymes were practiced and ancient rhymes were lost. This constituted the first change in the study of rhymes.

Coming down to the Tang period, *shi* and *fu* were used to select scholar-officials, and their rhymes were unified by taking Lu Fayan's *Qieyun* as a standard.[6] Although there were notes on single and combined rhymes, the division of rhyme groups never changed. When it came to the Jingyou reign period of the Song dynasty [1034–1037], there were some minor changes. In the later years of Emperor Li Zong [r. 1225–1264], Liu Yuan of Pingshui reduced the 206 rhymes to 107.[7] In the Yuan period, Huang Gongshao wrote his *Yunhui* following this, which has lasted to the present time.[8] As a result, Song rhymes were practiced and Tang rhymes were lost. This was the second change in the study of rhymes.

As an age becomes daily more distant, so its transmission is daily more error strewn, and the loss of the Way has taken place over more than two thousand years. I have looked deeply into the matter over the years, but it was only when I acquired a copy of the *Guangyun*[9] that, for the first time and from all aspects, I came to an understanding of its theories. As a result, I relied on the Tang writers as the basis for correcting Song errors, and the ancient classics as the basis for correcting the errors of Shen Yue and the Tang writers. Further, the rhymes of the Three Dynasties and before were divided up and put in order, a matter of considerable complexity, but one that cannot be left in a state of confusion. Then I set out the changes of ancient and modern rhymes and examined the reasons for the differences, preparing the *Yinlun* in two *juan*. I examined and corrected the rhymes of the Three Dynasties and before and made notes on the 305 odes to create the *Shibenyin* in ten *juan*. I annotated the *Book of Changes* [*Yi Jing*] to create the *Yiyin* in three *juan*. I distinguished Shen Yue's errors of classification and, using the ancient rhymes one by one, corrected them to create the "Tang Yunzheng" in twenty *juan*. I arranged the ancient rhymes in ten groups, creating the "Guyin Biao" in two *juan*.

From this, the writings of the Six Classics can be read. The books of the other philosophers have variations and correspondences, but they are not far apart. "Heaven will never lose this writing," so, of necessity, a sage will again arise who will bring modern-day speech back to the purity of ancient times. Confucius said, "I returned from Wei to Lu, and afterward music was corrected, and the *ya* and *song* each were brought back to what they should be."[10] Truly, there is hope that someone will do this in the times to come.

2.3 PREFACE TO THE FIRST EDITION OF THE *RIZHI LU*

I copied out the work I wrote—the *Record of Daily Knowledge*—because many of my friends wanted me to, being anxious that I would not be able to give it to them. Subsequently, in the year *shangzhang yan* [*gengxu*, the ninth year of the Kangxi reign period—1670], I printed these eight *juan*. Now, six or seven years have gone past. I am older and have made some progress. In days past I began to regret the limitations of my learning—my opinions were not very enlightened. There are frequent omissions in the book, but it is already out there in the world and it is not possible to hide them. I have gradually made additions and amendments and now have twenty or so *juan*. I would like to print it again but still don't presume to think it is in its final form. Therefore, I have first given the old edition to those of like mind. Now, the pattern [*li* 理] of all under

Heaven is without limit, and the noble man's purpose lies in the Way [*dao* 道]. If he doesn't complete this purpose, he is unsuccessful. And so my past attainments are not enough to brag about. The work's completion in the days to come doesn't allow me to limit myself. If what I wish for is enlightened scholarship, correction of men's minds, and reform of a disordered age by bringing its affairs to a great peace, then this won't be completed by this printing. After I finally put down my brush, I must "hide this in a famous mountain,"[11] where it will lie waiting to be sought out by someone who seeks to bring peace to the world and order to the ten thousand things. It will be fortunate indeed if he doesn't cast this printing aside because of its shallowness!

3

SWJ 3

LETTERS 1

Section 3: This section contains twenty-four letters. The first seven are relatively long letters to friends on specific topics, notably scholarship (3.1), the *Changes* (3.2, 3.3), and disciples (3.6). The remaining seventeen are addressed to particular individuals. Five of these are replies.

3.1 LETTER TO A FRIEND DISCUSSING LEARNING

Recently, during my travels north and south, I was much indebted to my friends for holding someone in high regard who is only a day or so older than themselves and for asking the way from a blind man. I have sighed with regret because, over the past hundred years or more, those who are deemed scholars have frequently spoken of mind]*xin* 心] and nature [*xing* 性] and yet have completely failed to gain an understanding [of these terms]. The decree of Heaven [*ming* 命] and *ren* 仁 [loving-kindness, benevolence, humanity] were things the Master seldom spoke of. Nature and the Way of Heaven were things Zigong never heard of. The *li* 理 [principle, pattern, coherence] of the decreed nature [*xing ming* 性命] was set out in his commentary on the *Changes* so he [Confucius] did not often tell people about them. In reply to those who enquired about [the meaning of] "scholar," he said, "In your conduct, let there be a sense of shame" and, with regard to learning, "love what is ancient and diligently seek it." In speaking with his disciples on the statement passed from Yao to Shun about "wavering, subtle, discriminating, and undivided," he said nothing at all. He only said, "Strongly hold fast to the center. If, within the four seas, there is distress and want, the heavenly revenue will come to a perpetual end." Indeed, how plain and simple is the Sage's learning; how easy it is to follow![1]

Thus, [the Master] said, "I study what is below and yet I aspire to an understanding of what is above." Master Yan was almost a sage and yet he could still say, "He broadened my mind with learning." In telling Duke Ai of the merit of making clear what is good, he gave first place to wide learning. From Zengzi onward, there was no one like Zixia in regard to sincerity and truthfulness. In speaking of *ren* 仁, he said, "[It is to be found in] broad learning and a sincere will, eagerness in questioning, and thinking of what is close at hand." The noble men of the present day are not like this. They gather guests and disciples, seeking scholars—thousands of men who, "like plants and trees, have to be separately treated according to their kinds." And yet they speak with all of them about mind and nature. They set aside "study much and commit it to memory" and "seek the method of one thread."[2] They dismiss talk of distress and want within the four seas, all the time expounding the theory of "wavering, subtle, discriminating, and undivided," in the certainty that their way is higher than the Master's and their disciples more worthy than Zigong.[3] They overlook the "school of eastern Lu" [Confucians] and see themselves as directly continuing the transmission of mind of the two emperors [Yao and Shun]. I dare not approve of this.

Mencius, in his book, speaks of mind and nature but is also very cautious. Then, when it comes to what questions Wan Chang, Gongsun Chou, Chen Dai, Chen Zhen, Zhou Xiao, and Peng Geng asked and what Mencius's answers were, they were always about going forth and staying at home, retiring from and taking up office, rejecting and accepting, and taking and giving. In considering Yi Yin as being a great sage and the outstanding virtue and great merit of Yao and Shun in ruling their people, the basis of these things was in "not looking at a thousand teams of horses" and "not taking a single straw."[4] Bo Yi and Yi Yin were not the same as Confucius, but they were alike in this: "Neither of them would have committed one unrighteous act or put to death one innocent person in order to obtain all under Heaven."[5] This is why nature, the decree of Heaven, and Heaven itself were things the Master seldom spoke about, and yet they are what noble men of the present day constantly speak about. The distinctions between going forth and staying at home, retiring from and taking up office, rejecting and accepting, and taking and giving are what Confucius and Mencius constantly spoke about, and yet they are what noble men of the present time seldom speak about. To speak of loyalty and purity as not reaching to *ren* 仁 and yet not to know that there can be talk of *ren* 仁 without loyalty and purity is a matter of ignorance. To speak of not hating and not coveting as being not sufficient to complete the Way [*dao* 道], and yet not to know that in a lifetime of hatred and covetousness it is possible to speak of the Way [*dao* 道], is a matter of ignorance. I dare not presume knowledge of this.[6]

What is it that I speak of as the Way [*dao* 道] of the Sage? I mean, "to widely study the writings"; I mean, "to have a sense of shame in one's actions."[7] From the individual life right up to the empire and its kingdoms, everything is a matter of learning. From [the obligations incumbent on a] son, subject, younger brother, and friend right up to going out and entering, coming and going, rejecting and accepting, and taking and giving—all are matters in which there is a sense of shame. Shame, in relation to a man, is a very great matter. This is not "to be ashamed of bad clothing and bad food" but "to be ashamed of ordinary men and women not receiving their due blessings."[8] Therefore, it is said, "The ten thousand things are all complete in ourselves; when I look at myself, there is *cheng* 誠 [genuineness, integrity]."[9] Ah, alas! To be a scholar and not first speak of shame is to be a man without a foundation. If one does not love the ancients and listen assiduously, then one's learning is empty and without substance. To be a man without a foundation and expound learning that is empty and without substance, I see as becoming more remote from the matters of the Sage every day. Although this is something I hardly dare speak of, nevertheless, with my trivial thoughts, I look forward to your enlightening reply.

4

SWJ 4

LETTERS 2

This is the second section devoted entirely to letters, of which there are forty-three in all. There are multiple letters or replies to the following people: Li Zide (three), Pan Cigeng (four), Li Zhongfu (two), and Wang Shanshi (two). There are then twenty-five short letters to unnamed friends (seven of which are presented in the following) followed by one longer letter, which exists in two versions.

4.18–41 LETTERS TO FRIENDS

1. If a man who is a scholar does not make progress every day, then every day he slips back. If he studies alone, without a companion, then he becomes limited and shallow, and it is difficult for him to achieve anything. If he lives for a long time in one place, then he may fall into bad habits without realizing it. If he has the misfortune to live in a poor and remote region without the use of a horse and cart, he should still study widely and inquire carefully, using the teachings of the ancients to seek out where truth and falsehood lie. Perhaps, then, he can achieve some measure of success—say five or six parts out of ten. If he does not venture abroad and also does not read books, then he is a scholar who doesn't study. Although he may be the equal of Zi Gao and Yuan Xian in worthiness,[1] ultimately he brings no benefit to the world. The Master said, "Certainly, in a hamlet of ten families, someone may be found who is as loyal and true as I am, but not someone who loves learning as I do."[2] If a sage such as Confucius still needs to retain a love of learning, how can the men of the present time not be as assiduous?

2. There is nothing a sage sees and hears that is not in the *Changes*. If you were to say you sweep aside what you see and hear and devote your attention entirely to studying the *Changes*, this is to put that classic beyond what is seen and heard. The 64 diagrams and the 384 lines are all used to inform men's actions. This is what is called "consider it, and afterward speak; deliberate on it, and afterward act."[3] As for "letting body and limbs drop away, casting out mind and intellect,"[4] these are the theories of Zhuang Zhou and Lie Yukou and have nothing to do with the *Changes*.

6. Of the friends one meets in the course of one's life, those who, through poverty or age, fall into a decline and become dispirited number seven or eight out of ten. Chi Bao[5] was a noble man who lived for a long time in Jiangdong. How could he do otherwise than sigh with disappointment? Earlier, when he was in Zezhou, he received my poem and was deeply moved. Later he wrote, saying, "If one is old, one must rest; one cannot escape weariness." These words are wrong. The Master said, "Let me return, let me return."[6] Not for one day did he forget the world. Thus, the studies of the noble man end only with his death.

9. When I look with my own eyes at the trends of the times, then I know that the key to whether there is good order or disorder must lie within the minds and customs of the people. And what changes the minds and hearts of the people and rectifies their customs cannot be lacking in the civilizing influence of education and the application of the laws. If this is maintained continuously for a hundred years or a complete generation, it is still not enough. If it is neglected for one day and one night, it is still too much.

20. If some gentleman should wish to publish his own writings in order to seek fame in the world, it would be like someone losing his footing and falling into a well. If someone then were to add a preface to his works, how would this not be like casting a stone on top of him? Before he has fallen, there is still time to stop him from this enterprise. If you try to stop him but he pays no heed, then a well may be considered an appropriate domicile for him. I have said all I need to say!

21. When Zheng Kangcheng was in his seventy-fourth year, he was compelled by Yuan Benchu [Yuan Shao] to go to Yuancheng, but he died en route. And yet Cao Mengde subsequently put out the story that Zheng Kangcheng got drunk while on the journey, lay on the ground, and died, thinking to have Benchu held responsible for the crime. It would be fortunate if retired scholars in later times were not like Kangcheng and that people did not treat them like Benchu.[7]

23. The ability to write doesn't make someone a writer. The ability to explain [the classics] doesn't make someone a teacher. In my view, those who are writers and teachers of the classics at the present time are all motivated by the desire for fame as writers and teachers. Did the Master not say, "This is notoriety, not distinction"? He also said, "To be silent and yet to understand it."[8] As Confucius said, even though I may not be a clever man, I must try to put these statements into practice.

4.42 LETTER TO A FRIEND

Twenty-five years have passed from the year Dingyou [1657] to the present.[9] During this time I have not received any news from you. Whenever I travel over mountains, along rivers, or across strategic passes, I regret we two are not together and know we are both the same. And I think back to the high hills and fast-flowing streams between Rao and She,[10] which were like places at the very edge of heaven. Before, when you sent me a letter, I was at Wuhu,[11] and I made a record of it in my notebook. But my notebook was stolen by robbers, so subsequently I didn't know your address, and when I asked at Taiyuan Ford, I couldn't get it. This autumn, people came from the capital and brought three letters from you, so I know you are well and haven't been troubled with ill health. I know, too, that in your travels by the Yellow and Fen Rivers, you have been accompanied by many men of the likes of Fang and Du,[12] so my joy is unbounded. I unrolled and read your substantial writings, in which you speak at length of present and past. I know you think kindly of your old friend and fear that his writings from an earlier time will not be transmitted. How solicitous you are! Nevertheless, twenty-five years have gone by and I have made some progress in the matter.

The noble man pursues his studies to clarify the *dao* [Way] of government and to save the world. Devoting oneself solely to poetry and elegant essays and nothing else—a trivial skill. What benefit does it bring? Since I turned fifty, I have directed my attention to the classics and histories and have achieved some depth in my studies of phonology. Now there is the *Wushu* [*Yinxue Wushu—Five Books on Phonetics*] to continue the long-interrupted interpretation of the three hundred odes. Apart from this, there is the *Rizhi Lu* [*A Record of Daily Knowledge*]—thirty or so *juan* in all—comprising a first section on the study of the classics, a middle section on the *dao* of government, and a final section on general studies. If a king were to arise who would use the material in the conduct of affairs, he might return the world to the glories of the rulers of ancient times. But this is something I hardly dare speak about with men of the present time. The works I previously published and circulated were but a small fragment.

Now, at Huaxia [Huayin], I have begun the building of an ancestral temple to Zhu Xi as a way of showing what was, at the time, the meaning of my reply to Zijing's letter. Here the place is bleak and desolate in the extreme. I would like to visit my parents' graves in Jiangzuo province once more and build a shrine to my late mother, but I don't know where they are exactly. I am an old man now and not likely to go to the capital again, but our letters must not stop. I would hope that from time to time you might write to me through my nephew Yan. It would be as if we were continuing our discussion. I am adding six poems to this letter.

5
SWJ 5
RECORDS, INSCRIPTIONS, AND OTHER WRITINGS

This section contains twenty-three pieces: nine are *ji* 記 (records); two are *hou* 後 (postscripts, postfaces); two are *zhuang* 狀 (descriptions); three are *ming* 銘 (inscriptions); four are about visiting the imperial tombs; and three are miscellaneous, of which one is about his shrine to Zhu Xi.

5.2 THE PEI VILLAGE RECORD

Alas! Since the progressive decline in the *dao* [Way] of government, the state has been without a strong clan system. Being without a strong clan system means the state is not properly established, and if the state is not properly established, this means the people are dispersed within and there is rebellion without, until finally the state comes to be destroyed. Is preservation of the clan system not, then, how people are made correct in their conduct and the power of the state strengthened?

I came to Pei village in Wenxi district and visited the ancestral hall of Jin Gong [Pei Du],[1] where I asked about his ancestry. There were still one or two hundred people, and there were farm implements and accompanying visitors. I came out of the village and reached the side of the official residence, where I read the inscription from Tang times recording the genealogy in the family register. Then I climbed the bank and looked into the distance. Within ten *li* there were burial mounds running continuously together. There were more than a hundred men whose surnames, styles, and official ranks could be examined. Now, the prominence of the recent past did not go back beyond the Tang, and yet in the region of the Yellow River, there were recent areas of imperial domains. The land was topographically important and the clans were many, like the Liu of Jiezhou and the Pei of Wenxi; both served in succession over several hundred years in an official capacity. The Xue clan of Fengyin relied on the Yellow River to protect themselves from Shi Hu,[2] creating the boundaries of Fujian to set up an independent regime, and yet they never had a single person at the court who was an official. The Fan clan of Yishi county and the Wang clan raised a volunteer force to ward off the attack by the hordes of Gao Huan.[3] These were not the methods of the Three Dynasties still being preserved, and yet those among them who were worthy led them in the *dao* 道 [Way] of protecting the family and guarding the clan—how otherwise would they have been able to escape destruction for so long?

Since the fall of the Tang, the records detailing clan succession have all been completely destroyed. Nevertheless, Pei Shu took a party of six or seven men who still had misgivings about Zhu Quanzhong[4] and waited at the White Horse postal relay station to kill him and seize the Tang throne. The relationship the clans had to the state was like this. When it came to the time of the Five Dynasties, the position of the emperor was much like it is in chess, and the rich families sunk to become like messengers. With the Jingkang change [1126] there was not one family in the succession that was able to lead a force to protect themselves. Sima Shi from Xia county led his whole family in the southern crossing, and they didn't return to their native village for a hundred years. Ah, alas! This is how the *dao* 道 [Way] of government each day plummets downward. Then suddenly there is a change, and the ruler cannot depend on the great officials, the people of the state cannot depend on the great families, and they lead one another to flee and hide away, seeking to avoid the issue of right and wrong. Is this a situation that must inevitably come about? If this is why the emperors of the Tang honored the noble families and followed the practice of increasing officials, I presume we know that the *fengjian* system [feudalism] cannot return, and yet we can lodge the concept in the great officers, and by means of this, in one sudden moment of compulsion, can defend ourselves. This is also undoubtedly something that later rulers are unable to understand.

Previously, I visited in succession Shandong and Hebei. Since the fighting arose, the subprefectures and districts that were able to avoid destruction and ruin in many cases relied on the strength of the great and powerful families and were not completely dependent on the administration [magistrate]. When I came to the district east of the Yellow River [Shanxi], I asked why Li Zicheng[5] was able to make a push down to the Three Jin and was not prevented from causing harm. Someone answered and said that during the late part of the Chongzhen reign period [1628–1644], there was a man from Quwo county, Li Jiantai,[6] with the title "bulwark of government." When the rebel entered Xi'an, the emperor gave him an audience and sighed. Jiantai replied, saying, "Our prefecture is about to become an important path for the rebel. I ask to be allowed to lead forth our whole clan and men from the district, and I will contribute resources amounting to a million taels to defend the Yellow River for our kingdom." The emperor was very pleased and ordered that Jiantai be made a supervisor of armies. Then he personally accompanied his departing visitor to the main gate of the city. He raised a drinking vessel that had been handed down over successive dynasties and poured wine into it, which he gave him. Jianbai had not yet sent troops into battle when Pingyang and Taiyuan prefectures fell in quick succession. He didn't know what to do. The troops stopped at Zhending, and the rebel had already entered through Juyong Pass. This shows that Jiantai was a man of limited ability—certainly inferior to Wang Duo and Zhang Jun.[7] And yet there was no authority to give to a superior man and no method of linking up with such a person. This was a problem that didn't spring up overnight. Now, to expect these great officers to have the empty reputation of the paltry term "bulwark official" [*zaifu*] and to involve them in the task of peace and danger to the altars of soil and grain is surely a plan that cannot be realized.

In the *Rites of Zhou* [*Zhou Li*], under the heading "Tai Zai," there is, "Take nine to be paired with the people of the country; . . . The fifth is called *zong* and by means of clans gains the people."[8] If you look at the Pei clan's connection with the preservation or loss of the Tang, the broad outline can be discerned here. Now, it is not possible to return to the *fengjian* system of government, and yet if you wish to rely on the power of officials to establish government, this lies in the important clans! Yes, this lies in the important clans!

6

SWJ 6

MISCELLANEOUS

This section, titled *buyi* 補遺 (supplementary material), contains a miscellany of twenty-four essays. The first four are the four early "constitutional" essays on military matters (6.1); geographical issues, particularly with military implications (6.2); agriculture (6.3); and monetary matters (6.4), respectively. There is one additional *bian* and then seven additional prefaces and postfaces, including the preface to Gu's substantial work on historical geography, the *Tianxia Junguo Libing Shu* (6.8). There is an essay on wide-ranging learning (6.13), another ten letters (6.14–23), and finally a memorial for his adoptive mother, Wang (6.24).

6.1 ON MILITARY SYSTEMS

If the laws don't change, it won't be possible to remedy the present situation. To be in a situation of being unable to do otherwise than change, and yet to still avoid the realities of change, thus temporarily preserving the name of not changing, will most certainly lead to great harm. Can the military system of today not be said to be the military system of Gao Huang Di [Ming Tai Zu, r. 1368–1399]?[1] In name it may be so, but in reality it has changed. Moreover, if both superiors and subordinates join with one another in preserving the status quo to an extreme degree and align themselves with a policy of not changing, how can this be fulfilling the intention of the military system? Gao Huang Di said, "I have nurtured a million soldiers without wasting one grain of the people's rice." Speaking of this from the viewpoint of the present day, is there waste or not? And where are the million soldiers? To consider this to still be like the original system is based on deception.

In the past, when I studied in the *Spring and Autumn Annals* and the *Rites of Zhou* the ancient concept of letting soldiers lodge among peasants, I never failed to heave a deep sigh, considering the division of soldiers and farmers into two separate groups to be a common failing from the Three Dynasties on. But the division of officers [*jun*] and rank-and-file soldiers [*shi*] into two groups as well began with our own dynasty. To take a whole people and divide it into those who are farmers and those who are soldiers, and to have the former support the latter, creates an intolerable burden. To take the rank-and-file soldiers as one group and divide them into *jun* 軍 and *bing* 兵 is to have one group of farmers supporting two groups of soldiers, which adds even more to the burden. To take soldiers as one and divide them into guarding troops, militiamen, and mercenary recruits is to have one group of farmers supporting three groups of soldiers, which further increases the burden. If there is not a prompt change, there will be no end to the matter until everyone is driven to be a soldier. Drive the people to be soldiers, and the affairs of the nation will become too unbearable to discuss.

The system of the Two Ancestors [Ming Tai Zu and Ming Chengzu, r. 1403–1425] was as follows: In the capital, 5 chief military commissioners and 72 guards were established. In the imperial domain, 50 guards were established. In each province, a regional military commissioner (of whom there were therefore 21 in all) was established, and also officers left on guard, 2 in number, guards to the number of 191, independent battalions, state farm battalions, and herd battalions to the number of 211. In the border regions, 95 chief officers for pacification were established, as well as frontier native military commission guards and 107 battalions. Some 5,600 men constituted a guard, 1,120 a battalion [*qianhusuo* 千戶所], and 112 a company [*baihusuo* 百戶所]. The soldiers were given agricultural land, and camps and walled villages were established so that there was both plowing and guarding.[2] Each person received 50 *mou* of arable land with a grain tax of 24 piculs. Half of this was returned to the individuals paying and half used for official salaries. There was also an instruction to those guarding the cities to set out at daybreak and come back in the evening. In this way, how could the empire be distressed by having soldiers, and how could such a system be reestablished? A long period of peace resulted in a relaxation of preparations, so the organization was damaged and the military ranks depleted. In the later part of the Zhengtong reign period [1436–1449], there was first an order to the prefectures and districts to select militiamen. During the Hongzhi reign period [1488–1505], there was a regulation that all the village and township assistants should provide 2, 4, or 5 men, who were to be sent on an expedition; the officials would give these men the necessary provisions. In the Zhengde reign period [1506–1521], the grain tax received from the population was the basis for local authorities themselves determining the silver for military purposes, and if, among the people, the year's produce was in excess of 7 *liang*, then in all cases a land tax was imposed on them. This was referred to as the quick organization of a people's militia that is strong. And yet for every increase in soldiers, there was an associated change in regulations. Also, preparations were protracted and benefits were dissipated; robbers arose in Yong and Yu[3] and then spread to a number of provinces. The militia were insufficient for the purpose, so new troops were levied and their salaries doubled, considering them to be an army for long campaigns. And so the soldiers were again increased and the system again changed. Those who were encampment guards would say, "What do I know about being a soldier? My duty is to transport tax grain; guard duty is not my responsibility." Therefore, there was the organization of a militia, and encampment guards were not used. Those who were militiamen would say, "What do I know about being a soldier? My duty is the provision of service; the levying of duty is not my responsibility." Therefore, those who were newly recruited militiamen were men of no use. I previously calculated the combined *weisuo* 衛所[4] soldiers in the empire and came up with a number of not less than 2 million. If a kingdom has an army of 2 million, it cannot have no enemies and not use a single man. If it has the fields of 2 million men, it cannot be said there is not enough, and yet not a single *sheng* or *ge* need be used. Therefore, I say the method of Gao Huang Di is lost.

If this is the case, should all the *weisuo* soldiers be changed to become regular army soldiers, and should all the *weisuo* officials be changed to become generals? I say this is not possible. Or, if the *weisuo* army were to be disbanded, should the allocated fields all be taken away? I say this is not possible. I would submit that in an unchanging situation, if there is recourse to a regulation effecting change following circumstances that have already changed, restore the method of creation. There should be enquiry into all the military registers[5] to see whether there are vacancies, and if so, how many. Then the fields should be reclaimed and the vacancies filled with new soldiers. There should be a gathering together of all the squads and an examination to determine whether they were successful in military terms. If they were not successful but fled, then their fields should be confiscated and they, themselves, replaced with new soldiers. Every five years, there should be a review, with rehabilitation of those in poor condition and promotion of those who have been valiant, without necessarily granting them hereditary status. If things were done in this way, then not one coin from the public purse would be wasted. If every garrison were to obtain a certain number of men for use, then as far as the empire was concerned, the 2 million soldiers could be completely restored. Furthermore, those soldiers who at the present time occupy the halting places on the empire's southern circuit and have responsibility for dragging the barges are each year reduced several fold. Viewed as soldiers, their position can be considered to be strong, and as farmers they can be considered to be rich, but they don't come up to what is appropriate for the time. If these 10 million men are allowed to take over the name of soldier and waste the military provisions, and yet they are unable to draw a bow or loose an arrow, then they are not of the slightest use to the country. If the kingdom completely discards these 10 million men together with their fields, then in terms of resources, how can there not be a shortfall, and in terms of military organization, how can there not be weakness and decay? Also, how can hostilities be foreseen and planned for and the merits of victory achieved?

6.2 ON GEOGRAPHY

In former times, there were eight dynasties in all that established their capitals in the south—these were Wu, Eastern Jin, Song, Qi, Liang, Chen, Southern Tang, and Southern Song. At the time of Wu, there was a three-way confrontation, the state being bounded by Baqiu in the west and Wancheng and Ruxu in the north. When Wu was lost, the strategically important Changjiang [Yangzi River] first came under Jin control.[6]

At the time of the southern crossing, during the Yongjia reign period [307–312], Jing, Yu, Qing, Yan, and half of Xu fell under the control of Liu Yuan and Shi Le, while Liang and Yi fell under the control of Li Xiong, and Hefei, Huaiyin, Shouyang, Sikou, and Jiaocheng became places of strategic importance.[7] When it came to the upheavals of Fu, Yao, and Murong, [the prefectures of] Qing, Yan, Liang, and Yi were the first to be gained [by Jin], and Song perpetuated this.[8] When it came to the northern attack during the Yuanjia reign period [424–453] and the loss of the army at Que'ao, Fuli's horses and camping at Guabu were a consequence of guarding the Changjiang.[9] Tuoba had complete possession of the central plain, while Qi and Liang, in succession, ruled east of the Yangzi, and regions both north and south of the Huai became battlefields.[10] There was the Taiqing internal calamity, the Chengsheng seeking after soldiers, Qi's seizure of Huainan, Wei's taking of Shu and Han, and Jiangling's ruination.[11] In Chen Shi's rise, he did not gain Shu and Han in the west, while in the north he lost Huai and Fei. He took the Changjiang as the frontier and as a result defended it.[12] The area of the kingdom grew less each day and its prosperity progressively diminished, while the armies at Caishi and Jingkou at that same time crossed the river and were finally swallowed up by Sui. When the Southern Tang lost Huainan, it also took Changjiang as a boundary, and the kingdom was subsequently unable to sustain itself.[13]

The Song established a capital at Lin'an and concluded a treaty of alliance with the Jin people, establishing as a boundary between them the waters of the Huai, while in the west they resisted Da Sanguan. During the Duanping reign period [1234–1236], they destroyed the Jin [province of] Caizhou and threw down the gauntlet to the Mongols. During the Baoyou reign period [1253–1258], they lost Shu, and during the Xianchun reign period [1265–1274], they lost Xiang and Fan. The Yuan forces moved south, and the young lord appeared with his hands tied behind his back and the jade seal [*pi*] in his mouth.[14] Is this not a reflection of the general trend of events?

Previously, when I examined the reasons for the rise and fall of the eight dynasties in historical sequence and considered these in relation to the empire as a whole, then I regarded Jingzhou and Xiangyang to be the throat of the kingdom, Shu to be the neck, and the two Huais and Shandong to be the back. Shu is where the upper reaches of the nation's rivers are. In former times, those who established kingdoms in the south could be certain that, if first they lost Shu, danger and destruction would follow. If Shu were an independent kingdom and not combined with the central kingdom, it was still possible for there to be peace. Sun Wu's coexistence with Han, and Eastern Jin's coexistence with Li Xiong, were instances of this.[15] If Shu were joined with the central kingdom, thus combining the empire's strengths, then relying on the power of possessing the upper reaches of the nation's waterways, I would consider our enemy to be in danger. Wang Jun's eastward progress from Baqiu and Liu Zheng's plan to take Shu as a means to occupy Song were cases in point.[16] Therefore Shu should be defended first. If there is an assembly of the men of Shu and use is made of its wealth, then by sending out soldiers from Qin, Feng, Jing, and Long, it would not be difficult to shake the foundations of the empire. Therefore Shu should be attacked first.

Zhao Ding said, "Plans to control the central plain start from Guanzhong; control of Guanzhong starts from Shu; progress to Shu begins from Jing and Xiang." Chen Liang said, "Jing and Xiang occupy the eastern side of the upper waters of the Changjiang. To the west, Ba and Shu adjoin. To the north there could be control of Guanzhong and Luoyang. The men of Chu used this as a basis for casting covetous eyes on Qi and Jin and to fight with Qin for the emperorship. From Eastern Jin on, places of strategic importance were established to guard the central plain." Meng Gong said, "Xiang and Fan are the foundations of the kingdom. After many battles to recover them, it is fitting that they be governed properly."[17] The ideas of the Song people were like this.

When the Yuan seized Song, they passed as expected from Xiangyang and Fancheng through Ezhou. Therefore, taking these [two places] to be the nation's strength, they surrounded them for five years. After they crossed the Changjiang, they took Lin'an in less than two years. So without Shu it is still possible to establish a kingdom—Eastern Jin is a case in point.[18] Without Jing and Xiang it is not possible to establish a kingdom; Chu leaving Chen and moving to Shouchun is a case in point. Not to hold the north-south course of the Huai and to use the Changjiang as a defense will result in its loss. The Zhenming reign period of Chen [587] and the Baoda reign period of the Southern Tang [943–957] are cases in point. Therefore, it is of the utmost importance to make Jing and Xiang substantial. In ancient times, those skilled in guarding put their reliance on places of strategic importance, and certainly any surplus strength was devoted to the regions beyond such strategic places. Thus, those defending the Huai did not do so at the Huai itself but at Xuzhou and Suzhou; those defending the Yangzi did not do so at the Yangzi itself but at the two Huais. These things being so, my method, whether attacking or defending, would be to have an excess of land so the kingdom could flourish. Therefore it is critically important to establish opposition at the two Huais. Someone said that Gao Huang Di formerly used the south to take the north, so why do you speak only about guarding it? I say this is right. Those who would take the empire must certainly occupy the area of the upper reaches of the rivers, and after this they can govern the people. If military heroes have no territory for the deployment of their forces, then matters cannot be brought to a satisfactory conclusion. Moreover, although people know that Gao Huang Di established a capital at Jinling, they don't know how he took the empire. At that time, because the territory east of the Yangzi River was not settled, he first deployed a large force to capture Xiang and Han, suppress Huai'an, and subdue Xuzhou and Suzhou, and subsequently moved north to seize the central plain.[19] This is to use military force first in gaining control of strategically important positions.

Moreover, Chu established its hegemony at the battle of Bi;[20] in Han Gao Zu's rise, he entered Qin from Pei, and from Nanyang he entered Xi and Li;[21] Guang Wu rose up from Nanyang;[22] Song Wu destroyed Nan Yan, entered Si from Huai, and destroyed Qin, entering the Yellow River region from Bian.[23] These examples, all from ancient times, present clear evidence of an attack on the north being launched from the south, and of beginning operations from an advantageous position. In my view, there should be a uniting of the two halves of the empire to make it one, and it should be used like the snake of Changshan.[24] Then, even if there were the great mass of Fu Qin's one million soldiers[25] or Wanyan's thirty two armies,[26] they could not look with avarice on our land. Moreover, there should be conservation of strength and building up of fighting spirit, with strong and valiant troops awaiting the moment of the enemy's relaxation; then an effective result can be obtained. This, then, is the plan applicable to both attack and defense and the best method for the utilization of military forces.

6.3 ON AGRICULTURE

There are two aspects to the great wealth of the world; the first can be termed plowing [fields] and the second, tending [animals]. For a state this is also the case. "It was through their fields and farming that Qin and Yang became one region."[27] It was through their animal husbandry that Wu Shi and Qiao Yao were classed as feudal lords and in so doing enriched their families.[28] Qi made his grain luxuriant and was enfeoffed with Tai.[29] Fei Zi increased what was produced, and Qin conferred [honors] on him.[30] These are instances of enriching the state. In affairs, if plans are vague and poorly formulated, it is difficult to put them into effect, and ultimately it can be said that in unifying the states of the world and serving their people, there is nothing as good as the plowing of fields.

In the past I read the memorial of Wei Liaoweng of Song, in which he put forward the following considerations: "Men in ancient times guarded the frontier fortresses. In this way it was possible to preserve the people's energies for other uses and still be fully aware of the situations of enemies. Attention could then be solely devoted to agricultural matters, and the accumulation of grain could become the fundamental activity." He also said,

> There is "land given to military colonists" [*tuntian* 屯田—state farms],[31] and there are reclaimed lands. After large-scale military activities, many of the fields are uncultivated and lie fallow. The people should be encouraged to cultivate the fallow fields that lie in the various provinces and be made to open up wasteland for cultivation, so they could again have a livelihood. In that way the true yield of raising crops would often be greater than with the *tuntian* system. Moreover, if the lands near the borders have been uncultivated and not plowed for a long time, grain is expensive. If it is expensive, the people disperse, and if they disperse, the army becomes weak. Certainly, if the land is opened up and cultivated widely, grain is cheap. If it is cheap, the people gather together, and if they gather together, the army becomes strong. I ask that no attention be given to the empty term *tuntian* and that first there be a calculation of the real profits to be obtained from reclaimed land. If one calls on those of the local gentry who are loyal and right

acting, officials will be helped, and it will be convenient to open up wasteland. It may also be possible to plan to cultivate several thousand *qing* [one *qing* is approximately sixteen acres], so that in the next year at the same time, the profits of the land can be reaped and cheap grain made available. Moreover, all the people engaged in land cultivation can be used in a military capacity, and if there happens to be a prior warning, families themselves provide defenders and people themselves fight. This is altogether different from overhasty banishment for crimes. If there is not the name *tuntian* but in reality this system does exist, there is not the expense of providing for soldiers, and it is also possible to manage arrogant and ruthless military men unobtrusively. Indeed, not only is it possible to manage prisoners but also it is possible in this way to guard against the comings and goings of other robbers. Within a few short years the borders will be well provided for and prosperous. Then, if there is a war, it can be won, and if there is a need for guarding, it can be secure.[32]

I think this would correct the pressing problems of the present time. In periods of peace, there was a master for each field. Nowadays, in the central plain, weeds are everywhere. Truly, landowners must work diligently at plowing; those who don't work hard should have their land confiscated and given to new owners, since we cannot allow our kingdom to have wasteland. In this way, the people will submit—this will be the first change. In times of repeated bumper crops, grain will become cheap. Nowadays warfare is continuous, so for successive years there is great famine, making food hard to come by for many people, and they must be urged to till the fields—this will be the second change. The border villages of the ancients were in many instances in barren regions [deserts]. Nowadays the land south of the Yellow River is soft and muddy. The low-lying [paddy] fields of Yangzhou and the dry fields of Ying and Shou will restore the historical traces of Yang Hu and Du Yu and return to the *tuntian* system of the Shangyuan reign period [674–676]—this will be the third change.[33] After a long period of noncultivation, the productive capacity of the land will not be readily released, and there must be a double harvest of grain—this will be the fourth change.

Nevertheless, there are three difficulties. If the Ministry of Agriculture informs the court that there are deficiencies and that it is necessary to provide several hundred thousand pieces of gold to seek a benefit after a period of three to four years; this is the first difficulty. If the court is unable to make long-term appointments, the people are not willing to labor alone, and they beg for a man of strength to shoulder the responsibility for several years; this is the second difficulty. If Heaven brings drought and floods and over the years there is an excess of misfortune—for example, in He Chengju's[34] first year of planting rice the frost was early and the grain did not mature, so the expected yield was prevented—this is the third difficulty.

I ask that a contribution of several hundred thousand pieces of gold be given to the officials responsible for agriculture to encourage them, and that they not be questioned on their earnings and expenditures. Then, after three years, by the profit and loss and by the cheapness or otherwise of the grain in the border regions, their merits can be assessed. If this one person wishes to find a surplus of border grain, he must do his utmost to plow and plant, he must trade, and he must make the repayments secure. If the people are peaceful and settled and the border corn abundant, then our resources will be rich, the army will have adequate numbers, the cities and frontiers will be strong, and the emperor will receive a profit without speaking about it. This will allow the great riches of the empire to accumulate.

6.4 ON MONETARY SYSTEMS

There is nothing as good as the monetary system of the present [Ming] dynasty but nothing as bad as its utilization of money. If the matter is examined in the *Histories*, King Jing [544–519 B.C.E.] cast the *daqian* 大錢, and Zhou coinage underwent one change. Han inherited the Qin *banliang* 半兩 and then made [the following coinage]: *jiaqian* 莢錢, *sizhu* 四銖, *sanzhu* 三銖, *wuzhu* 五銖, *chize* 赤仄, and *sanguan* 三官. When it came to Emperor Ling [168–188] and Emperor Xian [189–220], they made *sichu* 四出 and *xiaoqian* 小錢. Han coinage thus had nine changes in all. Tang cast the *kaitong* 開通 and afterward also cast the *daqian* 大錢. Then there was the *ganfeng* 乾封, *ganyuan* 乾元, and *zhongleng* 重稜, Tang coinage having, in all, four changes. Song followed the old style of the *kaitong*. When troubles arose on the western frontier, they cast the *daqian* 大錢, casting during the Chongning reign period [1102–1106] the equivalent of ten copper cash and during the Jiading reign period [1208–1224], the equivalent of five. This was also combined with the use of iron coinage—the *jiaozi* 交子 and *kuaizi* 會子—and the system came close to ruin. Song coinage, then, also underwent three or four changes. With every change of coinage, articles of merchandise jumped in price, there was no constancy of value, and the people suffered from this. Our dynasty, from the Hongwu reign period [1368–1398] to the Zhengde reign period [1506–1521], had ten emperors but only four castings, and with the later emperors, one casting. When it came to the Wanli reign period [1572–1619], the coinage produced became increasingly refined. The coinage style was such that every one hundred coins weighed thirteen taels. The perimeter of the coins was perfectly regular, and the characters and figures particularly clear. Indeed, they followed the ancients in their intent not to do shoddy work or use inferior materials. Moreover, for three hundred years, there was no change in the edict. Market prices remained constant, the monetary system was not confusing, and people found it convenient to use. This was an excellent monetary system.

However, when we come to the present, commodities become more expensive every day, while every day money diminishes in value. Private coinage is becoming increasingly common, and the power the emperor holds by virtue of his control of the weights of the myriad things no longer exists. Why is this so? The ancients, in their utilization of money, not only distributed it to those below but also gathered it into the emperor's coffers. According to Han law, people paid a personal tax of 120 *qian* 錢, and this poll tax was received in the form of money. In the "Yance" chapter of the *Guanzi* [it states], "A kingdom of ten thousand files of soldiers is worth, in monetary terms, thirty million."[35] This is a case of the salt and iron taxes being received in the form of money. For resident and traveling merchants, strings of cash to the value of 4,000 are taxed at 1 *suan* 算. The light carts of the *san lao* [elders] and the mounted officers of the northern regions are taxed at 1 *suan*, the light carts of merchants and traders at 2 *suan*, and boats of five *zhang* or more in length are taxed at 1 *suan*. These are instances of the income from the frontier passes and markets being received in the form of money. An order was given that the people be taxed on the selling of wine at a rate of 4 *qian* per pint, this being an instance of levying the toll on liquor sales in the form of money. The princess of Longlü[36] paid a ransom for the life of her son in money [10 million], this being an instance of a penalty being received in the form of money.

At the time of the Jin family's southern crossing [317],[37] for all contracts on land, dwellings, male and female slaves, horses, and oxen, there was a tax of 400 for every value of 10,000. This was an example of a contract tax being received in the form of money. Zhang Fangping[38] said that the government tax on houses and dwellings, the money levied on tea, salt, wine, and vinegar, and the methods of the *muyi* and the *qingmiao* were to collect money throughout the empire and to direct it to the emperor, the money being distributed as official salaries. This is a method I consider useful. For money to pass from above down and from below up, circulating freely without obstruction, is the desired method of monetary organization. Nowadays, the money that is below does not go upward, and this is the reason why counterfeit money daily circulates, and the money officially designated for circulation is obstructed [i.e., prevented from circulating]. Indeed, it is always so for this reason. I ask that the regulations of the former dynasties be imitated, and that whatever is retained or dispersed by the regions and districts be replaced by money. This would have the effect that, within the empire, officials would not dare to receive anything other than the standardized money, so strengthening the standard currency. If the standard currency is strengthened, the emperor's power is likewise strengthened.

Jia Shan had this to say: "Money in itself is a useless commodity, but it can be exchanged for wealth and honor. Wealth and honor are the means whereby the ruler holds power. Let the people create them, and they will share power with the ruler, but this is a state of affairs that cannot long endure." Therefore, the benefits from calculating capital and computing interest are small, whereas the benefits to be derived from return of power to the ruler are substantial. Nowadays, the money from the marketplace is debased, and the standard currency is also debased. For this reason, the money in the marketplace is worth little, and the standardized currency is also worth little. This means that the ruler is devoid of authority because it has passed to those below. What benefit is there to the emperor in this? If the emperor does not receive it, it is no different from money not being important. Therefore I, in my foolishness, say there is nothing as bad as the present dynasty's usage of money. This is what Jia Sheng referred to as "doing away with the seven blessings and bringing about widespread misfortune."[39]

6.19 LETTER TO YANG XUECHEN

I think of you as the new year comes in, hoping your life is peaceful, your health good, and that each day your resplendent virtue is renewed.[40] What I especially admire in you is your not publishing your writings and so not contending for fame with the men of our time. When one is among friends and looks at them as those of later generations might, one can see how difficult it is to reproduce the worthiness of those of former times and continue their virtue and kindness. Your sons search wide and deep in ancient writings, and yet they don't sit the examinations. This is also something students of the present day ought to emulate. If men everywhere studied the Five Classics and had a working knowledge of writings on historical matters, they could acquire a thorough understanding of the affairs of the world.[41] The calamity is to be deceived by the lure of fame and benefit without being aware of it.

Previously, when the *Rizhi Lu* [*Record of Daily Knowledge*] was printed, you were kind enough to approve of it despite its failings. Now, my scholarship has progressed somewhat and I realize there are many amendments to be made. My intention is to dispel disorder and cleanse what is unclean. It is to follow ancient models and use the Xia.[42] My book will inform many scholars if they care to listen to what it has to say, but it really awaits a later king who will impose unity and good order. I myself believe this book must be handed down, and yet I don't dare show it to others. Like the *Yinxue Wushu*, it is the work of a whole lifetime. It is also adequate to use as an aid in studying the Six Classics—unlike the largely useless discussions of the present times. But I am unwilling to give it to other men as something written for their use, like that already printed by the banks of the Huai waters.[43]

The purpose of my whole life is to know myself well. I used to think, in years gone by, I would find myself alone and solitary, floating along buffeted by wind and rain. And now it is my relatives who have reached prominent positions. I think of the chariot of the returning Confucius, but I fear it is more like Bo Luan's stove.[44] I have, moreover, passed through seven of the nine regions and climbed four of the five sacred mountains, but I still have never seen a "noble man"—just those like our own "great officers." The difficulty of practicing the Way is something we can already know. So I will walk to and fro on the bank of the Wei River and linger on the eastern peak of Huashan. I'm going to farm a small plot of land, living in seclusion where the smoke of the others' hearth fires cannot be seen, and where fields in spring and orchards in autumn are traversed by the crisscrossing paw prints of tigers. But I must rely on the manor house to build my own house, and I must beg my neighbors for firewood. When you look at the ancients who perched on mountains or hid themselves in valleys, this is hardly the same thing! But the world now is like a land deluged by floodwaters while heaven remains dark and indifferent. I don't know whether or not we shall ever meet again in this life, so at an appropriate time I shall send you some writings detailing my devoutly held ideas.

III

POEMS FROM *COLLECTED POEMS AND ESSAYS* (*TINGLIN SHIWENJI—SWJ*)

Gu Yanwu wrote many poems during his lifetime, although poetry was not his major concern, and he was not regarded as a leading poet. As well as writing poems, he expressed views on the technical aspects of writing poetry and the role of poetry in society. These views are recorded in his essays and letters. In addition, his work on phonology is directly relevant to the composition of poetry. His surviving poems, which number over three hundred, are preserved in several works—specifically, the *Gu Tinglin Shiwenji* and the edition with detailed annotations by Xu Jia 徐嘉, the *Gushi Jianzu* in seventeen *juan*, printed in 1897. There are two relatively modern editions of his extant verse that include 332 poems arranged chronologically; in the more recent of the two, there is division according to five periods of his life after 1644. Gu destroyed all his poems written prior to that year as part of his response to the Manchu conquest.

The numbering of the poems is that in the "Shiji" section of the *Shiwenji*, but the two works just mentioned were used for the translations. The translated poems are grouped under the five periods of his post-1644 life.

1. 1644–1649

These were particularly critical years for Gu Yanwu, as they were for the country as a whole. At a national level, in 1644 the capital fell, first to Li Zicheng, and then to the Manchus, who established the Qing dynasty. The last Ming emperor (Ming Si Zong) took his own life, and following the occupation of the capital, the Manchus continued their advance south. At a personal level, several of Gu's relatives were either killed or injured during this advance, and his adoptive mother, Wang, so influential in his upbringing, took her own life in 1645 rather than live under the alien regime. During these years the direction of Gu's life changed dramatically. He devoted himself primarily to attempting to restore the Ming dynasty. His first significant statecraft writings date from this time, while some of his poems from the period have a strong martial flavor.

1.1 Lament on the Death of an Emperor

If the divine vessel has no center, it will fall,
but brave and brilliant, descendants will follow.
The purple dragon has met his death by the sword,
and under the red sun the royal carriage ascends.
By the great decree the Yin king succeeds,
while the magic tally of Dai Di is received.
Heaven's majesty respectfully issues a warning.
An ancestor's traces continue in his virtues.
His place of repose displays the king's frugality.
His carved bowls are images of his reverent fear.
His favor is like water offered in summer heat.
His cautious heart is like walking on ice in spring.

But the age fell into the path of decline;
so many men, but all just servile followers.
When he sought officers, he found only great rats;
managing the army, he found no hungry vultures.
Manchu invaders are every year more aggressive,
and rebellious peasants every year more numerous.
When closing the door, the iron bolt was lost,

while in the royal chamber bindings were loosed.
Mist rises to cover the Zhaoyang mirror,
as the wind shakes the Jiaguan lantern.
As foretold, the Yi Waters are exhausted,
and the Qi world's collapse ensues.
The Way is blocked;
no recourse to a benevolent sage.
The times are perilous;
no help from officers and ministers.

The sadness is the same as at Wang Di's transformation,
while the spirit looks to climb aboard white clouds.
There is a secret prophecy to return to Xinye,
while popular feelings turn toward Youreng.
In the king's chamber his officers let their tears flow.
No road ahead—just the wailing at Qiaoling.

Note: This poem—the first in his collected verse—is a lament for the last Ming emperor. It is replete with literary and historical allusions. There are three distinct sections, as follows:

1. Optimism surrounding the ascent of Si Zong: The divine utensil or vessel is the emperor or empire (see *Daodejing* 29). The first two lines refer to Xi Zong's death and Si Zong's establishment as emperor in 1628. In 1627 the powerful and scheming eunuch Wei Zhongxian hanged himself and was disemboweled after his death. Dai Di was the son of the first Han emperor, Han Gao Zu, and was enfeoffed as Dai Wang.

2. The catastrophic deterioration that led to the fall of the last Ming emperor, Si Zong, and culminated in the end of the dynasty. Zhaoyang and Jiaguan are references to Han Wu Di's palace. There is particularly a reference to Li Zicheng's entering Beijing, which directly led to the emperor's suicide by hanging.

3. Reference to previous similar events. Wang Di was the name given to a Shu king, Du Yu, a descendant of the Yellow Emperor, who ruled the territory of Shu under the Zhou. When his territory was saved from the ravages of a severe flood by Bie Ling, who cut a passage through the Wu mountains, Du Yu resigned in favor

of the savior and retired to devote himself to study. The legend is that he turned into a nightjar. The second and third lines make reference to *Zhuangzi* 33 in relation to Si Zong's dying in the service of the empire. The subsequent two lines refer to events during the restoration of the Han dynasty after Wang Mang's usurpation. Xinye is the place where Guang Wu Di, first emperor of the Later Han, raised troops, and Youreng Shi was the mother of his son, Shao Kang. Qiaoling refers to the place of burial of the Yellow Emperor.

1.8 Autumn Hills 1

Autumn hills, still more autumn hills,
and autumn rain joins the hills in red.
Yesterday, fighting was at the river mouth;
today, there is fighting on the hillsides.
I hear the right flank is already dispersed,
and see the left driven back and destroyed.
Flags and banners lie buried in the earth,
ladders and battering rams beat against the walls.
In a single morning Changping was lost,
and fallen bodies lie strewn all around.
Three hundred barges have left for the north;
barge after barge bearing fresh-faced girls.
Wu men crowd together with camels,
and pipes sound as they enter the Yan gates.
In an earlier time the men of Yan and Ying
were still to be found south of the city.

Note: In this description of war two eras are referred to: the present, in that the Manchus entered Beijing through the Yan gates and passes and the girls were captives being sent north to the capital; and the past, in that Changping was the site of a particularly bloody battle between the armies of Qin and Zhao in the third century B.C.E. in which a great number of Zhao soldiers were killed, while Yan (different from the previous Yan) and Ying were major cities in the southern state of Chu in ancient times.

1.8 Autumn Hills 2

Autumn hills, still more autumn rains,
and autumn flowers still retain their red.
A fierce wind blows over hills and mounds,
and flickering fires come to light the town.
The "heavenly dog" sinks behind Wu Gate.
A bright rainbow surrounds the fortifications.

How sad that in a previously prosperous land,
brambles and weeds spring up in a single day.
You can't return the heads of the worthy men,
for their necks are now forever severed.
The men of Chu certainly set fire to Jun,
perhaps they liked the flavor of old sacrifices.
Gou Jian perched within the mountains,
and his countrymen were all prepared to die.
I breathe a sigh, thinking of men of old.
Survival or death really start from now.

Note: As with the first poem, the focus is on the depredations of war. The final two characters in lines 4 and 5 are taken as indicating Suzhou. The reference to the men of Chu is to events described in the *Zuo Zhuan* for the fifth year of Duke Ding. Gou Jian was the leader of the Yue forces in an ongoing battle with Wu.

1.31 The Jingwei Bird

So many matters and no peace to be found,
why then do I let myself suffer in vain?
Going on so long with this little body,
bearing wood and stones in my mouth to the end.
My wish is to fill the great Eastern Sea.
Although my body decays,
my mind will never change.
But the great sea will never be leveled,
and my own heart will never find peace.
Ah me! Do you not see in the Western Hills,

the great throng of birds?
Magpies come, swallows depart,
each completing its own nest.

Note: The Jingwei was a mythical bird, said to be like a pheasant, which was the reincarnation of the daughter of the founding father of agriculture, Shen Nong, who perished while traveling by the Eastern Sea. According to the legend, the bird attempted to fill the sea by repeatedly carrying stones and wood in its beak that it dropped into the water. The translation takes Gu to be picturing himself as the Jingwei bird.

2. 1650–1656

During these years, as the prospect of a Ming restoration seemed increasingly remote, Gu started to focus more on how the problems related to the Manchu conquest and the resultant oppression of the Han Chinese majority might be addressed. He was also personally involved in a particularly unpleasant altercation over his family's land that resulted in an attempt on his life. Gu and his associates killed his would-be assassin. For this, Gu was imprisoned, although he was freed after less than a year.

2.4 The Boatmen's Song 1

Our dwellings lie on a midriver island;
our oars dip briskly like free-flying birds.
Once Jin soldiers reached the northern bank,
by foot and carriage and surrounded Jin Shan.

2.4 The Boatmen's Song 2

In Zhenzhou city men are strong and resolute.
At Jingkou on the river there are no concerns.
Mooring my boat at night by the south bank,
I wonder if a leader of the southern court will come.

Note: These two short poems allude to the Manchu invasion and overthrow of the Ming by speaking of the earlier Mongol invasion and overthrow of the Song. Zhenzhou and Jingkou are two relatively southerly places of particular relevance to the earlier invasion.

2.5 Wandering About

I wander between Wu and Gui;
which land is my land?
Climbing high, I gaze over the Nine Regions;
wilderness only as far as the eye can see.
Cold waters rise against the setting sun,
mingling together, fish and shrimps in a frenzy.
Night comes, but the hungry birds don't rest,
while ever a crescent moon still gives them light.

As dawn breaks I climb Beigu Tower,
and in my sadness tears fall like rain.
Carefully I cut the hair at my temples,
and changed my attire to seem like a merchant.
Looking back five years have come and gone;
staying as I was will only lead to suffering.
There are fearful journeys to go by water and land,
with my enemies lurking always at the gates.
Not a single night have I spent in my village,
wandering far since I left my old home.
Time and again I have crossed passes and bridges,
nor have I avoided cities and townships.

A man of purpose harbors larger concerns,
but is there one single path he can choose?
Let me not be the instrument of lesser men.
Let me not throw rotting meat to hungry tigers.
All my great thoughts are on the central plain,
as I swear a vow on the bank of the great river.
The time will come for merit and reputation.
Then I shall whip my horse and follow Guang Wu.

Note: This poem was written in 1650 and signals Gu's intention to travel north. There is also reference to his tonsorial modification to conform to the Manchu edict. Guang Wu was Li Tai Wang of the state of Han.

3. 1657–1662

These years saw the beginning of Gu's extensive travels, which included the northern regions. To all intents and purposes, he left his home in Kunshan and embraced the wandering life from this point on. He had no fixed abode, staying with friends and associates for short periods while he thought, wrote, and gathered material for his various studies.

3.20 I Laugh at Myself

Another year and I laugh at myself, still I have not returned.
A cup of wine and a book of verse, what else shall I rely on?
As dawn breaks I call the boy and ask him to bring my horse;
before winter comes I must find a woman to mend my clothes.
I have no Yellow Ears to bring me a letter with news from home.
Now I am old and have time to think, I recall the mountains.
Then I am transformed and become a wild goose heading south.
Next I chase the west wind, flying on toward the Li Marshes.

Note: Yellow Ears was the legendary dog belonging to the poet Lu Ji (261–303). It is said to have borne messages between Lu, who had moved to Luoyang after the fall of Wu, and his younger brother Lu Yun, who had remained at home. The Li Marshes in Jiangsu province were the site of a famous ancient battle between the states of Wu and Yue.

3.49 Baixia

Fallen leaves invade Baixia, driven by winds from the west.
Again I come to this place, again climb up to look around.
Clear sounds of pipes, a bright moon, autumn drapes the walls.
The wilderness burns as cold stars come forth over the forest.
Rivers and hills go back to ancient times, wild peaks seek a master.
Year after year with weapons of war, we search each other out.

But if we each shed a handful of New Pavilion tears,
we will make the great river rise ten fathoms or more.

Note: Baixia was another name for the old southern capital Nanjing. This was where the alternative Ming government was briefly established after the fall of Beijing in 1644. North of the city was the important Baishi fortification. The New Pavilion (Xin Ting) was a meeting place for scholars.

3.50 Again I Visit the Southern Imperial Tombs

Eunuchs and monks among my old acquaintances
were much surprised by my wanderings when we met.
They asked me why I would travel three thousand *li*,
north to the imperial tombs in spring and south in autumn.

4. 1663–1673

Now over fifty, his wandering life continued, as did his prolific writing. He was again in trouble with the law—this time as one of a group of writers and intellectuals accused of anti-Qing activities. He was held in custody for six months but then exonerated.

4.12 In the Rain, Sent to Shen Hanguang

Ten years ago we met at a bend in the river Fen,
new poems still fresh, the sound of the cold jade.
Before Xuanweng Mountain a hundred streams flow,
below Taitai temple a thousand trees stand.
Boarding our carriage we push against the rain,
but the horse neighs in distress,
worried by the silken saddle cloth.
Beyond the city wall at Bingzhou
no travelers to be seen,
so we two, like Liu and Zu,
can hear the night cock crow.

Note: Shen Hanguang (1620–1677) was a noted poet from the northern regions who turned increasingly to philosophy in his later writings. He, like Gu, never served in an official capacity under the Qing. Taitai was the spirit of the Fen River. Bingzhou was the old name for Taiyuan. The reference in the final lines is to Liu Kun and Zu Ti from the third and fourth centuries, who became great friends and strove to outdo each other in resisting foreign incursion.

4.52 Handan

In the kingdom of Zhao the land lies untended,
towns crowd together and wilderness fires burn.
In Pingyuan and Mafu,
everything lies buried under withered plants.
Starving birds peck at the winter snow,
a lone wild goose calls at the edge of town.
There may be plans, but what use will they be
to wipe clean a thousand bright swords?
Who will hear the Xiao king come,
leaving the north at Yuyang with brave men?
Lying down by day near Wenming Hall,
while the ordinary people weep and wail.
I sigh—again what is there to say?
All I can do is deal with what I meet!

Note: Handan was the capital of the state of Zhao during the Warring States period (it is a city in present-day Hebei). Pingyuan and Mafu were places within the state. The fourth couplet is a reference to the *Zuo Zhuan* for the twelfth year of Duke Wen. The Xiao king is Han Guangwu Di, who restored the Han dynasty in 25 C.E.

5. 1674–1682

This was the last decade of Gu's life, and his writings necessarily reflect the trials of growing old. Although he continued to travel widely, he did establish a study in Shanxi province through the good offices of a friend. He also acquired a concubine. His wife, who had remained in Kunshan throughout Gu's many years of travel, died during these years. These last years saw him become more involved in family matters generally. In 1682, as he was setting out on yet another journey, he fell while mounting his horse and died from his injuries a few days later.

5.9 Harvesting My Crop below Changbai Mountain

Bearing my plow I reach the eastern state.
Year after year I come and then depart.
The corn droops as the day's light fails,
fruit falls and wild birds come to rest.
I eat what I grow, retaining my integrity;
to rely on others is a shameful thing.
The road leads away to Yellow Turban city,
and there is only Zheng Gong mountain.

Note: This poem relates to Gu's agricultural venture late in his life and the wider significance of being able to provide for oneself. Ku Wei-ying, in his dissertation, attaches particular importance to the complex allusion in the final lines. He quotes from the *Asahi Shinbun* as follows: "The main theme in this poem is Gu's emphasis on agriculture as the basic occupation and his use of an agricultural economy as the main force for resisting the Manchu regime." Yellow Turban city is a reference to both the Yellow Turban rebellion in Han times and a city of importance in the Northern Qi period. Zheng Gong refers to the noted Han scholar Zheng Xuan, who was, in many ways, the model for the "Han learning" of the Qing period.

5.59 Sent to the Man of Letters Kang Naixin on Returning to Heyang

The house where Zixia read his books
is by the riverbank looking out on all sides.
The hills follow Thunder Mountain and depart,
the waves go away from Dragon Gate and return.
Sadly the great Way will be discarded;
abandoning the classics doubles the sorrow.

If there is no prince who truly loves the ancients,
who will there be to clear away moss and lichen?

Note: Kang Naixin (1643–1707) was a scholar who loved the ancients. Zixia is Pu Shang, one of the leading Confucian disciples. He is associated with one of two stone cottages on the banks of a tributary of the Yellow River as described in the *Water Classic*.

5.60 An Old Friend Comes and We Sit Together Composing Poems

Being of no use is what we relied on
to let us live out our allotted spans.
It is what let us perch so long
beside the swift rushing torrent.
We send word to our old friends
that we are happy in ourselves.
Casting off the green and purple—
approaching the world of spirits.

Note: This is a reference to the oft-repeated story from the early Daoist classic the *Zhuangzi* about an old tree, bent and gnarled, that has been able to avoid the axe of woodman or carpenter because its timber is taken to be useless. "Green and purple" refers to the life of an official.

5.67 Mourning

I sit alone beside the cold window looking out
at the chopper and block.
What words are there to describe growing old?
Where now are the vows of our young hearts?
Who knows where the wandering man went
when he left you for the edge of heaven?
Who can bear the emptiness
of inner apartments
in the depth of night?

Note: This relates to Gu's wife, who remained at home in Kunshan during the many years of his travels. The "wandering man" is of course Gu himself.

Appendix 1
Biographical Summary

1613: Gu Yanwu was born in Qiandun, a village some twenty-four *li* south of Kunshan city in what was then Jiangnan province, on the twenty-eighth day of the fifth month of the forty-first year of the Wanli reign period (1613). At first he was named Jishen; this was later changed to Jiang. His *zi* (style) was initially Zhongqing (loyal and pure). He was the second son of Gu Tongying, a minor scholar and noted poet, but was later adopted as the heir of Tongying's paternal uncle, Gu Shaofei, and Shaofei's deceased son, Tongji. When he died in 1601, at the age of eighteen, Tongji was betrothed to a woman named Wang, who did not subsequently marry but attached herself to Shaofei's household and gained renown as a model of propriety and rectitude.

1615: At the age of three, Gu contracted smallpox, which left him with a permanent disfigurement of one eye.

1618–1623: When Gu was six, his paternal grandmother, Li Shuoren, died. At this point his adoptive mother, Wang, assumed management of the household and was largely responsible for Gu's early education. At the age of seven, he began attendance at the local school. His grandfather, Shaofei, now took over supervision of his studies.

1626: In this year, Gu is said to have completed his reading of the *Comprehensive Mirror* with his adoptive grandfather. According to Willard Peterson, their practice was to compare what they had read in the older work with what appeared in the *Capital Gazette* ("The Life of Ku

Yen-wu [1613–1682]," *Harvard Journal of Asiatic Studies* 28 [1968]: 125). Also in this year, aged fourteen, he passed an examination in Suzhou to become a government student and is said also to have joined the Society for Restoration (Fushe). In this year Gu Tongying died at the age of forty-two.

1630: Now aged eighteen, Gu was placed twentieth in the first rank of the preliminary examination in Suzhou but failed the subsequent triennial examination held later that year in Nanjing.

1631: Gu was placed eleventh in the first rank of the annual examination. In this year, he married a woman of the surname Wang from Taicang and changed his name to Gu Jiang.

1632: Gu was again placed in the first rank of the annual examination, this time in fourteenth position.

1633: In this year Gu was placed in the third (lowest) rank of the preliminary examination.

1634: Gu's adoptive mother received official recognition of her virtue when the title "chaste and filial" was given to her for her gate by a regional inspecting censor.

1636: In this year, to quote Peterson, "another regional inspecting censor memorialized the throne for permission to grant her [Wang] the title 'chaste and filial.' The petition was approved, and, when the imperial honor was bestowed, all of Gu Shaofei's and Gu Jiang's friends from the surrounding districts came with gifts and congratulations" ("Life of Ku Yen-wu," 128–29). Gu was then in his twenty-fourth year.

1638: In both the annual examinations and the preliminary examinations for this year, Gu was placed in the third rank.

1639: In the seventh month of this year, Gu again failed the triennial examination, being ranked in the second class. As Peterson has noted, the prefaces to his two geographical compilations (the *Zhaoyu Zhi* and the *Tianxia Junguo Libing Shu*) refer to 1639 as the year in which he began to gather geographical materials ("Life of Ku Yen-wu," 131).

1640: Gu attempted the annual examination again in this year and was ranked in the second class.

1641: In the spring, when Gu was twenty-nine, his adoptive paternal grandfather, Gu Shaofei, died. The period of mourning following this death marked the end of Gu's examination attempts.

1642: Gu's older brother, Gu Xiang, died, thus making Gu Jiang the head of the household. Faced with the expenses of two funerals in quick succession and beset by financial pressures, he mortgaged part of the family estate to one Ye Fangheng, a matter that became the subject of an ongoing dispute.

1643: In this year Gu purchased rank in the National University.

1644: Impelled by the fall of Beijing and the inevitable progress of the Manchu army south, Gu moved his adoptive mother and the remainder of the household to Tangshi in Changshu district in the fourth month and, in the tenth month, to the family residence in Qiandun. In the twelfth month, Gu moved his household again, this time to a village called Yulianjing, between Kunshan and Changshu. During this time the alternative Ming government was being established in Nanjing. Late in 1644, the magistrate of Kunshan, Yang Yongyan, submitted Gu's name to the Ming court as a recommended candidate for office, and Gu was called to serve as *bingbu siwu* (associated with the Ministry of War).

1645: During this year, Kunshan was captured, and several of Gu's relatives were directly involved in the conflict. Two of his younger brothers were killed, and his biological mother was injured. It seems probable that Gu himself was not involved in the fighting. Earlier in the year, he had gone to Nanjing, ostensibly to take up his position with the Ministry of War, but this never eventuated. The Manchu forces entered Nanjing, and, in the sixth month, Gu retired to Yulianjing, where, in all probability, he remained during the hostilities in Kunshan. At the end of this year, Gu's adoptive mother starved herself to death rather than submit to the alien regime. The year also saw Gu's presentation of four substantial essays on political matters and his change of name from Gu Jiang to Gu Yanwu (literally, "warlike and blazing"). This was accompanied by the destruction of all his previously written poems.

1646: For this and several succeeding years, relatively little is known of Gu's activities. According to Peterson, in the spring of 1646 he was summoned to the court of the Prince of Tang in Yanping but did not go, in part at least because his adoptive mother had remained unburied, awaiting the hoped-for Ming restoration ("Life of Ku Yen-wu," 147).

1647: With no prospect of a Ming restoration in sight, Gu's adoptive mother was buried, and in the twelfth month, Gu returned to Yulianjing. Prior to this, he had traveled with his close friend Gui Zhuang to Wuxing.

1648–1650: After completion of his mourning in Yulianjing, Gu began a period of travel, first in the Suzhou area and then in the south. To facilitate his travels, he assumed an appearance somewhat in accordance with Manchu requirements. His long poem "Wandering About" alludes to this. Indeed, his poems from this period, which represent a new beginning poetically, reflect his travels and his thoughts on the devastation of war.

1651: In this year, aged thirty-nine, Gu made the first of a series of visits to the tomb of Ming Tai Zu (r. 1368–1398) in Nanjing.

1652–1654: During these years, Gu resided in Nanjing, although his wife continued to live in Kunshan. In the spring of 1654, he set up a residence in Shenlie Shan, which facilitated his continuing visits to Ming Tai Zu's tomb.

1655: Now aged forty-three, Gu returned to Kunshan and became involved in a serious legal matter involving a servant, Lu En, a longtime member of the Gu household, who had transferred his allegiance to Ye Fangheng, with whom Gu was contesting a property dispute. Perhaps with the connivance of Ye, Lu sought to discredit Gu by informing local officials that he had been connected with the southern Ming court in Fuzhou. On his return to Kunshan in the fifth month of 1665, Gu and his associates seized Lu and drowned him. Gu was arrested and held by the associates of Ye. His initial trial, at which he was sentenced to forced labor, was also influenced by Ye. Ultimately, through the intercession of his friends, in particular Gui Zhuang and Lu Zepu, he was retried in a different court and his sentence reduced to a beating. He was released in the spring of 1656.

1656: Following his release, Gu returned to Kunshan. Shortly thereafter, his natural mother, He, died. In the intercalary sixth month, Gu set out for Nanjing. During this journey, he was attacked by an assassin sent by Ye Fangheng and was fortunate to escape with only a head wound thanks to the intervention of a bystander. Also in this year Gu's household in Kunshan was robbed by Ye's ruffians.

1657: In the spring, Gu returned to Kunshan, but realizing he was unable to contest effectively any legal battle with Ye, he again left his home area and departed on his northern travels. Thus began a period of extensive travel and also of substantial literary production. It was during the years from 1657 to 1677 that the major part of the *Rizhi Lu* was written.

1658: In the spring of this year, now aged forty-six, Gu went to Tai'an and climbed Mount Tai. He then traveled to Yanzhou and on to Qufu and Zouxian, where he visited the temples of Confucius, Mencius, and the Duke of Zhou. Traversing Zhangqiu, Changshan, Qinan, and Laizhou, he reached the capital. He left Beijing late in the year.

1659: Gu, based in Shandong since 1657, continued his travels, passing through Shanhaiguan, a place of obvious strategic importance, and then journeying in a southwesterly direction along the coast. In the autumn of this year, Gu went to Yangzhou but returned to Tianjin later in the year. This year also saw his first visit to Shisanling, site of the northern Ming tombs at Tianshou Shan, north of Beijing. Also in 1659 Gu visited Lingyan Temple, southwest of Qinan in Shandong, and obtained there, in the ruined building, a number of inscriptions from the Tang period. Thereafter, his travels were at least in part aimed at the gathering of such materials.

1660: This year saw Gu's return to Jiangnan and to Nanjing.

1661: In the spring of this year, Gu resumed his travels, traversing Suzhou and Hangzhou before reaching Shaoxing. Finally, in the autumn, he returned to Shandong. Apropos of these journeys, Peterson has written, "It is difficult to discern why he traveled in the south at this time," suggesting subsequently that it may have been to attend to his property and "to reconnoiter the area and estimate the extent of Qing consolidation" ("Life of Ku Yen-wu," 208). In the last month of the year, he returned to Shandong and completed his short work *Shandong Kaogu Lu*.

1662: In this, his fifty-first year, Gu's travels continued, including a visit to Shanxi, during which he located an old text of interest at a temple at Mount Huo, in the southern part of the province. In this year, he wrote the preface to his extensive geographical work, the *Tianxia Junguo Libing Shu*, begun in 1639, for which he had been collecting materials throughout his travels.

1663: In this year, Gu's travels included visits to Taiyuan, Wutai Shan, Huayin, and Xi'an. He called on Wang Hongzhuan and, later, the renowned Shaanxi scholar Li Yong. Also, while in Shaanxi, he visited Zhu Cungang, a descendant of the Ming imperial house, by whom he was asked to edit and write a preface for a compilation of Zhu's father's poems. This was also the year of the trial of literati in northern Zhejiang involved in the preparation of an unofficial Ming history. Although Gu himself was not directly implicated in the case, some of his friends were, and he later wrote an account of the matter.

1664: Gu's travels during this year included Changping, a further visit to the northern Ming tombs, and to Henan, where he called upon the noted scholar Sun Qifeng, in Huixian in the northern part of the province.

1665: This year, after travels through Tai'an and Dezhou, saw Gu's return to Qinan, where he established a farm in Zhangqiu, taking over some property of one Xie Zhangji, who had been in his debt. He also traveled to Qufu, where he again visited Confucius's tomb, and to Queli, the site of the Sage's home.

1666: Gu, now fifty-four, continued his travels from his Shandong base and included a visit to the residence of Chen Shangnian, where the young scholar Li Yindu, with whom Gu had previously become acquainted, was working as a family tutor. Also in this year, in conjunction with twenty or so others, he was involved in the development of some uncultivated land north of Yanmen.

1667: Gu's travels during this year included his last trip south, to Jiangnan. It was in this year that his well-known work on phonetics, the *Yinxue Wushu*, was first published, with the aid of Chang Shao, in Shanyang in Jiangsu.

1668: This was a momentous year for the fifty-six-year-old Gu. On the fourteenth day of the second month, while residing in a monastery in Beijing, he learned of his implication in a trial in Shandong. He traveled back to Qinan, arriving in the third month to find that he had been accused of sedition by a certain Jiang Yuanheng. The charge involved a number of scholars said to have been sympathetic to the Ming and slanderous, in their writings, toward the Qing rulers. Gu remained in custody for approximately six months, being released in the tenth month of that year.

1669: Gu's northern travels continued, especially between Shandong and the capital. He also went to Zhangqiu to resolve the issue of ownership of the farm he had acquired in 1665 and that had been taken over by others during his imprisonment. It was toward the end of this year that Pan Lei traveled from Shanyang to Qinan to become Gu's student.

1670: This year, Gu, now fifty-eight, saw the first publication of the *Rizhi Lu* in eight *juan*.

1671: In the spring of this year, Gu was visited by two young nephews, sons of two of Gu's younger brothers. Later in the year, he was summoned by the Qing official Xiong Cilü and asked to collaborate in the compilation of the Ming history, a request he declined. Following this, he left the capital and traveled to Taiyuan in Shaanxi, where he was engaged in some literary work, which included the punctuation of a commentary on the Han history.

1672: Despite reaching the age of sixty, Gu's travels continued. He journeyed from Shanxi back to the capital, where he stayed with his nephew, Xu Yuanwen, for two months before returning, in the fifth month, to Qinan. In the eighth month, he again returned to the capital, staying with Xu as before, and later traveled to Dezhou and through Henan back to Shanxi.

1673–1674: Gu's travels continued, taking in Shandong, Shanxi, and Henan.

1675: Gu, now aged sixty-three, established a study in Qixian, southern Shanxi, in a house built for him there by Dai Tingshi, who had supported a number of Ming loyalists.

1676: In the first month, Gu returned from Shanxi to Shandong and, in the second month, entered the capital. He is said to have taken a concubine in Jingle and subsequently ordered Gu Yansheng, the son of one of his distant cousins whom Gu had adopted as his own son, to come north to meet him. This he did in Dezhou, where, according to Peterson, they "fulfilled the rites of father and son" ("Life of Ku Yen-wu," 244).

1677: Aged sixty-five, Gu continued to travel, leaving the capital in the fourth month and journeying to Dezhou. In the ninth month, he went to Shaanxi, where he visited Li Zhongfu. Toward the end of the year, he traveled to Huayin, visiting Wang Hongzhuan before returning to Qixian. While with Wang he apparently discussed the possibility of setting up a residence in Shaanxi. Gu moved his books to Huayin and a plot of land was purchased.

1678: This year was notable for an attempt to involve the sixty-six-year-old Gu in Qing officialdom. In the fourth month, while in Fuping in Shaanxi, he was invited to the magistrate's yamen. He refused this and a subsequent invitation, as he also refused a request later in this year from the son of the commander in chief in Gansu, Zhang Yunyi, to go to that province. The same Zhang had earlier (in 1671) contributed to the cost of publication of Gu's short work *Zuo Zhuan Dujie Buzheng*.

1679: Early in the year, Gu again visited Wang Hongzhuan in Huayin and joined with him in planning a shrine and academy there to commemorate a visit by Zhu Xi to the place in 1185. Also in this year, he petitioned the History Board for the inclusion of his adoptive mother in the biographies of women in the Ming history.

1680: In the first month Gu went again to Fuping. Subsequently, while with his adopted son in Fenzhou, he received news of the death of his wife, who had remained in Kunshan throughout the period of her husband's extensive northern travels. He met his mourning obligations while staying at a friend's house and sent a poem to mark the occasion of her death. Later in the year, he returned to Huayin in relation to his work with Wang Hongzhuan on the shrine to Zhu Xi.

1681: The first part of this year found Gu, now aged sixty-nine, back in Fenzhou, which he left in the second month to travel to Quwo and thence to Jiezhou. In the fourth month, he again went to Huayin to see Wang Hongzhuan. On the second day of the eighth month, he began what was to be his last journey, setting out to travel, via Yuncheng, to Quwo. On the eleventh day of the eighth month, three days after he arrived in Quwo, he became ill and had difficulty walking. In the tenth month, he moved to the house of Han Xuan. In this year he completed the rites of adoption with his nephew Gu Yansheng and while there arranged the marriage of his adopted son to the daughter of an eminent local family.

1682: The start of this, his final year, found him, now aged seventy, still staying with Han Xuan in Shanxi. Although his health had shown improvement, on the eighth day of the first month his foot slipped as he was mounting his horse and he fell to the ground. There was a marked decline in his condition, and he died early on the morning of the ninth day of the first month of 1682. Han Xuan attended to his funeral arrangements, and, in the third month, his coffin accompanied by his adopted son, Gu Yanwu was returned to Kunshan, where he was buried.

Appendix 2
Works by Gu Yanwu

Gu Yanwu was a prolific writer, and his works reflect the breadth of his interests, covering philosophy, phonetics, philology, textual criticism, historical geography, and verse. Within these broad categories there are further subdivisions, so the range of topics is indeed extensive. There are no pre-1644 writings extant, although it is probable that the collection of data for his first two important works on historical geography with strategic implications—the *Zhaoyu Ji* and the *Tianxia Junguo Libing Shu*—began in 1639. A detailed list of works is included in Jean-François Vergnaud, *La pensée de Gu Yanwu (1613–1682)* (Paris: École française d'Extrême-Orient, 1990), 203–20. This is based on the very detailed study by Jan Hagman, *Bibliographical Notes on Ku Yen-wu (1613–1682)* (Stockholm: Föreningen för Orientalisker Studier, 1973), and contains eighty titles grouped as follows:

classical (10 titles)
historical (27 titles)
philosophical (7 titles)
miscellaneous (14 titles)
collections (6 titles)
various unclassified (16 titles)

The following somewhat abbreviated list is subdivided according to the categories given by the *Siku Quanshu* (*SKQS*). The works listed in the *SKQS Zongmu Tiyao* are marked with an asterisk.

1. CLASSICS (*JING* 經)

*i. *Jiujing Wuzi* 九經誤字, one *juan*: This short work examines textual inaccuracies in the Nine Classics. In his preface, Gu draws attention to the numerous errors and omissions in the then current editions of the classics put out by the Imperial Academy. The purpose of the work was to correct these errors by comparison with old texts, including stone engravings, seeing this exercise as being of benefit to later scholars.

*ii. *Zuo Zhuan Dujie Buzheng* 左傳杜解補掙, three *juan*: In this short work Gu examines errors and omissions in the early commentary by the Jin scholar Du Yu 杜預 (222–284).

iii. *Wujing Tongyi* 五經同異, three *juan*: This work is concerned mainly with textual criticism relating to the Five Classics (*Changes*, *Documents*, *Odes*, *Spring and Autumn Annals*, and *San Li*). Its purpose is somewhat different from the sections on the classics in the *Rizhi Lu*, being focused primarily on the commentaries of Song, Yuan, and Ming Confucians.

*iv. *Yinxue Wushu* 音學五書, thirty-eight *juan*: This is one of Gu's most important works and is listed in the *SKQS* in the classics section under the philology subdivision. In the *Zongmu Tiyao* the five component books are listed separately. In this work, he continues the method established by his Ming predecessor Chen Di 陳第. Fang Chao-ying writes, "Ku Yen-wu adopted Ch'en's method in his own more extensive phonetical researches and, by adducing still more examples to show its applicability, he so popularized it that it became one of the most effective tools of Ch'ing scholarship" (*ECCP*, 424). The work, which first appeared in 1667, printed at Shanyang in Jiangsu with the collaboration of Zhang Chao 張弨, is subdivided into the following five sections: "Guyin Biao" 古音表, two *juan*, a catalogue of ancient sounds; "Yiyin" 易音, three *juan*, a study of phonetics in the *Changes*; "Shi Benyin" 詩本音, ten *juan*, an examination of rhymes in the *Odes*; "Tang Yunzheng" 唐韻正, twenty *juan*, a comparison of Tang sounds with those used in ancient times; and "Yinlun" 音論, three *juan*, a general discussion of the subject.

*v. *Yunbu Zheng* 韻補正, one *juan*: This short work, written after Gu had compiled the "Tang Yunzheng" 唐韻正 section of the *Yinxue Wushu* and published in 1657, was based on the *Yunbu* 韻補, by the Song scholar Wu Yu 吳棫 (d. 1154). It is about errors in ancient rhymes and irregularities in the contemporary use of rhymes. This work is also included in the philology division of the classics section of the *SKQS* and is in the *Tinglin Yishu* 亭林遺書.

2. HISTORICAL WORKS (*SHI* 史)

*i. *Changping Shanshui Ji* 昌平山水記, two *juan*: This short work consists of miscellaneous notes on the district of Changping in Zhili (near the capital), including details of the thirteen Ming *lu* and the nature of the land near the capital. For the most part the writings were based on close personal observation. Wang Hong 王宏, in his *Shanzhi* 山志, attests to the detail of Gu's observations.

ii. *Zhaoyu Zhi* 肇域志, one hundred *juan*: Gu began (at least as far data collection was concerned) this extensive work on historical geography in 1639, but it was never published in a completed form. Gu, in his preface, indicates the breadth of the background reading done in preparation for the work: "This book was begun in . . . [1639]. First I took the general gazetteers of the empire, then the gazetteers of each of the *sheng*, *fu*, *zhou*, and *xian*. Then I took the twenty-one dynastic histories and various works, reading in all more than one thousand works." According to Fang, who likens the work to Gu Zuyu's 顧祖禹 (1631–1692) *Dushi Fangyu Jiyao* 讀史方輿紀要 (*ECCP*, 424), two incomplete manuscripts of this compendium of historical geography were preserved in the Guoxue Library in Nanjing. A breakdown of the contents is given by Zhang Shunhui 張舜徽 in his *Gu Tinglin Xueji*, 8–9.

*iii. *Jinshi Wenzi Ji* 金石文字記, six *juan*: This work, printed by Pan Lei around 1695 in the *Tinglin Shizhong* 亭林十種, continued the epigraphical tradition of Ouyang Xiu 歐陽修 and Zhao Mingcheng 趙明誠, to whom Gu acknowledges his debt in the preface to this work. The works in question were Ouyang Xiu's *Jigu Lu* 集古錄 and Zhao Mingcheng's *Jinshi Lu* 金石錄 (see *SB*, 199 and 201, respectively). Gu's work is a record of his study of over three hundred post-Han stone inscriptions, compiled during his travels. For each inscription there is a commentary, an account of the origin and other details, along with a discussion of textual errors. This work was also published in the *Tinglin Yishu* 亭林遺書.

*iv. *Jingdong Kaogu Lu* 京東考古錄, one *juan*: This brief work, concerning place-names and antiquities east of the capital, was published by Wu Zhenfang 吳震方 in his *Shuoling* 說鈴. According to several sources, all the material is included in either the *Rizhi Lu* or the *Changping Shanshui Ji*.

*v. *Qiugu Lu* 求古錄, one *juan*: This work is a record of stone inscriptions extending from the Han period to the Ming period, in all fifty-six inscriptions, with Gu's notes and textual criticisms.

*vi. *Juegu Shishi* 譎觚十事, one *juan*: This brief work on geographical matters has been said to have been prepared in collaboration with Li Huanzhang 李煥章 of Yue'an, but this is probably not so. The material is said to be included in the *Rizhi Lu*.

*vii. *Gu Shi Puxi Kao* 顧氏譜系考, one *juan*: This brief work concerns the history of the surname Gu of the Gu family and is included in the historical biographies section of the *SKQS*.

*viii. *Lidai Diwang Zhaijing Ji* 歷代帝王宅京記, twenty *juan*: This is the third of Gu's major topographical studies (after the *Zhaoyu Zhi* and *Tianxia Junguo Libing Shu*). The work was, according to Fang (*ECCP*, 424–25), completed toward the end of Gu's life and first printed in 1808. It is a record of the establishment of cities through successive dynasties. The first two chapters are in the form of a general introduction, while the remaining eighteen record in detail the establishment of cities and suburbs, palaces and mansions, capitals, monasteries, and temples.

ix. *Mingji Shilu* 明季實錄, one *juan*: This is a collection of official documents, including imperial edicts, memorials, and official dispatches for the later part of the Ming period. The work was published in the *Tinglin Yishu* 亭林遺書.

*x. *Shandong Kaogu Lu* 山東考古錄, one *juan*: This brief work, said to have been compiled in 1661, examines errors in the recording of Shandong's ancient place-names, names of people, and historical biographies. It was included in the *Tinglin Yishu* 亭林遺書 and is similar in scope to the *Jingdong Kaogu Lu*.

xi. *Sheng'an Jishi* 聖安紀檢事, two *juan*: This work, also titled *Sheng'an Huang Di Benji* 聖安皇帝本紀, concerns events surrounding the establishment of the Hongguang emperor in Nanjing after the fall of the Ming in 1644.

*xii. *Shijing Kao* 石經考, one *juan*: This work is essentially one of textual criticism of the stone carvings of the classics from various periods. It includes examination of sources and details as well as textual errors and also compares previous opinions and criticisms. According to Fang (*ECCP*, 425), the work itself was corrected and criticized by Hang Shijun 杭世駿. It was included in the *Tinglin Yishu* 亭林遺書.

*xiii. *Tianxia Junguo Libing Shu* 天下郡國利病書, one hundred twenty *juan*: This substantial work is a collection of material from historical records, veritable records, local records, collected works, and various other official documents, supplemented and corrected by Gu's observations made during his extensive travels. It is said that whatever had a bearing on the nation's economy and the people's livelihood was thought worthy of examination and recording. Particular stress is laid on places of strategic military importance, taxation, and waterways. The collection of data was begun in 1639 and the preface written in 1662. It is said that the original draft, in Gu's hand, was reproduced in 1936 in the third section of the *SBCK*.

*xiv. *Yingping Erzhou Diming Ji* 營平二州地名記, one *juan*: It is said that Gu, who during his northern sojourn repeatedly visited these two *zhou*, was asked by the people to remedy the topographical records. In response, he collected materials concerning the histories of the two ancient *zhou*, compiling and preparing a work titled *Yingping Erzhou Shishi* in six *juan*. The *Yingping Erzhou Diming Ji* was apparently part of that work. It is an incomplete work.

3. PHILOSOPHICAL WORKS (*ZI* 子)

*i. *Jingshi Pian* 經世篇, twelve *juan*: There is little information about this work. According to Zhang Shunhui 張舜徽 (*Gu Tinglin Xueji*, 7), it consisted of a series of sections devoted to examination topics, and its purpose was to assist in the taking of the examinations. In the *SKQS* it is listed in the category of miscellaneous reference works but was apparently unpublished.

*ii. *Qiuwen Gelun* 求文格論, one *juan*: This brief work is devoted to the ancients' recording of matters related to times, seasons, reign titles, official names, place-names, and the like, and questions relating thereto. In the *SKQS* it is listed under the works of miscellaneous scholars, and its contents are said to be included in full in the *Rizhi Lu*.

*iii. *Rizhi Lu* 日知錄, thirty-two *juan*: Probably Gu's best-known and most influential work, this book was first published in 1670 in eight *juan*. Finally, after numerous revisions and amplifications under the editorship of Pan Lei, it was published in its present form of thirty-two *juan* in Fujian in 1695. The next edition appeared in 1795 based on the 1695 publication but with some differences. What became the definitive edition, prepared by Huang Rucheng 黄汝成, was published in 1834 and republished in 1868, 1869, 1872, and subsequently. This edition is included in the *SBBY* of the Zhonghua Shuju and the Guoxue Jiben Congshu of the Commercial Press. The *Yuanchaoben Rizhi Lu* was published in Taiwan in 1958.

iv. *Ruzhi Luzhi Yu* 日知錄之餘: The four *juan* grouped under this title were included as supplementary notes in the 1795 edition of the *Rizhi Lu* but not in the original 1695 edition. These four sections concern calligraphy, legal restrictions, Buddhism and Daoism, and miscellaneous theories. This work is appended to Huang Rucheng's 黄汝成 edition of the *Rizhi Lu*. It was reprinted by Zou Fubao in 1910.

*v. *Guzhong Suibi* 菰中隨筆, one *juan*: This work is described by Zhang Shunhui 張舜徽 as containing "miscellaneous notes from Gu Yanwu's daily readings." He goes on to say, "Although it is slight and defective and of a trifling nature, yet it has material bearing on textual research" (*Gu Tinglin Xueji*, 7). It, too, is appended to the Huang Rucheng 黃汝成 edition of the *Rizhi Lu*. According to Fang, this collection of miscellaneous notes was never printed, "but a manuscript copy once owned by Lu Xinyuan 陸心源 is in the Seikado Bunko, Tokyo. Apparently a work bearing the same title and printed in the *Tinglin Yishu Huiji* 亭林遺書彙輯 is not authentic" (*ECCP*, 425).

vi. *Zalu* 雜錄, one *juan*: This collection of miscellaneous notes is now included in the *Rizhi Lu*.

4. MISCELLANEOUS WORKS (*JI* 集)

i. *Gu Tinglin Xiansheng Shi Jianzhu* 顧亭林先生詩箋注, seventeen *juan*: This collection of Gu's verse was annotated by Xu Jia 徐嘉, from Shanyang, and printed in 1897. The work also contains a chronological biography.

ii. *Tinglin Yishi* 亭林軼詩, one *juan*: This short collection of Gu's verse was published by Zhu Jirong 朱記榮, of Wuxian.

iii. *Tinglin Shiji* 亭林詩集, five *juan*: The is the most complete collection of Gu's verse and was initially published as part of the *Tinglin Yishu* 亭林遺書. This collection is currently available both in the *Gu Tinglin Shiwen Ji* 顧亭林詩文集 and (in six *juan*) in the *Gu Tinglin Shiji Huizhu* 顧亭林詩集彙注 with detailed annotation.

iv. *Tinglin Wenji* 亭林文集, six *juan*: This miscellaneous collection of Gu's writings contains some of his most influential pieces, including the four essays on current affairs (geographical, military, economic, and agricultural) prepared in 1645 after the fall of the Ming. The sections are, broadly, as follows: *juan* 1, exposition and argumentation; *juan* 2, prefaces and postscripts; *juan* 3 and 4, correspondence; *juan* 5, narratives, tables, and inscriptions; *juan* 6, addenda (miscellaneous). The collection is currently available in the *Tinglin Shiwen Ji*.

v. *Tinglin Yuji* 亭林餘集, one *juan*: This collection of twelve essays was originally prepared during the early years of the Qianlong reign period and published by Peng Shaosheng 彭紹升. The collection is also currently included in the *Tinglin Shiwen Ji*.

Appendix 3
Zhang Binglin's Preface to Huang Kan's *Rizhi Lu Jiaoji*

Previously, when I read the *Record of Daily Knowledge*, I was surprised that Gu Yanwu, who had served the Ming as a young man, would refer to it as Ming in his work, no differently from any other dynasty. I suspected that some later person had tampered with the work. Also, the essay titled "Su Yidi Xing Hu Yidi" had been completely removed from the work.[1] This, too, could be something taken out as being offensive to the Qianlong emperor. Later I acquired a copy of Pan Cigeng's first edition[2] and found this to be no different, so I assumed it had already become Gu Yanwu's "true record," and for a long time I had been unhappy with this subterfuge. Last year I heard that a friend, Zhang Ji, had found a lost manuscript dating from the Yongzheng reign period of the Qing dynasty [1723–1735]; no loss was recorded, therefore the work still existed. Also, there was an additional essay, "Hu Fu,"[3] which consisted of more than a thousand characters. Instead of writing *ming* 明, he wrote *ben chao* 本朝. If taboos involving *ming* existed, then he used these two characters, therefore I believed this to be Gu's true work. So my former doubts on this matter were at once confirmed. Gu's writing in red and yellow ink in various places couldn't be photographed to show scholars. In the spring of that year, my student Huang Kan, during his time of working on the *Jiaoji*, made a comprehensive comparison [to show] what the present edition lacked, recording this completely in notes and writing it out for every character and sentence. His achievement was both reliable and diligent. It seems rather strange that Cigeng, an outstanding student of both Master Gu and Xu Zhaofa, and a man who received very personal teaching from them, would not be expected to differ from other, ordinary people. And yet, in editing his teacher's book, he could turn around and make its true appearance impossible to see with one's own eyes! How ungrateful would this be to his teacher! It could, however, be the case that he was mindful of the warnings from history and did so against his will. Now, the *Jiaoji* has already come out, and everyone can read it carefully and assess its genuineness, so Master Gu's "thousand autumn will" cannot but be appreciated, and Kan's achievement makes it so that he can be joined together with the wise men of former times. This comes at a time when there is military misfortune, chaos, and appropriation—a year when Emperor Puyi's northern retreat [Jehol] was seized by the Japanese [and made part of Manchuria].

Appendix 4
On the Feudal System (*Fengjian Lun*)—Liu Zongyuan

Liu Zongyuan (773–819) was an important writer and intellectual of the later part of the Tang period. He is listed as one of the "eight great prose writers of the Tang and Song." He was also active politically, especially during the problems that followed the An Lushan Rebellion in the middle of the eighth century. Here the interest is in his celebrated essay on the feudal (*fengjian* 封建) system. Gu himself refers to Liu—for example, in the essay "The Governing of Townships (*Xiang* 鄉) and Neighborhoods (*Ting* 亭)" (*RZL* 8.5)—while Thomas Bartlett makes the point that the nine-part *SWJ* essay "Junxian Lun" should be read with Liu's essay in mind ("Gu Yanwu," in *ECP*, 273). Ku Wei-ying writes, "In his provocative essay on the *fengjian* system, Liu dealt a seemingly fatal blow to the myth which had upheld the *fengjian* system—that it had been the ingenious design of the ancient sage rulers—and declared that, on the contrary, the system had been the result of an historical necessity forced upon them by social developments" ("The Political Theories of Ku Yen-wu and the Manchu Conquest" [PhD diss., University of British Columbia, 1983], 4). The essay is translated here in full.

Did heaven and earth really have no beginning? I have no way of knowing this. Did mankind really have a beginning? I have no way of knowing this. In that case, then, what is closer to reality? I say that having a beginning is closer. How am I clear about this? Through the feudal system I am clear about it. The feudal system was something that continued through the time of the ancient sage-kings—Yao, Shun, Yu, Tang, Wen, and Wu—and they were never able to do away with it. Now, this was not because they didn't want to do away with it; it was because the circumstances didn't allow them to do so. Was the coming of such circumstances the beginning of mankind? Without such a beginning, there would have been no way for feudalism to exist. The feudal system was not a concept of the sage-kings.

Now, there was that beginning [of mankind], and the ten thousand things all arose with them. All the grasses and trees grew wild, and deer and pigs went around in groups, but people were unable to seize and bite; moreover, they had no fur or feathers to preserve and protect them. It was as Xun Qing said—they had to avail themselves of things and regard them as being of use.[1] Now, those who avail themselves of things inevitably contend, and when their contention finds no resolution, there must be someone who is able to decide what is right and wrong, and they must listen to his decree. Those who have wisdom and clarity must overawe the multitudes and inform them in a straightforward way without vacillating, and they must inflict pain on them so they are afraid. Because of this, rulers and leaders created a punitive administration. Therefore, those who lived gathered close together stayed close together to become a large group. When large groups are split into smaller groups, contention inevitably becomes very great. When it becomes very great, the options are military force and moral persuasion. Also, when it becomes very great, there must be leaders of the multitude, and they must be listened to such that they pacify those they are leading. This is why the class of feudal lords arose. But then contention between them also became very great. In the case of moral authority being great, the class of feudal lords listened to the command and in this way pacified their fiefdoms. As a result, there were the classes of regional earls and commandery governors, and then the contention again became very great. If there was someone whose moral authority was great, the regional earls and commandery governors listened to their commands and in this way pacified their people. Subsequently, the world could be unified under one person. For this reason, there were first village chiefs, then there were district leaders; first there were district leaders, then there were feudal lords; first there were feudal lords, then there were regional earls and commandery governors; first there were regional earls and commandery governors, then there was the Son of Heaven. From the Son of the Heaven down to the village chiefs, when one who was virtuous among the people died, they would seek out his descendants as leaders. Therefore, the feudal system was not a concept developed by the sages. It arose out of circumstances.

Now, Yao, Shun, Yu, and Tang belong to the distant past. By the time of Zhou, matters were much more complex. When the Zhou held sway over the world, the land was divided up, and five ranks were established.[2] Feudal lords were enfeoffed with territories that were scattered all over the place like the stars in the sky. The four corners of the world were like the spokes of a wheel connected to the axle. The feudal lords came together to have an audience with the ruler. They separated again to be officers guarding their territories, like shields and city walls. Nevertheless, when it came to the time of King Yi of Zhou [869–858 B.C.E.], he did harm to *li* 禮 [ritual practice, propriety] and damaged honor by coming down from the hall to receive those seeking an audience. When it came to the time of King Xuan [827–782 B.C.E.], he relied on restoring the virtue of ancient times and the power of south-north contention but ultimately was unable to establish a successor to the Marquis of Lu.[3] The decline continued until the time of You and Li, when the royal house moved east [from present-day Xi'an to Luoyang] and the ruler of Zhou himself became a feudal lord. From that time on, there were several notable events: [King Zhuang of Chu] asking about the weights of the tripods; the arrow of [Zhuang of Zheng] striking [Huan of Zhou] in the shoulder; the kidnapping of Fan Bo; and the killing of Chang Hong.[4] Perversion spread throughout the world, and rulers were not treated as rulers. In my view, Zhou had long since lost its power and had only an empty title above that of duke and marquis. Isn't this the fault of the burgeoning strength of the feudal lords—of the tail being too big [for the body]? Subsequently, there was division into twelve states, which were later merged into seven. The power was divided among the enfeoffed states [Han, Wei, Zhao, and Qi], and the state [of Zhou] was wiped out by the later-enfeoffed state of Qin. So then, the cause of the fall of the Zhou lay in this.

When Qin held sway over the world, the capital cities of the feudal lords were abolished and in their place commanderies [prefectures] and districts were established. The positions of feudal lords protecting the emperor were abolished, and in their place senior officials [governors and magistrates] protecting the land were appointed. Qin occupied an imposing position at the apex of the arrangement of the world, controlling the Six Directions and joining the whole country under its central control. This is what Qin is thought to have achieved, but it wasn't long before the empire collapsed. The reasons for this were as follows: forced enlistment of large numbers of men, cruel and vicious punishments, exhaustion of its goods and wealth, and sending those who worked on the land to fight at the frontier. People looked at one another and joined forces to become a mob. At the time, then, there were rebellious peasants, but no rebellious officials. The people were resentful below while officials were timorous above. Throughout the land governors and magistrates were seized and killed one after the other. The fault lay with the people's resentment, and not with the failure of the system of commanderies [prefectures] and districts.

When Han held sway over the world, it righted the wrongs of the Qin by following the system of Zhou, dividing the territories within the seas and establishing the sons of its own clan or enfeoffing meritorious officers. For many years there was a pressing need to recover from the damage, and yet there was not enough time to do so. [The emperor] suffered a series of setbacks: there was the difficulty at Pingcheng [in 200 B.C.E.],[5] and he was hit by a flying arrow [in 195 B.C.E.]. There was a gradual decline, which the next three emperors[6] could not reverse. Later, the emperor's counselors offered suggestions about reducing the size of the fiefs of the feudal lords, and yet they only needed to protect their own territories. Nevertheless, at the beginning of the feudal system, half the empire was still commanderies and half states. At that time, there were only rebellious states but not rebellious commanderies. What advantage the Qin system achieved is also clear from this. The imperial system following Qin that continued from the Han can still be recognized, even though a hundred generations have passed.

When the Tang flourished there was a system of regions and districts and the establishment of territorial administrators. This was considered to be what was appropriate. Nevertheless, those who were vicious and cunning arose at the time and rampaged through the regions and districts. The failing did not lie with the regions; it lay with the armies [of the warlords]. At the time, then, there were rebellious generals, but not rebellious regions. The setting up of regions and districts certainly cannot be done away with.

Someone might say, "Those who are feudal lords will definitely regard their land as their own private land, will treat their vassals as their own children, adapt to their customs, cultivate their control, and facilitate transformation and change. If those who are territorial administrators devote their minds to thinking about advancing their own rank and that is all, how will they be able to administer?" I also think this is wrong.

The traces of the affairs of Zhou can definitely still be seen. The various dukes were proud and discontented; they were constantly greedy and warlike. In general, many states were in disorder; only a few were well ordered. Marquises and earls were unable to change their form of administration, and the Son of Heaven was unable to change his princes. On the matters of "private land" and "vassals as children," there was not even one in a hundred who could achieve this. The failing lay in the system; it did not lie in the management of it. The affairs of Zhou were like this.

The traces of the affairs of Qin can also definitely still be seen. That there were policies for regulating people and that these were not delegated to commanderies and fiefs is right. That there were ministers for regulating the people and that these were not the creation of territorial administrators is right. Commanderies and fiefs were unable to rectify their policies; territorial administrators were unable to carry out their controls. There were cruel punishments and the sufferings of forced labor. The myriad people looked askance, but the failings lay in the administration and not in the policies. The Qin dynasty was like this.

When Han flourished, the administration of the Son of Heaven was carried out in the commanderies and not in the states. The policies were those of territorial administrators and not those of marquises and kings. Even if marquises and kings were disorderly, they could not change things. Even if the people of the states were in distress, this could not be eliminated. Now, when it came to the stage of large-scale rebellion, they were secretly seized and moved away or the army was sent to exterminate them. While a great rebellion was not yet manifest, they gained illicit benefits, extorted money, abused power, and were intimidating, treating the people harshly, and nothing could be done about it. When it came to the commanderies and districts, it could be said there was regulation as well as peace. How can I say this? Because Han knew of Meng Shu through Tian Shu, found Wei Shang through Feng Tang, heard about King [Huang] Ba's enlightened examination of things, and saw Ji An's simple pacification.[7] This is how they could be honored and restored to their positions and Han could be content in delegating to them the stabilization of one region.

Those at fault could be identified and dismissed; those who were able could be identified and rewarded. If the court appointed them in the morning but they did not carry out their duties, it could dismiss them in the evening. If they were appointed in the evening but did not comply with the laws, it could dismiss them in the morning. If all the cities and districts of the Han house were under the control of marquises and kings, and they were allowed to bring disorder to the people, all they could do was grieve over it. The methods of Meng Shu and Wei Shang would never have been discovered and implemented; the transformation of Huang Ba and Ji An would never have been discovered and put into practice. When the marquises and kings were clearly reprimanded, they would be compliant, but once the audience was over and they withdrew, they immediately disobeyed. If they were ordered to reduce their fiefdoms, they would plan to form a close alliance with others of the same class, and then they would turn to one another with angry looks and suddenly fly into a rage. If, by good fortune, they did not rise up, then their fiefs were reduced by half. If their fiefs were reduced by half, then the people would still suffer. Why not abolish the fiefdoms altogether and protect the ordinary people? The affairs of Han were like this.

At the present time the country has gone over completely to the system of commanderies [prefectures] and districts, appointing one territorial administrator after another. It is certainly impossible to change this. If there is skillful control and careful selection of officers, there is a peaceful administration.

Someone might also say, "Xia, Shang, Zhou, and Han implemented the feudal system and were long lasting. Qin implemented the system of commanderies and districts and was short-lived." This particularly can be described as not knowing about administrative order. Wei succeeded Han, and the feudal system was further established. Jin continued on from Wei and followed the same system without change. And yet the two clans[8] were ruined, and no one heard of a long-enduring series of emperors. Now this has been reformed and changed, and there has been continuity for two hundred years, so the great foundation is increasingly secure. How has this any connection to feudal lords?

Someone might also suppose that Yin and Zhou had sage-kings and yet they didn't change their system, so further discussion is pointless. This is absolutely not the case. Now Yin and Zhou not changing just affirms that they had no alternative. In fact, there were three thousand feudal lords subject to Yin, and Yin relied on them to get rid of Xia. Tang did not succeed and was destroyed. There were eight hundred feudal lords subject to Zhou, and Zhou relied on them to overcome Yin. King Wu was not able to make a change. He complied with the system to preserve peace and stability. Conforming with this was considered to be the custom, and Tang and Wu had no alternative. Now, the reason they had no alternative was not because the public interest was most important but because private interests were strong, and private interests offered the best protection for their descendants. Why the Qin made a change was because they thought their system was in the best interests of the people generally. With regard to their feelings of self-interest, then privately the power was vested in one person—the emperor himself—and everyone was subject to him. Nevertheless, the beginnings of a general concern with the world started with Qin.

Now, the way of the world is that a good and stable administration gains the support of the people. If worthy people occupy leading positions and the lesser people occupy lower positions, there can subsequently be a good and stable administration. Now, when there is a feudal system, one generation succeeds another in governing. If this is the case, are those in the higher positions certainly worthy? Are those in the lower positions certainly unworthy? So then, whether there is going to be good order or disorder cannot be known. If the wish is going to be to bring benefit to the altars of soil and grain [the kingdom] as a way of bringing unity to the experience of the people, there should also be those who possess the hereditary fiefdoms and completely use what is within the boundaries. But if sages and worthies lived in this time, they, too, would have no way of establishing themselves in the world because the feudal system would have had no use for them. Did the system of the sages come to this point! I certainly say power is not the purpose of the sage.

NOTES

INTRODUCTION

1. The book in French is that by Jean-François Vergnaud, *La pensée de Gu Yanwu (1613–1682): Essai de synthèse* (Paris: École française d'Extrême-Orient, 1990). The four dissertations in English are, in chronological order, Ku Wei-ying, "The Political Theories of Ku Yen-wu and the Manchu Conquest" (PhD diss., University of British Columbia, 1983); Thomas C. Bartlett, "Ku Yen-wu's Response to the 'Demise of Human Society'" (PhD diss., Princeton University, 1985); Ian Johnston, "Ku Yen-wu's *Record of Daily Knowledge*" (PhD diss., University of Sydney, 1992); John Patrick Delury, "Despotism Above and Below: Gu Yanwu's *Record of Daily Learning* on Power, Money and Mores" (PhD diss., Yale University, 2007). An example of an article on Gu Yanwu is Lung-chang Young, "Ku Yen-wu's Views on the Ming Examination System," *Ming Studies* 23 (spring 1987): 48–63. Two general books that give consideration to Gu Yanwu are Liang Ch'i-ch'ao [Qichao], *Intellectual Trends in the Ch'ing Period*, trans. Immanuel C. Y. Hsü (Cambridge, Mass.: Harvard University Press, 1959), and Benjamin A. Elman, *From Philosophy to Philology: Intellectual and Social Aspects of Change in Late Imperial China* (Cambridge, Mass.: Council on East Asian Studies, Harvard University, 1984).
2. The most detailed account in English of Gu Yanwu's life is Willard J. Peterson, "The Life of Ku Yen-wu (1613–1682)," *Harvard Journal of Asiatic Studies* 28 (1968): 114–56, 29 (1969): 201–47.
3. Ibid., 117–18.
4. Ibid., 123.
5. Ibid., 127.

6. For a detailed account of these events, see ibid., 227–33.
7. Chen Zuwu, "Rizhi Lu Bajuanben Mo Yi," *Dushu*, January 1982, 136–37.
8. *ECCP*, 424.
9. Ku Wei-ying, "Political Theories," 29–31.
10. Delury, "Despotism," 9.
11. See "Notes on the Translations" in this introduction.
12. The precise number varies from 1,013 to 1,022 according to the edition.
13. *ECCP*, 424.
14. Thomas C. Bartlett, "Gu Yanwu," in *ECP*, 275–76.
15. Delury, "Despotism," 3.
16. *Tinglin Shiwenji*, 3.41.
17. Ibid., 2.41.
18. *Mencius*, VIIB.3.
19. The numbering and translations of the essays and letters from the *SWJ* follow the *Xinyi Gu Tinglin Wenji* (Taipei: Sanmin Shuju, 2000).
20. Peterson, "Life of Ku Yen-wu," 134–35.
21. See, e.g., Bartlett, "Gu Yanwu," 273, where these men, proponents of *shixue*, are likened to Gu in their approach to learning.
22. Ku Wei-ying, "Political Theories," 279. The Chinese text is reprinted on page 1445 of Zhang Jinghua's recent edition of the *Rizhi Lu*.
23. *Dai Zhen Wenji*, 146, quoted in Elman, *From Philosophy to Philology*, 29.
24. Yü Ying-shih, "Some Preliminary Observations on the Rise of Ch'ing Confucian Intellectualism," *Tsing Hua Journal of Chinese Studies* 11 (1975): 126.
25. Ku Wei-ying, "Political Theories," 283.
26. Paul A. Cohen, *Between Tradition and Modernity: Wang T'ao and Reform in Late Ch'ing China* (Cambridge, Mass.: Harvard University Press, 1974), 274.
27. Elman, *From Philosophy to Philology*, 176.
28. Ku Wei-ying, "Political Theories," 291–92.

1. *RZL* 1–7: THE CLASSICS

1. Bao Xi Shi 包羲氏, better known as Fu Xi 伏羲, was the first of the Five Emperors of the legendary period at the start of the second millennium B.C.E. He is said to have been responsible for the construction of the eight diagrams, deriving them from the markings on the shell of a tortoise.
2. *Changes, Xi Ci* (pt. 2), *SSJZS*, 1.173. The middle period of antiquity extended from the rise of the Zhou dynasty to the Confucian era.
3. Ibid., 1.175. The Yin dynasty was superseded by the Zhou dynasty in 1112 B.C.E. Zhou, the last tyrannical ruler of the Yin dynasty, died in the flames of his own palace when finally overthrown by King Wu, the son of King Wen; see James Legge, *The I Ching* (New York: Dover, 1963), 5.
4. *Mozi* 31.6–8; Ian Johnston, *The Mozi: A Complete Translation* (New York: Columbia University Press, 2010), 284–87.

5. A form of divination using plant stalks or bamboo. See *Zuo Zhuan* V, 15; LCC, 5.164.
6. *Zuo Zhuan* V, 15; LCC, 5.164, 167—"That fox in Ku must be the Marquis of Chin" (Legge's trans.).
7. *Zuo Zhuan* VIII, 16; LCC, 5.391.
8. Fei Zhi 費直 was the earliest of the Han commentators and initiator of the tradition continued by Ma Rong 馬融 (79–166) and Zheng Xuan 鄭玄 (127–200)—see the *Gu Zhou Yi* reference in *SB* 12 and *Han Shu* 88, 11.3602. Zheng Xuan was a noted commentator on the *Changes* and other classics and a pupil of Ma Rong's. Wang Bi 王弼 (226–249) was noted for his commentaries on the *Changes* and *Daodejing*. The former appears in both the *SBCK* and *SSJZS* versions of the *Changes*.
9. The *Yichuan Yizhuan* 伊川易傳 of Cheng Yi 程頤 was published in 1099 and covered "the whole of the classic and those appendixes scattered over it in the modern text, but not the five appendixes that follow it" (*SB*, 3–4).
10. Chao Yuezhi 晁說之 (1059–1129) compiled the *Lu Gu Yi* 錄古易 in eight chapters (see *SB*, 12).
11. Lü Zuqian 吕祖謙 (1137–1181) was a scholar and official of the Song period and also a contemporary of Zhu Xi's—see the entry on the *Gu Zhou Yi* in *SB*, 12–13.
12. *Zhou Yi Benyi*, i.
13. See *SB*, 11: "In spite of Zhu Xi's intentions, his explanations are attached to Cheng Yi's in the *Wujing Daquan* [*Great Collection of Commentaries on the Five Classics*], which served as the standard for the civil service examinations for several hundred years."
14. *Zhou Yi Benyi*, 2, following the first section headed "Tuan Yue."
15. *Yi Jing* under *qian* 乾—*SSJZS*, 1.10.
16. *Zhou Yi Benyi*, 2, following the first section headed "Xiang Yue."
17. *Yi Jing* under *qian* 乾—*SSJZS*, 1.11.
18. *Yi Jing*, *SSJZS*, 1.12.
19. See *Zhu Wengong Wenji* 66, 2.1154ff. The remainder of the paragraph is taken largely from this work.
20. Cao Mao 曹髦 (221–260) was the grandson of Cao Pi 曹丕 and was made Gaogui Xianggong 高貴鄉公 at the age of four. In 254 he succeeded Cao Fang as the fourth Wei emperor.
21. This sentence is in the *Sanguo Zhi* but not in Gu Yanwu.
22. For this dialogue, see the *Sanguo Zhi* 4, 1.136.
23. *Han Shu* 88, 11.3602.
24. *Zhu Wengong Wenji* 66, "Zazhu."
25. *Yi Jing*, *SSJZS*, 1.83. See also Zhu Xi's *Zhou Yi Benyi*, 29, for a discussion of the use of *yi* 亦. The meaning of this is somewhat obscure. See also Legge, *I Ching*, 123, 305, and Richard Wilhelm, trans., *The I Ching; or, Book of Changes* (Princeton: Princeton University Press, 1950), 124, 545.

26. Hu Anguo 胡安國 (1074–1138) prepared his commentary on the *Spring and Autumn Annals* at the direction of Emperor Gao Zong. In this commentary he relates current events to those reported in the *Spring and Autumn Annals* in an attempt to learn from the lessons of history and thereby improve the administration of the day. See the article by Ueda Sanae in *SB*, 40, which also gives details of the editions of Hu's commentary.
27. *Shefu* was a literary and word game in which a third word, relating to each member of a given pair of words, is sought.
28. Dan Zhu 啖助 and Zhao Kuang 趙匡 were Tang commentators on the *Spring and Autumn Annals*. Their writings can be found in the *Chunqiu Jijie* 春秋集解 compiled by Lü Benzhong 呂本中 in the Song period. See *SB*, 40.
29. See *Han Shu* 30, 6.1705–6, and *Han Shu* 88 for Fu Sheng 伏勝 (伏生). See also LCC, 3, prolegomena, 15ff., for a detailed discussion of the views of Kong Anguo 孔安國 (second century B.C.E.) and others on the old text–new text issue.
30. For an account of the extraordinary events of 92–90 B.C.E., see Michael Loewe, *Crisis and Conflict in Han China* (London: Allen and Unwin, 1974), 37ff.
31. *Han Shu* 30, 6.1706. See also LCC, 3, 23–25.
32. For this sequence, see *Han Shu* 88, 11.3607. Kong Anguo was a descendant of Confucius's who was involved in analysis of the text of the *Documents* found in the walls of the Master's house, as described in this essay. Detailed consideration of the nature and fate of his commentary is given by Legge in the prolegomena to his translation of the classic (see note 29). Liu Xin 劉歆 was a noted scholar and son of Liu Hsiang, who rose to prominence during Wang Mang's interregnum. He was in large part responsible for the establishment of the "old learning," or old text, school, being described by Fung Yu-lan with reference to the old learning as "its most illustrious protagonist" (*HCP*, 2.133–36); see also *CHC*, 1.760ff., and *Han Shu* 36, 1967ff.
33. *Han Shu* 88, 11.3607. Legge gives a brief mention of Zhang Ba 張霸 on page 30 of his prolegomena to the *Shu Jing*; see also 30n11.
34. *Hou Han Shu* 79a, 9.2560. LCC, *Shu Jing*, 3(prolegomena).30, states, "In the next reign, and extending on to a.d. 124, we meet with a K'ung He [K'ung Hsi 孔僖], then chief of the K'ung family, in which it is said, 'the ancient text had been handed down from Gan-kwo [Kong Anguo], from father to son, without break.'"
35. *Hou Han Shu* 79a, 9.2566—see Legge's prolegomena for consideration of Du Lin's 杜林 text and the commentaries on this.
36. Ibid., 79a, 9.2546.
37. Ibid., 7.1849.
38. There is a textual error here as the "Yiwen Zhi" is, in fact, in the *Xin Tang Shu*—see 57, 5.1427 for the listing referred to. Ma Rong and Zheng Xuan

referred to here and elsewhere were both outstanding scholars of the Later Han period, the latter being the pupil of the former—see *CHC*, 1.813ff.

39. Lu Deming, *Jingdian Shiwen* 經典釋文, 1.
40. This is a partial quote from the *Sui Shu* 32, 2.915. Mei Ze 梅賾 (fl. 317–322) presented a text titled *Kong Anguo Shang Shu* to the new Imperial Library established by the Jin in the early fourth century—see *ECT*, 383.
41. I am grateful to Thomas Bartlett for drawing my attention to a passage in the *Sui Shu*, "Jingjizhi," which states that Yao Fangxing 姚方興 purchased the book at a floating market in Nanjing—hence the reference to "large boat."
42. Liu Xuan 劉炫 (d. 613) was a Sui scholar of the period of the north-south division. For biographical details and his work on the classic, see *Sui Shu* 75, 3.1719ff.
43. *Mencius* VIIB.3(1); LCC, 2.479. See also Legge's note on the same page.
44. *Mencius* VA.4(1); LCC, 2.351, and *Documents*, LCC, 3.40.
45. The references given to the *Zuo Zhuan* (LCC, vol. 5) are as follows: III(8), 81; V(24), 190; V(27), 200; VI(7), 247; IX(5), 426; IX(21), 487; IX(23), 500; IX(26), 521; XII(6), 808; XII(18), 851.
46. *Guoyu*, "Zhouyu" (*shang*), *SBCK* 14(*Guoyu*).10.
47. These are the first words of *The Counsels of the Great Yu*; see *Documents*, LCC, 3.52. Gu takes this as further evidence to support his view that this book was a retrospective compilation and should be included in the Books of Xia.
48. *Documents*, LCC, 3.76. See also Legge's note on the same page.
49. *Documents* V, XXII(29) and V.XXIII(1); LCC, 3.560 and 562.
50. See Legge, *Odes*, prolegomena II; LCC, 4.38.
51. *Shiji* 24, 4.1235.
52. The five poems are as follows: Mao 48 (LCC, 4.78), Mao 95 (LCC, 4.148), Mao 77 (LCC, 4.127), Mao 91 (LCC, 4.145), and Mao 117 (LCC, 4.179). Duan 段 was the brother of Zhuang Gong 莊公.
53. *Odes*, Mao 76; LCC, 4.125.
54. *Odes*, Mao 82; LCC, 4.134.
55. *Odes*, Mao 93; LCC, 4.146.
56. *Odes*, Mao 138; LCC, 4.207.
57. See *Jiu Tang Shu* 86, 9.2828.
58. A collection of essays and poems by the Song scholar Zhen Dexiu 真德秀 (1178–1235).
59. The *Gushi Shijiushou* 古詩十九首 is an early verse collection of disputed origin—see *ICCL*, 489–91. For an English translation with the Chinese text, see Ian Johnston, *Waiting for the Owl: Poems and Songs from Ancient China* (Lauderdale, Tas., Aus.: Pardalote Press, 2009), 14–29.
60. *Nineteen Old Poems*, 13.
61. *Odes*, Mao 115; LCC, 4.176.

62. *Nineteen Old Poems*, 16.
63. *Odes*, Mao 33; LCC, 4.51.
64. *Nineteen Old Poems*, 7, and *Odes*, Mao 203.
65. *Nineteen Old Poems*, 8, and *Odes*, Mao 218.
66. Xiao Tong 蕭統 (501–531) was Crown Prince Zhaoming 昭明 of the Liang period and compiler of the *Wen Xuan*.
67. Xu Qin 徐擒 and Yu Xin 庾信 were writers from the Six Dynasties period whose names are often linked.
68. *Odes*, Mao 212; LCC, 4.381.
69. *Odes*, Mao 154; LCC, 4.230.
70. For this phrase, see *Zuo Zhuan* I(8); LCC, 5.25.
71. *Odes*, Mao 162; LCC, 4.247, and Mao 40; LCC, 4.66. Note there is a textual difference here.
72. *Lunyu* XV.25; LCC, 1.301. The term *shi* 史, which Legge translates as "historiographer," is rendered by Charles Hucker as "scribe" and is said to refer to a "lowly or unranked post identifiable only by a prefixed agency name" (*A Dictionary of Official Titles in Imperial China* [Stanford, Calif.: Stanford University Press, 1985], p. 421, no. 5199). Legge, in his note on page 302, amplifies the point of the statement: "A historiographer, on any point about which he was not sure, would leave a blank, so careful were they to tell the truth."
73. *Spring and Autumn Annals* II(17); LCC, 5.67. See also the note on page 67, paragraph 8, where Legge points out that this eclipse took place on October 3, 694 B.C.E., on the seventh day of the cycle and, further, that "the day of the cycle is not given in the text, because, according to Tso-she, the officers had lost it."
74. *Zuo Zhuan* II(17); LCC, 5.67.
75. *Spring and Autumn Annals* V(15); LCC, 5.163.
76. *Zuo Zhuan* for the same year (Legge, 164). In his note on page 167 (para. 5), Legge remarks that "there was no eclipse in all this year visible in Lu. There was, indeed, an eclipse of the sun on January 28th, b.c. 644; but it could not have been seen there."
77. *Mencius* IVB.26(3); LCC, 2.332.
78. There are five references to the burial of Duke Hui 惠公 in the *Spring and Autumn Annals*, as follows: I.1(4), LCC, 5.1; VII.10(10), LCC, 5.306; XI.4(6), LCC, 5.749; XII.4(3), LCC, 5.803; XII.10(10), LCC, 5.820.
79. The references here are to the *Spring and Autumn Annals*, as follows: III.26(3), LCC, 5.110; VIII.15(9), LCC, 5.386; VI.8(8), LCC, 5.250.
80. The references here are to the *Spring and Autumn Annals*, as follows: IX.7(10), LCC, 5.429; X.19(11), LCC, 5.568; XII.10(3), LCC, 5.819.
81. The final words of the *Spring and Autumn Annals* are "In the spring of the 14th year some hunters in the west captured a *lin*" (XII.14[1]; LCC, 5.833). Zuo Shi continued on from there to year twenty-eight of Duke Ai as well as the fourth year of Duke Tao—see also Legge's note on page 834.

82. *Lunyu* II.18(2); LCC, 1.151.
83. See Legge's note on the *Lunyu* (LCC, 1.151). Zizhang, one of the Confucian disciples, was studying "with a view to official emolument."
84. *Zuo Zhuan* IX, 24; LCC, 5.505.
85. Duke Hui was the father and predecessor of Duke Yin 隱公. See the *Spring and Autumn Annals* I,1(4); LCC, 5.1, and also Legge's note on page 3.
86. *Spring and Autumn Annals* I.1(4); LCC, 5.1, and Legge's note on pages 6–7.
87. *Spring and Autumn Annals* I.3(2); LCC, 5.10. Legge has the following: "In the third month, on the day keng-hsu, the king by heaven's grace died. In the *Tso Chuan* however it is stated that the King P'ing actually died on the day jen-hsu i.e.12 days earlier but that the official communication gave the wrong date, which was therefore recorded."
88. *Spring and Autumn Annals* II.5(1); LCC, 5.45, and the *Zuo Zhuan* for the same date.
89. For these concepts of medicine, reference is made to the treatise *Bencao Gangmu* 本草綱目 by the renowned Ming pharmacologist and physician Li Shizhen 李時珍 (1518–1593).
90. *Zhou Li* 5, "Shi yi," *SSJZS*, 3.72.
91. Chunyu Yi 淳于意 was a native of Linzi in Han times and a student of medicine—see *Shiji* 105, 9.2817.
92. *Changes*, *SSJZS*, 1(*Zhou Yi*).58, and Wilhelm, *I Ching*, 77.
93. Zhang Ziwen 張子文 (Zhang Qian—d. 5 B.C.E.) served under Emperor Wu Di of the Former Han—see *Han Shu* 81, 10.3349–52.
94. Li Linfu 李林甫 (d. 752) was a major statesman during the reign of Xuan Zong of the Tang—see *CHC*, 3(i).409–47.
95. Xu Yunzong 許允宗 was a native of Yixing in Tang times and was skilled in medicine.
96. The quotation is a combination from the *Old Tang History* and *New Tang History* but predominantly the former—see *Jiu Tang Shu* 191, 16.5091, and *Xin Tang Shu* 204, 18.5800.
97. Hua Tuo 華陀 was a famous physician and surgeon of the Later Han period who attended Cao Cao—see *Hou Han Shu* 82, 10.2736.
98. See the *Changes* for the seventh diagram (*shi*), *SSJZS*, 1(*Zhou Yi*).35–36, and Wilhelm, *I Ching*, 31–35, 420–25.
99. *Documents* 47, "Establishing Government"; LCC, 3.513.
100. *Odes*, Mao 250, "Duke Lin," verse 4; LCC, 4.487.
101. The *Daxue* (texts 2 and 4); LCC, 1.356–58. See also Legge's note to paragraph 2, page 356, and *Laozi* 44.
102. The *Daxue* (commentary), III(2); LCC, 1.362, and *Odes*, Mao 235; LCC, 4.427: "[How] profound was King Wen. In continuity and brightness did his reverence rest" (trans. after Legge, 429).
103. *Zhongyong*, XXVII(3); LCC, 1.422.
104. *Odes*, Mao 260; LCC, 4.541.

105. *Mencius* IVB.19(2); LCC, 2.325.
106. *Documents*, LCC, 3.320. This was with regard to how the government of the empire should be conducted. He was informed of the "Great Plan" with nine divisions that Yu received from Heaven. See Legge, *Documents*, note to chapter 1, LCC, 3.321–22.
107. Ji Zi 箕子 was one of the nobles under Zhou Xin, the last emperor of the Yin dynasty, and putative author of the Great Plan; *Documents* V, IV; LCC, 3.320. See Legge's note on page 320 and *Shiji* 3, 1.91ff.
108. Zengzi 曾子 is Zeng San 曾參, and Zi You 子游 is Yan Yan 言偃. Both were among Confucius's leading disciples. For their dialogues with the Master, see, e.g., *Lunyu* I.4; LCC, 1.139, and II.7; LCC, 1.148.
109. *Mencius* VIIA.4; LCC, 2.450.
110. *Changes* (*jia ren* 家人), *SSJZS*, 1.89.
111. *Li Ji*, "Ai Gong Wen," *SSJZS*, 5.851.
112. *Lunyu* XVII.9(7); LCC, 1.323.
113. *Mencius* VIIA.46(1); LCC, 2.476.
114. *Lunyu* XII.13; LCC, 1.257, and the *Daxue* (commentary) 4; LCC, 1.364.
115. A very similar idea is expressed in *Zhongyong*, XV; LCC, 1.396. This is immediately followed by observations on ghosts and spirits.
116. See also *Zhongyong*, XIX; LCC, 1.404.
117. *Xiao Jing* 18, "Sang Qin," *SSJZS*, 8(*Xiao Jing*).55–56.
118. For this phrase, see *Zhongyong*, XIII.4; LCC, 1.394.
119. *Mencius* IVA.2(1); LCC, 2.292.
120. *Zhongyong*, XII.4; LCC, 1.393.
121. *Li Ji* 47, "Jiyi," *SSJZS*, 5.807.
122. *Xiao Jing* 18, "Sang Qin," *SSJZS*, 8(*Xiao Jing*).55–56.
123. *Zhongyong*, XVI.3; LCC, 1.397–98.
124. *Li Ji* 20, "Wen Wang Shizi," *SSJZS*, 5.391.
125. *Li Ji* 47, "Jiyi," *SSJZS*, 5.808–9; translation (in part) after James Legge, *Li Chi: Book of Rites* (New Hyde Park, N.Y.: University Books, 1967), 2:212–13. The quote from the *Odes* is from Mao 196; LCC, 4.333.
126. *Li Ji* 47, "Jiyi," *SSJZS*, 5.807–18.
127. *Lunyu* XI.11; LCC, 1.240—see in particular Legge's note on pages 240–41.
128. These comments by Cheng Zi and Zhang Zai are to be found in reference to *Zhongyong*, XVI.1; LCC, 1.397: "The Master said, How abundantly do spiritual beings display the powers that belong to them." The comments of the two Song neo-Confucians are given in Zhu Xi's *Zhongyong Zhangju* (*Zhongyong*, 11).
129. *Changes*, "Shuo Gua," *SSJZS* (*Zhou Yi*), 1.184.
130. *Changes* (*qian*), *SSJZS*, 1.17.
131. *Lunyu* VII.24; LCC, 1.202. Legge, in his note on pages 202–3, quotes the definitions of these terms in the *Sishu Beizhi* as follows: *wen* 文—"letters"; *xing* 行—"what is daily used in the relations of sages"; *zhong* 忠—"not a

single thought not exhausted"; *xin* 信—"not a single thought without its reality." Zhu Xi, in his *Sishi Jizhu*, quotes Cheng Zi on this matter.

132. *Lunyu* V.12; LCC, 1.178. Zhu Xi remarks that "when it comes to nature and the way of Heaven, this was something that the Master seldom spoke of and his students could not hear" (*Sishu Jizhu*, 28).
133. *Lunyu* VII.23; LCC, 1.202.
134. *Lunyu* V.12; LCC, 1.177.
135. *Lunyu* XVII.19 (2 and 3); LCC, 1.326.
136. *Mencius* IIA.2(22); LCC, 2.194.
137. See *Lunyu* X.1; LCC, 1.227. "The Master in his village was simple and unassuming as if he were not able to speak. In the ancestral temple or the court he was cautious and precise, but his words were exhaustive. When at court and speaking to the officers of a lower rank, he was direct and to the point. While with the officers of a higher rank he was reserved and formal."
138. *Mencius* VIIB.33(2); LCC, 2.495.
139. *Mencius* VIIB.33(1): "Mencius said, Yao and Shun were what they were by nature. Tang and Wu returned to this."
140. *Lunyu* XIV.16; LCC, 1.281. Zhu Xi, in his note (*Sishu Jizhu*, 97) states, "The two dukes . . . gave an oath to punish the barbarians as a means of venerating the Zhou house."
141. *Mencius* IIIB.9(11); LCC, 2.283: "Confucius completed the *Spring and Autumn Annals*, and rebellious ministers and villainous sons were struck with terror."
142. For details of Hu Anguo's commentary on the *Spring and Autumn Annals*, see *SB*, 39–40.
143. *Lunyu* XVII.19(2); LCC, 1.376.
144. A commentary on the *Yi Jing* attributed to either King Wen or Confucius.
145. The references to the *Changes* in the *SBCK* are as follows: 1(*Yi Jing*).45; 1(*Yi Jing*).49; 1(*Yi Jing*).49; 1(*Yi Jing*).51.
146. *Changes*, "Xici," *SBCK* 1(*Yi Jing*).52, and Wilhelm, *I Ching*, 349.
147. The three references to the *Lunyu* are as follows: XIII.19, LCC, 1.271; XII.2(2), LCC, 1.251; XII.1(1), LCC, 1.250.
148. Two of Confucius's leading disciples (two of the "Four Associates of the Master"). Yan Hui (Ziyuan, 514–483 B.C.E.) is said to have been the favorite disciple (see, e.g., *Lunyu* XII; LCC, 1.250). Zeng San (Ziyou, 505–437 B.C.E.) was esteemed especially for his filial piety and is said to have been involved in the composition of the *Highest Learning* and the *Classic of Filial Piety* (see, e.g., *Lunyu* I.4; LCC, 1.139, and note thereto, as well as *Lunyu* XIX.16–18; LCC, 1.344–45).
149. The three quotes from Zhu Xi are as follows: *Hui'an Ji* 38 ("Reply to Lin Qianzhi"); *Yulei* 19; *Hui'an Ji* 35 ("Reply to Liu Zideng").
150. The references to the *Lunyu* are as follows: V.12, LCC, 1.177; I.1(1), LCC, 1.137; IV.15(31), LCC, 1.169; XV.2(3), LCC, 1.295.

151. The references to the *Mencius* are as follows: IA.1(3–6), LCC, 2.126–27; IA.3(11), LCC, 2.129.
152. The terms here are used for two schools of thought. Lian refers to Zhou Dunyi 周敦頤, the Song neo-Confucian, and Luo to Luoyang, indicating the Cheng brothers.
153. A work by the Song scholar Huang Zhen 黃震. The full title is *Cixi Huangshi Richao* 慈溪黃氏日鈔—see *SB*, 232; for this statement, see *Huangshi Richao* 28.
154. The initial four branches of study were morality (*dexing* 德行), speaking (*yanyu* 言語), administration (*zhengshi* 政事), and literature (*wenxue* 文學)—see *Lunyu* XI.2(2); LCC, 1.237.
155. Five non-Han barbarian tribes from the north of China that caused considerable trouble during the Jin period. There is a textual discrepancy here. The Huang Rucheng edition has Liu [and] Shi, referring to Liu Yuan 劉淵 (d. 310), a Turkic chieftain, and Shi Le 石勒 (273–332), also of Turkic descent; both were involved in active rebellion at the end of the Han period. I have followed the *Yuanchaoben* edition. "Pure talk" (*qing tan* 清談) is described in *HCP* as "the art of conversing about philosophy and abstract topics only, and avoiding all mundane matters. This type of conversation was very popular among the neo-Taoists of the period" (2.206n1).
156. See note 150 and *Lunyu* XVII.19(1 and 2); LCC, 1.326.
157. Wang Yan 王衍 (256–311) was a scholar of the Jin dynasty and cousin of Wang Rong. He was renowned as a talker, particularly on Daoism, and during conversation was said to have waved a yak's tail set in jade. Subsequently, as a military leader under the Prince of Chengdu, he was defeated and put to death by Shi Le. For the basis of the comparison, see *Jin Shu* 43, 4.1236. Zigong 子貢 was Duanmu Zi, one of the foremost of Confucius's disciples. According to Legge (*Lunyu* I.10[2], note on page 142),he was conspicuous "for his readiness and smartness in reply, and displayed on several occasions practical and political ability" Shi Le was a successful military commander who seized the throne in 318 on the death of Liu Zong.
158. *Jin Shu* 43, 4.1238.
159. There is an original note as follows: Huang Shi, in his *Richao*, "Du Wang Zhi," says, "In a society based on agriculture, all salaries, of necessity, come from agriculture, and in the case of those above the highest agricultural, this is without plowing" (*Huangshi Richao* 16).
160. *Mencius* VIA.11(4); LCC, 2.414.
161. *Lunyu* XV.30; LCC, 1.302.
162. *Mencius* IVB.28(1); LCC, 2.333.
163. *Mencius* VIA.9(3); LCC, 2.410.
164. Du You 杜佑 (735–812) was a noted scholar of the Tang period whose work (*Tong Dian* 通典) referred to here was a substantial treatise, published ca. 800, in eight sections on administrative and political matters—see *CHC*, 3(i).605, and

ICCL, 528. The person whose memorial is mentioned is He Xun 賀循 (d. 310), a scholar and statesman who served in various roles under the first Jin emperor. The memorial quoted here does not appear in his biography in *Jin Shu* 6.1824.

165. *Tong Dian* 53.
166. Xun Song 荀崧 was a scholar of the Eastern Jin period. His biography appears in *Jin Shu* 75, 7.1975ff. The memorial here incompletely quoted can be found on pages 1977–78.
167. Wang Dun 王敦 (d. 324) was responsible for large-scale military activity during the reign of Emperor Yuan of the Eastern Jin; for details, see *Jin Shu* 98, 8.2553–65, and *Song Shu* 14.
168. The following statement by Li Yuancui 李元瓘, titled "Qingjin Gongjuren Xizhouli Dengjingshu" 清今貢舉人習周禮等經疏, can be found in *Quan Tang Wen* 304, 4.3095.
169. For details of this examination, see Gu's essay *RZL* 16.l.
170. Yang Yang 楊瑒 was a Tang official. Biographical details are given in *Jiu Tang Shu* 185, 15.4819, and *Xin Tang Shu* 130, 14.4494. The substance of the memorial and the response to it can be found in *Jiu Tang Shu* 15.4820.
171. *Song Shi* 155, 11.3618.
172. *Zhu Wengong Wenji* 14, 1.150.
173. Ibid., 76, 2.1336. Here this is quoted incompletely and somewhat inaccurately. Xie Chuozhong 謝綽中 is Xie Yu 謝譽 (1098–1143)—*Songren Zhuanzhi Ziliao Suolin*, 4113.

2. *RZL* 8–12: ADMINISTRATION AND ECONOMICS

1. *Han Shu* 3, 19.742.
2. Ibid., 1, 1.33.
3. Guan Zhong 管仲 (d. 645 B.C.E.) became minister of state under Duke Huan of Qi and is the putative author of the *Guanzi*. Wei Ao 蔿敖 was a Chu statesman from the Spring and Autumn period—see *Zuo Zhuan*, twelfth year of Duke Huan. Zi Chan 子產 was a Zheng ruler from the same period—see *Lunyu* V.15; LCC, 1.178.
4. *Zhou Li*, *SSJZS*, 3.182ff. A summary of Charles Hucker's (*A Dictionary of Official Titles in Imperial China* [Stanford, Calif.: Stanford University Press, 1985]) entries on each of the titles follows:

zhou chang: "responsible . . . for sacrifices, other rites, education, and general administration in his township" (p. 178, no. 1334)

dang zheng: head of a local self-government unit in the royal domain "who was reportedly popularly elected" (p. 486, no. 6282)

zu shi: "head of one hundred families constituting a precinct in local self-government organization of the populace" (p. 528, 7054) *lü xu:* "actual head of a village responsible to one of two supervisors of villages for such matters as census, taxes, state service assignments, and public morality" (p. 325, no. 3884)

bi chang: head of a "five family unit in which residents of the royal domain were organized for local sacrificial, fiscal, and security purposes" (p. 375, no. 4570)

xian zheng: head of a local self-government unit comprising five wards (*bi*) and "responsible for properly classifying people and lands, adjudicating disputes, promoting agriculture and morality, and raising a local militia when called on" (p. 240, no. 2492)

bi shi: "responsible for maintaining peace, propriety, and law among the five hundred families constituting his jurisdiction, a ward outside the royal domain" (p. 376, no. 4585)

zan chang: cuo was the precinct comprising four neighboring villages (*li*), each with twenty-five households; the *chang* was responsible for "local ceremonial, military, agricultural, and craft activities" (p. 516, no. 6845)

li zai: responsible for "promoting agriculture, collecting taxes, etc." in a village [*li*] of twenty-five households (p. 308, no. 3643)

lin chang: head of a local self-government unit outside the royal domain (p. 312, no. 3717).

5. The memorial is recorded in *Wei Shu* 110, 8.2855.
6. See *Wei Shu* 33, 4.1179ff., for biographical details.
7. See ibid., 79 (*xia*), 53 and 110; *Bei Shi* 100.
8. Su Chuo 蘇綽 (498–546) prepared his "Six Articles" in 544 at Yuwen Tai's 宇文泰 behest. It has been described by Arthur Wright as "a kind of epitome of statecraft and administration." See *CHC*, 3(i).70, and *Zhou Shu* 22, 2.382.
9. *Zhou Shu* 23, 2.388.
10. See, in the present work, Liu Zongyuan's "On the Feudal System," appendix 4.
11. *Hou Han Shu* 48, 6.1618.
12. *Han Shu* 89, 11.3637.
13. *Ming Shilu* (*Tai Zu Shilu* 232), 8.3396.
14. *Quan Tang Shi* 149, 5.1541.
15. *Ming Shilu* (*Xuan Zong Shilu* 4).
16. *Han Shu* 1, 1.34; see also Burton Watson, trans., *Records of the Grand Historian of China* (New York: Columbia University Press, 1961), 1:96.
17. *Han Shu* 63, 9.2744, and 2745n2.
18. Heir apparent to Han Wu Di.
19. Li An 李安—for biographical details, see *Ming Shi* 145, 13.4090.
20. See *Ming Shilu* 78, 20.1818. I can find no other information on Zhang Zheng 張政.

21. *Ming Shi* 132, 13.3861–62.
22. *Lunyu* VI.1; LCC, 1.184.
23. *Documents* V, XIX, 13 and 14; LCC, 3.517.
24. *Shiji* 6, 1.258. See also 259n4.
25. *Shiji* 122, 10.3131.
26. From "Shugu" (poem 2), by Du Fu. See *Dushi Yinzhi, juan* 21, p. 1818.
27. From "Xiehuai" (poem 2), by Du Fu. See *Dushi Xiangzhi*, vol. 4, *juan* 8.
28. *Han Shu* 4, 1.124.
29. Zhuge Liang 諸葛亮 (181–234). While leading a simple life of withdrawal from public affairs, his assistance was twice sought by Liu Bei 劉備, whom he had helped to take the throne of Shu and whose fortunes prospered under the guidance of his revered minister.
30. Cao Cao 曹操 (155–220) ruled in Wei during the time of Zhuge Liang's prominence in Shu and Sun Quan's 孫權 (181–252) rule in Wu.
31. Shu Xiang 叔向 was Yang Shexi 羊舌肸 of Qin in the Spring and Autumn period. Zi Chan was Gongsun Qiao 公孫僑 of Zheng 鄭 (581–521 B.C.E.). For the exchange referred to, see *Zuo Zhuan* X, 6; LCC, 5.607.
32. Du Yuankai 杜元凱 (Du Yu 杜預, 222–284) was a noted commentator on the *Zuo Zhuan*. His comments here are with reference to the twelfth year of Duke Xuan. See *Zuo Zhuan*, *SSJZS*, 6.329.
33. *Han Shu* 56, 8.2518.
34. Ye Shi 葉適 (1150–1223) was a noted scholar of the Song period who defended Zhu Xi on his impeachment by Lin Piao 林栗. See also *SB*, 426–27. For biographical details, see *Song Shi* 434, 37.13889–94. The first quote is from his "Shilun" (2), and the second and third quotes are from his "Shimou." For both these essays, see *Shuixin Xiansheng Wenji* 4, *SBCK*.
35. Chen Liang 陳亮 (1143–1194) was a noted Song scholar and contemporary of Ye Shi. His collected works, *Longchuan Wenji*, can be found in the *SBBY*. See also *SB*, 426, and, for biographical details, *Song Shi* 436, 37.12929–43. For the memorial here quoted (*Shang Xiao Zong Huang Di Sanhu*), see *Chen Liang Ji* (*shang*), *juan* 1, p. 13.
36. *Ming Shilu* 85, 4.1510–11.
37. Ye Shi: this idea is expressed in "Zouyi Jigang" 2 of his *Shuixin Xiansheng Wenji*, *SBCK* 59.59–60. The quote is not exact.
38. Chen Tang 陳湯 was a Han official noted for his love of literature from an early age—see *Han Shu* 70, 9.3007ff.
39. Mei Cheng 枚乘 (d. 140 B.C.E.) was a Former Han scholar. His writings can be found in *QSGW* 20, vol. 1 (Han). See also *Han Shu* 51, 8.2359ff. Sima Xiangru 司馬相如 (d. 117 B.C.E.) was a noted poet and scholar-official of the Former Han period—see *Han Shu* 57, 8.2529ff.
40. For Guan Zhong, see note 3. Sun Wu 孫吳 (sixth century B.C.E.) was from Qi; he was the author of a treatise on warfare, *The Art of War* (*Bingfa* 兵法).
41. See *Zuo Zhuan* XII(15); LCC, 5.842.

42. *Mozi* 9.5; Ian Johnston, *The Mozi: A Complete Translation* (New York: Columbia University Press, 2010), 68–69.
43. See *Lü Shi Chunqiu*, John Knoblock and Jeffrey Riegel, *The Annals of Lü Buwei: A Complete Translation and Study* (Stanford, Calif.: Stanford University Press, 2000), 13/6 ("Wuben"), 296.
44. Liu Fen 劉蕡 was a Tang scholar—see *Jiu Tang Shu* 190 (*xia*) and *Xin Tang Shu* 178, 17.5303.
45. Yang Pu 楊溥 (1372–1446) was a renowned statesman and scholar who was recalled to the court after a somewhat checkered early career and became a major adviser to Ren Zong—see *DMB*, 2.1525–28, and *CHC*, 7(i).277–84.
46. *Ming Shilu* (*Xuan Zong Shilu*) 69, 19.1623. The quote from Dong Zhongshu 董仲舒 is to be found in *Han Shu* 56, 8.2512.
47. See *Zhou Li*, *SSJZS*, 3.160.
48. *Huiyao* 83, "Zushui Shang," and *Jiu Tang Shu* 9, 1.218.
49. A form of taxation introduced during the economically difficult period after the An Lushan Rebellion in the Tang era—see *Xin Tang Shu* 51, 5.1348, and D. C. Twitchett, *Financial Administration under the T'ang Dynasty* (Cambridge: Cambridge University Press, 1970), 20ff.
50. Lu Zhi 陸贄 (754–805) was a Tang scholar and official who became a close adviser to De Zong. For a detailed account of his life and views, together with reference to his original writings, see D. C. Twitchett, "Lu Chih (754–805): Imperial Advisor and Court Official," in *Confucian Personalities*, ed. Arthur F. Wright and Denis Twitchett, 84–122 (Stanford, Calif.: Stanford University Press, 1962).
51. *Lu Xuangong Zouyi* 6.
52. *Jiu Tang Shu* 49; *Huiyao* 83.
53. *Quan Tang Shi* 343, 10.3850.
54. An encyclopedic work compiled by Ma Duanlin 馬端臨 completed around 1308—see *SB*, 74–75.
55. On the Three Offices (*san si* 三司), see Hucker, *Dictionary of Official Titles*, pp. 401–2, no. 4912).
56. This is, in part, referred to in *Jiu Wu Dai Shi* 146, 6.1947.
57. *Odes*, Mao 113; LCC, 4.172.
58. Xie Junzhi 謝君直 (Xie Fangde 謝枋得, 1226–1289). For biographical details, see *Song Shi* 425, 36.12687–89. I have been unable to find the quote given here.
59. *Odes*, Mao 113; LCC, 4.172.
60. Yu Qian 虞謙 was a Ming official; for biographical details, see *Ming Shi* 150, 24.4167ff.
61. *Han Shu* 5, 1.148. During Xiao Jing's reign the method of numbering the years underwent a transition (see *CHC*, 1.687). For details of the changes in the monetary system at this time and the penalties attendant upon debasing or counterfeiting, see *CHC*, 1.585–90.

62. *Shiji* 30, 4.1439. See also Watson, *Records*, 2:101–2. For Ru Chun's note, see *Shiji* 4.1440.
63. *Song Shi* 2, 1.33.
64. *Jiu Tang Shu* 17(i), 2.531–32.
65. On these two offices, Hucker has, for the first, *shuiheng duwei*, "from 115 B.C. a major official of the central government . . . in general supervisory control of the Imperial Forest Park and many revenue-producing and manufacturing activities associated with it; his subordinate directors (*ling*) controlled such disparate things as coinage, granaries, stables, and steel manufacturing" (*Dictionary of Official Titles*, p. 438, no. 5497). For the second, *zhijin*, he has "responsible for administering laws relating to precious metals and for handling fines levied in gold or other precious objects" (ibid., p. 157, no. 962).
66. *Mencius* VIIB.12(3); LCC, 2.483.
67. *Taizu Shilu* 131.
68. *Xin Tang Shu* 100.
69. *Taizu Shilu* 145.
70. *Xin Tang Shu* 134, 15.4557–68 (particularly 4567). The subjects are Yuwen Rong 宇文融, Wei Jian 韋堅, Yang Shenqin 楊慎矜, Wang Hong 王鉷, and Yang Guozhong 楊國忠. The quote from *Mencius* is from IA.1(4); LCC, 2.126. Consideration of the schemes of Yuwen Rong and the others can be found in *CHC*, 3(i).382ff and 420ff.
71. *Guoyu*, "Zhouyu" (*shang*), *SBCK* 14(*Guoyu*).5.
72. *Mencius* IA.1(4); LCC, 2.126.

3. *RZL* 13–15: CUSTOMS AND MORES

1. The final sentence in the *Spring and Autumn Annals*, XII(14), i.e., the fourteenth year of Duke Ai of Lu. For consideration of the *lin*, see LCC, 5.834.
2. *Zuo Zhuan* XII(27). Regarding Duke Ai, the *Shiji* states, "The people of the kingdom welcomed his return, and he died in [the house of] You Shan Shi" (33, 5.1545). According to the note, Duke Ai reigned from 497 to 471 B.C.E., although this does not tally with the chronology given in the *Ci Hai*. You Shan Shi 有山氏 was an official in Lu.
3. Also known by the posthumous titles Wen Hou 文侯, Lie Hou 烈侯, and Jing Hou 景侯.
4. Tian He 田和 was a descendant of the ruling house of Qi—see Legge's note in the *Zuo Zhuan* XII(14); LCC, 5.840.
5. Su Qin 蘇秦 was a native of Luoyang whose initial attempts to gain official employment in Qin were unsuccessful. He later conceived the idea of federating the six states in an alliance against the rapidly growing power of Qin in the west. He achieved great power but after the breakdown of the alliance was disgraced and later assassinated.

6. There is an original note referring to a passage in *Shiji* 5 (1.203) on these events.
7. King Wen of Zhou, named Chang 昌, and his son King Wu, named Fa 發, who overthrew the Shang to assume control of the empire.
8. See *QSGW* 39, 1.11, and *Han Shu* 22.
9. Dong Zhongshu 董仲舒 was a renowned Confucian scholar of the Former Han period—see *HCP*, 2.32–46.
10. The first three emperors of the Later Han, ruling from 25 to 57, 58 to 75, and 76 to 88, respectively. See also *Lunyu* VI.22; LCC, 1.192.
11. For the opening two paragraphs, see Qinshi Huang's biography in *Shiji* 6, 1.233ff. The three quotations can be found on pages 243, 252, and 262, respectively.
12. Gou Jian 勾踐 was a prince of the Yue state. For biographical details, see *Shiji* 41. He came to the throne of Yue in 496 B.C.E. and was involved in a long-running struggle with the state of Wu, and in particular Fu Chai, who came to the Wu throne in 495 B.C.E.
13. *Guoyu*, "Yueyu" (*shang*), *SBCK* 14(*Guoyu*).146. This also appears in *Wu Yue Chunqiu* 10, *SBCK* 15.68.
14. Zixu 子胥 (Wu Yuan 伍員) was a native of Chu who served Prince Liao of Wu and was involved in the war with Yue. See *Taiping Yulan* 47 and *Shiji* 66, 7.2171ff.
15. Wang Mang 王莽 (33 B.C.E.–23 c.e.) was a nephew of the consort of the Emperor Yuan. During the declining years of the Former Han dynasty he gained increasing political power, finally assuming the regency in 9 c.e., after the death of Emperor Ping. In his endeavors he was greatly encouraged by sycophants and flatterers.
16. In the later part of the Eastern Han, particularly under the reign of Huan Di (147–167), the power of the eunuchs greatly increased. This trend was somewhat restrained by the actions of upright officials such as Li Ying 李膺, but fortunes were later reversed and the faction was proscribed—see *Hou Han Shu* 67, 8.2183.
17. *Odes*, Mao 90; LCC, 4.143. See also Legge's note on page 143 on the different views as to the significance of this verse. Gu Yanwu obviously subscribes to the view that it represents "a longing for superior men to arise and settle the disturbed state of Ch'ing [i.e., Cheng], men who would do their duties as the cocks in the darkest and stormiest night."
18. Fan Ye 范曄 (398–446) was a Song (north-south division) scholar and author of the *Hou Han Shu*—see 79, 9.2589.
19. *Hou Han Shu* 61, 7.2043.
20. Mengde 孟德 (Cao Cao 曹操, 155–220). Jizhou 冀州 was one of the nine divisions of ancient China, but from Han times on it was the name of a region—see *Han Shu* 28, 6.1541, and the map of the Han empire at 140 in *CHC*, 1.252–53 (map 12).

21. Dong Zhao 董昭 was a Wei official who served under the second Wei emperor (Ming Di). This quote is part of a memorial sent up in the fourth year of the Taihe reign period (230)—see *Sanguo Zhi* 14, 2.436–42 for Dong Zhao's biography and page 442 for the memorial.
22. The first three emperors of the Later Han: Guang Wu Di (25–57), Ming Di (58–75), and Zhang Di (76–88).
23. Deng Yu 鄧禹 (1–58) was an official and general of the early part of the Later Han period who served Emperor Guang Wu. For his biography, which includes the subsequent sentence, see *Hou Han Shu* 16, 3.599–607.
24. Fan Zhong 樊重 was the maternal grandfather of Guang Wu Di and father of Fan Hong 樊宏—see *Hou Han Shu* 62, 4.1119ff, and *CHC*, 1.573 and 624.
25. Cai Yong 蔡邕 (133–192) was an important scholar of the Later Han period and one of those primarily concerned with the preparation of the Han Stone Classics. According to B. J. Mansvelt Beck, he was one of the "great scholars" who were "intimidated into joining his [i.e., Dong Zhuo's] government" (*CHC*, 1.346). See *Hou Han Shu* 60, 7.1979ff. In relation to the episode described, Herbert Giles writes, "He had just been ennobled as Marquis when Tung Cho himself fell, and for words of regret which he thoughtlessly uttered he was once more thrown into prison where he died in spite of great efforts to obtain his release" (*A Chinese Biographical Dictionary* [London: Quaritch, 1898], 754).
26. Dong Zhuo 董卓was a general of the Later Han period who briefly gained what was in effect supreme power during the reigns of Shao Di and Xian Di from 189, when he entered the capital, to his death in 192. He coerced Cai Yong among others into serving him (see n. 25)—see *Hou Han Shu* 72, 8.2319ff, and *CHC*, 1.341–50.
27. Bojie 伯喈: Cai Yong 蔡邕—see note 25.
28. Wei Ming Di ruled from 227 to 239 (see *Sanguo Zhi* 3). On his death, Shao Di assumed the throne (see *Sanguo Zhi* 4). He ruled from 240 to 253. The Zhengshi reign period extended from 240 to 248. Sima Yi 司馬懿, who initially served under Cao Cao, was subsequently in command of the army under three successive emperors. Cao Shuang 曹爽, a close associate of Ming Di's, later gave himself over to a life of debauchery and was put to death in 249 for conspiracy. See *Sanguo Zhi* 4, 1.123.
29. *Jin Shu* 36, 4.1067. Wang Dun 王敦 (d. 324) was a son-in-law of Jin Wu Di's and rose to high office under Yuan Di. Wei Jie 衛玠, renowned for his beauty, was the son of Wei Huan, a high official under Jin Hui Di.
30. For biographical details of Zhi Dun 支遁 and some account of his writings, see *HCP*, 2.249–52.
31. *Song Shu* 54, 5.1536. Tai Zu was the Song emperor Wen Di, who reigned from 424 to 453. Yang Xuanbao 羊玄保 was a high official of that period. "The bamboo grove" refers to the Seven Worthies of the Bamboo Grove.

32. This indicates the Daoist concept of dwelling in quiescence and nonactivity. See *Song Shu* 62, 6.1669.
33. *Nan Qi Shu* 33, 2.600.
34. *Nan Shi* 30, 3.782.
35. *Jin Shu* 91, 8.2346.
36. Zheng Xuan 鄭玄 (127–200) was a pupil of Ma Rong's and one of the most celebrated commentators on the classics. Wang Su 王肅 (d. 256) was another noted Confucian scholar and commentator on the classics. He was also the editor or putative author of the *Kongzi Jiayu*.
37. Wang Bi 王弼 (226–245) was a scholar noted for his commentaries on the *Changes* and the *Daodejing*. He Yan 何晏 was a scholar noted particularly for his work on the *Changes*. He was also known as a keen student of Lao Zi and Zhuang Zhou and, with Xiahou Xuan 夏侯玄 and others of the Wei period, indulged in "pure talk."
38. *Mencius* IIIB.9; LCC, 2.283.
39. *Mencius* IIIB.9; LCC, 2.282.
40. Ji Shao 嵇紹 (253–304) rose to be imperial librarian under Emperor Wu Di of the Jin dynasty. He fell in battle bravely defending Emperor Hui Di, whose robes were spattered with Shao's blood. It is said that the emperor refused to allow the blood to be washed off the garments. See *Jin Shu* 89, 8.2298–2301. Ji Kang 嵇康 (223–262) was one of the Seven Worthies of the Bamboo Grove, described by Fung Yu-lan as "a group of Taoistically minded men who used to meet in a bamboo grove for convivial and often bibulous conversation" (*HCP*, 2.205n2). He was denounced to Emperor Wen Di and condemned to death.
41. Shan Tao 山濤 (205–283) was an official who rose to high office under Wu Di of Jin (i.e., Sima Yan). He was one of the Seven Worthies of the Bamboo Grove—see *Jin Shu* 43, 4.1223–28 and *Shishuo Xinyu* III.8.
42. Dangyin 蕩陰 was situated in what is now Henan province and was the place of Ji Shao's death defending Emperor Hui.
43. Wang Pou 王裒 of the Jin period was one of the twenty-four examples of filial piety. He, like Ji Shao, had a father put to death, but unlike Shao, he thenceforth lived in retirement and refused to serve the Jin house—see *Jin Shu* 88, 7.2279–80.
44. Liu Cong 劉聰 and Shi Le 石勒 combined on behalf of Liu Yuan 劉淵, who, in 308, had proclaimed himself the first emperor of the new Han dynasty and attacked the imperial armies, gaining control over a large area of land. Subsequently both men sought, and relatively briefly attained, great power.
45. See *Li Ji*, "Wang Zhi," *SSJZS*, 5.256; James Legge, *Li Chi: Book of Rites* (New Hyde Park, N.Y.: University Books, 1967), 1:232; *Documents*, "Bi Ming," V.XXIV.7; LCC, 3.574.
46. *Jin Shu* 70.
47. *Song Shu* 3, 1.52.

48. There is an original note here stating that proclamations from Qi, Liang, and Chen all say *xi chu* first in the notes. At that time *xiang lun* and *qing yi* were items recorded in the notes.
49. *Jin Shu* 82, 7.2137–38, *Shishuo Xinyu*; Liu I-ch'ing [Liu Yiqing], comp., *Shih-shuo Hsin-yü: A New Account of the World*, trans. Richard B. Mather, 2nd ed. (Ann Arbor: Center for Chinese Studies, University of Michigan, 2002), 538.
50. See *Shishuo Xinyu*, 33; Mather, *Shih-shuo Hsin-yü*, 511.
51. *Shishuo Xinyu* 23, *SBCK* 24(*Shishuo Xinyu*).118–19.
52. *Song Shu* 53, 5.1524, *Nan Shi* 19, 2.537.
53. *Liang Shu* 33, 2.474–79, *Nan Shi* 31.
54. See *Liang Shu* 33 and *Nan Shi* 31.
55. The description of this pavilion in the *Zhongwen Da Cidian* is taken from the *Rizhi Lu*.
56. *Taizu Shilu* 147.
57. Ibid., 172.
58. *Shiji* 129, 10.3271. See also Burton Watson, trans., *Records of the Grand Historian of China* (New York: Columbia University Press, 1961), 2:491–92.
59. *Yiwen Leiju* 21; *Quan Jin Wen* 86.
60. *Nan Shi* 74, 6.1851.
61. Li Ling 李陵 was a grandson of the renowned general of the Former Han period Li Kuang 李廣, the family being from Chengji in Longxi province. The chronicle of the family is given in both *Shiji* 109 and *Han Shu* 54. For Li Ling's surrender to the Xiongnu, see *Shiji* 109, 9.2877–78. Burton Watson has a translation in *Records*, 2:153–54—see in particular 154n4 for the relationship of Li Ling's surrender to Sima Qian's castration. For Duan Ganmu 段干木, see *Shiji* 44, 6.1839 and the note on the same page for details.
62. This statement is from *Mencius* VIIA.26: "The philosopher Mo loves all equally. If by rubbing smooth his whole body from the crown to the heel he could have benefited the kingdom, he would have done so" (trans. after Legge).
63. Huang Xian 黃憲 was a man of the later Han period known for his virtue. His style was Shudu 叔度—see *Hou Han Shu* 53. Qin Jia 秦嘉 was a man of the Later Han period from Longxi who retired because of the illness of his wife, Xu Shu 徐淑.
64. The quote is from the memorial by Xie Qianguang 薛謙光, a Tang official. His biography is found in *Jiu Tang Shu* 101, 10.3136–41. The memorial is on pages 3137–39.
65. Fan Wenzheng 范文正 is Fan Zhongyan 范仲淹 (989–1052), a renowned scholar and administrator of the Song period—see *Song Shi* 314, 29.10267–76. Yan Yuanxian 晏元獻 is Yan Shu 晏殊 (984–1046), a poet and official of the Song period—see *Song Shi* 311, 29.10195–98. Yao and Shun were the last emperors of the legendary period and renowned for their good works. Jie is Jie Gui 桀癸 (d. 1763 B.C.E.). He was the last emperor of

the Xia dynasty. Zhou is Zhou Xin 紂辛 (d. 1122 B.C.E.). He was the last emperor of the Yin dynasty. Both are renowned for their cruelty, lust, and extravagance, which brought their respective dynasties to an end. For the Eight Good Ones and the Four Wicked Ones, see *Zuo Zhuan* VI.18; LCC, 5.280, and Legge's translation on pages 282–83. They were, in brief, descendants of early emperors who manifested good and bad characteristics, respectively.

66. Gongsun Hong 公孫弘 (d. 121 B.C.E.) "is remembered in the annals of Chinese history as the classic case of a man who rose from the humblest circumstances of a keeper of pigs to the office of chancellor, highest in the land, which he held from 124–118 BC" (*CHC*, 1.109—see also pages 769–70, and *Han shu* 58, 8.2613–24). For the reference to his being recommended for office for the second time, see *Shiji* 112, 9.2949. Sunshu Ao 孫叔敖 was a man of Chu who, according to Giles, "thrice became prime minister without feeling joy and thrice suffered dismissal without feeling resentment" (*Chinese Biographical Dictionary*, 694). See also *Zuo Zhuan* VII.12; LCC, 5.311ff, and *Shiji* 119, 10.3099. For reference to the matter alluded to here, see *Shiji* 126, 10.3201.
67. The two place-names, Fufeng 扶風 and Zhuojun 涿郡, represent two Han officials, Yin Wenggui 尹翁歸 and Han Fu 韓福, respectively. See *Han Shu* 76, 10.3206–10 and 72, 10.3083ff. Details of these allusions can be found on pages 3209 and 3083, respectively.
68. *Han Shu* 58, 9.2624.
69. These three men, Xu Mao 徐貌, Hu Zhi 胡質, and Tian Yu 田豫, were of the Wei period. For their biographies see *Sanguo Zhi* 27, 3.739–41, 741–43, and 26.726–29, respectively. The proclamation is referred to in part on page 729 and in detail on page 740, although the wording differs somewhat from that in Gu's text.
70. Li Mi 李謐 was a scholar of the Northern Wei period so devoted to study that he eschewed all official appointments. For his biography, see *Wei Shu* 90, 6.1932–39. The proclamation quoted can be found on pages 1938–39. It is not clear who Hui 惠 and Kang 康 were. The former may refer to Hui Shi, a philosopher of the School of Names and a friend of Zhuang Zhou's, while the latter may refer to Ji Kang, one of the Seven Worthies of the Bamboo Grove. Xuanyan Xiansheng was the soubriquet of the Jin scholar Huangfu Mi (215–282), whose biography can be found in *Jin Shu* 51, 5.1409ff.
71. The *Tang Liudian* 唐六典 was a work compiled by Emperor Xuan Zong—see *Liudian* 14, "Taichang Boshi."
72. These were Ming officials—see *Ming Shi* as follows: Qi Biaojia 祁彪佳 275, 23.7051–55; Gui Zimu 歸子慕 87, 24.7383.
73. See *Xin Tang Shu* 174, 17.5229. Niu Sengru 牛僧孺 was an important statesman of the Tang era. Detailed consideration of his significance can be found in *CHC*, 3(i).639ff.

74. Hu Ying (1375–1463) was a particularly long-serving Ming official whose family home was in Wujin—see *Ming Shi* 169, 15.4534–37, and *DMB*, 1.643.
75. Feng Dao 馮道 served as a high official under several of the Five Dynasties emperors—see *Xin Wu Dai Shi* 54, 2.612–15, and *Jiu Wu Dai Shi* 126, 5.1655–66.
76. *Guanzi* 1, *SBCK* 18(*Guanzi*).4.
77. *Xin Wu Dai Shi* 54, 2.611.
78. *Lunyu* XIII.20; LCC, 1.271.
79. *Mencius* VIIA.6; LCC, 2.451.
80. *Mencius* VIIA.7; LCC 2.451–52.
81. The sources of these three quotations are as follows: Lunyu IX.27, LCC, 1.225; *Odes*, Mao 90, LCC, 4.143; and *Chu Ci* 楚辭, "Yufu" (*Qufu Xinbian* 屈賦新編, 2.535).
82. Yan Zhitui 顏之推was a scholar and official who served under several emperors of the north-south division and finally of the Sui period. See *Bei Qi Shu* 45, 2.617–26. The Xianbei 鮮卑 was a barbarian tribe from southeastern Mongolia. For the quote, see *Yanshi Jiaxun*, *SBCK* 22 (*Yanshi Jiaxun*), 4.
83. *Odes*, Mao 196; LCC, 4.333ff. In his notes to this poem, Legge writes, "Some officer in a time of disorder and misgovernment urges on his brothers the duty of maintaining their own virtue and of observing the greatest caution."
84. *Mencius* VIIB.37(9); LCC, 2.500.
85. Luo Congyan 羅從彥 (Zhongsu 仲素, 1079–1135) was a prominent neo-Confucian thinker and follower of Yang Shi 楊時—see *Song Shi* 428, 36.12743–45. For the quote, see *Yuzhang Wenji* 豫章文集 17.
86. The *Wuzi* 吳子 was a work on the art of war in one chapter compiled by Wu Qi 吳起 in the Zhou period. For the quoted passage, see *Wuzi*, "Tuguo" 1, *CSJC* (new ser.) 32.
87. The *Weiliaozi* 尉繚子 was also a work on warfare, compiled by Wei Liao, probably of the Wei state in the period of the Warring States. The quote is from 1(4), "Zhanwei Pian," *CSJC* (new ser.) 32.
88. This is a summary of Duke Tai's statement that can be found in *Liu Tao* 六韜 3; see *SBCK* 18 (*Liu Tao*) 12.
89. *Odes*, Mao 7; LCC, 4.13ff.
90. Zhang Huan 張奐 was a general of the Later Han period. His biography is in *Hou Han Shu* 65, 8.2138–45. The reference is to page 2138—see also *CHC*, 1.428ff.
91. Liaodong 遼東 was established as a *jun* in Qin times corresponding to part of what is now Liaoning province.
92. Lianpo 廉頗 was a renowned general of the Zhao state in the Warring States period. He was said to have been overtly jealous of Lin Xiangru, a minister of that time who was ranked above him. He was, however, made to feel shame by Lin's courteous and deferential attitude toward him. It is presumably this shame that is referred to here. See *Dushi Yinde* 1.74.

93. Wang Bi 王佖 was a Tang official. For this quotation, see *Jiu Tang Shu* 123, 11.3686.
94. The phrase *ying shu yan shuo* 郢書燕說 is a reference to *Han Feizi* 11, *SBCK* 18(*Han Feizi*).56. According to this story, Ying, while writing to Yan, called upon his attendant to raise the light higher. Unthinkingly, Ying incorporated the instruction in his writing. This was interpreted by Yan as a guide to conduct with beneficial effect.
95. Lü Dalin 呂大臨 (1044–1093) was a noted scholar of the Song period and a student of Cheng Yi's. His biography can be found in *Song Shi* 340, 31.10848–49; this exchange with Fu Bi is quoted there. Fu Bi 富弼 was also a noted Song scholar who gained renown for his dealings with the Tartars. He was unable to reconcile himself with the doctrines of Wang Anshi and resigned on the grounds of old age in 1068.
96. According to Charles Hucker, *san gong* was "from antiquity a collective reference to dignitaries who were officially considered the three paramount aides to the ruler and held the highest possible ranks in officialdom" (*A Dictionary of Official Titles in Imperial China* [Stanford, Calif.: Stanford University Press, 1985], p. 399, no. 4871).
97. *Mencius* VB.1(2); LCC, 2.370.
98. *Doctrine of the Mean* XXV.3; LCC, 1.418.
99. For this exchange, see Sima Guang's *Zizhi Tongjian* for 718, summer, fourth month (*Tongjian* 212).
100. *Mencius* IIIA.4(13); LCC, 2. 254.
101. Huang Zhen 黃震 (1213–1280) was a scholar of the Southern Song and author of the *Cixi Huangshi Richao* 慈溪黃氏日鈔 (Huang Zhen's diary), a work in ninety-seven chapters—see *SB*, 232–33.
102. There is a note here referring to *Song Shi* 105 ("Li Zhi").
103. This can be seen in *Lunyu* II.18 and XII.6; LCC, 1.151 and 253, respectively. Legge comments first that "it would appear that inferior motives sometimes ruled" (151) and subsequently that "he was always seeking to be wise about things lofty and distant and therefore Confucius brings him back to things near at hand, which it was more necessary for him to attend to" (253).
104. Lu Xiangshan 陸象山 was the literary name of Lu Jiuyuan 陸九淵 (1139–1193), the Song philosopher described by Fung Yu-lan as "the real founder of the rival idealistic (*xinxue* 心學) school [of neo-Confucianism]" (*HCP*, 2.572)—see Fung (ibid.) for Lu's response to You Ruo and subsequently (572–92) for a discussion of his thought.
105. *Huangshi Richao* 3, "Reading Mencius."
106. In *Lunyu* 1, You Ruo is thrice referred to as You Zi (Philosopher You; 1.2, 1.12, and 1.13), while Zeng Can 曾參 is mentioned once in like manner (1.9). As Legge observes (LCC, 1.138, note to 1.2) (You) and Zeng Can are the only two of Confucius's disciples who are mentioned in this style in the *Lunyu*.
107. *Shiji* 47, 6.1945.

108. *Li Ji* ("Tan Gong," *xia*), *SSJZS*, 5.166.
109. A final note says, "Mencius did not say You Ruo was like Confucius; he said You Ruo was like a sage. The *Shiji* says that You Ruo looked like Confucius. This is an important mistake."
110. Suo Lin 索綝 was a Jin scholar and official, the son of Suo Jing 索靖. His biography can be found in *Jin Shu* 60, 6.1650–52. Baling 霸陵 and Duling 杜陵 were established for Han emperors Wen Di and Xuan Di, respectively. Biographical details can be found in *Han Shu, Dili Zhi*. For some discussion of the practice of the Han emperors of filling their tombs with treasure, see *CHC*, 1.209–10. "The Red Eyebrows" was a peasant-based movement involved in the overthrow of the usurper Wang Mang and the restoration of the Han dynasty—for details see *CHC*, 1.243–54 The quotation is from *Jin Shu* 60, 1651.
111. *Shiji* 10, 2.433.
112. Liu Xiang 劉向 (80–9 B.C.E.), a descendant of the Han founder, Liu Bang, was a noted scholar of the Former Han period who held office under a succession of emperors—for the memorial, see *Han Shu* 36, 7.1950ff.
113. *Han Shu* 59, 9.2643.
114. *Zuo Zhuan* VIII.2; LCC, 5.341 (trans. after Legge).
115. For the phrase *zhong bi* 重閉 (doubly enclosing), see *Zuo Zhuan* VIII.8; LCC, 5.366, and the "Yueling" chapter of the *Li Ji* (*SSJZS*, 5.345).
116. *Shiji* 126, 10.3200, and note 2 on the same page.
117. The quotation is from the *Lü Shi Chunqiu*—see *SBCK* 22(*Lü Shi Chunqiu*).57–58, and John Knoblock and Jeffrey Riegel, *The Annals of Lü Buwei: A Complete Translation and Study* (Stanford, Calif.: Stanford University Press, 2000), 10/2.1–4, 227–30.
118. The quotation is from the *Lü Shi Chunqiu*—see *SBCK* 22(*Lü Shi Chunqiu*).58–59, and Knoblock and Riegel, *Annals*, 10/3.1–5, 230–33.

4. *RZL* 16–17: THE EXAMINATION SYSTEM

1. Details of the meaning and significance of these categories can be found in *Xin Tang Shu* 4.1159–81. Charles O. Hucker, *A Dictionary of Official Titles in Imperial China* (Stanford, Calif.: Stanford University Press, 1985), has entries for the following terms: *xiucai* (cultivated talent—p. 248, no. 2633); *mingjing* (classicist—p. 333, no. 4007); *jinshi* (presented scholar or metropolitan graduate—p. 167, no. 1148); *mingfa* (law graduate—p. 333, no. 4009), and *daoju* (Daoist recruit—p. 489, no. 6311). The first three terms are the subjects of essays 1, 2, and 4 of the present section.
2. Amplification of the subcategories of *mingjing* is also to be found in *Xin Tang Shu* 4.1159–81. See also Hucker's entry for *mingjing* (*Dictionary of Official Titles*, p. 333, no. 4007).

3. This term, used from Tang to Qing times and rendered by Hucker as "special recruitment," was "a designation for civil service recruitment examinations given by decree irregularly in search of extraordinarily talented men from within or without the service" (*Dictionary of Official Titles*, p. 157, no. 969). See also *Xin Tang Shu* 4.1169.
4. Yao Chong 姚崇 was a prominent official who rose to high office under Xuan Zong. He is described by Denis Twitchett as "a pragmatic statesman adept at dealing with practical affairs" (*CHC*, 3[i].337). The phrase is used with reference to Yao in *Xin Tang Shu* 124, 14.4381. For further discussion of his activities in relation to the examination system, see *CHC*, 3(i).327, 331–54, and 375.
5. Zhang Jiuling 張九齡 (673–740) was a major political figure during the reign of Tang Ming Huang. For some consideration of his observations and recommendations on the examination system, see *CHC*, 3(i).352, and 404–5. The phrase "way like Yi and Lü" is seen as applied to his own examination success (*Xin Tang Shu* 126, 14.4424). Yi is Yi Yin 伊尹, a legendary figure said to have aided the founder of the Shang dynasty, Cheng Tang 成湯. Lü is Tai Gong 太公, or Lü Shang 呂尚, who is said to have been, in his last years, counselor to King Wen and subsequently to King Wu.
6. An original note says that in *Kunxue Jiwen* 14 it is stated that the names of the Tang system of recommendation numbered as many as eighty-six.
7. On Wang Weizhen 王維楨, see *Ming Shi* 286, 24.7349.
8. The term *keju* 科舉, applicable from the Tang to Qing periods, is defined by Hucker (*Dictionary of Official Titles*, p. 279, no. 3193) as recruitment by examination or regular recruitment as distinct from special recruitment by irregular special examinations.
9. The term *zhiju* 制舉 is rendered "special recruitment" by Hucker (ibid., p. 157, no. 969) and described as a designation for civil service recruitment examinations given "by decree irregularly in search of extraordinarily talented men from within and without the service; distinguished from regular scheduled examination recruitment." It is similar to *zhike*.
10. For this phrase, used here and subsequently, see *Shiji* 10, 2.422.
11. *Xin Tang Shu* 44, 4.1169–70.
12. *Song Shi* 156, "Xuanju."
13. *Dake* 大科 was an examination for those with special talents. It was conducted by the emperor himself, and he was also responsible for selecting the examination topics. It was therefore similar in intent to the *zhike* of the title. The *Zhongwen Da Zidian* has an extensive quote from this essay in explication of the term (2.1461). There is also an original note with reference to Ye Zuqia's 葉祖洽 biography in *Song Shi* 354 and *Shaoshi Wenjian Lu*, "Qianlu," 9.
14. Xu Du 徐度 published his *Quesao Bian* 卻掃編 around 1130—see *SB*, 105–6. What follows is a long quotation from that work.

15. See Hucker, *Dictionary of Official Titles*, p. 242, no. 2516, on this recommendation category.
16. For the quotation, see *CSJC* (new ser.) 84.715–16.
17. Erudite literatus, a category first established in the Tang period. See Hucker, *Dictionary of Official Titles*, p. 388, no. 4732, and Miyazaki, *China's Examination Hell*, 108–10.
18. *Tong Jian* 238, Yuanhe seventh year, first month.
19. Ibid., 241, Yuanhe fifteenth year, first month.
20. *Hou Han Shu* 93.
21. *Fengsu Tong* 4, "Guoyu."
22. *Sanguo Zhi* 1 for the ninth month of the sixteenth year of Chuping.
23. *Jinshi Cuibian* 金石萃編 8.
24. *Lishi* 隸釋 8. For Liu Min 柳敏, see *Zhou Shu* 32, 2.560–62.
25. *Jin Shu* 66.

5. *RZL* 18–21: LITERATURE AND PHILOSOPHY

1. *Li Ji* 38 ("Yueli"), *SSJZS*, 5.682.
2. An original note states that the *Cefu Yuangui* (52) quotes the *Tang Huiyao* as saying that in the second month of the second year of the Kaicheng reign period (837), Wang Yanwei prepared a work in twelve *juan* titled *Neidian Zilu*.
3. Sengzhao 僧肇 (384–414)—see his *Zhaolun* 肇論.
4. There is a significant textual variation in the later part of this opening paragraph. In the HRC edition there is an original note, a note by the editor, and a long note by Qian Xiaozheng. The text followed in the translation is that given in Chen Yuan's 2011 edition.
5. The *Cixi Huangshi Richao* 慈溪黃氏日鈔 is a work compiled by the Song scholar Huang Zhen 黃震—for details, see *SB*, 232. Xie Shi is Xie Liangzuo 謝良佐 (1059–1103)—for his writings, collected and collated by Zhu Xi, see *SB*, 221–22.
6. The quote is from *Huangshi Richao* 2.
7. For Chu Shaosun 褚少孫, see *Han Shu* 88, 11.3610. The "Huaji Zhuan" of the *Shiji* is *juan* 126.
8. See *Hou Han Shu* 112 *shang* (preface), and *Sanguo Zhi* 11, "Wei Zhi."
9. See *Hou Han Shu* 58 (*shang*).
10. This essay begins with a long quotation from Huang Zhen's (1213–1280) *Cixi Huangshi Richao*—a work often quoted in the *RZL*.
11. The four quotes from the *Documents* are as follows: II.II.2(15), LCC, 3.61; II.II.2(17), LCC, 3.63; II.II.2(16), LCC, 3.62; II.II.2(17), LCC, 3.63. See also Zhu Xi's preface to the *Zhongyong* 中庸 in his *Sishu Zhangju*, included in Ian Johnston and Wang Ping, trans., *Daxue and Zhongyong* (Hong Kong: Chinese University Press, 2012), 400–405.

12. Cai Jiufeng 蔡九峰 is Cai Shen 蔡沈 (1167–1230), a Song scholar who retired early and devoted himself to a life of scholarship. His commentary on the *Documents* (*Shangshu Jizhuan*) is an important text on the ancient work—see *SB*, 22–23. For the quote in question, see *Shangshu Jizhuan*, 14.
13. I.e., the *Zhuangzi* 莊子 and the *Liezi* 列子.
14. The quote is from *Huangshi Richao* 5.
15. This is the prefatory statement to the opening section of the *Zhongyong*—see Johnston and Wang, *Daxue and Zhongyong*, 406–7.
16. The three quotes from the *Lunyu* are as follows: II.4(6), LCC, 1.147; VI.5, LCC, 1.186; XVII.22, LCC, 1.329. For the last, Arthur Waley has, "The Master said, those who do nothing all day but cram themselves with food and never use their minds are difficult" (*The Analects of Confucius* [London: Allen and Unwin, 1938], 215).
17. *Mencius* VIA.9(4); LCC, 2.409. This statement is attributed to Confucius.
18. *Mencius* VIA.8(2); LCC, 2.408.
19. Tang Renqing 唐仁卿 (Tang Boyuan 唐伯元) was a Ming scholar and a *jinshi* in the second year of the Wanli reign period (1574). He had a particular aversion to the works of Wang Shouren. See *Ming Shi* 282, 24.7257. I am unable to locate the text of this letter.
20. The three references are as follows: *Lunyu* IV.6(2), LCC, 1.167; *Lunyu* XII.1, LCC, 1.250; *Changes*, *SSJZS*, 1(*Yi Jing*).9, and Richard Wilhelm, trans., *The I Ching; or, Book of Changes* (Princeton: Princeton University Press, 1950), 374.
21. This is a tripartite comparison between Yan Hui, the most favored disciple (*Lunyu* VI.2; LCC, 1.185, and XI.6; LCC, 1.239), and the other disciples and people in general.
22. See *Lunyu* XII.1; LCC, 1.250.
23. *Mencius* (VIIA.25; LCC, 2.464) contrasts the disciple of Shun, diligent in the pursuit of virtue, with the disciple of the robber Zhi, diligent in the pursuit of gain. Legge, in his note, opines that the point here is the distinction between the public mind and the selfish mind and the slightness of the separation between them.
24. *Mencius* VIA.13(4); LCC, 2.414: "The great end of learning is nothing else but to seek for the lost mind."
25. *Lunyu* IV.2; LCC, 1.165.
26. The quote is from Xie Liangzuo 謝良佐 (1050–1103), a disciple of Cheng Hao's. This statement is part of his comment on the passage given by Zhu Xi, *Sishu Zhangju Jizhu*, 92.
27. *Documents* V.1(1); LCC, 3.199.
28. *Zhongyong* VIII; LCC, 1.389.
29. Han Yu 韓愈 (768–824) was, apart from his political career, one of the most noted of Chinese poets and essayists, having, in the early Tang period, a profound influence on literary thought and style. For a full translation

of this long poem and reference to the original, see Stephen Owen, *The Poetry of Meng Chiao and Han Yü* (New Haven: Yale University Press, 1975), 271–73.

30. Liu Zhi 劉摯 (1014–1081) was a scholar and official from Dongguang—see *Song Shi* 340, 31.10849–58.
31. Yang Ziyun 揚子雲 is Yang Xiong 揚雄 (52 B.C.E.–18 c.e.). He was a scholar and official who rose to prominence at the end of the Former Han period and subsequently served under Wang Mang. He was a major force in the old-text school of Han Confucians—see *HCP*, 2.136ff. For the reference, see his *Fayan Wenming* 法言文明, *SBCK* 18(*Fayan*).15.
32. Huang Luzhi 黄魯直 is Huang Tingjian 黄庭堅 (1050–1110), an official who rose to a high position in the Imperial Academy and was a noted poet of the Song period—see *Song Shi* 444, 37.13109–11. For the reference, see *Huang Wengong Quanji*, "Bieji" 18, "Letter to Hongsheng Junfu."
33. The three people referred to are, respectively, Lu Shen 陸深 (1477–1544) (see *DMB*, 1.999); Liu Jian 劉健 (1433–1526), a somewhat older contemporary of Lu Shen's from Loyang (see *DMB*, 1.938, and *Ming Shi* 181, 16.4810); and Kongtong 空同, or Li Mengyang 李夢陽, a Ming scholar (see *Ming Shi* 286, 24.7346 ff).
34. Ouyang Yongshu 歐陽永叔 is Ouyang Xiu 歐陽修 (1007–1072), a renowned scholar of the Song period who rose to high office. In 1071 he retired in protest against the policies of Wang Anshi—see *Song Shi* 319, 30.10381.
35. Fan Zongshi 樊宗師 was a Tang scholar from Nanyang particularly opposed to plagiarism. He was well regarded by Han Yu—see *Xin Tang Shu* 159, 16.4953. The quote can be found in *Han Changli Wenji Jiaozhu*, 552.
36. *Lunyu* XV.40; LCC, 1.305.
37. *Mencius* IIB.10(4); LCC, 2.226.
38. *Mencius* IVB.33; LCC, 2.340–41.
39. *Mencius* VA.2(4); LCC, 2.347–48.
40. Liu Qizhi 劉器之 is Liu Anshi 劉安世 (1048–1125), a notably outspoken official who nevertheless rose to high office—see *Yuancheng Yulu* 元城語錄 (*xia*).
41. This quote can be found in the "Jin Tang Shubiao" at the end of *Xin Tang Shu*, 20.6471–72.
42. The *Gu Shi* 古史 was one of the works of Su Che 蘇轍. It is described in the *Sung Bibliography* as "a study of antiquity in criticism of Sima Qian" (*SB*, 400). For the two *Shiji* quotes, see 71, 7.2307 and 2310.
43. For the phrase *li yan* 立言 (to establish one's words or teachings), see *Zuo Zhuan*, twenty-fourth year of Duke Xiang; LCC, 5.505: "I have heard that the highest meaning of it is when there is established (an example of) virtue; second, when there is established (an example of) successful service; and the third, when there is established (an example of) wise speech" (trans. after Legge, 507).

44. *Odes*, Mao 301; LCC, 4.633.
45. See Cheng Yi's 程頤 *Yichuan Yizhuan* 伊川易傳 in *Er Cheng Quanshu* 二程全書, *SBBY* edition, vol. 12, *juan* 4. The diagram is number 64. See Wilhelm's comments on the positions of the lines (*I Ching*, 248, 362, 714).
46. *Documents* II.I.5(24); LCC, 3.48.
47. *Li Ji*, "Wang Zhi," *SBCK* 1.39.
48. *Xunzi* 27.92, "Dalue"—see John Knoblock, *Xunzi: A Study and Translation of the Complete Works; Volume 3, Books 17–32* (Stanford, Calif.: Stanford University Press, 1994), 3:230.
49. *Mencius* IVB.21(1); LCC, 2.327.
50. This is part of an exchange between Yang Xiong and an unnamed questioner on the value of the *fu* of Jing Cha, Tang Le, Song Yu, and Mei Cheng. On the issue of "excess," Yang Zi says, "The *fu* of those who wrote *shi* style verse achieved beauty by means of standards. The *fu* of those who wrote *ci* style verse achieved beauty by going to excess." See Jeffrey S. Bullock, *Yang Xiong: Philosophy of the "Fa yan"* (Highlands, N.C.: Mountain Mind Press, 2011), p. 46, no. 2.2.
51. Bai Juyi was a noted Tang poet. He formed a friendship with Yuan Weizhi (Yuan Zhen 元稹, 779–831), a child prodigy who subsequently became a poet of renown and originator of the Yuanhe style. The letter can be found in *Bai Juyi Ji* 45, 3.959ff. Liang Hong 梁鴻 was a scholar of the Later Han who, during his travels, composed the poem "Wuyi" 五噫. This poem was said to have offended the emperor to such a degree that he ordered Liang Hong's arrest, although this was not effected (see *Hou Han Shu* 83, 2765). I could find no trace of Deng Fang. Tang Qu is said to have been a man given to easy weeping and to have wept on listening to Bai Juyi's verse.
52. *Zuo Zhuan* IX.24; LCC, 5.505.
53. Ge Hong 葛洪 (281–341) was something of a recluse who loved learning and was particularly interested in the supernatural and the pharmacological aspects thereof. He styled himself Baopu Zi 抱朴子—see *Jin Shu* 72, and, for the quote, *Baopuzi Waipian* 40, *SBCK* 27.224.

6. *RZL* 22–32: MISCELLANEOUS

1. *Shang Shu* (*Documents*), *SSJZS*, 1(*Shang Shu*).42.
2. Zou Yan 騶衍 (fourth century B.C.E.) was a pre-Qin philosopher of the Five Phases (Elements) school. For details of his doctrines, see *HCP*, 1.159ff. His geographical observations referred to here can be found on pages 160ff.
3. An original note states that the character 州 *zhou* was originally 洲 *zhou* (i.e., "island").
4. An original note refers to the *Li Ji* (*SSJZS*, 5.821), where mention is made of the northern, eastern, southern, and western Seas, as indeed occurs in other works.

5. *Erya*, *SBCK* 1(*Erya*).16.
6. *Zhou Li*, *SSJZS*, 3.496.
7. *Yi Jing*, *SSJZS*, 1(*Zhou Yi*).130.
8. *Li Ji*, *SSJZS*, 5.1008 and James Legge, *Li Chi: Book of Rites* (New Hyde Park, N.Y.: University Books, 1967), 2:443.
9. *Documents* (*Shu Jing*), LCC, 3.77.
10. *Documents* (*Shu Jing*), LCC, 3.132. See also Legge's extensive note on pages 133–34.
11. *Documents* (*Shu Jing*), LCC, 3.150.
12. Hong Mai 洪邁 (1123–1202) was a noted scholar and writer of the Song period. His comments reported here are to be found in the *Rongzhai Suibi Wuji* 容齋隨筆五集, in the essay titled "Sihai Yiye," 3, 1.33.
13. *Zhuangzi* 1, Guo Qingfan, *Zhuangzi Jishi*, 4 vols. (Beijing, Zhonghua Shuju, 1978), 1.14.
14. *Li Sao*, *Qufu Xinbian*, 1.268.
15. Cheng Dachang 程大昌 (1123–1195) was a Song scholar from Xiuning in Huizhou. For biographical details, see *Song Shi* 433, 37.12858–61. His work, the *Yonglu* 雍錄, can be found in *Gujin Yishi* 古今逸史, vols. 22–26 (see also *SB*, 152). I have not been able to locate the quotation given. Tiaozhi is the name of an ancient kingdom (Mesopotamia)—see *Shiji* 123.
16. Ban Chao 班超 (31–101) was the younger brother of Ban Gu, the historian. He traveled widely beyond the confines of the kingdom, achieving major military successes in central Asia. Gan Ying 甘英 was a subordinate of Ban Chao's who was appointed as envoy to Rome but actually reached Tiaozhi 條支, a country on the shores of the Persian Gulf—see *CHC*, 1.579.
17. Huo Qubing 霍去病 (d. 117 B.C.E.) was a military man of the Former Han period who rose to the rank of president of the Board of War and gained a number of victories over the Xiongnu. Lang Juxu Mountain was situated in the northwest of Wuyuan district of Suiyuan province on the northern bank of the Yellow River. Han Hai 瀚海 (or "Northern Sea") refers to the Gobi Desert.
18. Su Wu 蘇武 was an official under Emperor Wu of Han. He was dispatched on a mission of peace to return the Xiongnu envoys who had been detained by the Chinese but was himself imprisoned by the Xiongnu—see *Han Shu* 54, 8.2459–69. Guo Ji 郭伋 (38 B.C.E.–47 C.E.) was an official who served first under Wang Mang and subsequently under the first emperor of the Later Han dynasty. He was also imprisoned by the Xiongnu—see *Hou Han Shu* 31, 4.1091–93.
19. The Guligan 骨利幹 were an aboriginal people—see *Xin Tang Shu* 217a, 19.6112). Gu's text has *Tang Shi*.
20. There is a textual variation here between the Huang Rucheng edition, which has *hua yi* 華裔 (Chinese descendants), and the *Yuanchaoben*

edition, which has *di xia* 夷夏 (barbarians and Chinese); the latter has been followed.

21. Juyan Hai 居延海 was the name of a lake—see *Shiji* 110. Qing Hai 青海 was also a lake, in what is now Qinghai province. Dian Hai 滇海 was in the southern part of Kunming district, Yunnan.
22. The *Tong Dian* 通典 is a work compiled by the Tang scholar Du You 杜佑; it is an extensive treatise on matters of government—see *CHC*, 3(i).604ff., and *SB*, 173 and 176.
23. *Bei Shi* 36, 5.1326.
24. An original note here quotes Cheng Dachang's *Yonglu* as saying that the site of the academy was to the right of Daming Palace and within the Yintai gate.
25. Officials of the Tang period. The following references to *CHC*, 3(i), give some indication of their roles in the Tang administration: Zhang Yue 張說 (348–56, 352–53, 376–91); Lu Jian 陸堅 (386); Zhang Jiuling 張九齡 (352–53, 388–89, 397–409); Zhang Ji 張吉 (449–50).
26. *Jiu Tang Shu* 43, 6.1853.
27. The *Tang Liudian* 唐六典 was a compilation initiated by Xuan Zong and completed in 738. According to Denis Twitchett, it provides "much of our detailed knowledge of Tang administrative law" (*CHC*, 3[i].354 and 415).
28. See *Jiu Tang Shu* 43, 6.1853.
29. Lu Zhi 陸贄 was a Hanlin academician who became a very influential adviser to De Zong—see *CHC*, 3(i).584ff. Wu Tongxuan 吳通玄 was a Hanlin academician and official. For details of his disagreement with Lu Zhi, see *Jiu Tang Shu* 190b, 15.5057–58. On the term *dai zhao* 待詔, rendered as "expectant official," see Charles O. Hucker, *A Dictionary of Official Titles in Imperial China* (Stanford, Calif.: Stanford University Press, 1985), p. 475, no. 6127.
30. Brief details of the men listed are as follows: Wu Yun 吳筠 was a Confucian scholar; see *Jiu Tang Shu* 142, 16.5129–50. Han Ying 韓穎 gave prognostic advice to Xuan Zong; he held a position of attendant at the gate to the heir apparent. Wang Shuwen 王叔文 and Wang Pi 王伾—the former a lowly official, the latter a scribe who was appointed a Hanlin academician in 805—were both closely involved in the clique that, disaffected with De Zong's administration, gathered around the heir apparent Shun Zong; see *CHC*, 3(i).601–7, and Bischoff, *La forêt des pinceaux*, 42, 60–62. With reference to Liu Mi 柳泌 and Datong 大通, see *Jiu Tang Shu* 131, 11.3642 and *Xin Tang Shu* 167, 16.5114. I have not been able to track down the following three men: Liu Xuan 劉烜, Wang Yi 王倚, and Sun Zhun 孫準.
31. Li Gan 黎幹 was an expert in star divination and magical calculations—see *Jiu Tang Shu* 118, 10.3426.
32. Ibid., 14, 2.405.
33. Ibid., 17a, 2.52.

34. Zhao Lin 趙璘 was a Tang scholar who became a *jinshi* during the Kaicheng reign period. His *Yinhua Lu* appears in *Shuofu* 15, but I could find no mention of Wen Zong there.
35. *Xian Zong Shilu* 49.
36. Details of these events, including part of the text of the memorial in which the three Hanlin compilers took the occasion of the lantern festival to voice a protest against Zhu Jianshen's preoccupation with pleasure, can be found in *Ming Shi* 13, 1.164 and 179, 16.4751–55. Details of their punishment, demotion, and subsequent reinstatement are also to be found therein.
37. *Shiji* 4, 1.142–44; see also 144n1.
38. An original note refers to Yan Shigu's note to "The List of Ancient and Present-Day People" in the *Han Shu*, as follows: *Gong* was the state, *bo* was the rank—i.e., "earl," and He was his name.
39. *Annals of the Bamboo Books* for Li Wang 厲王; see LCC, 3(prolegomena).153–54.
40. *Zuo Zhuan* X(26); LCC, 5.714.
41. *Lü Shi Chunqiu*, 21/1.1, "Kai Chun," John Knoblock and Jeffrey Riegel, *The Annals of Lü Buwei: A Complete Translation and Study* (Stanford, Calif.: Stanford University Press, 2000), 548.
42. *Zhuangzi* 28, 4.983 (Guo Qingfan)—see, in particular, notes 1 and 2 on pages 982–84. The translation follows Burton Watson, trans., *The Complete Works of Chuang Tzu* (New York: Columbia University Press, 1968), 319.
43. See *Zuo Zhuan* 1.1, *SSJZS*, 6.36, where the note referred to immediately follows the statement about Tai Shu's flight.
44. This statement, in fact, is to be found in *Shiji* 44, "Wei Shi Jia" (6.1862). There is nothing resembling this entry in the "Chun Shen Jun Chuan."
45. *Shiji* 46, 6.1903—see particularly 1903nn1, 2, 3.
46. The entry actually reads *gong yan hou lu ba shi* 共嚴侯旅罷師, *Han Shu* 16, 2.591.
47. See *Jiu Tang Shu* 39, 5.1491.
48. *Han Shu* 35, 7.1904.
49. *Hou Han Shu* 1a, 1.25.
50. Ibid., 67, 8.2210.
51. Ibid., 10b, 2.445. There is some uncertainty about this statement. Not only have I been unable to identify the people concerned other than in this statement, but also the term *fu* 父 is not present in the *Hou Han Shu* passage.
52. Ibid., 79a, 9.2545. In the *Hou Han Shu* text quoted, the character *mao* 毛 is omitted.
53. Ibid., 9.2546.
54. Ibid., 79b, 9.2569.
55. Ibid., 25, 12.3572.
56. Ibid., 8, 2.344.

57. *Xunzi* 15, "Yi Bing," *SBCK* 17(*Xunzi*).102. I have followed Homer H. Dubs, *The Works of Hsuntze* (Taipei: Ch'eng-wen, 1973), 160, in the translation. Burton Watson has "it will be smashed, crushed, broken, defeated, and forced to fall back" (Burton Watson, *Hsün Tzu: Basic Writings* [New York: Columbia University Press, 1963], 58), adding in a note, "This last clause contains seven characters that are quite unintelligible. Commentators generally agree that they must have the meaning given in the translation, though efforts to interpret or amend the individual characters are scarcely convincing." The note on page 232 of the *Xunzi Xinzhu* states that the intention is to convey the impression of an army defeated and fleeing in panic.
58. *Jiu Tang Shu* 61, 10.2366.
59. *Bei Shi* 59, 7.2114.
60. The term *xi di* 席地 indicates the use of some sort of cotton or calico mat placed on the ground for sitting or reclining—see, e.g., *Nan Qi Shu* 22, 2.417.
61. The *Daming Huidian* 大明會典 was a compilation in 180 chapters prepared by Li Tongyang and others and first completed in 1509.
62. *Zhou Li* 25, "Tai Zhu," *SSJZS*, 3.387. Gu Yanwu's quote differs somewhat from the original text.
63. *Li Ji*, *SSJZS*, 5.488. Translation after Legge—see Legge, *Book of Rites*, 1:423.
64. *Zuo Zhuan* V(23); LCC, 5.185. The ode in question is Mao 177 (LCC, 4.281).
65. *Zuo Zhuan* IX(3); LCC, 5.418.
66. *Zuo Zhuan* IX(24); LCC, 5.505. Legge's translation is followed.
67. *Zuo Zhuan* XII(17); LCC, 5.849.
68. *Guoyu*, "Chuyu" (*shang*), *SBCK* 14(*Guoyu*).9–11. There are some discrepancies between the two texts.
69. Biographical details for both Li Ling 李陵 and Su Wu 蘇武 can be found in *Han Shu* 54, 8.2450 and 2459, respectively. Exchanges between them are given on pages 2464ff, although not as quoted.
70. Chen Xiangdao 陳祥道 (1058–1093) was one of the many commentators on the *Zhou Li*. His work, the *Li Shu* 禮書, in 150 *juan*, is included in the *SKQS*.
71. *Documents*, LCC, 3.206–7.
72. *Documents*, LCC, 3.424; see particularly the note on the same page.
73. Although the quote is not exact, this is probably from *Yi Li* 8, *SSJZS*, 4.254.
74. *Zuo Zhuan* VI(7); LCC, 5.246.
75. *Zuo Zhuan*, twenty-fifth year of Duke Zhao.
76. A short original note follows referring to *Li Shu* 87, "Baiyi," *shang*.
77. *Xunzi* 27.27; John Knoblock, *Xunzi: A Study and Translation of the Complete Works; Volume 3, Books 17–32* (Stanford, Calif.: Stanford University Press, 1994), 3:214; *Xunzi Xinzhu* 27, 447, and note thereto.
78. *Lunyu* XI.17(4); LCC, 1.243.
79. *Mencius* IIIA.4(14); LCC, 2.255.
80. *Song Shu* 52, 5.1506.
81. Ibid., 51, 5.1482.

82. *Shishuo Xinyu* 25, *Shishuo Xinyu Jianshu* 25.792.
83. *Shishuo Xinyu* 13, *Shishuo Xinyu Jianshu* 13.595. The general referred to is Wang Dun 王敦 of Jin (d. 324).
84. *Shishuo Xinyu* 26, *Shishuo Xinyu Jianshu* 26.848.
85. *Bei Shi* 29, 4.1047.
86. *Bei Qi Shu* 35, 2.467.
87. Gongyang Gao 公羊高 was one of the major early commentators on the *Spring and Autumn Annals*; he was from Qi. The *Huainanzi* 淮南子 was supposedly compiled by Liu An 劉安 (d. 122 B.C.E.), the son of Liu Bang 劉邦—i.e., Han Gao Di.
88. *Liang Shu* 48, 3.678.
89. Li Yexing 李業興 was a native of Changzi in the later Wei period who was noted for his learning. He was subsequently enfeoffed as Earl of Changzi. See *Bei Shi* 81, 9.2721–25.
90. Yan Zhitui 顏之推 (531–595) was a scholar and high official in the Northern Qi and Sui periods. His writings include a treatise on family education (*Yanshi Jiaxun*)—see *Bei Qi Shu* 45, 2.617–26.
91. This reference is to the new-text version of the classic. For some considerations on the controversy between old- and new-text schools, see *HCP*, 2, chapters 2 and 4, and *CHC*, 1.760ff. For the *Jin Shu* reference, see 135, 4.2891.
92. The character *an* 案 is frequently used in the *Xunzi* (thirty-seven entries in the Harvard-Yenching concordance) for the more usual *an* 按. *Qiang* 羌 was a commonly used particle in Chu writings—see, e.g., *Qufu Xinbian*, 1.223, sec. 15, and the following note.
93. See Liu Hsieh, *The Literary Mind and the Carving of Dragons*, trans. Vincent Yu-chung Shih (New York: Columbia University Press, 1959), 356–57, for the original text and English translation. Zhang Hua 張華 (232–300) was a scholar of the Jin period. Shiheng 士衡 is Lu Ji 陸機 (261–303).
94. *Odes*, Mao 154; LCC, 4.226 (and note on page 227).
95. *Odes*, Mao 118; LCC, 4.179 (and note on page 180 for the three stars).
96. *Odes*, Mao 232; LCC, 4.422.
97. *Zuo Zhuan*, fifth year of Duke Xi; LCC, 5.144.
98. For Fan Shen 樊深, see *Ming Shi* 207, 18.5481–82. The "Lü Shu" 律書 is *juan* 25 of the *Shiji* (4.1239–54). Yang Shiqi 楊士奇 was a noted Ming scholar—see *Ming Shi* 148, 14.4131; *DMB*, 2.1535–38; and *CHC*, 7.277–84, 302ff. The *Tianyuan Yuli Xiangyi Fu* is a work by Zhu Gaochi 朱高熾, who later became, for one year only, Emperor Ren Zong—see Joseph Needham, *Science and Civilisation in China: Volume 3, Mathematics and the Sciences of the Heavens and the Earth* (Cambridge: Cambridge University Press, 1959), 475.
99. Er Shi 貳師 is a place-name. In Han times it was a city in Fergana but here indicates Ershi Jiangjun, or Li Guangli 李廣利, a renowned Han general and frequent opponent of the Xiongnu who captured the city in one of his

campaigns. Biographical details of Li Guangli are to be found in *Han Shu* 61, 9.2699ff., and the incident referred to in *Han Shu* 94a, 11.3781—see also *CHC*, 1.168–69, and 175ff.

100. The beheading of Ran Min 冉閔 by Murong Jun 慕容儁 at Longcheng is recorded in *Jin Shu* 110, 9.2833. See also *Jin Shu* 107.
101. *Wei Shu* 28, 2.682. The text in Gu Yanwu differs slightly from that in the *Wei Shu*. I have followed the latter in the use of the Duke of Jianxing, Gu Bi 古弼, whereas Gu Yanwu has You Bi 右弼, which Hucker, *Dictionary of Official Titles*, renders as "Supporter on the Right" (p. 586, no. 8067) (the *SBBY* edition of the *Rizhi Lu* has Gu Bi).
102. Boyou 伯有 is a style and refers to Liang Xiao 良宵 of Zheng 鄭 in the Spring and Autumn period. See, e.g., *Spring and Autumn Annals* IX(30); LCC, 5.551, which records the death of Liang Xiao. For Boyou as an evil spirit, see *Zuo Zhuan* X(7); LCC, 5.613, and Legge's translation on page 618.
103. *Shiji* 43, 6.1789. Details of Zhao Xiangzi 趙襄子 are given in this chapter.
104. *Shuijing Zhu* 水經注—see *SBCK* 16.189. Mei Fu 梅福 was a scholar and official of the Former Han period. He disappeared on the accession of Wang Mang—see *Han Shu* 67.
105. *Shiji* 7, 1.321.
106. Ibid., 8, 2.369, 385, and 389. Jinyang 晉 was a *xian* (district) established during the Qin dynasty, corresponding to what is now Taiyuan district in Shanxi, as Gu points out—see also *Han Shu* 4, 1.105.
107. *Han Shu* 10, 2.413.
108. Ibid., 425. Note the discrepancy in the number of years in the two texts, and see also the same entry in *Han Shu* 4, 1.119, and the note on *fu* 復, page 120. See also the original note referring to Ru Chun's 如淳 contention that Jinyang was the first capital, with a subsequent move to Zhongdu.
109. *Han Shu* 10, 2.423.
110. Ibid., 46, 7.2200.
111. *Documents*, LCC, 4.159 (trans. after Legge).
112. *Zuo Zhuan*, twelfth year of Duke Xuan; LCC, 5.315, and translation on page 321.
113. *Li Ji*, "Quli," *SSJZS*, 5.78. See also Legge's translation in *Book of Rites*, 1:107.
114. *Chu Ci*, "Jiu Ge," "Da Siming," *Qufu Xinbian*, 1.325; and Arthur Waley, *The Nine Songs: A Study of Shamanism in Ancient China* (New York: Grove Press, 1956), 38.
115. *Chu Ci*, "Jiu Bian," *Qufu Xinbian*, 1.139.
116. *Zuo Zhuan*, second year of Duke Xuan; LCC, 5.288 (trans. after Legge, 289). For details of Hua Yuan, see Legge's note on page 289.
117. *Documents*, II, I, 3(8); LCC, 3.36, and see note on page 39.
118. *Lunyu* IX.23; LCC,1.224.
119. There is an original note here to the effect that the ancients considered the characters *ru* 如, *ruo* 若, and *nai* 奈 to have the one meaning, although not necessarily the one pronunciation.

120. See *Sanguo Zhi* 28, 3.766–77, for the text of the letter in which this observation is included.
121. *Song Shu* 47, 5.1410. Xuan is Huan Xuan 桓玄 (369–404), the son of Huan Wen. After military successes, he established himself as Emperor of Chu in 403, but his reign was short-lived and his end violent.

1. *SWJ* 1: STATECRAFT ESSAYS

1. Charles O. Hucker, *A Dictionary of Official Titles in Imperial China* (Stanford, Calif.: Stanford University Press, 1985), p. 2518, no. 993, uses "District Magistrate" for both these terms, taking *zhi xian* 知縣 to apply to the Song-Qing period and *xian ling* 縣令 to the Qin-Jin period.
2. See ibid., p. 539, no. 7229, for the range of official positions included in the term *dufu sidao* 督撫司道. Basically they were overseeing positions.
3. Wu Shi 烏氏 is Luo 裸 of Wu Shi (Wu Shi Luo). He was ennobled by Qinshi Huang Di for his work in animal husbandry—see *Shiji* 129, 10.3260. Qiao Yao 橋姚 was from the Han era and renowned for the rearing of domestic animals—see *Shiji* 129, 10.3280, and *Rizhi Lu* 10.10, "Ma Zheng" 馬政.
4. In the Warring States period Qufu 曲阜 was the capital of Lu; it was also the birthplace of Confucius.
5. This refers to Yang Yinglong 楊應龍, a minority leader who rebelled against the Ming administration—see *CHC*, 7(i).564ff.
6. Liu Yuan 劉淵 (d. 310) was the descendant of a Turkic chieftain who, in 308, proclaimed himself the first emperor of a new Han dynasty. Shi Le 石勒 (273–332) was a onetime slave noted for his great strength who rose to a high position under Liu Yuan—see *CHC*, 1.370–71. Wang Xianzhi 王仙芝 was a bandit leader of great notoriety during the reign of Tang Xi Zong (874–888). Huang Chao 黃巢 (d. 884) was a confederate of Wang Xianzhi's. Initially a member of the official class, he later turned to banditry. For a detailed consideration of the activities of both Wang and Huang, see *CHC*, 3(i).722–50.
7. *Lunyu* XX.2; LCC, 1.351.
8. Ye Shi 葉適 (Ye Zhengze 葉正則, 1150–1223) was a scholar and official of the Song period. His collected works, the *Shuixin Wenji* 水心文集, contain material discussing government, institutions, and politics (see *SB*, 426–27). For this quote, see *Lixu* 3.
9. San Fu 三府 is an unofficial reference to the *san gong* 三公 (Three Dukes), although there are also other meanings—see Hucker, *Dictionary of Official Titles*, p. 399, no. 4871; *CHC*, 1.493–502; and Bartlett, "Gu Yanwu," in *ECP*, 189–90.
10. Yan Yuan 顏淵 (Yan Hui) was Confucius's favorite disciple. He died young and presumably did not serve—see *Lunyu* VI.2; LCC, 1.185. Min Zi (Min

Sun 閔損) refused to serve—see *Lunyu* VI.7; LCC, 1.187. Qidiao Kai 漆雕開 was also a disciple of Confucius's who considered himself not able for official employment—see *Lunyu* V.5; LCC, 1.174, and Legge's note on the same page. Zeng Xi 曾晳 was another of the Confucian disciples, who, however, chose differently from the others when asked how he would conduct himself in office—see *Lunyu* XI.25(7); LCC, 1.248.

11. Yu 禹 was the founder of the Xia dynasty, traditional date 2206 B.C.E. Tang 湯 was the founder of the Shang dynasty, traditional date 1766 B.C.E.
12. Yang Yan 楊炎 (727–781) was a prominent Tang official. For his introduction of the "two-tax" system, see *CHC*, 3(i).580–82.
13. See *Han Shu* 24b, 4.1152.
14. Yang Yuling 楊於陵 was a Tang official—see *Jiu Tang Shu* 164 and *Xin Tang Shu* 163.
15. There follows here an extensive original note that is essentially an extract from *Jiu Tang Shu* 16, 2.480.
16. Xu Zhigao 徐知誥 was the assumed name of Li Bian 李昪, an orphan brought up initially by Yang Xingmi and subsequently by Xu Wen 徐溫, whose name he took. He became emperor of the Southern Tang, with his capital at Nanjing. Song Qiqiu 宋齊丘 was an official in his service—see *Jiu Wudai Shi* 134, 6.1784–87.
17. There follows here an extensive note comprising quotations from the three Tang writers mentioned. In the first, taken from the second part of Lu Zhi's *Shang Junjie Caifu Liushi*, the author rails against the two-tax system (*liangshui fa*) introduced in 780 (see *CHC*, 3[i].496ff.). In the second, taken from an essay titled "Shugai Shuifa," in Li Ao's *Collected Writings*, the author argues against the collection of taxes as money, reflecting on the burden this imposes on farmers. In the third, from Bai Juyi's poem "Zengyou," the writer makes a similar point. The farmer produces grain but is taxed in cash. Each year the price of money increases and the value of grain diminishes. Bai, as do the other writers quoted, looks back to earlier times when the system was more equitable.
18. The last two emperors of the legendary period, Yao 堯 (r. 2356– 2256 B.C.E.) and Shun 舜 (r. 2255—2205 B.C.E.) (traditional dates). The Sixiong 四凶 (four great criminals of the empire) are considered in *Documents*, "Canon of Shun," LCC, 3.39. The criminals were Gong Gong 共工, Huan Tou 驩兜, Gun 鯀, and San Miao 三苗, the last being a place-name. The first three are mentioned in the "Canon of Yao."
19. *Han Shu* 1b,1.54–55. See also 56nn16, 21.
20. *Mencius* IA.7(16 and 17); LCC, 2.145–46.
21. This refers to Qinshi Huang Di—see *Wen Xuan*, "Kong Anguo," 2(4).222.
22. A famous sword of ancient times. See *Shiji* 69, 7.2251, and 2252n16.
23. See, e.g., Ouyang Xiu's *Ji Jiuben Hanwen Hou* in *Ouyang Xiu Quanji* 1(3).136, for the use of this term, which Bartlett translates as "model essay" ("Gu Yanwu," 1999).

24. *Lunyu* II.11; LCC, 1.149. Legge's translation of the section in full is, "The Master said, 'If a man keeps cherishing his old knowledge so as continually to be acquiring new, he may be a teacher of others.'" See also Legge's note on page 149.

2. *SWJ* 2: PREFACES

1. The six categories of Chinese characters: self-explanatory, pictographic, pictophonetic, ideographic (associative compounds), mutually explanatory, and phonetic loan.
2. See, respectively, *Li Ji* 39, *SSJZS*, 5.663, and *Zhou Li* 37, *SSJZS*, 3.565.
3. Shun was one of the exemplary rulers of the legendary period during the third millennium B.C.E. His date of accession is traditionally given as 2255 B.C.E. Gaoyao 皋陶 was his minister—see *Documents* 2, 4, and 5; LCC, 3.29ff., 68ff., and 76ff., respectively. Ji Zi 箕子 (Viscount Ji—twelfth century B.C.E.) was a leading noble under the reviled Zhou, last emperor of the Yin. He was imprisoned for speaking out against the tyrant, but, when released by King Wu, he retired rather than serve his rescuer because the latter was, strictly speaking, a usurper—see *Documents* 32; LCC, 3.320ff. The "appendixes of King Wen and the Duke of Zhou" refer to the *Changes*, *tuan* and *yao*, respectively.
4. Zhou Yong 周顒 (fifth century) and Shen Yue 沈約 (441–513) are the two men credited with first devising the system of four tones. The former wrote a work called *Sisheng Qieyin*, while the latter, himself a noted poet, claimed priority in the matter.
5. Ban Gu (32–92), perhaps most noted as the grand historian of the Later Han, was also an important writer of *fu*, of which his *Liangdu Fu* (*Fu of Two Capitals*) is the most well known. Zhang Heng (78–139) was particularly renowned as a mathematician and astronomer but was also a poet of note, as were the Caos—the father, Cao Cao (155–220), founder of the Wei dynasty, and two of his sons, Cao Pi (188–227) and Cao Zhi (192–232). Liu Zheng (d. 217), who served under Cao Cao, was one of the "Seven Masters of the Jian'an Period."
6. The *Qieyun*, a phonetic dictionary arranged under 206 finals (*yun*), dates from the late sixth century (the date of the preface is 600) and was prepared by Lu Fayan with assistance from Yan Zhitui.
7. Liu Yuan prepared a work titled *Libu Yunlue*.
8. Huang Gongshao's work, the *Gujin Yunhui*, dates from 1292.
9. The full title of this work, completed during the Song period by Chen Pengnian and others and based on the *Qieyun*, was *Da Song Zhongxiu Guangyun*.
10. The two references to the *Lunyu* are IX.5(3) and IX.14, respectively.
11. See *Shiji* 130, 10.3320 and 3321n14.

3. *SWJ* 3: LETTERS 1

1. The *Lunyu* references are as follows: IX.1, V.12, XIII.20(1), and VII,19. The reference to the transmission from Yao to Shun is an abbreviated form of what is given in the *Documents*, *The Counsels of Yu*—see LCC, 3. 61, and also Zhu Xi's preface to the *Zhongyong* 中庸 in his *Sishu Zhangju*.
2. The references, all from the *Lunyu*, are, in order, XIV.37(2), IX.10(2), XIX.6, XIX.12(2), and XV.2(1–3). Master Yan is Yan Hui (Yan Yuan), possibly Confucius's favorite disciple. In *Zhongyong* 14, Confucius responds to the question from Duke Ai (of Lu) about government (Ian Johnston and Wang Ping, trans., *Daxue and Zhongyong* [Hong Kong: Chinese University Press, 2012], 291ff.). Zengzi is Zeng Shen (505–437 B.C.E.), a first-generation disciple traditionally credited with the writing of the *Daxue* (*Highest Learning*). Zixia is Bu Shang (b. 507 B.C.E.), another disciple.
3. Zigong is Duanmu Ci (b. 520 B.C.E.), one of the Master's foremost disciples. He was noted particularly for his devotion to Confucius and is said to have been present at the Master's death.
4. Yi Yin (eighteenth century B.C.E.) was, despite his great reluctance, persuaded to serve as minister to Cheng Tang, the first emperor of the Shang dynasty. He is regarded as the epitome of the wise and selfless counselor. For the *Mencius* reference, see VA.7(2).
5. Bo Yi (twelfth century B.C.E.) was an example of great filial piety. For the comparison of Yi Yin and Bo Yi with Confucius, see *Mencius* IIA.2(22).
6. This is a somewhat terse and opaque expression of what is recorded in *Lunyu* V.18.
7. *Lunyu* VI.25 and XIII.20(1).
8. The two references here are to *Lunyu* IV.9 and *Mencius* VA.7(6).
9. *Mencius* VIIA.4(1 and 2).

4. *SWJ* 4: LETTERS 2

1. Both were disciples of Confucius. Zi Gao was noted for his *ren* and filial piety—see, e.g., *Lunyu* XI.17(1). Yuan Xian was renowned for his pursuit of truth and disregard of worldly benefits—see, e.g., *Lunyu* VI.3(3).
2. *Lunyu* V.27.
3. See *SSJZS*, 1(*Zhou Yi*).151.
4. *Zhuangzi* 6—see *Zhuangzi Jishi*, 1.284.
5. It is not clear who Chi Bao is; there is no listing of this name in any of the major sources. The term *chi bao* 赤豹 is found in the *Odes*, Mao 261; LCC, 4.551, and in the "Nine Songs" (*Qufu Xinbian* 屈賦新編, 1.340); Arthur Waley, *The Nine Songs: A Study of Shamanism in Ancient China* [New York:

Grove Press, 1956], 53). It is translated variously as "red panther" or "red leopard."

6. *Lunyu* V.21; LCC, 1.181.
7. Zheng Kangcheng is Zheng Xuan 鄭玄 (127–200), a noted Confucian scholar of the Later Han period and disciple of Ma Rong 馬融. After the Yellow Turban rebellion, he retired from official life but in 200 was summoned by Yuan Shao 袁紹 (d. 202), who, at about this time, had declared his opposition to Cao Cao 曹操 (155–220). The details of the incidents referred to can be found in *Hou Han Shu* 35, 5.1211.
8. The *Lunyu* references are XII.20(4), LCC, 1.259; VII.2, LCC, 1.191: XII.2, LCC, 1.251.
9. This letter appears in part as the last of the immediately preceding twenty-five letters to friends.
10. Rao and She are two *zhou*, the first in Jiangxi, the second in Anhui.
11. Wuhu was a lake situated in southwestern Wuhu *xian* in Anhui. This *xian*, which may be what is being referred to here, was first established in Han times with the name Wuhu. For reference to Gu's journey to Wuhu, see Willard J. Peterson, "The Life of Ku Yen-wu (1613–1682)," *Harvard Journal of Asiatic Studies* 28 (1968): 153.
12. Fang Xuanling 房玄齡 (578–648) and Du Ruhui 杜如晦 (d. 630) were officials under Tang Tai Zong and worked in close concert. Howard Wechsler writes, "Tu Ju-hui and Fang Hsuan-ling were complementary characters and worked smoothly together. Between them they staffed and set in operation the whole executive side of government. Unfortunately Tu died of an unspecified illness in 630, at the very peak of his power" (*CHC*, 3[i].16). Biographical details for both can be found in *Jiu Tang Shu* 66, 7.2459–69 and the *Xin Tang Shu* 96, 12.3853–60.

5. *SWJ* 5: RECORDS, INSCRIPTIONS, AND OTHER WRITINGS

1. Jin Gong 晉公 is Pei Zhongli 裴中立, whose designation was Pei Du 裴度.
2. Shi Hu 石虎 was a descendant of Shi Le 石勒. In the Jin period he became ruler of the Later Zhao.
3. Gao Huan 高歡 (496–547), from Northern Qi, rose to high office in Northern Wei and forced the emperor (Xiao Wu) to flee, establishing himself as leader of the Eastern Wei—see *History of the Northern Qi* 1.
4. See *Xin Tang Shu* 140 and *Wudai Shi* 12.
5. Li Zicheng 李自成 (1606–1645) was the leader of the rebel forces that entered Beijing in 1644. His triumph was short-lived and he was defeated in battle by Wu Sangui 吳三桂, the Ming general who transferred his allegiance to the Manchus on learning of Li Zicheng's exploits.

6. On Li Jiantai 李建泰, Thomas Bartlett has the following two notes: "(i) See Li's biography in Chang T'ing-yü et al., *Ming-shih* 253, 'Wei Tsau-to chuan: [fu] Li Chien-t'ai.' The exact date of the emperor's reception for Li is given in ibid., ch. 24, 'Chuang-lieh-ti pen-chi 2,' p. 334. Nineteen days before the emperor died, Li initiated a proposal that Ch'ung-chen remove to Nanking, which was seconded by other officials, but vetoed by the emperor (ibid.). (ii) Ku Yen-wu's opinion of Li may also have been affected by the knowledge that Li failed to carry out an attempt at honorable suicide after his capture by a subordinate of Li Tzu-ch'eng, and that Li Chien-t'ai went on to hold office as a Grand Secretary under the Ch'ing dynasty, before finally dying in rebellion ("Ku Yen-wu's Response to the 'Demise of Human Society'" [PhD diss., Princeton University, 1985])."
7. See Gu's original note on Wang Duo and Zhang Jun.
8. *Zhou Li*, *SSJZS*, 3.32.

6. *SWJ* 6: MISCELLANEOUS

1. Gao Huang Di was the first Ming emperor. He established the *weisuo* 衛所 military system. Edward Dreyer writes, "During the wars of dynastic founding, the Ming armies had expanded by enrolling troops of defeated enemies. The 1364 reorganization that created the *wei-so* system arose from the need to establish regular procedures for processing the large numbers of troops gained this way" (*CHC*, 7[i].104). I am unable to identify the precise source of the quote attributed to Gao Huang Di in the present essay.
2. For a consideration of the Ming military organization and its relationship to earlier systems, see ibid., 104–6, 244ff. See also Charles O. Hucker, *A Dictionary of Official Titles in Imperial China* (Stanford, Calif.: Stanford University Press, 1985), 75ff., and the entries for the individual titles (the translation of which follows Hucker in all cases except for *baihu suo*, which is not listed). See also *Ming Shi* 89–92, 2175–2278.
3. Both Yong 雍 and Yu 豫 were numbered among the nine ancient *zhou*; Yong corresponded to parts of Shansi and Gansu, while Yu corresponded to part of Henan.
4. For more on the *weisuo* system, see *CHC*, 7(i).104–6, 248ff., and 319ff.
5. The term "military register" (*chi ji* 尺籍) derives from the foot-long wooden board on which military matters were recorded—see *Shiji* 102, 9.2759 and 119, 10.3101.
6. In 280 the ruler of Wu was deposed by Sima Yan 司馬炎 (236–290) and the territory annexed to Jin, which had been founded in 265.
7. The three people referred to here are Liu Yuan 劉淵 (d. 310) (see *Jin Shu* 101); Shi Le 石勒 (273–332) (see *Jin Shu* 104 and 105, *Wei Shu* 95); and Li Xiong 李雄 (d. 334) (see *Jin Shu* 121).

8. The three people referred to here, all militarists and statesmen of the turbulent north-south division period, are Fu Jian 苻堅 (337–384) (see *Jin Shu* 113 and 114); Yao Chang 姚萇 (330–393) (see *Jin Shu* 116); and Murong Chui 慕容垂 (326–396) (see *Jin Shu* 123, *Wei Shu* 95).
9. For the northern campaign of Wang Xuanmou 王玄謀 (386–467), see *Song Shu* 5, 1.99ff. Fuli is Tuoba Tao 拓跋燾 (d. 452).
10. Tuoba Tao succeeded his father to become the third emperor of the Northern Wei dynasty. He subsequently annexed Liang, subdued Yan, and gained control of much of central China; see Wolfram Eberhard, *A History of China* (New York: Cosimo, 2005), 138–49.
11. The several events referred to here are as follows: In the third year of the Taiqing reign period of the Liang dynasty (549), Hou Jing 侯景 (502–552) seized Liang Wudi in the capital and put him under house arrest. In the Chengsheng reign period of the Liang dynasty (552–554), Xiao Cha 蕭察 (538–562), whose claim to the throne had been set aside, gathered a large force while military superintendent of the territory north of the Yangzi and, after the capture of Jiangling by the Western Wei, became emperor of the Minor Liang dynasty. Huainan was a prefecture in what is now Anhui province. Wei's taking of Shu and Han concerned events involving Yuwen Tai 宇文泰 (506–557), founder of the Western Wei dynasty, while Jiangling was a district in what is now Hubei and was seized by Chen Baxian (see following note) prior to the overthrow of Liang Yuandi by Xiao Cha.
12. Chen Baxian 陳霸先 (503–559) was a general and statesman who initially served the Liang dynasty but subsequently (in 557) compelled the abdication of the last Liang emperor and established the short-lived Chen dynasty. See *Chen Shu* 1 and 2 and *Nan Shi* 9.
13. The Southern Tang was one of the ten kingdoms of the Five Dynasties period and had its capital at Nanjing. It existed from 937 to 975—see *Xin Wudai Shi* 62.
14. The Southern Song was established by Gao Zong in 1127 and extended through twelve emperors to 1278, coexisting in part with the Jin and Yuan dynasties. The description of the emperor's surrender is taken from *Zuo Zhuan* V(7); LCC, 5.146.
15. In the Three Kingdoms period the two southern kingdoms of Shu and Wu coexisted, while later, during the Eastern Jin period, Li Xiong 李雄 established a separate kingdom in an area occupying much of Sichuan—see note 7.
16. Wang Jun 王濬 was a Western Jin general—see *Jin Shu* 42, 1207. Liu Zheng 劉整 was from Wei during the Three Kingdoms period—see *Sanguo Zhi* 4.
17. Zhao Ding, Chen Liang, and Meng Gong were soldiers and statesmen of the Southern Song period. Biographical details are as follows: Zhao Ding 趙鼎, *Song Shi* 360. The quoted remarks are on 32.11286. Chen Liang 陳亮, *Song Shi* 436. The statement in the essay does not appear

verbatim in the history, but something very similar can be found on 37.12937. Meng Gong 孟珙, *Song Shi* 412. The quoted remarks are on 35.12376.

18. Reference here is to events of the pre-Qin period when, in 241 B.C.E., the southern state of Chu moved its capital to Shouchun 壽春, which was in what is now the Shou district of Anhui province.
19. Ming Tai Zu, the founder of the Ming dynasty. For details of his military successes, see *CHC*, 7(i).44ff.
20. Bi 邲 is an ancient place-name. It was situated in what is now the Cheng district of Henan province and was, in ancient times, the site of a battle between Jin and Chu.
21. For details of the military events leading up to the establishment of the Han dynasty, see *CHC*, 1.110ff.
22. Guang Wu is Guang Wudi 光武帝, founder of the Later Han dynasty.
23. Liu Yu 劉裕 (356–422) was the founder of the Liu Song dynasty and later called Song Wudi.
24. See Sun Wu 孫吳, *The Art of War* (*Bingfa* 兵法). This phrase is used to indicate skill in the deployment of military forces.
25. Fu Qin is Fu Jian 苻堅 (337–384).
26. Wanyan Liang 完顏亮 (d. 1161) was the fourth emperor of the Jin dynasty. He held sway in northern China for twelve years until 1161, when he launched a large-scale, but unsuccessful, attack on the Song.
27. Qin 秦 and Yang 楊 were, in the early Han period, renowned for their agriculture—see *Shiji* 129, 10.3282, and *Han Shu* 91, 11.3694.
28. Qiao Yao 橋姚 was from the Han period and renowned for the rearing of domestic animals—see *Shiji* 129, 10.3280. Wu Shi is Wu Shi Luo 烏氏裸. He was ennobled by Qinshi Huang Di for his work in animal husbandry—see *Shiji* 129, 10.3260.
29. Qi 棄 was a minister of agriculture under Emperor Shun—see *Documents* II.I.5; LCC, 3.43.
30. Fei Zi 非子 of the Zhou state was noted for his animal husbandry—see *Shiji* 5, 1.175ff.
31. Hucker, *Dictionary of Official Titles*, p. 550, no. 7409, has a detailed and informative entry on this term.
32. Wei Liaoweng 魏了翁 was a Song neo-Confucian scholar of note who rose to high office—for biographical details, see *Song Shi* 437, 37.12965–71. I am unable to locate the exact source of the quotes here from Wei Liaoweng. His collected works, *Zhongjiao Heshan Xiansheng Daquanji*, appear as vol. 60 of the *SBCK*.
33. Yangzhou 揚州 was one of the nine ancient divisions corresponding to part of what is now Jiangsu province. Ying 潁 and Shou 壽 are presumably Yingzhou and Shouzhou, the former originally established in the Eastern Wei period in an area corresponding in part to Henan province and the

latter corresponding to part of present-day Anhui. Yang Hu 羊祜 (d. 278) and Du Yu 杜預 (222–284) were officials of the Jin dynasty—see *Jin Shu* 34, 4.1013–25 and 1025–34.

34. He Chengju 何承矩 was from the Song period. For details of his activities, see *Song Shi* 273, 27.9327ff.
35. *Guanzi* 22, *SBCK* 18(*Guanzi*).128.
36. Longlü was a district established in Han times. I haven't been able to find an account of this incident.
37. Reference here is to Emperor Yuan of Jin's crossing of the Yangzi River from north to south in 317 and setting up the Eastern Jin.
38. Zhang Fangping 張方平 (1007–1091) was a Song scholar and trenchant opponent of Wang Anshi—see *Song Shi* 318, 30.10353–59.
39. The two men referred to are the scholar-officials of the Former Han Jia Shan 賈山 and Jia Yi 賈誼. The statements can be found in *Quan Shanggu Sandai Jin Han Sanguo Liuchao Wen*, 1.14 and 16, respectively.
40. There are two references to the *Zhou Yi* in this opening statement: (1) *su lü* 素履, *SSJZS*, 1(*Zhou Yi*).40; (2) *ri xin sheng de* 日新盛德, "Xici" (*shang*), *SSJZS*, 1 (*Zhou Yi*).149.
41. The Five Classics referred to here are the *Odes* (*Shi* 詩), *Documents* (*Shu* 書), *Rites* (*Sanli* 三禮—*Li Ji*, *Zhou Li*, *Yi Li*), *Changes* (*Zhou Yi* 周易), and *Spring and Autumn Annals* (*Chunqiu* 春秋). I have taken the term *shi jian* to refer to historical writings generally (featuring as they do so much in Gu's writings), although here it may be a specific reference to the *Shiji* 史記 and the *Zizhi Tongjian* 資治通鑑.
42. The reference here is to *Mencius* IIIA.4(12); LCC, 2.253–54. D. C. Lau's translation is as follows: "I have heard of the Chinese converting barbarians to their ways, but not of their having been converted to barbarian ways" (*Mencius* [New York: Penguin, 1970], 117).
43. The three provinces Henan, Anhui, and Jiangsu.
44. Mention of Confucius's chariot is a reference to his returning to Lu to teach there after a long absence—see *Lunyu* 5.22. Bo Luan 伯鸞 was a servant of a high official in Han times. The story is that he used the stove to cook his meals after others had done so in order to avail himself of the heat they had created—see *Dongguan Hanji*, "Liang Hong Zhuan."

APPENDIX 3. ZHANG BINGLIN'S PREFACE TO HUANG KAN'S *RIZHI LU JIAOJI*

1. This essay appears as 9.8 in the *Yuanchaoben* version, immediately before "Gui Shen," which is 6.45 in the Huang Rucheng edition.
2. This was published in 1695 and was the first complete edition.
3. The essay is 29.11 in the *Yuanchaoben* version.

APPENDIX 4. ON THE FEUDAL SYSTEM (*FENGJIAN LUN*)—LIU ZONGYUAN

1. This is not an exact quote—the idea is expressed in *Xunzi* 1, "Quanxue."
2. The five ranks were *gong* 公 (duke), *hou* 侯 (marquis), *bo* 伯 (earl), *zi* 子 (viscount), and *yong* 男 (baron).
3. See *SBCK* 14(*Guoyu*).3–11.
4. The four references are, respectively, *Zuo Zhuan*, third year of Duke Huan, LCC 5.292–93; *Zuo Zhuan*, fifth year of Duke Huan, LCC 5.297–98; *Spring and Autumn Annals*, seventh year of Duke Yin, LCC 5.22; *Zuo Zhuan*, third year of Duke Ai, LCC 5.801–2. The years were, respectively (all B.C.E.), 708, 706, 715, 493.
5. *Han Shu* 1 (*xia*), 1.63.
6. After Liu Bang there followed Hui, Wen, and Jing.
7. The four references are (1) *Shiji* 104, Burton Watson, trans., *Records of the Grand Historian of China* (New York: Columbia University Press, 1961), 1:556–61; (2) *Shiji* 102, Watson, *Records*, 1:539–42; (3) *Shiji* 96 (8.2688), *Han Shu* 89 (11.3627–34); (4) *Shiji* 120, Watson, *Records*, 2:343–52.
8. Cao in Wei and Sima in Jin.

BIBLIOGRAPHY

WORKS BY GU YANWU

Gu Tinglin Shi Jianshi 顧亭林詩箋釋. Ed. Wang Jimin 王冀民. 2 vols. Beijing: Zhonghua Shuju, 1998.

Gu Tinglin Shiji Huizhu 顧亭林詩集彙注. Ed. Wang Quchang 王蘧常. 2 vols. Shanghai: Shanghai Guji Chubanshe, 1983.

Gu Tinglin Shiwenji 顧亭林詩文集. Ed. Hua Chenzhi 華忱之. Beijing: Zhonghua Shuju, 1959.

Gu Tinglin Wenji 顧亭林文集. Ed. Liu Jiuzhou 劉九洲. Taipei: Sanmin Shuju, 2000.

Gu Yanwu Quanji 顧炎武全集. Ed. Huang Shen 黃珅, Yan Zuozhi 嚴佐之, and Liu Yongxiang 劉永翔. 22 vols. Shanghai: Shanghai Guji Chubanshe, 2011.

Rizhi Lu Jiaoshi 日知錄校釋. Ed. Zhang Jinghua 張京華. 2 vols. Hunan: Yuelu Shushe, 2011.

Rizhi Lu Jiaozhu 日知錄校注. Ed. Chen Yuan 陳垣. 3 vols. Anhui: Anhui Daxue Chubanshe, 2007.

Rizhi Lu Jishi 日知錄集釋. Ed. Huang Rucheng 黃汝成. 2 vols. Taipei: Shijie Shuju, 1984.

Yuanchaoben Rizhi Lu 原抄本日知錄. Taipei: Wenshizhi Chubanshe, 1979.

WORKS IN CHINESE

Chen Zuwu 陳祖武. *Gu Yanwu Pingzhuan* 顧炎武評傳. Beijing: Zhongguo Shehui Chubanshe, 2009.

——. "Rizhi Lu Bajuanben Mo Yi." *Dushu*, January 1982, 136–37.

Congshu Jicheng 叢書集成. Taipei: Xinwenfeng, 1989.

He Yikun 何貽焜. *Tinglin Xueshu Shuping* 亭林學術述評. Taipei: Zhengzhong Shuju, 1944.

Huang Xiuzheng 黃秀政. *Gu Yanwu Yu Qingchu Jingshi Xuefeng* 顧炎武與清初經世學風. Taipei: Shangwu Yinshuguan, 1987.

Jian Mingyong 簡明勇 et al. *Gu Yanwu, Wang Fuzhi, Li Yong, Yan Yuan* 顧炎武，王夫之，李顒，顏元. 中國歷代思想家 15. Taipei: Shangwu Yinshuguan, 1999.

Jiang Fan 江藩. *Hanxue Shicheng Ji* 漢學師承積. Taipei, 1972.

Qian Mu 錢穆. *Zhongguo Jin Sanbainian Xueshushi* 中國近三百年學術史. Taipei: Shangwu Yinshuguan, 1976.

Quan Shanggu Sandai Qin Han Sanguo Liuchao Wen 全上古三代秦漢三國六朝文. 9 vols. Taipei: Shijie Shuju, 1982.

Shen Jiarong 沈嘉榮. *Gu Yanwu Lunkao* 顧炎武論考. Nanjing: Jiangsu Renmin Chubanshe, 1994.

Shisanjing Zhushu 十三經注疏. Taipei: Yiwen Yinshuguan, 2001.

Sibu Congkan 四部叢刊. Taipei: Shangwu Yinshuguan, 1979.

Siku Quanshu 四庫全書. Hong Kong: Digital Heritage. Online version.

Siku Quanshu Zongmu Tiyao 四庫全書總目提要. Taipei: Shangwu Yinshuguan, 1983.

Xie Guozhen 謝國楨. *Gu Ningren Xiansheng Xuepu* 顧寧人先生學譜. Taipei: Shangwu Yinshuguan, 1957.

Zhang Mu 張穆. *Qing Gu Tinglin Xianshengyanwu Nianpu* 清顧亭林先生炎武年譜. Taipei: Shangwu Yinshuguan, 1980.

WORKS IN OTHER LANGUAGES

Bartlett, Thomas C. "Gu Yanwu." In *Encyclopedia of Chinese Philosophy*, ed. Antonio S. Cua, 272–76. New York: Routledge, 2003.

——. "Ku Yen-wu's Response to the 'Demise of Human Society.'" PhD diss., Princeton University, 1985.

Ch'ien, Edward T. *Chiao Hung and the Restructuring of Neo-Confucianism in the Late Ming*. New York: Columbia University Press, 1986.

Cohen, Paul A. *Between Tradition and Modernity: Wang T'ao and Reform in Late Ch'ing China*. Cambridge, Mass.: Harvard University Press, 1974.

Cua, Antonio S., ed. *Encyclopedia of Chinese Philosophy*. New York: Routledge, 2003.

de Bary, Wm. Theodore. *Neo-Confucian Orthodoxy and the Learning of the Mind-and-Heart*. New York: Columbia University Press, 1981.

Delury, John Patrick. "Despotism Above and Below: Gu Yanwu's *Record of Daily Learning* on Power, Money and Mores." PhD diss., Yale University, 2007.

Elman, Benjamin A. *From Philosophy to Philology: Intellectual and Social Aspects of Change in Late Imperial China*. Cambridge, Mass.: Council on East Asian Studies, Harvard University, 1984.

Fung Yu-lan. *A History of Chinese Philosophy*. Trans. Derk Bodde. 2 vols. Princeton: Princeton University Press, 1952.

Goodrich, L. Carrington, and Chaoying Fang, eds. *Dictionary of Ming Biography, 1368–1644*. 2 vols. New York: Columbia University Press, 1976.

Hagman, Jan. *Bibliographical Notes on Ku Yen-wu*. Stockholm: Föreningen för Orientalisker Studier, 1973.

Hervouet, Yves, ed. *A Sung Bibliography (Bibliographie des Song)*. Hong Kong: Chinese University Press, 1978.

Hucker, Charles O. *A Dictionary of Official Titles in Imperial China*. Stanford, Calif.: Stanford University Press, 1985.

Hummel, Arthur W. *Eminent Chinese of the Ch'ing Period, 1644–1912*. Washington, D.C.: Government Printing Office, 1943–1944.

——. "Manuscripts of Ku Yen-wu." In *Annual Report of the Librarian of Congress*, 170–74. Washington, D.C.: Government Printing Office, 1937.

Johnston, Ian. "Ku Yen-wu's *Record of Daily Knowledge*." PhD diss., University of Sydney 1992.

——. *The Mozi: A Complete Translation*. New York: Columbia University Press, 2010.

Johnston, Ian, and Wang Ping, trans. *Daxue and Zhongyong*. Hong Kong: Chinese University Press, 2012.

Kessler, Lawrence D. "Chinese Scholars and the Early Manchu State." *Harvard Journal of Asiatic Studies* 31 (1971): 179–200.

Knoblock, John, and Jeffrey Riegel. *The Annals of Lü Buwei: A Complete Translation and Study*. Stanford, Calif.: Stanford University Press, 2000.

Ku Wei-ying. "The Political Theories of Ku Yen-wu and the Manchu Conquest." PhD diss., University of British Columbia, 1983.

Legge, James. *The Chinese Classics*. 5 vols. Hong Kong: Hong Kong University Press, 1960.

——. *The I Ching*. New York: Dover, 1963.

——. *Li Chi: Book of Rites*. 2 vols. New Hyde Park, N.Y.: University Books, 1967.

Liang Ch'i-ch'ao [Qichao]. *Intellectual Trends in the Ch'ing Period*. Trans. Immanuel C. Y. Hsü. Cambridge, Mass.: Harvard University Press, 1959.

Loewe, Michael. *Early Chinese Texts: A Bibliographical Guide*. Berkeley: Society for the Study of Early China and the Institute of East Asian Studies, University of California, 1993.

Nienhauser, William H., Jr., ed. *The Indiana Companion to Traditional Chinese Literature*. Bloomington: Indiana University Press, 1986.

Peterson, Willard J. "The Life of Ku Yen-wu (1613–1682)." *Harvard Journal of Asiatic Studies* 28 (1968): 114–56, 29 (1969): 201–47.

Santangelo, Paolo. "Gu Yanwu's Contribution to History: The Historian's Method and Tasks." *East and West* 32, no. 1/4 (December): 145–85.

Twitchett, Denis, and John K. Fairbank, eds. *The Cambridge History of China*. 15 vols. Cambridge: Cambridge University Press, 1978–2015.

Vergnaud, Jean-François. *La pensée de Gu Yanwu (1613–1682): Essai de synthèse*. Paris: École française d'Extrême-Orient, 1990.

Watson, Burton, trans. *The Complete Works of Chuang Tzu*. New York: Columbia University Press, 1968.

——, trans. *Hsün Tzu: Basic Writings*. New York: Columbia University Press, 1963.

——, trans. *Records of the Grand Historian of China*. 2 vols. New York: Columbia University Press, 1961.

Wilhelm, Richard, trans. *The I Ching; or, Book of Changes*. Princeton: Princeton University Press, 1950.

Wright, Arthur F., and Denis Twitchett, eds. *Confucian Personalities*. Stanford, Calif.: Stanford University Press, 1962.

Young, Lung-chang. "Ku Yen-wu's Views on the Ming Examination System." *Ming Studies* 23 (spring 1987): 48–63.

Yü Ying-shih. "Some Preliminary Observations on the Rise of Ch'ing Confucian Intellectualism." *Tsing Hua Journal of Chinese Studies* 11 (1975): 105–46.

INDEX

TRANSLATIONS FROM THE ASIAN CLASSICS

Major Plays of Chikamatsu, tr. Donald Keene 1961

Four Major Plays of Chikamatsu, tr. Donald Keene. Paperback ed. only. 1961; rev. ed. 1997

Records of the Grand Historian of China, translated from the Shih chi of Ssu-ma Ch'ien, tr. Burton Watson, 2 vols. 1961

Instructions for Practical Living and Other Neo-Confucian Writings by Wang Yang-ming, tr. Wing-tsit Chan 1963

Hsün Tzu: Basic Writings, tr. Burton Watson, paperback ed. only. 1963; rev. ed. 1996

Chuang Tzu: Basic Writings, tr. Burton Watson, paperback ed. only. 1964; rev. ed. 1996

The Mahābhārata, tr. Chakravarthi V. Narasimhan. Also in paperback ed. 1965; rev. ed. 1997

The Manyōshū, Nippon Gakujutsu Shinkōkai edition 1965

Su Tung-p'o: Selections from a Sung Dynasty Poet, tr. Burton Watson. Also in paperback ed. 1965

Bhartrihari: Poems, tr. Barbara Stoler Miller. Also in paperback ed. 1967

Basic Writings of Mo Tzu, Hsün Tzu, and Han Fei Tzu, tr. Burton Watson. Also in separate paperback eds. 1967

The Awakening of Faith, Attributed to Aśvaghosha, tr. Yoshito S. Hakeda. Also in paperback ed. 1967

Reflections on Things at Hand: The Neo-Confucian Anthology, comp. Chu Hsi and Lü Tsu-ch'ien, tr. Wing-tsit Chan 1967

The Platform Sutra of the Sixth Patriarch, tr. Philip B. Yampolsky. Also in paperback ed. 1967

Essays in Idleness: The Tsurezuregusa of Kenkō, tr. Donald Keene. Also in paperback ed. 1967

The Pillow Book of Sei Shōnagon, tr. Ivan Morris, 2 vols. 1967

Two Plays of Ancient India: The Little Clay Cart and the Minister's Seal, tr. J. A. B. van Buitenen 1968

The Complete Works of Chuang Tzu, tr. Burton Watson 1968

The Romance of the Western Chamber (*Hsi Hsiang chi*), tr. S. I. Hsiung. Also in paperback ed. 1968

The Manyōshū, Nippon Gakujutsu Shinkōkai edition. Paperback ed. only. 1969

Records of the Historian: Chapters from the Shih chi of Ssu-ma Ch'ien, tr. Burton Watson. Paperback ed. only. 1969

Cold Mountain: 100 Poems by the T'ang Poet Han-shan, tr. Burton Watson. Also in paperback ed. 1970

Twenty Plays of the Nō Theatre, ed. Donald Keene. Also in paperback ed. 1970

Chūshingura: The Treasury of Loyal Retainers, tr. Donald Keene. Also in paperback ed. 1971; rev. ed. 1997

The Zen Master Hakuin: Selected Writings, tr. Philip B. Yampolsky 1971

Chinese Rhyme-Prose: Poems in the Fu Form from the Han and Six Dynasties Periods, tr. Burton Watson. Also in paperback ed. 1971

Kūkai: Major Works, tr. Yoshito S. Hakeda. Also in paperback ed. 1972

The Old Man Who Does as He Pleases: Selections from the Poetry and Prose of Lu Yu, tr. Burton Watson 1973

The Lion's Roar of Queen Śrīmālā, tr. Alex and Hideko Wayman 1974

Courtier and Commoner in Ancient China: Selections from the History of the Former Han by Pan Ku, tr. Burton Watson. Also in paperback ed. 1974

Japanese Literature in Chinese, vol. 1: *Poetry and Prose in Chinese by Japanese Writers of the Early Period*, tr. Burton Watson 1975

Japanese Literature in Chinese, vol. 2: *Poetry and Prose in Chinese by Japanese Writers of the Later Period*, tr. Burton Watson 1976

Love Song of the Dark Lord: Jayadeva's Gītagovinda, tr. Barbara Stoler Miller. Also in paperback ed. Cloth ed. includes critical text of the Sanskrit. 1977; rev. ed. 1997

Ryōkan: Zen Monk-Poet of Japan, tr. Burton Watson 1977

Calming the Mind and Discerning the Real: From the Lam rim chen mo of Tsoṇ-kha-pa, tr. Alex Wayman 1978

The Hermit and the Love-Thief: Sanskrit Poems of Bhartrihari and Bilhaṇa, tr. Barbara Stoler Miller 1978

The Lute: Kao Ming's P'i-p'a chi, tr. Jean Mulligan. Also in paperback ed. 1980

A Chronicle of Gods and Sovereigns: Jinnō Shōtōki of Kitabatake Chikafusa, tr. H. Paul Varley 1980

Among the Flowers: The Hua-chien chi, tr. Lois Fusek 1982

Grass Hill: Poems and Prose by the Japanese Monk Gensei, tr. Burton Watson 1983

Doctors, Diviners, and Magicians of Ancient China: Biographies of Fang-shih, tr. Kenneth J. DeWoskin. Also in paperback ed. 1983

Theater of Memory: The Plays of Kālidāsa, ed. Barbara Stoler Miller. Also in paperback ed. 1984

The Columbia Book of Chinese Poetry: From Early Times to the Thirteenth Century, ed. and tr. Burton Watson. Also in paperback ed. 1984

Poems of Love and War: From the Eight Anthologies and the Ten Long Poems of Classical Tamil, tr. A. K. Ramanujan. Also in paperback ed. 1985

The Bhagavad Gita: Krishna's Counsel in Time of War, tr. Barbara Stoler Miller 1986

The Columbia Book of Later Chinese Poetry, ed. and tr. Jonathan Chaves. Also in paperback ed. 1986

The Tso Chuan: Selections from China's Oldest Narrative History, tr. Burton Watson 1989

Waiting for the Wind: Thirty-six Poets of Japan's Late Medieval Age, tr. Steven Carter 1989

Selected Writings of Nichiren, ed. Philip B. Yampolsky 1990

Saigyō, Poems of a Mountain Home, tr. Burton Watson 1990

The Book of Lieh Tzu: A Classic of the Tao, tr. A. C. Graham. Morningside ed. 1990
The Tale of an Anklet: An Epic of South India—The Cilappatikāram of Iḷaṅkō Aṭikaḷ, tr. R. Parthasarathy 1993
Waiting for the Dawn: A Plan for the Prince, tr. with introduction by Wm. Theodore de Bary 1993
Yoshitsune and the Thousand Cherry Trees: A Masterpiece of the Eighteenth-Century Japanese Puppet Theater, tr., annotated, and with introduction by Stanleigh H. Jones Jr. 1993
The Lotus Sutra, tr. Burton Watson. Also in paperback ed. 1993
The Classic of Changes: A New Translation of the I Ching as Interpreted by Wang Bi, tr. Richard John Lynn 1994
Beyond Spring: Tz'u Poems of the Sung Dynasty, tr. Julie Landau 1994
The Columbia Anthology of Traditional Chinese Literature, ed. Victor H. Mair 1994
Scenes for Mandarins: The Elite Theater of the Ming, tr. Cyril Birch 1995
Letters of Nichiren, ed. Philip B. Yampolsky; tr. Burton Watson et al. 1996
Unforgotten Dreams: Poems by the Zen Monk Shōtetsu, tr. Steven D. Carter 1997
The Vimalakirti Sutra, tr. Burton Watson 1997
Japanese and Chinese Poems to Sing: The Wakan rōei shū, tr. J. Thomas Rimer and Jonathan Chaves 1997
Breeze Through Bamboo: Kanshi of Ema Saikō, tr. Hiroaki Sato 1998
A Tower for the Summer Heat, by Li Yu, tr. Patrick Hanan 1998
Traditional Japanese Theater: An Anthology of Plays, by Karen Brazell 1998
The Original Analects: Sayings of Confucius and His Successors (0479–0249), by E. Bruce Brooks and A. Taeko Brooks 1998
The Classic of the Way and Virtue: A New Translation of the Tao-te ching of Laozi as Interpreted by Wang Bi, tr. Richard John Lynn 1999
The Four Hundred Songs of War and Wisdom: An Anthology of Poems from Classical Tamil, The Puṟanāṉūṟu, ed. and tr. George L. Hart and Hank Heifetz 1999
Original Tao: Inward Training (Nei-yeh) *and the Foundations of Taoist Mysticism*, by Harold D. Roth 1999
Po Chü-i: Selected Poems, tr. Burton Watson 2000
Lao Tzu's Tao Te Ching: *A Translation of the Startling New Documents Found at Guodian*, by Robert G. Henricks 2000
The Shorter Columbia Anthology of Traditional Chinese Literature, ed. Victor H. Mair 2000
Mistress and Maid (Jiaohongji), by Meng Chengshun, tr. Cyril Birch 2001
Chikamatsu: Five Late Plays, tr. and ed. C. Andrew Gerstle 2001
The Essential Lotus: Selections from the Lotus Sutra, tr. Burton Watson 2002
Early Modern Japanese Literature: An Anthology, 1600–1900, ed. Haruo Shirane 2002; abridged 2008
The Columbia Anthology of Traditional Korean Poetry, ed. Peter H. Lee 2002
The Sound of the Kiss, or The Story That Must Never Be Told: Pingali Suranna's Kalapurnodayamu, tr. Vecheru Narayana Rao and David Shulman 2003

The Selected Poems of Du Fu, tr. Burton Watson 2003
Far Beyond the Field: Haiku by Japanese Women, tr. Makoto Ueda 2003
Just Living: Poems and Prose by the Japanese Monk Tonna, ed. and tr. Steven D. Carter 2003
Han Feizi: Basic Writings, tr. Burton Watson 2003
Mozi: Basic Writings, tr. Burton Watson 2003
Xunzi: Basic Writings, tr. Burton Watson 2003
Zhuangzi: Basic Writings, tr. Burton Watson 2003
The Awakening of Faith, Attributed to Aśvaghosha, tr. Yoshito S. Hakeda, introduction by Ryuichi Abe 2005
The Tales of the Heike, tr. Burton Watson, ed. Haruo Shirane 2006
Tales of Moonlight and Rain, by Ueda Akinari, tr. with introduction by Anthony H. Chambers 2007
Traditional Japanese Literature: An Anthology, Beginnings to 1600, ed. Haruo Shirane 2007
The Philosophy of Qi, by Kaibara Ekken, tr. Mary Evelyn Tucker 2007
The Analects of Confucius, tr. Burton Watson 2007
The Art of War: Sun Zi's Military Methods, tr. Victor Mair 2007
One Hundred Poets, One Poem Each: A Translation of the Ogura Hyakunin Isshu, tr. Peter McMillan 2008
Zeami: Performance Notes, tr. Tom Hare 2008
Zongmi on Chan, tr. Jeffrey Lyle Broughton 2009
Scripture of the Lotus Blossom of the Fine Dharma, rev. ed., tr. Leon Hurvitz, preface and introduction by Stephen R. Teiser 2009
Mencius, tr. Irene Bloom, ed. with an introduction by Philip J. Ivanhoe 2009
Clouds Thick, Whereabouts Unknown: Poems by Zen Monks of China, Charles Egan 2010
The Mozi: A Complete Translation, tr. Ian Johnston 2010
The Huainanzi: A Guide to the Theory and Practice of Government in Early Han China, by Liu An, tr. and ed. John S. Major, Sarah A. Queen, Andrew Seth Meyer, and Harold D. Roth, with Michael Puett and Judson Murray 2010
The Demon at Agi Bridge and Other Japanese Tales, tr. Burton Watson, ed. with introduction by Haruo Shirane 2011
Haiku Before Haiku: From the Renga Masters to Bashō, tr. with introduction by Steven D. Carter 2011
The Columbia Anthology of Chinese Folk and Popular Literature, ed. Victor H. Mair and Mark Bender 2011
Tamil Love Poetry: The Five Hundred Short Poems of the Aiṅkuṟunūṟu, tr. and ed. Martha Ann Selby 2011
The Teachings of Master Wuzhu: Zen and Religion of No-Religion, by Wendi L. Adamek 2011
The Essential Huainanzi, by Liu An, tr. and ed. John S. Major, Sarah A. Queen, Andrew Seth Meyer, and Harold D. Roth 2012

The Dao of the Military: Liu An's Art of War, tr. Andrew Seth Meyer 2012

Unearthing the Changes: Recently Discovered Manuscripts of the Yi Jing (I Ching) *and Related Texts*, Edward L. Shaughnessy 2013

Record of Miraculous Events in Japan: The Nihon ryōiki, tr. Burton Watson 2013

The Complete Works of Zhuangzi, tr. Burton Watson 2013

Lust, Commerce, and Corruption: An Account of What I Have Seen and Heard, *by an Edo Samurai*, tr. and ed. Mark Teeuwen and Kate Wildman Nakai with Miyazaki Fumiko, Anne Walthall, and John Breen 2014

Exemplary Women of Early China: The Lienü zhuan *of Liu Xiang*, tr. Anne Behnke Kinney 2014

The Columbia Anthology of Yuan Drama, ed. C. T. Hsia, Wai-yee Li, and George Kao 2014

The Resurrected Skeleton: From Zhuangzi to Lu Xun, by Wilt L. Idema 2014

The Sarashina Diary: *A Woman's Life in Eleventh-Century Japan*, by Sugawara no Takasue no Musume, tr. with introduction by Sonja Arntzen and Itō Moriyuki 2014

The Kojiki: *An Account of Ancient Matters*, by Ō no Yasumaro, tr. Gustav Heldt 2014

The Orphan of Zhao *and Other Yuan Plays: The Earliest Known Versions*, tr. and introduced by Stephen H. West and Wilt L. Idema 2014

Luxuriant Gems of the Spring and Autumn, attributed to Dong Zhongshu, ed. and tr. Sarah A. Queen and John S. Major 2016

A Book to Burn and a Book to Keep (Hidden): Selected Writings, by Li Zhi, ed. and tr. Rivi Handler-Spitz, Pauline Lee, and Haun Saussy 2016

The Shenzi Fragments: *A Philosophical Analysis and Translation*, Eirik Lang Harris 2016

GPSR Authorized Representative: Easy Access System Europe, Mustamäe tee 50, 10621 Tallinn, Estonia, gpsr.requests@easproject.com

www.ingramcontent.com/pod-product-compliance
Lightning Source LLC
Chambersburg PA
CBHW020932310726
48980CB00007B/743/J

* 9 7 8 0 2 3 1 1 7 0 4 8 2 *